The Widening
Circle of Genocide

The Widening Circle of Genocide

Genocide: A Critical Bibliographic Review
VOLUME 3

Edited by Israel W. Charny

With a foreword by Irving Louis Horowitz

Routledge
Taylor & Francis Group

LONDON AND NEW YORK

First published 1994 by Transaction Publishers

Published 2017 by Routledge
2 Park Square, Milton Park, Abingdon, Oxon OX14 4RN
711 Third Avenue, New York, NY 10017, USA

First issued in paperback 2018

Routledge is an imprint of the Taylor & Francis Group, an informa business

Library of Congress Catalog Number: 93-46257

Library of Congress Cataloging-in-Publication Data

The Widening circle of genocide / edited by Israel W. Charny ; with a
    foreword by Irving Louis Horowitz.
        p. cm. — (Genocide ; v. 3)
    "A Publication of the Institute on the Holocaust and Genocide."
    Includes bibliographical references and index.
    ISBN 1-56000-172-0 (cloth)
    1. Genocide—Bibliography. I. Charny, Israel W. II. Institute on the Holocaust
and Genocide (Jerusalem) III. Series
Z7164.G45G45   1988 vol. 3
[HV6542]
016.364′51—dc20   93-46257
                                                                 CIP

ISBN 13: 978-1-138-51714-1 (pbk)
ISBN 13: 978-1-56000-172-0 (hbk)

Dedicated with great respect, and in warm friendship to the doyen of scholarship of genocide

Prof. LEO KUPER, University of California

A great pioneer in scholarship of genocide, dedicated leader in active efforts to introduce new ways of coping with, intervening, and preventing genocide, and a dear decent, positive person.

Contents

Contributing Editors

Israel W. Charny is Executive Director, Institute on the Holocaust and Genocide, Jerusalem; and Professor of Psychology & Family Therapy and Director, Program for Advanced Studies in Integrative Psychotherapy, Dept. of Psychology & Martin Buber Center, Hebrew University of Jerusalem

Vahakn N. Dadrian is Professor, Department of Sociology, Sate University of New York, Geneseo, and Director of Genocide Study Program, H.F. Guggenheim Foundation Grant, Conesus, N.Y.

James Dunn, a foreign affairs adviser and one time consul in East Timor, was sent to Timor on an official fact-finding mission, and was again there leading an aid mission when Indonesia's invasion began. He later testified before the U.S. Congress and U.N. Committees [13 Percy Davis Drive, Moruya NSW, Australia].

Leonard B. Glick is Professor of Anthropology, Hampshire College, Amherst, Massachusetts

George Kent is Professor, Department of Political Science, University of Hawaii, Honolulu, Hawaii

Rosanne Klass established and directed the Afghanistan Information Center at Freedom House in New York (1981-1991), and is co-founder and vice-president of the Afghanistan Relief Committee

Robert Krell is Professor of Psychiatry, Department of Psychiatry, Health Sciences Center Hospital, University of British Columbia, Vancouver, B.C., Canada

R.J. Rummel is Professor of Political Science, University of Hawaii at Manoa, Honolulu, Hawaii

Marc I. Sherman is Director of the Holocaust and Genocide Computerized Bibliographic Database Project at the Institute on the Holocaust and Genocide in Jerusalem, and Director of Academic Research Information Systems at the Research Authority of Tel Aviv University

Samuel Totten is Associate Professor, College of Education, University of Arkansas, Fayetteville, Arkansas

Gabrielle Tyrnauer, an anthropologist, is Associate Director of the Refugee Research Project, and of Living Testimonies, a project for videotaping oral histories of Jewish and Gypsy Holocaust survivors at McGill University, Montreal, Quebec, Canada

Martin van Bruinessen, an anthropologist, is Research Associate/Lecturer at the University of Leiden in The Netherlands

Foreword

There are many characteristics to the work of Israel Charny that are unique—and that makes him a singular figure in the dismal "science" of genocide studies. I should like, in this brief space, to draw attention to three such properties: the first theoretical, the second organizational, and third moral. I do so not to celebrate a colleague—although he merits and has earned such encomiums, but rather to highlight what social science can contribute to the course of civilization when done properly and decently.

Charny's opening statement provides such a pelucid account of the contents of each section that my task in this Foreword is greatly eased. Clearly, his notion of *The Widening Circle of Genocide* as a concept rather than a title is two-edged: on one side there is a growing sense that the numbers of human beings trapped in circles of despair leading to dismemberment continue to exceed our wildest earlier estimates; while on the other, there is an appreciation that this widening circle is one of recognition—early awareness and early actions that can deter, or at least limit, the practice of genocide.

That our thinking on genocide has progressed to the point of taking the subject to intervention and prevention, and beyond moaning and groaning over what has been, itself raises controversial issues that are being debated daily in policy discourse over Somalia, Bosnia, and Haiti. But this in itself marks a level of consciousness with respect to genocidal practices that did not exist say in 1944—a bare fifty years ago. Indeed, the implication of Charny's work—and those of his colleagues herein assembled—is clear. Had a higher level of political awareness and action been manifest in the Allied powers' response to Nazism, the worst features of that odious system might have been muted, if not averted. In this particular "if then," we are talking of millions of innocent lives who were consigned to destruction in the ashes of the Holocaust.

What then are the special contributions made by Charny and his associates to this painful subject? First, there is the unity of life struggles as such, that is, to the unitary character of taking lives—whether in Armenia in the past as described by my good friend Vahakn Dadrian or in the present in such seemingly exotic places as Afghanistan, East Timor, or East Europe. For the fact is that genocide is an ongoing concern, not a historical remnant. The broad theoretical issue of the distinction between the collective murder of a people, such as the fate of European Jewry between 1941 and 1945; or the selective murder of a people, such as the fate that continues to haunt other peoples, while significant, is of a second order of significance. The theoretical ink spilled over who has claims to higher victim totals must surely pale in contrast to the actual blood spilled by real individuals and communities.

Charny's great virtue is that his focus, and that of all contributors to this volume, has never wavered from holding in suspension judgments as to who suffers most; while pursuing mechanisms for reducing suffering as such. In this connection, I should like to note the terrible seamless character of genocidal practices; a seamlessness that brings into sharp focus the difference between real theory and nit-picking; or between primary and secondary issues involved in the practice of, as well as the prevention of, genocide. Since this third volume in the series Genocide: A Critical Bibliographic Review does not deal with the Nazi onslaught against the Jewish people, reference to the Holocaust will hopefully not appear amiss.

Let me quote, necessarily at some length, the following from a report filed by Timothy W. Ryback in *The New Yorker* (15 November 1993). It illustrates the unitary character of genocide, whatever be its variations. and intensities.

In June, 1940, nine months after the occupation of Poland, the Germans established the *Konzentrationslager* Auschwitz in the brick buildings of a Polish military camp that dated back to the First World War. A former ammunitions depot on the edge of the camp was converted into a crematorium to incinerate the corpses of inmates who had been executed or had perished from disease, exhaustion, or abuse. Poison gas is reported to have first been used in Auschwitz that September, when six hundred Soviet prisoners of war and two hundred and fifty sick prisoners were locked in basement rooms of Block XI and exposed to Zyklon B. Later that month, nine hundred Soviet soldiers were crammed into the morgue of the Auschwitz crematorium and gassed. Rudolf Höss, who observed both operations, recalled the latter one in his memoirs, written in prison after the war: "The Russians were ordered to undress in an anteroom: they then quietly entered the mortuary, for they had been told they were to be deloused. The whole transport exactly filled the mortuary to capacity. The doors were then sealed and the gas shaken down through the holes in the roof. I do not know how long this killing took. For a little while a humming sound could be heard. When the powder was thrown in there were cries of 'Gas!,' then a great bellowing, and the trapped prisoners hurled themselves against both the doors. But the doors held. They were opened several hours later, so that the place might be aired. It was then that I saw, for the first time, gassed bodies in the mass. On January 20, 1942, the Nazi leadership convened a secret meeting at a villa in Wannsee, on the outskirts of Berlin, to discuss plans for the mass extermination of Europe's Jews and other minority groups. Auschwitz, because of its relative isolation and its proximity to major rail links, became the end point for the Nazis' final solution.

Now the importance of this, beyond its obvious historical interest, is not simply a search for pedestrian mechanisms of law to preserve artifacts to "prove" that a Holocaust took place, but rather to note how what was initially tried out on 900 Red Army troops, presumably non-Jewish for the most part, became the engineering and chemical prototype for the destruction of six million Jews, and perhaps an equal number of non-Jews. So whatever be the disputations on the meaning of the Holocaust, the truth of a pre-emptive genocide cannot be doubted. An early detection system, a rapid deployment of military response, a mass communications participation: each of these might have blunted the blade of the killers. While the deaths of several hundred Red Army troops does not weigh on the same scale as the death of a whole people, the central fact is that they are linked events in history. That, I submit, is a theoretical insight of great importance; and the work of Israel Charny must be seen as central in this regard.

I suspect that Charny would be the last person to deny that problems in this line of argument exist. When should random killing be described as systematic? Is this a matter of counting bodies, or some other form of measurement? When is a rapid deployment of military personnel warranted to prevent or bring to a halt, genocidal practices? Whose troops should be used and under whose auspices should they serve? And when does mass communication blunt sensibilities rather than spur actions. Do pictures of starving and maimed children provide outrage or sublimate responses in a voyeuristic series of excesses? These issues are now being addressed—perhaps not or as fully as one would like. Nonetheless, the level of awareness is so much higher than a half century ago that we are entitled to salute the pioneering efforts of people like Charny, Kuper (to whom this book is dedicated), Rummel (whose own books have been widely published by Transaction), and Dadrian—of whom we have already spoken.

Now let me turn briefly to the organizational efforts involved in Charny's work—or what can best be described as the conspiracy of conscience, or the public representation of private sentiments. For behind the theory is an organizational concept—a belief that issues of life and death frame any realignment of the social sciences. This certainly has been a characteristic of my own work—from *Radicalism and the Revolt Against Reason* in the 1960s to *Taking Lives* in the 1970s and 1980s, and, finally, to my current interest in linking the reformation of social science to the study of life-taking systems at one end and life-giving societies at the other. For in this shared pursuit, our "conspiracy" shall, nay must, triumph over the furtive efforts in dark corners to hatch new varieties of the murder of innocents. The professional identities of the contributors to *The Widening Circle* tells the story: Charny from psychology, Dadrian from sociology, Dunn from public administration, Glick and van Bruinessen from anthropology, Kent and Rummel from political science, Krell from psychiatry, Totten from education. The key here is transitive: each of these people has had something to say about specific issues or peoples related to genocide. Past professional identities may have helped shape present analysis. But, in fact, as a result of such efforts as Charny has launched through his Institute on the Holocaust and Genocide, the professional review of genocide has secured a foothold in the world of social research, and in so doing, helps contribute to what Frances Bacon might well have called the new great instauration of our times.

Now we turn to the final point to note about this collective effort: the moral undertones that help inform the empirical analysis. For without such controlled passions that distinguish right from wrong, life from death, all is lost in a bag of pure relativism. It is the normative standpoint, derived perhaps more from a medical than a social-scientific model, that provides the fuel bringing life to these papers. For while such ethical premises do not of themselves assure quality scholarship, without such premises the work itself could never be conceived, much less carried out.

One does not risk so much for the sake of gaining so little, in personal reward at least, without some Kantian imperative lighting the way. The study of genocide is a value unto itself because life is a good into itself. The "reward" may not be reflected in emoluments or distinctions within traditional departments or societies, but it is surely reflected in the millions of people for whom the Holocaust and the many genocides that dot our century is now part of their *Geist*. Every debate among the *Historiker streit* in Germany; every trial of an Eichmann in Jerusalem; every archive opened in a Turkish vault gives evidence to the moral fervor that makes possible renewal not only of professional life, but of life in general. The work of Israel Charny deserves recognition as a key building block in this effort. *The Widen-*

ing Circle of Genocide is but one of several such foundation blocks, and deserves, nay commands, our intellectual attention and personal respect as a result.

IRVING LOUIS HOROWITZ

Introduction

The Widening Circle of Genocide: The Third Volume in the Series, *Genocide: A Critical Bibliographic Review* is as the full title conveys, an addition to the series which began with the publication of *Genocide: A Critical Bibliographic Review* in 1988 (London: Mansell Publishing Co.; and New York; Facts on File), and *Genocide: A Critical Bibliographic Review, Volume 2* in 1991 (London: Mansell Publishing Co.; and New York: Facts on File). The now three volumes, each separate from one another, together constitute the beginning of a small encyclopedia of scholarship of genocide:

- its history, unfolding and dynamics;
- the possibilities, problems and potentials in memorial and education about genocide;
- scholarship probing the root causes and dynamic patterns of individual and collective human availability to commit genocide, including analyses of the roles of the major societal institutions of religion, law, and the roles of professionals;
- the significance and limitations of various forms of narrative testimony and recording of the events of genocide as well as the interpretation of genocide in various art forms;
- the impacts of genocide, not only on the tragic victims who go to their death, but on myriads of survivors and their families and communities;
- patterns of mass destruction of human life, if not genocidal in the strict definition of the prevailing tradition of the definition of genocide as *intentional* destruction of a specific targeted community, nonetheless statements of human malice and/or indifference towards even millions of human lives - such as the millions of children who go to their deaths because of starvation and woeful health conditions around the world each year;
- the portents of further future mass destruction through weapons systems that ultimately threaten millions of human beings' lives, and then even the existence of planetary civilization;

- and, more than anything else, a search for innovative ideas and initiatives to reduce genocide: possible interventions in cases of genocide that might be limited in their scope if only society responds knowledgeably and courageously at an early time; responses in law to punish and perhaps to deter these heinous crimes; and proposals of new international mechanisms for the possible prevention of potential genocide before it ever takes place.

Overall, obviously, these volumes are dedicated to *the search for means of intervention and prevention of genocide*. The assembly of informations in these volumes about genocide can have no other meaning, or at least no other meaning that should be acceptable to sensitive human beings or cultures that seek to promote human welfare.

All three volumes in this series are designed around chapters by Contributing Editors who are experts in a given field of the study of genocide. They have been asked to compile first, in an authoritative, encyclopedic-form, though at times also pioneering investigation of, the knowledge base in the subject matter about which they write; followed by a selection of the critical, most representative and most useful bibliographic items in their field presented in citations which will make these bibliographic items accessible to the reader relatively easily, followed by descriptive and also critical annotations of these important items in the literature.

The volumes are intended as basic research tools to be referred to over and over again by generalists in the field of genocide studies, and by scholars who are focusing on a particular dimension of the study of genocide. Nothing has been more gratifying to me as the editor of this series than to see with my own eyes the obviously hard-at-work, dogeared first two volumes of the series on the most-often-used shelves of colleagues in different universities and institutes where I have visited professionally.

♦

In the present volume, the reader and user will find some important and original tools for the study of genocide. Part I of the book, *Democracy and the Prevention of Genocide*, is devoted to the work of political scientist, R.J. RUMMEL, of the University of Hawaii who, in recent years, painstakingly, and brilliantly, has amassed the most extensive empirical and evidential record of the tolls of genocide in one country/political region after another. Correct or incorrect, Rummel's explicit assembly of the informations renders them far more accessible than has any previous scholar to critical evaluation and revision.

In the chapter in this volume, Rummel sums up the conclusions he reaches based on the evidential record. He argues in a way that no serious thinker about society can ignore that only the democratic form of societal organization has shown itself capable of limiting the extent of genocidal practices. Many liberal thinkers would ask that greater attention, and social protest, be devoted by him to the genocidal massacres and larger cases of mass murder that have also been committed by democracies, and that the largest conclusion must be that *no* organization of human beings has proven itself exempt of the possibility of committing the worst crime men can commit. Yet, there is no question that R.J. Rummel has given us perhaps the single most important key yet proven towards the possibility of limiting genocidal activities.

♦

Part II of this book, *Religion and Genocide*, by anthropologist, LEONARD GLICK of Hampshire College contributes a piece long missing and needed in the literature of genocide. This is an appropriate place to tell that over the years of the preparation of the first two volumes in this series, numerous efforts were made to recruit a senior scholar of religion to be the Contributing Editor for this chapter. Unlike virtually any other topic for which invitations were sent out, in the case of the subject of religion and genocide there were several instances where scholars declined; but even more remarkable was the fact that in three different instances the assignment was accepted and then at a much later date word was sent that the assignment would *not* be completed after all, a phenomenon one certainly encounters in scholarly projects but which was otherwise rare in the course of the preparation of these volumes. The unusual concentration of resistances to this one topic gave me reason to wonder whether it is a topic which frightens scholars. I have decided for myself, *yes*, particularly in view of the facts that the three who did commit themselves and then were unable to deliver were, in each case, professors of religion, each also strongly identified with the Establishment of their respective faiths. It is my considered guess that they, and generally scholars and leaders in religion, are not easily capable of concluding as Leonard Glick does in the present chapter, "It appears that if we are ever to reach the point where genocidal massacres will have become a thing of the past, it will not be owing to religions: they are part of the problem" (p. 61). We are very grateful to Leonard Glick for breaking the taboo and giving us a vital statement about the crucial issue of genocide originating in "proto-genocidal attacks on neighboring groups identified as alien or 'other,' [and the] conviction that one's own deities approve of such attacks and promote their success" (p. 46).

♦

Part III, *Compelling Confirmations of the Armenian Genocide in German and Austrian Sources*, is devoted to a new contribution by the intrepid, far-ranging scholar of the Armenian Genocide, VAHAKN DADRIAN of the State University of New York. The Armenian Genocide is noteworthy for many things, including its being the earliest instance of a vast genocide in the murderous twentieth century, and which many have recognized as a "dress rehearsal" for the Holocaust which in turn then 'achieves' an archetypal meaning as the quintessential event of genocide to date, but far from the largest and not really entirely different from many other events of mass destruction of peoples.

The Armenian Genocide is a vivid case example of carefully state-organized and orchestrated premeditated genocide. It is also noteworthy in its being the most extensively denied, and, sadly, at times the most 'successfully' denied case of recorded genocide. The far-ranging instances of denial are primarily a result of the extensive and expensive organized efforts of the Turkish government to suppress and censor public informations about the Armenian genocide and the Turks' devotion to a major disinformation campaign, as well as, amazingly, the cooption of even major democratic societies such as the U.S., and even the Holocaust-sensitive democratic society of Israel, in serving what they perceive as their realpolitik interests by cooperating with Turkey's demands that various cultural and scholarly institutions and public media be stopped from producing the real record of the Armenian Genocide.

Dadrian's chapter produces a still new group of incontrovertible evidences and informations about the Armenian Genocide. In the previous volume in this series, Dadrian documented tracings of the Armenian genocide even in the records of the Turks who do so much to suppress the information. Now, in this volume, Dadrian brings together countless trails of observation and documentation by the Germans, the Turks' closest allies during the period of the Armenian genocide. It is also not lost upon the reader that in this powerful record, Dadrian touches on the chilling pattern of connections in awareness, cooperation, and support by the government of the people who had previously been responsible for genocide of an African tribe, the Hereros, and who were shortly to become responsible for the unique devotion of all of modern man's finest scientific, technological and organizational resources to the best-organized and most 'effective' campaign of persecution, terror, torture, and consummate destruction, in the Holocaust of the Jewish people, as well as others including the Gypsies.

◆

Part IV, *Case Histories, Including Much-Avoided and Denied Major Events of Genocide*, a presents a series of case histories, one more troubling than the other in its information of human bestiality and the relentlessness of commitment of state resources to the mass murders of another people. All of these cases are enormously disturbing because *even today*, our Western world, notwithstanding an emergent concern with the horrors and criminality of genocide, has organized itself to know relatively little about each of these events. I often call to the attention of my students in Israel that when they, as Jews and Israelis, are hurt and enraged at the fact that the world chose largely not to know about the Holocaust, on the level of knowing or information, and also on the level of failing to take action even when information was available, they must be aware that, in virtually all cases, they too, years after the awesome lessons of the Holocaust, know nothing about most other events of genocide in the world, past and present.

It has been a privilege to locate and gain the cooperation of each of the four scholars who contribute their respective chapters in this section on genocide in Afghanistan, genocide of the Kurds, genocide in East Timor, and the genocide of the Gypsies in the Holocaust.

Each of these Contributing Editors is clearly an intrepid and devoted scholar, literally fighting to amass, preserve and bring to the attention of the world body of scholars the informations about these cases of genocide. As

I said earlier, every one of these cases has been largely unrecognized, avoided and/or compromised by realpolitik forces who are interested in whatever practical issue of stabilizing a region, not "embarrassing" the perpetrator government, or doing lucrative political and economic business with the perpetrator government.

In the exceptional case of the poor Gypsies, of course, there are hardly motivations of lucrative self interest, for who will care one way or the other about Gypsy constituencies in the European countries where, though they constitute sizable populations, they are inevitably consigned to the lowest class, without representation or power, and are still subject to powerful institutional and populist prejudice and discrimination? I do not know of an instance where there is a government that has sought to suppress the record of what happened to the Gypsies in order to avoid giving them any additional strength politically or economically. Yet, even here, denial and suppression of the record are evidenced, and amazingly no less than at the hands of any number of devoted Holocaust scholars and institutions devoted to commemoration of the Holocaust, in their cases, they sometimes say, because they fear that recognition of the fate of the Gypsies in the Holocaust might in some way detract from their claims of specialness and uniqueness of the fates of the Jews. Oh, how the human need to be competitively first invades and contaminates even the subject of victimhood.

Three of the subjects in this part of the book are still *ongoing processes of destruction of a people* at the time of preparation of this book, if not necessarily of mass genocide, then of continued attacks on the victims, denials of the genocides that have taken place, and threats of further extermination.

Rosanne Klass, an independent scholar in New York, formerly with Freedom House, documents, convincingly and touchingly, that during 14 years of Soviet rule, 1.5 to 2 million Afghan civilians were killed—by Soviet forces and by a variety of others who assisted them including the communist regimes set up in Kabul, and the East Germans, Bulgarians, Czechs, Cubans, Palestinians and Indians. The pattern included systematic efforts to depopulate selected areas on an ethnic basis. Bombing reduced villages to rubble; helicopters slaughtered fleeing civilians; villages were singled out for massacres. Stringent controls were imposed to prevent information from reaching the outer world, including the Red Cross being ordered to leave the country. Notes Klass only too correctly, "As in other cases, reports of genocide in Afghanistan initially met with disbelief. Subsequently they received only sporadic attention" (p. 134). The reader will soon find that throughout, Rosanne Klass' work is studious, yet involving, clearly drawn out of her own ongoing commitment and caring about the human loss and tragedy.

Martin van Bruinessen, an anthropologist resident in Indonesia, and Research Associate/Lecturer at the University of Leiden in Holland, has assembled an important chapter about past and recent massacres and genocide of the Kurdish people in what appears to be a pattern of unending persecution and destruction through most of the twentieth century that continues to this very day. The Kurds have the distinction also of being the subjects of genocide by *several* governments, including the Turks, Iraqis, Iranians and Soviets. A new peak was reached in the course of the 1980s when Saddam Hussein's Iraqi government bombed the Kurdish town of Halabaja in March 1988 with chemical warheads killing, according to the most widely accepted estimate, some 5,000 people. The world's reaction, notes van Bruinessen, was essentially indifferent—in this case notwithstanding an initial outcry. "Appropriate pressure might conceivably have dissuaded Iraq from further use of chemical weapons against the Kurds. As it was, Iraq used war gasses again on a wide scale between February and September 1988, in anti-Kurdish military campaigns of unprecedented brutality they were given the ominous code-name of *Anfal* ('Spoils')" (p. 173). I would add that there have been many observers who have suggested that had Saddam Hussein been confronted fully on the issue of this mass murder by gassing, the events leading to the annexation of Kuwait and the Gulf War, including its missile attacks against Israel and Saudi Arabia, might well have been averted, but, again, the world did not know to act when required. Van Bruinessen's chapter is a long-needed introduction for Western scholars to a case history of persecution of a substantial people, who number 18 to 20 million strong in this world today, and whose outcome has not even yet been determined.

James Dunn of the Human Rights Council of Australia, formerly a diplomat, writes forcefully that the virtually unknown genocide and pattern of political repression in East Timor, which continues to this day, "provides the ultimate test of the commitment of the international community to the upholding of human rights" (p. 211).

East Timor is a small country in size and in population. The population in 1975 was about 680,000 people, of whom as many as 60,000, or almost 10 percent, may have died in the first year of the invasion. The Indonesians engaged in orgies of indiscriminate killing, large-scale public executions, rape and torture to a point where James Dunn refers to East Timor becoming, in the four years following the invasion, no less than "a killing field." To this day, the Indonesians have kept a tight occupying-power grip on East Timor. I have heard periodic reports by Amnesty International as recently as this year that the cumulative and continuing effects of the genocide and repression of the East Timor people by the Indonesian government has resulted in actual negative population growth.

The invasion of East Timor in 1975 by Indonesia was ignored by two of the world's great democracies, neighboring Australia and the world leader, the United States. "The Indonesian military action was virtually facilitated by their compliance, and their accommodating acceptance of the status quo helped seal the fate of East Timor" (p. 193).

The story of the East Timorese, a politically and strategically 'unimportant' people, raises no less fearfully than do major events of numerically larger cases of genocide all the questions that need to be asked about the responsibilities of other governments to intervene, and about the moral limits of cooperation with the perpetrator government even when it is in the interest of another country. Of course, East Timor also underscores the necessity of developing an effective international system to respond to mass murders.

The last chapter in this part of the book has to do with the relatively well-known fate of the Gypsies in the Holocaust. Yet, Gabrielle Tyrnauer, an anthropologist who is Associate Director of the Refugee Research Project, and of Living Testimonies at the Documentation Archive at McGill University, decries the extreme scarcity of information about the Gypsy fate. Wryly, she notes, "One cannot attribute the paucity of research on the Gypsy genocide to malevolent intent on the part of historians and survivors of the Holocaust, for, as noted above, most acknowledge the importance of the omission and express hopes that some day it will be remedied" (p. 221). She continues, "A cynical but perhaps realistic answer is suggested by (a reported) account of the conversation with an old French doctor. 'Of course they will be ignored,' the old man said, for 'everybody despises the Gypsies'" (p. 221).

Gabrielle Tyrnauer's excellent scholarship on the Gypsies is not only an outstanding example of diligence and academic work, but a reminder that all human communities need to become responsive to the fates of all peoples at all times.

◆

Part V of the book, "The Widening Circle of Destruction and Trauma," presents three powerful chapters, the first a comprehensive and highly original survey of the psychiatric treatment of Holocaust survivors, the second a review of literature on the massive mortality of children in our world, and the third a review of the ominous issue of horizontal nuclear proliferation and its genocidal implications.

Psychiatrist, Robert Krell of the University of British Columbia, himself a child survivor of the Holocaust, brings together a comprehensive review of the history and literature on mental health treatment of survivors of the Holocaust. He takes note of the major errors that were committed by even devoted psychiatrists at the outset in efforts to treat these traumatized people in the years immediately following World War II. He also describes, critically, the amazing and terrible silence on the part of many therapists over the course of many years who refused to encounter the centrality and overwhelming importance of the Holocaust traumatization of survivors they were treating, as if the subject were not relevant to the problems and symptoms they presented in other aspects of their lives.

In a chapter that is remarkably readable for non-mental health professionals and at the same time conveys important and original challenges for the most advanced professionals in the field, Robert Krell goes on to "speculate" that one of the fundamental hallmarks of psychiatric theory about Holocaust survivors, namely the concept of survivor guilt, is often an unconscious maneuver to protect therapists from dealing with the far more powerful force that would be awesome and frightening to encounter, namely "survivor rage." He writes: "To witness atrocity, to endure barbarity and to be helpless in face of it, engenders rage" (p. 256). The problem is that many survivors are not able consciously to express this rage; and it is only clinicians who are courageous enough to track and trust the indicators of hidden unconscious processes, and clinicians who are sensitive to the social reality that Holocaust survivors, traumatized by conditions that were so enormously out of their control, had very little place to go with their pent up needs for vengeance when the war was over, who will be able to deal with Krell's clarion call. "The suppression and containment of rage may well be the single most common feature in survivors" (p. 257). Krell concludes with a challenge that cannot be ignored by mental health professionals who deal with victim of many other extreme traumas, *"Future therapies of survivors of extreme trauma including those of torture and rape, must deal with the victim's rage, expressed or not"* (p. 257).

George Kent of the University of Hawaii writes about the massive mortality of children and analyzes the extent to which the deaths of no less than 12 million children each year (only a few years ago the figures were even higher) can and should be considered genocidal. Some scholars of genocide who have previewed this work, like some who responded to publication of earlier work by George Kent in *Internet on the Holocaust and Genocide*, the newsletter of the Institute on the Holocaust and Genocide in Jerusalem, are critical and even angry that such non-intentional deaths are included in the same context of work on genocide that has been undertaken as intentional state policy aimed at a specific target people. Yet, it is my conviction that any and all neglectful, exploitative, or abusive bureaucratic procedures, including unintentional failures of will and organization on the part of governments and international systems which result in major patterns of death to masses of human beings, in this case children, are to be considered murders of our species, along with actual intentional mass murder - although there are differences between these categories of genocide which should be identified and not blurred (see Charny, in press). And, thus, I have no hesitation in introducing all of us, including many who at this point only know that they care very deeply about certain specific events of genocide such as the Holocaust and Armenian Genocide, to the terrible issues of millions of our human children dying every year because, in a different but similar way, human society does not do what it needs to do to protect human life against the ravages of unnecessary human-caused death.

The last chapter in this section of the book probes, studiously and competently, the dangers of the spread of nuclear weapons. For the natural extension of all that is demonstrably genocidal in human systems is to utilize monstrous mega-weapons of destruction to destroy more and more and more human lives in the future. This is why no scholar of Holocaust or of any specific genocide dare, if he be human, which means committed to the humanity of his existence and the existence of all fellow creatures, ignore the dangers of known mega-weapons and systems of destruction, and by implication the incredible science-fiction weapons which are in the making.

Samuel Totten, who contributed to the first volume in this series a chapter on the fictional literature about nuclear and other futuristic weapons, here provides a responsible and sober review of the history of horizontal nuclear proliferation, as numerous and various nations strive to obtain nuclear weapons. He concludes honestly that the world does *not* show to date sufficient political will to prevent proliferation of nuclear weapons. "While the global community has much to rejoice over today as the U.S. and the Commonwealth nations set about making drastic cuts in their nuclear arsenals, one should be circumspect...The nuclear fire power that remains in the world is still awesome...There is a desperate need to awaken the world once and for all to the perils of nuclear proliferation...*before* nuclear weapons are used against a people once again" (pp. 307-308).

♦

The last section of this book, "Professional Study of Genocide and Its Prevention," is devoted to a chapter "Non-Governmental Organizations Working on the Issue of Genocide." This chapter is also by Samuel Totten who over the years has emerged as a devoted and prolific scholar of genocide, and who is in an excellent position for assembling and assessing information about organizations around the world and to evaluate critically the status of our societal efforts to stem genocide. In this chapter, readers will find information about the few organizations that have developed specific identities in respect of scholarship or activism to stem genocide, including the Society for Threatened Peoples in Germany, the Institute on the Holocaust and Genocide in Jerusalem; the Institute for the Study of Genocide in New York; International Alert, based in London; the Montreal Institute for Genocide Studies; and the Cambodian Documentation Commission in New York. Samuel Totten calls for the various individual organizations to form a more structured and formal network or coalition in order to strengthen overall efforts to prevent genocide. He also proposes that the time has come for the creation of a journal that focuses specifically on intervention and prevention of genocide. Himself a professor of education who has published extensively on teaching about Holocaust and genocide, he observes, "Current efforts to educate about genocide are neither as widespread nor as strong as they could or should be" (p. 339). Overall, he allows himself to conclude that, "There is a good deal to be hopeful about. A new field of genocide studies is emerging...The process has begun and that, in and of itself, is both a quantum leap but a vitally significant step in the right direction" (p. 342).

♦

As in the past, very special thanks are due the team of people who have completed this volume. In Volume 3, for the first time, two colleagues who have assisted me considerably in their various ways in the preparation of all three volumes are designated as associate editors. These are Marc I. Sherman, Director the Holocaust and Genocide Bibliographic Database Project at the Institute on the Holocaust and Genocide, who is also Director of Academic Research Information Systems at the Research Authority of Tel Aviv University, and Samuel Totten, Associate Professor at the College of Education, University of Arkansas. Our working together is not only a positive collaboration in getting a job done, but a constant source of support and validation of meaning because of the clearly deep devotion each member of the team has to the task not simply of putting another book out, however much we all enjoy that literary process and achievement, but to the main task of generating tools for scholarship of genocide that will, some day, contribute to interventions that will save human lives. I would also note at this writing that Marc I. Sherman will be the senior editor, along with me, of the forthcoming release of Version 2.0 of the Holocaust and Genocide Bibliographic Database to the professional public (Version 1.0 was submitted earlier only for use by the United States Institute of Peace Library in Washington, D.C., while the present version follows an extensive series of improvements and will be made available to the general public of scholars).

Coordination of the project has continued to be the province of Pauline Cooper, Managing Editor of *Internet on the Holocaust and Genocide*, as well as Project Coordinator of the Holocaust and Genocide Bibliographic Database Project. The combination of her skill and commitment are evidenced throughout the pulling together of the impossible collaborations of scholars in far-removed Indonesia, Hawaii, Canada, mainland United States, and Israel, each with their different work styles and office arrangements, and with the Tower of Babel of different computer languages. Much of the computerized production of the manuscript has been the province of Adina Bick to whom we are very grateful for cheerful and devoted work.

This third volume in the series is being published by a new publisher, namely Transaction Publishers, whose president is Irving Louis Horowitz, who also is contributing the Foreword to this book. What is unusual in this instance, and heartwarming, is that Professor Horowitz himself is, of course, one of the earliest and among the most significant scholars of genocide in his own right. His classic work on the patterns of state organization which commit themselves to the mass killing of populations was first published in 1976, and he has continued to write meaningfully on the subject of genocide. It is entirely clear that his acceptance and support of the publication of this volume are not only in his capacity as the director of a prestigious scholarly press which welcomes the social science research that we produce here, but that his heart and mind are devoted to the task to which we are devoted, namely increased awareness of, and commitment to, the development of a genuine field of study of genocide. It was therefore our honor to turn to him with the unusual request that he, our publisher, also undertake to write the Foreword to this work, for his devotion and scholarship on the subject mark him as a person who is entirely eminent to evaluate and launch the further original work that we seek to bring to the scholarly community in this volume.

We are very proud of the strong positive reviews that both first volumes in this series have earned, including selection of Volume 1 by *Choice* for its list of "Outstanding Academic Books of 1988-89" and by the American Library Association for its list of "Outstanding Reference Sources of 1989"; and we are pleased by many feedbacks from scholars about the usefulness of these volumes as resources for their ongoing research. This is also an opportunity to express further gratitude for the financial support, and also for the steady professional encouragement, under conditions of considerable work stress, given by the United States Institute of Peace in Washington, D.C., an agency of the United States Government, to the Holocaust and Genocide Bibliographic Database Project, which is the accompanying scholarly process to these volumes.

Finally, it is not hackneyed for me to repeat a personal note that has found a place in most of my major works during these years. I am fully aware of the grave demands in time and energy that this book and other work on genocide make on me, and therefore at the expense of the network of people whom I love and live with, and it is again and always appropriate for me to acknowledge and appreciate the support and love that I receive, especially from my wife, Judy Katz-Charny.

ISRAEL W. CHARNY
Jerusalem 1993

REFERENCES

Charny, Israel W. (Ed.) (1988). *Genocide: A Critical Bibliographic Review*. London: Mansell Publishing Co.; and New York: Facts on File.

Charny, Israel W. (Ed.) (1991). *Genocide: A Critical Bibliographic Review*. London: Mansell Publishing Co.; and New York: Facts on File.

Charny, Israel W. (in press, 1993). Towards a generic definition of genocide. In Andreopoulos, George (Ed.), *The Conceptual and Historical Dimensions of Genocide*. Philadelphia: University of Pennsylvania Press. [Presented at the Yale University Law School Raphael Lemkin Symposium on Genocide, February, 1991].

Dadrian, Vahakn N. (1991). Documentation of the Armenian Genocide in Turkish sources. In Charny, Israel W. (Ed.), *Genocide: A Critical Bibliographic Review, ibid.*, pp. 86-138.

Horowitz, Irving Louis (1976). *Genocide: State Power and Mass Murder*. New Brunswick, NJ: Transaction. [Revised in subsequent editions]

Kent, George (1990). "The Children's Holocaust." *Internet on the Holocaust and Genocide*, Issue 28.

Rummel, R.J. (1990). *Lethal Politics: Soviet Genocide and Mass Murder Since 1917*. New Brunswick, NJ: Transaction.

Rummel, R.J. (1991). *China's Bloody Century: Genocide and Mass Murder Since 1900*. New Brunswick, NJ: Transaction.

Rummel, R.J. (1991). *Democide: Nazi Genocide and Mass Murder*. New Brunswick, NJ: Transaction.

Totten, Samuel (1988). The literature, art, and film of nuclear and other futuristic destruction. In Charny, Israel W. (Ed.), *Genocide: A Critical Bibliographic Review*, Volume 2, *ibid.*, pp 86-138.

PART I

Democracy and the
Prevention of Genocide

1

Democide in Totalitarian States: Mortacracies and Megamurderers

R.J. Rummel

Democide: The murder of any person or people by a government.
Mortacracy: A type of political system that habitually and systematically murders large numbers of its own citizens.

THE NEW CONCEPT OF DEMOCIDE

The concept of genocide hardly covers the ruthless murder carried out by totalitarian states. It does not even account for most of those wiped out by the Nazis. A new concept is needed that covers the extent and variety of megamurders by these mortacracies.

In international conventions and the general literature, *genocide* has been defined as intentional killing by government of people because of their race, religion, ethnicity, or other indelible group membership. While killing people because of their politics or for political reasons has been explicitly excluded from the international Genocide Convention, some scholars nonetheless have included such killing in their study of genocide (Fein, 1984; Kuper, 1981; Porter, 1982). Some have extended the definition of genocide to cover any mass murder by government (Chalk and Jonassohn, 1988; Charny, 1991); some have even stretched it much further to characterize the unintentional spread of disease to indigenous populations during European colonization, including that of the American West (Stannard, 1992).

The problem is becoming conceptually acute. The early generic meaning of genocide was clear, although by its exclusion of political killing, controversial. The present extension of genocide's meaning, however, creates conceptual confusion and lumps together types of killing that theoretically should be kept distinct. If for example, genocide comes to mean all deaths due to government actions, whether lining up people and machinegunning them, executing prisoners of war, gassing Jews, creating a famine due to bad agricultural policies, the death of children because of ignorant welfare

3

policies, or the accidental creation of fatal disease among subject natives, then we would have to invent a concept to cover the intentional murder of people by virtue of their group identity. Since we already have the concept of genocide for that purpose, we really should create allied concepts to define other types of deaths due to government.

One concept, already suggested in the literature (Harff and Gurr, 1988; Rummel, 1990) is *politicide*. This defines that killing done intentionally by government for political-ideological purposes, including those killed because of their politics or political views. This is not purely exclusive of genocide, since there are cases, as in the Soviet deportation and murder of ethnic Germans during World War II, that are both genocide and politicide. Generally, however, I have found that this overlap will be but a smaller part of the politicide carried out by mortacracies, even for Nazi Germany. It usually would include, for example, executing purged Communist party members, or murdering anti-communists, counterrevolutionaries, social democrats, dissidents, or critics.

Another concept is *mass murder*, or government's intentional and indiscriminate murder of a large number of people. Obviously, in meaning this can overlap with genocide and politicide, but it can also include random executions of civilians, as in the German reprisals against partisan sabotage in Yugoslavia; working prisoners to death, as in the Soviet Kolyma mining camps; the blanket fire bombing of cities, as in the American bombing of Tokyo-Yokohama in 1945 or atomic bombing of Hiroshima and Nagasaki; or atrocities committed by soldiers, as in the 1937 Japanese rape and pillage of Nanking (which probably killed some 200,000 people).

But then there is killing that does not easily fit into any or these categories. There is, for example, murder by quota carried out by the Soviets, Chinese communists, and North Vietnamese. Government (or party) agencies would order subordinate units to kill a certain number of "enemies of the people," "rightists," or "tyrants," and the precise application of the order was left to the units involved. Moreover, millions of people died in labor or concentration camps not because of their social identity or political beliefs, but simply because they got in the way, violated some Draconian rule, did not express sufficient exuberance over the regime, innocently sat on a newspaper with the picture of Stalin showing, or simply was a body that was needed for labor (as the Nazis would grab women innocently walking along a road in Ukraine and deport them to Germany for forced labor). And there are the hundreds of thousands of peasants that slowly died of disease, malnutrition, overwork, and hunger in Cambodia as the Khmer Rouge forced them under penalty of death to labor in the collectivized fields, expropriating virtually their whole harvest and refusing them adequate medical care.

I have covered all this murder as well as genocide and politicide by the concept of *democide*. Table 1 provides the definition; Table 2 gives an overview of this and the other concepts mentioned above, placing them into the context of other sources of mass death.

Democide is meant to define the killing by states as the concept of murder does individual killing in domestic society. Here intentionality (premeditation) is critical. This also includes *practical* intentionality. If a government causes deaths through a reckless and depraved indifference to human life, the deaths were as though intended. If through neglect a mother lets her baby die of malnutrition, this is murder. If we imprison a girl in our home, force her to do exhausting work fourteen hours a day, not even minimally feed and clothe her, and watch her gradually die a little each day without helping her, then her inevitable death is not only our fault, but our practical intention. It is murder. Similarly, for example, the Soviet system for forcibly transporting prisoners to labor camps was lethal. In transit hundreds of thousands of political prisoners died at the hands of criminals or guards, or from heat, cold, or inadequate food or water. Although not intended (indeed, this deprived the regime of their labor), the deaths were still murder. They were democide.

THE CONCEPT OF A TOTALITARIAN STATE

There is much confusion about what is meant by *totalitarian* in the literature, including the denial that such systems even exist. I define a totalitarian state as one with a system of government that is unlimited constitutionally or by countervailing powers in society (such as by a church, rural gentry, labor unions, or regional powers); is not held responsible to the public by periodic secret and competitive elections; and employs its unlimited power to control all aspects of society, including the family, religion, education, business, private property, and social relationships. Under Stalin, the Soviet Union was thus totalitarian, as was Mao's China, Pol Pot's Cambodia, Hitler's Germany, and U Ne Win's Burma.

Totalitarian*ism* is then a political ideology for which a totalitarian government is the agency for realizing its ends. Thus, totalitarianism characterizes such ideologies as state socialism (as in Burma), Marxism-Leninism as in former East Germany, and Nazism. Even revolutionary Moslem Iran since the overthrow of the Shaw in 1978-79 has been totalitarian - here totalitarianism was married to Moslem fundamentalism.

In short, totalitarianism is the ideology of absolute power. State socialism. communism, Nazism, fascism, and Moslem fundamentalism have been some

Table 1. Definition of democide

Democide is any actions by government:

(1) designed to kill or cause the death of people

    (1.1) because of their religion, race, language, ethnicity, national origin, class, politics, speech, actions construed as opposing the government or wrecking social policy, or by virtue of their relationship to such people;

    (1.2) in order to fulfil a quota or requisition system;

    (1.3) in furtherance of a system of forced labor or enslavement;

    (1.4) by massacre;

    (1.5) through imposition of lethal living conditions;

    (1.6) by directly targeting noncombatants during a war or violent conflict.

(2) that cause death by virtue of an intentionally or knowingly reckless and depraved disregard for life (which constitutes *practical* intentionality), as in

    (2.1) deadly prison, concentration camp, forced labor, prisoner of war, or recruit camp conditions;

    (2.2) killing medical or scientific experiments on humans;

    (2.3) torture or beatings;

    (2.4) encouraged or condoned murder, or rape, looting, and pillage during which people are killed;

    (2.5) a famine or epidemic during which government authorities withhold aid, or knowingly act in a way to make it more deadly;

    (2.6) forced deportations and expulsions causing deaths.

(3) with the following qualifications and clarifications:

    (a) "government" includes de facto governance, as by the Communist Party of the People's Republic of China; or by a rebel or warlord army over a region and population it has conquered, as by the brief rule of Moslem Turks (East Turkistan Republic) over part of Sinkiang Province (1944-1946);

    (b) "actions by governments" comprise official or authoritative actions by government officials, including the police, military, or secret service; or such non-governmental actions (e.g., by brigands, press-gangs, or secret societies) receiving government approval, aid, or acceptance;

    (c) clause 1.1 includes, for example, directly targeting noncombatants during a war or violent conflict out of hatred or revenge, or to depopulate an enemy region or terrorize or force the population into urging surrender; this would involve, among other actions, indiscriminate urban bombing

(continued on next page)

(Table 1 - continued)

or shelling, or blockades that cause mass starvation;

(d) "relationship to such people" (clause 1.1) includes their relatives, colleagues, co-workers, teachers, or students;

(e) "massacre" (clause 1.4) includes the mass killing of prisoners of war or of rebels;

(f) "quota" system (clause 1.3) includes randomly selecting people for execution in order to meet a quota; or arresting people according to a quota, some of whom are then executed;

(g) "requisition" system (clause 1.3) includes taking from peasants or farmers all their food and produce, leaving them to starve to death;(h) and

excluding from the definition:

(h.1) execution for what are internationally considered capital crimes, such as murder, rape, spying, treason, and the like, so long as evidence does not exist that such allegations were invented by the government in order to execute the accused;

(h.2) actions taken against civilians during violent mob action or a riot (e.g., killing people with weapons in their hands is not democide);

(h.3) the death of noncombatants killed during attacks on military targets so long as the primary target is military (e.g., during bombing enemy logistics).

---

of its recent raiments. Totalitarian governments have been its agency. The state, with its international legal sovereignty and independence, has been its base. As will be pointed out, mortacracy is the result.

Totalitarian governments are the contemporary embodiment of absolute Power[1], as classically understood. And Power is a continuum, with limited and responsible Power at one end, and absolute Power - totalitarian governments - at the other end. In the middle are authoritarian governments, that is monarchies or dictatorships that leave social, economic, and cultural affairs and institutions largely free, but squash political opponents or critics (for example, in South Korea and Taiwan until recently, or Thailand and Greece under various military dictatorships). This then gives us a simple summary of relevant findings in the literature. The more unlimited the power of a government, the more likely it will kill. This can be put as a principle:

Power kills, absolute Power kills absolutely.

This Power Principle is the message emerging from research on the causes of war and current, comparative study of *democide* in this century. The more

Table 2. Sources of Mass Death

BASIS	TYPE/SUBTYPE	EXAMPLE

Intentionally By Government
    War
        international
        domestic

> **Democide**
>   **genocide (killing aspect)**
>   Nazi killing of Jews or Gypsies
>   Khmer Rouge killing of Vietnamese
>   Soviet killing of Volga Germans
>   **politicide**
>   Hitler's 1934 purge of the SA
>   Viet Minh murder of nationalists
>   Libya bombing of a civilian airliner
>   **mass murder/massacre**
>   Nazi reprisals in Yugoslavia
>   Vietnamese murder by quota
>   Japanese rape of Nanking
>   **terror**
>   Guatemala death squads
>   Stalin's 1936-38 purge of communists
>   Argentina's disappearances

Unintentionally
    Famine
        by nature
            China's 1936 famine
        government created [1]
            China's 1959-1962 Great Famine
    Disease
        by nature
            1918 influenza pandemic
        government created [1]
            Soviet 1918-23 typhus epidemic
    Disaster
        storm
        earthquake
        fire
        etc.

1. Intentionally man-made famine or disease is included under democide, and may constitute genocide, politicide, or mass murder.

power a government has, the more it can act arbitrarily according to the whims and desires of the elite, the more it will make war on others and murder its foreign and domestic subjects. The more constrained the power of governments, the more it is diffused, checked and balanced, the less it will aggress on others and commit democide. At the extremes of Power, totalitarian governments have slaughtered their people by the tens of *millions*, while many democracies can barely bring themselves to execute even serial murderers.

WHAT DO WE KNOW ABOUT DEMOCRACIES?

These above assertions about Power are extreme and categorical, but so is the evidence so far accumulated. First consider war. Table 3 shows the occurrence of war between nations since 1816. In no case has there been a war involving violent military action between stable democracies,[2] although they have fought, as everyone knows, non-democracies. Most wars are between nondemocracies. Indeed, we have here a general principle that is gaining acceptance among students of international relations and war. That is that *democracies don't make war on each other*. To this I would add that the less democratic two states, the more likely that they will fight each other.

Table 3. **Wars 1816 - 1991**

DYADS	WARS [1]
democracies vs. democracies	0
democracies vs. nondemocracies	155
nondemocracies vs. nondemocracies	198
TOTAL	353

1. Defined as any military action in which at least 1,000 are killed. The 1816-1965 count is based on Small and Singer (1976); that for 1966-1980 on Small and Singer (1982).

This belligerence of nondemocracies, that is, authoritarian and totalitarian states, is not an artifact of either a small number of democracies nor of our era. For one thing the number of democracies ("free" states) in 1991 numbered 75 out of 171, or about 44 percent of the world's states.[3] Yet we have had no war among them. Nor is there any threat of war. They create an oasis of peace.

Moreover, this is historically true of democracies as well. If one relaxes the definition of democracy to mean simply the restraint on Power by the participation of middle and lower classes in the determination of power holders and policy making, then there have been many democracies throughout history. And whether considering the classical Greek democracies, democratic forest states of Switzerland, or other historical democratic polities, they did not fight each other (depending on how war and democracy is defined, some might prefer to say that they rarely fought each other). Moreover, once those states that had been mortal enemies, that had frequently gone to war (as have France and Germany in recent centuries), became democratic, war ceased between them. Paradigmatic of this is Western Europe since 1945. The cauldron of our most disastrous wars for many centuries, in 1945 one would find few experts so foolhardy as to predict not only forty-six years of peace, but that at the end of that time there would be a European community with central government institutions, moves toward a joint European military force by France and Germany, and zero expectation of violence between any of these formerly hostile states. Yet such has happened. All because they are all democracies. Even among primitive tribes, it seems, where Power is divided and limited, war is less likely.

Were all to be said about Power is that it causes war and the attendant slaughter of the young and most capable of our species, this would be enough. But much worse is that even without the excuse of combat, Power also murders in cold blood even *more* of those helpless people it controls, *near four times more of them.*

Consider Table 4 and Figure 1, the list and its graph of this century's *megamurderers* - those states killing in cold blood, aside from warfare, 1,000,000 or more men, women, and children. At present count,[4] these eleven megamurderers have wiped out 142,902,000 people, almost *four times* the battle-dead in all this century's international and civil wars.[5] Absolute Power, that is the U.S.S.R., communist China, Nazi Germany, militarist Japan, Khmer Rouge Cambodia, communist Vietnam, and communist Yugoslavia account for 128,744,000 of them, or 90 percent. Absolute Power breeds mortacracies.

Then there are the *kilomurderers*, or those states that have killed innocents by the tens or hundreds of thousands, such as Communist Afghanistan, Angola, Laos, Ethiopia, North Korea, and Rumania, non-communist totalitarian Iran (post-1979) and Croatia (1941-44), as well as authoritarian Argentina, Burundi, Chile, Czechoslovakia (1945-46), Indonesia, Iraq, Rwanda, Spain, Sudan, and Uganda. These and other kilomurderers, and I am still counting, add an additional 8,361,000 people killed to the democide for this century, as shown in Table 4.

Table 4. **20th Century Democide**

REGIMES	YEARS	MURDERED [1]
MEGAMURDERERS		
U.S.S.R	1917-87	61,911,000
China (PRC)	1949-87	35,236,000
Germany	1934-45	20,946,000
China (KMT)	1928-49	10,075,000
Japan	1936-45	5,890,000 [2]
Cambodia	1975-78	2,035,000 [2]
Vietnam	1945-87	1,659,000 [2]
Poland	1945-47	1,583,000 [2]
Pakistan	1971	1,500,000 [2]
Yugoslavia	1944-87	1,067,000 [2]
Turkey	1915-18	1,000,000 [2]
TOTAL		**142,902,000** [2]
TOTALITARIAN TOTAL		**128,744,000** [2]
TOTALITARIAN PERCENT		**90** [2]
KILOMURDERERS		
PARTIAL SUBTOTAL		**8,361,000** [3]
PARTIAL WORLD TOTAL		**151,263,000** [3]

1. Includes genocide, politicide, and mass murder; excludes war-dead. Totalitarian states are outlined. Democide statistics are conservative mid-estimates in low to high ranges. From R.J. Rummel (1990, 1991, 1992).
2. Preliminary estimate; final figures are in Rummel (forthcoming).
3. Additional cases are in the process of being counted.

Now, democracies themselves are responsible for some of this democide. Detailed estimates have yet to be made, but preliminarily work suggests that some 2,000,000 foreigners have been killed in cold blood by democracies. This would include those killed in indiscriminate or civilian targeted city bombing, as of Germany and Japan in World War II.[6] It would include the large scale massacres of Filipinos during the bloody American colonization of the Philippines at the beginning of this century, deaths in British concentration camps in South Africa during the Boar War, civilian deaths due to starvation during the British blockade of Germany in and after World War I, the rape and murder of helpless Chinese in and around Peking in 1900, the atrocities committed by Americans in Vietnam, the murder of helpless Algerians during the Algerian War by the French, and the unnatural deaths of German prisoners of war in French and American POW camps after World War II.

Moreover, the secret services of democracies may also carry on subversive activities in other states, support deadly coups, and actually encourage or support rebel or military forces that are involved in democidal activities. Such was done, for example, by the American CIA in the 1952 coup against Iran Prime Minister Mossadeq and the 1973 coup against Chile's democratically elected President Allende by General Pinochet. Then there was the secret support given the military in El Salvador and Guatemala although they were slaughtering thousands of presumed communist supporters, and that of the Contras in their war against the Sandinista government of Nicaragua in spite of their atrocities. Particularly reprehensible was the covert support given to the Generals in Indonesia as they murdered hundreds of thousands of communists and others after the alleged attempted communist coup in 1965, and the continued secret support given to General Agha Mohammed Yahya Khan of Pakistan even as he was involved in murdering over a million Bengalis in East Pakistan (now Bangladesh).

All this killing of foreigners by democracies, complicity in such killing, or winking at allies doing such killing, may seem to violate the Power Principle, but really underlines it. For in each case, *the killing or related activities were carried out in secret, behind a conscious cover of lies and deceit* by those agencies and power-holders involved. In most cases they were shielded by tight censorship of the press and control of journalists. Even the indiscriminate bombing of German cities by the British was disguised before the House of Commons and in press releases as attacks on German military targets. That the general strategic bombing policy was to attack working men's homes was kept secret for long after the war.

The upshot is that even in democracies, Power can take root in particular institutions, remain unchecked and undisciplined, hide its activities, and murder en masse. Such Power usually flourishes during wartime, for then the military are often given far greater power, democratic controls over civilian leaders are weak, and the press labors under strict reigns. Indeed, democracies then become garrison states, Power is freed from many institutional restraints (note how easy it was during World War II to put tens

Figure 1.   20th Century Megamurderers

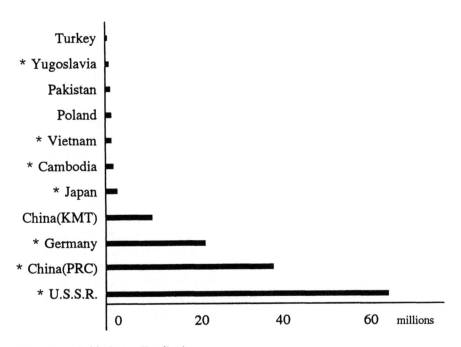

Note: From Table 2. * = Totalitarian

of thousands of American citizens - Japanese Americans - in concentration camps for nothing more than being of Japanese ancestry), and where it can become absolute, as in the military, it may kill absolutely. Witness Hiroshima and Nagasaki.[7]

THE DYNAMICS OF POWER

So Power kills and absolute Power kills absolutely. What then can be said of those alleged causes or factors in war, genocide, and mass murder favored by students of genocide? What about cultural-ethnic differences, outgroup conflict, misperception, frustration-aggression, relative deprivation, ideological imperatives, dehumanization, resource competition, overpopulation, and so on? At one time or another, for one state of another, one or more of these factors play an important role in democide. Some are essential for understanding some genocides, as of the Jews or Armenians; some politicide, as of "enemies of the people," bourgeoisie, and clergy; some massacres, as of competing religious-ethnic groups; or some atrocities, as of committed against poor and helpless villagers by victorious soldiers. But then neighbors in the service of Power have killed neighbor, fathers have killed their sons, faceless and unknown people have been killed by quota. One is hard put to find a race, religion, culture, or distinct ethnic group that has not murdered its own or others.

These specific causes or factors accelerate the likelihood of war or democide once some trigger event occurs and absolute or near absolute Power is present. That is, Power is a necessary cause for war or democide. When the elite have absolute power, war or democide is part of the following process (which I call the "conflict helix" [Rummel, 1991]).

In any society, including the international one, relations between individuals and groups is structured by social contracts determined by previous conflicts, accommodations, and adjustments among them. These social contracts define a structure of expectations that guide and regulate the social order, including Power. And this structure is based on a particular balance of powers (understood as an equation of interests, capabilities, and wills) among individuals and groups. That is, previous conflict and possibly violence determine a balance of power between competing individuals and groups and a congruent structure of expectations (as for example, war or revolution ends in a new balance of powers between nations or groups and an associated peace treaty or constitution). This structure of expectations often consists of new laws and norms defining a social order more consistent with the underlying distribution of relative power.

However, relative power never remains constant. It shifts as the interests, capabilities, and will of the parties change. The death of a charismatic leader, the outrage of significant groups, the loss of foreign support by outgroups, the entry into war and the resulting freedom of the elite to use force under the guise of war-time necessity, and so on, can significantly alter the balance of power between groups. Where such a shift in power is in favor of the governing elite, Power can now achieve its potential. Where also the elite have built up frustrations regarding those who have lost power or nonetheless feel threatened by them, where they see them as outside the moral universe, where they have dehumanized them, where the outgroup is culturally or ethnically distinct and the elite perceive them as inferior, or where any other such factors are present, Power will achieve its murderous potential. It simply waits for an excuse, an event of some sort, an assassination, a massacre in a neighboring country, an attempted coup, a famine, or a natural disaster that will justify beginning the murder en masse.

The result of such violence will be a new balance of power and attendant social contract. In some cases this may end the democide, as by the elimination of the "inferior" group (as of the Armenians by the Turks). In many cases this will subdue and cower the survivors (as the Ukrainians who lived through Stalin's collectivization campaign and intentional famine). In some cases, this establishes a new balance of power so skewed toward the elite that they may throughout their reign continue to murder at will. Murder as public policy becomes part of the new structure of expectations of the new social order. Consider the social orders of Hitler, Stalin, Mao, Pol Pot, and their henchmen.

As should be clear from all this, I believe that war and democide can be understood within a common framework. *It is part of a social process, a balancing of powers, where Power is supreme.*

It is not clear from this, however, why among states where Power is limited and accountable, war and significant democide do not take place. Two concepts explain this: *cross-pressures* and the associated *political culture.* Where Power is diffused, checked, accountable, society is riven by myriad independent groups, disparate institutions, and multiple interests. These overlap and contend; they section loyalties and divide desires and wants. Churches, unions, corporations, government bureaucracies, political parties, the media, special interest groups, and such, fight for and protect their interests. Individuals and the elite are pushed and pulled by their membership in several such groups and institutions. And it is difficult for any one driving interest to form. They are divided, weak, ambivalent; they are cross-pressured. And for the elite to sufficiently coalesce to commit itself to murdering its own citizens, there must be a near fanatical, driving interest. But even were such present among a few, the diversity of interests across the political elite and associated bureaucracies, the freedom of the media to dig out what is being planned or done, and the ever present potential leaks and fear of such leaks of disaffected elite to the media, brake such tendencies.

As to the possibility of war between democracies, diversity and resulting cross-pressures operate as well. Not only is it very difficult for the elite to unify public interests and opinion sufficiently to make war, but there are usually diverse, economic, social, and political bonds between democracies that tie them together and oppose violence.

But there is more to these restraints on Power in a democracy. Cross-pressures is a social force that operates wherever individual and group freedom predominates. It is natural to a spontaneous social field. But human behavior is not only a matter of social forces, it also depends on the meanings and values that things have and on individual norms. That is, democratic culture is also essential. When Power is checked and accountable, when cross-pressures limit the operation of Power, a particular democratic culture develops. This culture involves debate, demonstrations, protests, but also negotiation, compromise, and tolerance. It involves the arts of conflict resolution and the acceptance of democratic procedures at all levels of society. The ballot replaces the bullet, and particularly, people and groups come to accept a loss on this or that interest as only an unfortunate outcome of the way the legitimate game is played ("Lose today, win tomorrow").

That democratic political elite would kill opponents or commit genocide for some public policy is unthinkable (although such does occur in the isolated and secret corners of government where Power can still lurk). Even in modern democracies, publicly defining and dehumanizing outgroups has become a social and political evil. Witness the current potency of such allegations as "racism" or "sexism." Of course, the culture of democracy operates between democracies as well. Diplomacy, negotiating a middle-way, seeking common interests, is part of the operating medium among democracies. A detailed political history of the growth of the European Community would well display this. Since each democracy takes the legitimacy of the other and their interests for granted, conflict then is only a process of nonviolent learning and adjustment between them. Conferences, not war, is the instrumentality for settling disputes.

THE STATUS OF THE LITERATURE ON DEMOCIDE

This picture of Power and its human costs is new. Few are aware of the sheer democide that has been inflicted on our fellow human beings. That Hitler murdered millions of Jews is common knowledge. That he probably murdered overall some 20,946,000 Jews, Slavs, Gypsies, homosexuals, Frenchmen, Balts, Czechs, and others, is far less known. Similarly, that Stalin murdered tens of millions is becoming generally appreciated; but that Stalin, Lenin, and their successors murdered some 61,911,000 Soviet citizens and foreigners is little comprehended outside of the Soviet Union (where similar figures are now being widely published). Then there is Mao Tse-tung's China, militarist's Japan, Pol Pot's Cambodia, and other mortacracies listed in Table 4, who have murdered in the millions. Even those students of genocide who have tried to tabulate such killing around the world have grossly underestimated the toll. For example, a recent such accounting came up with a high of 16,000,000 killed in genocide and politicide since World War II (Harff and Gurr, 1988), an estimate that does not even cover half of the likely 35,236,000 murdered by just the Communist Party of China from 1949 to 1987 (Table 4).

Moreover, even the toll of war itself is not well understood. Many estimate that World War II, for example, killed 40,000,000 to 60,000,000 people. But the problem with such figures is that they include tens of millions killed in democide. Many war-time governments massacred civilians and foreigners, committed atrocities or genocide against them, and subjected them to reprisals. Aside from battle or military engagements, during the war the Nazis murdered some 20,946,000 civilians and prisoners of war; the Japanese, 5,890,000; the Chinese Nationalists, 5,907,000; the Chinese communists, 250,000; the Nazi satellite Croatians, 655,000; the Tito partisans, 600,000; and Stalin, 13,053,000 (above the 20,000,000 war-dead and democide by the Nazis of Soviet Jews and Slavs). I also should mention the civilian targeted bombing by the Allies that killed hundreds of thousands. Most of these deaths are usually included among the war-dead. But those killed in battle versus in democide form distinct conceptual and theoretical categories and should not be confused. That these separate categories have been consistently and sometimes intentionally combined helps raise the toll during World War II, for example, to some 60,000,000 people, way above the estimated 15,000,000 killed in battle and military action (Small and Singer, 1982). Even the almost universally accepted count of genocide during this war of "6,000,000" Jews has been generally included in the total dead for the war, which has further muddled our research and thought.[8]

Even more, our appreciation of the incredible scale of this century's democide has been stultified by lack of concepts and data. Democide is committed by absolute Power, its agency is government. The discipline for studying and analyzing power and government and associated genocide and mass murder is political science. But except for a few specific cases, such as the Holocaust and Armenian genocide, and a precious few more general works, one is hard put to find political science research specifically on this.

One university course I teach is "Introduction to Political Science." Each semester I review several possible introductory texts (the best measure of the discipline) for the course. At this stage of my research on democide, with the results shown in Table 4, I often just shake my head at what I find. *The concepts and views promoted in standard political science texts appear grossly unrealistic; they do not fit or explain, and are even contradictory to the existence of a Hell-State like Pol Pot's Cambodia, a Gulag-State like Stalin's Soviet Union, or a Genocide-State like Hitler's Germany.*

For instance, one textbook I recently read spends a chapter on describing the functions of government. Among these were law and order, individual security, cultural maintenance, and social welfare. Political scientists are still writing this even though we now have numerous examples of governments that kill millions of their own citizens, enslave the rest, and abolish traditional culture (it took only about a year for the Khmer Rouge to completely uproot and extinguish Buddhism, which had been the heart and soul of Cambodian culture). A systems approach to politics still dominates the field. Through this lens, politics is a matter of inputs and outputs, of citizen inputs, aggregation by political parties, government determining policy, and bureaucracies implementing it. There is especially the common and fundamental justification of government that it exists to protect citizens against the anarchic jungle that would otherwise threaten their lives and property. Such archaic or sterile views show no appreciation of democide's existence and all its related horrors and suffering. They are inconsistent with a regime that stands astride society like a gang of thugs over hikers they have captured in the woods, robbing all, raping some, torturing others for fun, murdering those they don't like, and terrorizing the rest into servile obedience. This is an exact characterization of many past and present governments, e.g., Idi Amin's Uganda, and it hardly squares with conventional political science.

Consider also that many books have been written on the possible nature and consequences of nuclear war and how it might be avoided. Yet, in the toll from democide, possibly even *more than 350,000,000 people killed* at the high end of the range, *we have experienced in this century the equivalent of nuclear war.* Yet to my knowledge, there is only one book dealing with the human cost of this "nuclear war" - Gil Elliot's *Twentieth Century Book of the Dead*, and to my knowledge he is not a political scientist.

What is needed is a reconceptualization of government and politics consistent with what we now know about democide and related misery. New concepts have to be invented, old ones realigned to correct our perception of Power. We need to invent concepts for governments that turn their states into a border-to-border concentration camp, that purposely starve to death millions of their citizens, that set up quotas of those that should be killed from one village or town to another (although murder by quota was carried out by the Soviets, Chinese communists, and Vietnamese, I could not find in any introductory or general political science texts even a recognition that governments can be so incredibly inhumane). *We have no concept for murder as an aim of public policy, determined by discussion among the governing elite in the highest councils, and imposed through government bureaucracy.* Indeed, in virtually no index to any general book on politics and government will one find a reference to genocide, mass murder, killed, dead, executed, or massacre. Such is not even usually indexed in books on the Soviet Union or China. Most even omit index references to concentration or labor camps or gulag, even though they may have a paragraph or so on them.

The preeminent fact about government is that some murder millions in cold blood. This is where absolute Power reigns. The second fact is that some, usually the same governments, murder tens of thousands more through foreign aggression and intervention. Absolute Power again. These two facts alone must be the basis of our reconceptualization and taxonomies; not, as it is today, only whether states are developed or not, third world or not, powerful or not, large or not. But what is also and more important is whether Power is absolute and has engaged in genocide, politicide, and mass murder - whether they are mortacracies or not.

THE LITERATURE IN ENGLISH
ON TOTALITARIAN DEMOCIDE

Turning specifically to the literature in English on totalitarian states, there has been virtually no interest in determining the nature and extent of their democide. The only exception to this is the Holocaust, for which a huge literature has grown and many fine works have concentrated on determining the how, why, when, and where of the genocide and the number of Jews murdered. But even then, hardly any such work has been undertaken for the Slavs, Gypsies, and others killed by the Nazis (the excellent collection of studies, *A Mosaic of Victims: Non-Jews Persecuted and Murdered by the Nazis*, edited by Michael Berenbaum (1990) is a notable exception). Moreover, virtually no systematic work has been done on the numbers killed and why in other totalitarian states.[9] Absolute Power's cost to human life is simply not of scholarly concern.

This is not to deny that there are some guesses and calculations about democide in the literature. Nor should one ignore the work on particular totalitarian engines of death, such as the Soviet labor or concentration camp or the secret police, although this work has also been terribly scarce compared to research on Soviet military power, political institutions, or economy. Indeed, besides my own, I could find only five works in English that have primarily focused on the *overall* democide of specific totalitarian states (Conquest, 1970; Dyadkin, 1983; Shalom, 1984, Walker, 1971, Wytwycky, 1980), and only one of them (Dyadkin) is a book.

As I have gone through stack after stack of books on a particular totalitarian state, I have been aghast at the number and detail of tables on such as their steel production, pigs, urban work force, tractors in use, railroads, exports, literacy, population, and on and on, by comparison to the lack of even snippets of data or "guesstimates" on concentration camps, forced laborers, arrests, executions, prison population, tortures, disappearances, massacres, genocide, suicides, deported, formally ostracized (in effect a sentence of death by starvation), famine deaths, and so on. Do economic, demographic, and trade statistics really matter, even where they are not falsified by the regime, when it is murdering hundreds of thousands, possibly even millions, of its citizens and millions more suffer and die at slave labor? Of what moment is it to know that the estimated 1976 gross national product for the Hell State of Cambodia under the Khmer Rouge was $540 million when Pol Pot was in the process of murdering between one-fourth to one-third of the total population. It is as though we concerned ourselves with the income and hours worked of our neighbor while he was starving his children to death. Going through this literature for information on democide is like mining gold: so many stacks of books will produce so many sentences of useful information. Then, sometimes one will hit a rich vein, such as the work of Robert Conquest (1968) on the Soviet Union or Hoang Van Chi (1964) on Vietnam.

In the following bibliography I have focused on the rare works in English that at least give an occasional nugget of information. Moreover, I have also included works that provide useful background for understanding when democide occurred and why. A frustrating amount of selectivity was required, and not all readers will agree that the works included are the best for this purpose. They are, however, the ones that I found most useful for my work on democide.

NOTES

1. Power capitalized stands for power and its holders (such as Stalin), agencies (such as government departments and bureaucracies), and instruments (such as armies, concentration camps, and propaganda).

2. An exception would appear to be barely democratic Finland, which joined Nazi Germany in its war on the Soviet Union during World War II and thus was technically at war with the Democratic Allies. No military action took place between Finland and the Allies, however.

3. See Freedom House's *Freedom Review*, 22 (January-February 1992), 6.

4. I am still in the process of collecting statistics and counting the democide for states and groups in this century. The final figures will be published in Rummel (forthcoming). Moreover, the totals for all states except the USSR, PRC, and Nazi Germany are preliminary totals.

5. The reason these figures are not rounded to millions or tens of millions is that they result from the summation and calculation of hundreds of sub-estimates, and therefore if rounded would differ from the correct sum, often by hundreds of thousands.

6. Deliberately targeting civilians with explosive and incendiary bombs simply because they happen to be under the command and control of an enemy Power is no better than lining them up and machinegunning them, a clear atrocity. In 1972, the International Red Cross held a conference of experts out of which came a Protocol to the 1949 Geneva Conventions defining the limits of air warfare. This has become widely accepted (although not ratified) and probably expresses customary international law. It outlaws any direct air attacks on civilians, including the type of terror and anti-morale attacks Great Britain and the United States carried out on German and Japanese cities.

7. Until I did a comparative study of democide, I had accepted the argument that this slaughter of civilians shortened the war and avoided perhaps more than a million being killed in the Allied invasion of Japan. However, this strategic reason for killing innocent civilians in wartime has been used throughout history. The Japanese terror bombing of Chinese cities during the Sino-Japanese War was justified as a method to shorten the war. The killing of all inhabitants of a city by the Mongols once its defenses were breached was justified by the terror it caused among inhabitants of

other cities, who would then surrender at once rather than suffer the same fate. Even the Nazi reprisal murders of tens of thousands of civilians in occupied countries was justified by them as a way of terrorizing civilians into compliance and served to protect German lives.

8. During the war the Soviets committed genocide against at least nine of their distinct ethnic-linguistic sub-nations, including ethnic Germans, ethnic Greeks, Crimean Tatars, and Balkars. Genocides by others include those of the Germans against Slavs, Gypsies, and homosexuals; Croatians against the Serbs, Jews, and Gypsies; the Serbs against Croatians and Moslems; the Hungarians against their Jews; the Serbs, Poles, and Czechs against their ethnic Germans.

9. The Turkish 1915-1918 genocide against the Armenians in 1915-1918 in which perhaps 1,000,000 or more were murdered is not included here. At the time, the government of the Young Turks was largely authoritarian, not totalitarian. Separate communities in Turkey had a great deal of autonomy, the economy was largely a free market, and the dictatorial government mainly restricted itself, as had the Ottoman Empire, to maintaining and assuring its power and repressing any political competition or opposition.

REFERENCES

Charny, Israel W. (February, 1991). A proposal of a new encompassing definition of genocide: Including new legal categories of accomplices to genocide, and genocide as a result of ecological destruction and abuse. Invited Address to the first Raphael Lemkin Symposium on Genocide, Yale University Law School.

Fein, Helen (1984). Scenarios of genocide: Models of genocide and critical responses, In Charny, Israel W. (Ed.), *Toward the Understanding and Prevention of Genocide: Proceedings of the International Conference on the Holocaust and Genocide*. Boulder: Westview Press, pp. 3-31.

Porter, Jack Nusan (1982). Introduction: What is genocide? Notes toward a definition. Porter, Jack Nusan (Ed.), In *Genocide and Human Rights: A Global Anthology*. Washington, D.C.: University Press of America, pp. 2-32.

Rummel, R.J. (1991). *The Conflict Helix: Principles and Practices of Interpersonal, Social, and International Conflict and Cooperation*. New Brunswick, NJ: Transaction Publishers. 297 pp.

Rummel, R. J. (forthcoming). *Death by Government: Genocide and Mass Murder in the Twentieth Century*.

Small, M., and Singer, J. David (1976). The war-proneness of democratic regimes, 1816-1965. *Jerusalem Journal International Relations, 1* (Summer), 50-69.

Small, Melvin, and Singer, J. David (1982). Resort to Arms: International and Civil Wars, 1816-1980. Beverly Hills: Sage Publications.

Stannard, David E. *American Holocaust: Columbus and the Conquest of the New World*. New York: Oxford University Press, 1992.

BIBLIOGRAPHY

General Works

These are sources providing general or comparative analyses that include totalitarian states, or statistics on democide in more than one of them. Throughout the annotations, when the authors use "genocide" broadly to mean what I am calling democide, I employ the latter term to describe their work.

Chalk, Frank, and Jonassohn, Kurt (1990). *The History and Sociology of Genocide: Analysis and Case Studies*. New Haven: Yale University Press. 461 pp. [Published in cooperation with the Montreal Institute for Genocide Studies]
   This is an important and seminal overview of democide throughout history. Through excerpts from major and often original works on genocide and mass murder, the authors also cover the most infamous cases of democide in this century. Most relevant here are their chapters on the Holocaust and Stalin's and Pol Pot's democides.

Charny, Israel W. (Ed.) (1984). *Toward the Understanding and Prevention of Genocide: Proceedings of the International Conference on the Holocaust and Genocide*. Boulder: Westview Press. 396 pp.
   This collection of papers on genocide and mass murder is a path-breaking contribution to our knowledge of such killing. Besides chapters dealing with the Holocaust, these papers also cover the genocide by China in Tibet, the Cambodian democide, and the Soviet genocidal famine in Ukraine.

Charny, Israel W. (Ed.) (1988). *Genocide: A Critical Bibliographic Review*. London: Mansell Publishing Co., and New York: Facts on File Publications. 273 pp.
   Has bibliographic chapters on the Holocaust, the Cambodian democide, and the Soviet genocidal famine in Ukraine.

Charny, Israel W. (1991). *Genocide: A Critical Bibliographic Review, Volume 2*. London: Mansell Publishing Co., and New York: Facts on File Publications, 432 pp.
   Has bibliographic chapters on the Holocaust and a number of general chapters relevant to democide by totalitarian states.

Glaser, Kurt, and Possony, Stefan T. (1979). *Victims of Politics: The State of Human Rights*. New York: Columbia University Press. 614 pp.
   In considering human rights, the authors comprehensively deal with all aspects of mass murder, including the Holocaust and Soviet and Communist Chinese democide. Moreover, these are treated as relevant in chapters on torture, forced labor, genocide (see particularly the chronology of genocide, mass expulsions and forced migrations, and the oppression of nationalities). This is one of the most comprehensive works on human rights in all its meanings and a useful starting work for those beginning study in this area.

Horowitz, Irving Louis (1980). *Taking Lives: Genocide and State Power*. [Third edition] New Brunswick, NJ: Transaction Books. 199 pp.
   In this revision of his 1976 *Genocide: State Power and Mass Murder*, he argues for a new typology of societies that would take into account their mass killing of human beings. At one side of a scale he suggests would-be genocidal societies, at the other permissive societies. This is an innovative work and ideal source for those doing conceptual-theoretical work on democide.

Kuper, Leo (1981). *Genocide: Its Political Use in the Twentieth Century*. New Haven, CT: Yale University Press. 255 pp.

This is a must read for students of democide. It overviews state murder, while covering the historical and political context and the relevant international conventions. It presents an helpful overview of theories of democide, and its social structure and process. His analysis of democide and the sovereign state is important for those who neglect this international legal framework that permits such mass murder.

Totten, Samuel, and Parsons, William S. (Eds.) (1991). Special Section: Teaching about Genocide. *Social Education, 55* (2), 84-133.

Articles deal with the Nazi genocide of the Jews and Gypsies, and the Cambodian and Soviet democides; presents a brief list of genocidal acts during this century (p. 129).

Veenhoven, Willem A., and Crum Ewing, Winifred (Eds.) (1975-1976). *Case Studies on Human Rights and Fundamental Freedoms: A World Survey, 5 v.* The Hague: Nijhoff. [Published for the Foundation for the Study of Plural Societies]

Includes chapters on Eastern Europe, communist China, and the Soviet gulag. Some articles, such as the one on gulag, provide much specific information on democide.

Wallimann, Isidor, and Dobkowski, Michael N. (Eds.) (1987). *Genocide and the Modern Age: Etiology and Case Studies of Mass Death*. NY: Greenwood Press. 322 pp. [Afterword by Richard L. Rubenstein]

Contains important taxonomic, theoretical, and overview chapters. The theoretical chapters on the Holocaust by John K. Roth, Alan Rosenberg, and Robert G.L. Waite are of particular relevance here.

Calculations of Overall Democide

Elliot, Gil (1972). *Twentieth Century Book of the Dead*. London: Allen Lane The Penguin Press. 242 pp.

Until recently this was the only work in English that tried to total all deaths from war and democide in this century. In many of the statistics the two are lumped together, and there usually are no sources given for them. Moreover, the usefulness of many of the subclassifications are questionable, such as those killed by "small guns" versus "big guns." However, as a pioneering effort it breaks new ground, and provides a helpful context for understanding a major democide by trying to see it through the eyes of an average victim. It concludes that major 20th century violence has caused 110,000,000 deaths (p. 215), which in the light of current research is much too low.

Foreign Affairs Research Institute (1979). The current death toll of international communism. Paper. London: 12 pp. [Arrow House, 27-31 Whitehall, London SW1A, United Kingdom]

Details, with citations, the democide in each communist state, and concludes that the toll "could not be lower than 70 million and must number at some point up to twice that conservative minimum" (p. 11).

Harff, Barbara, and Gurr, Ted Robert (1988). Toward empirical theory of genocides and politicides: Identification and measurement of cases since 1945. *International Studies Quarterly*, 32 (3), 359-371.

Pursuant to developing a typology of democide, the authors provide (without sources) what is meant to be a comprehensive listing of democides since World War II. The list is limited, however, as can be seen from their total of 7,000,000 to 16,000,000 killed (p. 370), the high being near half of the number probably killed by communist China alone since 1949. Nonetheless, this work is pioneering, and their list and typology useful.

Rummel, R.J. (1986). War isn't this century's biggest killer. *The Wall Street Journal*, (7 July). [Editorial page]
Presents the result of a preliminary survey of democide in this century, and gives the figure of 119,400,000 killed in democide (95,200,000 by communist states) compared to 35,700,000 battle-dead in all foreign and domestic wars.

Rummel, R.J. (1987). Deadlier than war. *IPA Review*, 41 (2), 24-30. [Institute of Public Affairs, 6th Floor, 83 William Street, Melbourne, 3000, Australia]
This presents the overall results given in the above *Wall Street Journal* article, in addition to a breakdown of the total for each country and the sources of information. A theoretical elaboration is also given, emphasizing the role of freedom in preventing democide.

Rummel, R.J. (1988). As though a nuclear war: the death toll of absolutism. *International Journal on World Peace, 5* (3), 27-43.
This is a republication of the above IPA article in a generally more accessible source.

Stewart-Smith, D. G. (1964). *The Defeat of Communism.* London: Ludgate Press. 482 pp.

A book-length narrative chronology of communism. Provides relevant war and democide statistics at points in the chronology. Concludes that the communists killed 83,500,000 people in war and democide, excluding World War II (p. 223).

SOVIET UNION

From 1917 to 1987, the communist party of the Soviet Union and its various leaders murdered in one way or another 28,326,000 to 126,891,000 citizens and foreigners, most conservatively 61,911,000 (54,767,000 citizens). The following general works shed light on this horrible and incredible democide and many contain overall figures of their own that tend to confirm this total.

General Works

Heller, Mikhail and Nekrich, Aleksandr (1986). *Utopia in Power: The History of the Soviet Union from 1917 to the Present.* New York: Summit Books, 1986. 877 pp. [Translated by Phyllis B. Carlos]
One of the best histories of the Soviet Union, it provides insight into motives and processes, while being sensitive to how, when, and what of democide.

Kravchenko, Victor (1946). *I Chose Freedom: The Personal and Political Life of a Soviet Official.* New York: Charles Scribner's Sons. 496 pp.
This is a must read. It is the first hand account of much of the party's thinking, democide, and related events by one intimately involved as an official. So damaging was the publication of this book that the Soviets launched a very effective propaganda

and disinformation campaign against it.

Calculations of Soviet Democide

Conquest, Robert (1970). *The Human Cost of Soviet Communism.* Washington, DC: United States Senate, 91st Congress, 2d Session, Committee on the Judiciary, Washington, D.C.: U.S. Government Printing Office, 25 pp.

A very useful overview of Soviet killing and one of the few attempts to calculate the overall Soviet democide. Conquest concludes by quoting the minimum of 20,000,000 dead calculated in his *Great Terror* (see below), and then adds that at least several million would have to be added to the figure for the Stalin-Yezhov period.

Dyadkin, Iosif G. (1983). *Unnatural Deaths in the USSR, 1928-1954.* New Brunswick, NJ: Transaction Books, 80 pp. [Translated by Tania Deruguine. Introduction by Nick Eberstadt]

Until recently, this was the only book in English wholly devoted to determining Soviet democide. A former professor of geophysics at the All-Union Geophysical Research Institute, Kalinin, USSR, Dyadkin wrote this former samizdat (underground literature) based on "census" returns. He calculated that for the years 1926 to 1954, repression cost 26,000,000 to 35,450,000 lives, excluding war-dead (pp. 41, 48, 55, 60). For the same period he determined that the population deficit was 78,000,000, including unborn, were there no repression (p. 59). For this samizdat he was imprisoned in the gulag for three years.

Maximoff, G. P. (1940). *The Guillotine at Work: Twenty Years of Terror in Russia (Data and Documents).* Chicago: The Chicago Section of the Alexander Berkman Fund. 624 pp. [Translated from Russian]

An important and statistics-filled attempt to document Lenin's democide in the years immediately following the Bolshevik coup in 1917. For example, Maximoff calculates a democide of at least 70,000 in 1921, including a "most conservative" 30,000 to 40,000 executed (p. 199). This is an eye opener for those who insist that Lenin had little blood on his hands.

Rummel, R.J. (1990). *Lethal Politics: Soviet Genocide and Mass Murder Since 1917.* New Brunswick, NJ : Transaction Publishers. 268 pp.

A historical and statistical analysis of Soviet democide. Concludes that 61,911,000 people probably were killed, including 54,767,000 citizens.

Stalin and His Period

In the bloody history of the Soviet Union, Stalin's reign from 1928 to 1953 was the most ruthless. At an absolute minimum, he and his communist henchmen murdered at least 19,641,000 people through terror, deportations, gulag, the intentional Ukrainian famine, purges, and collectivization, possibly as many as 91,685,000; a most reasonable figure is probably around 42,672,000. The following studies focus particularly on Stalin, but relevant figures also are given by most of the general or topical studies listed for the Soviet Union.

Antonov-Ovseenko, Anton (1981). *The Time of Stalin: Portrait of a Tyranny.* New York: Harper & Row. 374 pp. [Translated by George Saunders. Introduction by Stephen F. Cohen]

An in-depth treatment and analysis of this period, with helpful information on Stalin's various democides. He claims that Stalin killed 30,000,000 to 40,000,000 people (p. 126).

Conquest, Robert (1968). *The Great Terror: Stalin's Purge of the Thirties*. New York: Macmillan. 633 pp.
A thorough investigation into the background, reasons, and consequences of Stalin's great purge of the communist party from 1937 to 1938 in which perhaps 1,000,000 people were executed (p. 532). Packed full of details and useful information on the 1930s. Conquest presents an appendix in which he carefully considers diverse evidence on the human toll under Stalin and finds that for twenty-three years of his rule, "We get a figure of 20 million dead, which is almost certainly too low and might require an increase of 50 percent or so" (p. 533). This is perhaps the most widely quoted figure about Soviet democide in the literature.

Conquest, Robert (1990). *The Great Terror: A Reassessment*. New York: Oxford University Press. 570 pp.
Based on the most recent information revealed as a result of greater freedom in the Soviet Union, Conquest reconsiders the above calculated democide under Stalin and, without explicitly altering his above estimate, he concludes that "the sheer magnitudes of the Stalin holocaust are now beyond doubt" (p. 487).

Medvedev, Roy A. (1979). *On Stalin and Stalinism*. Oxford: Oxford University Press. 205 pp. [Translated by Ellen de Kadt]
As a judicious and insightful analysis of Soviet communism and Stalin's period by a Marxist historian, this work is an important corrective to the work of many Western Sovietologists. He cites demographer M. Maksudov's claim that from 1918 to 1953 there were 22,000,000 to 23,000,000 unnatural deaths (pp. 140-41).

Tolstoy, Nikolai (1981). *Stalin's Secret War*. New York: Holt, Rinehart and Winston. 463 pp.
A fact-filled and democide-sensitive analysis of Stalin's period and a good source of different kinds of democide statistics.

Gulag

The concentration and forced labor camps, the system of which is now known as *gulag*, were the most lethal Soviet institutions. Their major product was death, and only secondarily work. Established by Lenin, the camps were vastly developed by Stalin such that in the post World War II period they contained perhaps 12,000,000 prisoners, even possibly 20,000,000. The overall toll in gulag, including those dying in transit to or between camps, was probably from 15,919,000 to 82,281,000 prisoners, most likely 39,464,000. The following works help substantiate these figures while providing a feel for the slow and miserable deaths underlying these figures.

Conquest, Robert (1978). *Kolyma: The Arctic Death Camps*. New York: Viking Press. 254 pp.
A must read. This is a chilling and detailed history of the forced labor mining camps in Kolyma (northeastern Siberia). Life expectancy in some of these camps was measured in months; in some no one survived. The overall rough average death rate was 25 percent per year (p. 220); and Conquest calculates that from the 1930s to the

1950s, 2,000,000 to 5,500,000 died in these camps alone (pp. 227-28).

Kosyk, Volodymyr (1962). *Concentration Camps in the USSR*. London: Ukrainian Publishers.
This is a careful statistical analysis of the number of prisoners in the camps and approximate number of deaths for each year from 1927 to 1958. He concludes that overall 32,600,000 died in the camps, but he also says this figure is probably too low (p. 79).

Panin, Dimitri (1976). *The Notebooks of Sologdin*. New York: Harcourt Brace Jovanovich. 320 pp. [Translated by John Moore]
Written by a mechanical engineer who spent over a dozen years in the camps, this is an excellent analysis of Soviet democide and particularly of gulag. He estimates that 2,000,000 to 3,000,000 people were murdered from 1922 to 1928 (p. 93n), a period that many Sovietologists claim was relatively free of terror and mass killing. Overall, from 1917 to 1953, he puts the democide at 57,000,000 to 69,500,000 people (p. 93n).

Solzhenitsyn, Aleksandr I (1973). *The Gulag Archipelago 1918-1956: An Experiment in Literary Investigation*, Volumes I-II. New York: Harper & Row. 660 pp. [Translated by Thomas P. Whitney]
This and the following two volumes not only have received international acclaim for their personal, historical, and analytical description of gulag, but they caused many Westerners to reconsider their pro-communism or sympathy for the Soviet Union. These must be read by anyone wishing to get a feel for the camps, their administration, sheer misery, and death. Of particular worth is that the camps are treated as part of a process, beginning with the very nature of communist rule, its terror, the arrest, torture and sentencing, prison, transit to the camps, life and death in the camps, administrative resentencing, and for survivors, conditional release.

Solzhenitsyn, Aleksandr I. (1975). *The Gulag Archipelago 1918-1956: An Experiment in Literary Investigation, Volumes III-IV*. NY: Harper & Row. 712 pp. [Translated by Thomas P. Whitney]
Solzhenitsyn cites a professor of statistics, Kurnanov, who claims that "internal repression" cost 66,000,000 lives (p. 10).

Solzhenitsyn, Aleksandr I. (1978). *The Gulag Archipelago 1918-1956: An Experiment in Literary Investigation, Volumes V-VII*. New York: Harper & Row. 558 pp. [Translated by Harry Willetts]

Zorin, Libushe (1980). *Soviet Prisons and Concentration Camps: An Annotated Bibliography 1917-1980*. Newtonville, MA: Oriental Research Partners. 118 pp.

Ukraine Famine

From 1932 to 1933, Stalin purposely starved to death 5,000,000, maybe even 10,000,000 Ukrainians, probably to suppress Ukrainian nationalism and destroy peasant opposition to collectivism. Many works have recently been published on this, and only the most noteworthy can be listed here. Several excellent studies are also included in the general works listed earlier at the beginning of this bibliography.

Conquest, Robert (1986). *The Harvest of Sorrow: Soviet Collectivization and the*

Terror-Famine. New York: Oxford University Press. 412 pp.
This is the best work on the famine. It gives details and evidence not widely available. Conquest carefully considers whether the famine was in fact intentional, and after weighing opposing arguments he concludes that it had to be. He also evaluates separate estimates of the toll and gives his reasoning for selecting his estimate that 5,000,000 thus died in the Ukraine (p. 306).

Dalrymple, Dana G. (1964). The Soviet famine of 1932-1934. *Soviet Studies*, 15 (3), 250-284.
Perhaps the first scholarly study published on the famine that views it as intentional. He compares a variety of estimates of the toll and accepts a figure around 5,000,000 for the famine in and outside the Ukraine (p. 250).

Mace, James E. (1984). Famine and nationalism in Soviet Ukraine. *Problems of Communism*, (May-June), 37-50.
An excellent presentation of the information on the famine and its context. Mace argues that according to accepted international definitions, this famine was genocide (p. 37). Using demographic statistics, he calculates that 7,500,000 Ukrainians died as a result (p. 39).

Serbyn, Roman, and Krawchenko, Bohdan (Eds.) (1986). *Famine in Ukraine 1932-1933*. Edmonton: Canadian Institute of Ukrainian Studies, University of Alberta.
A collection of factual and significant studies on the famine.

World War II Repatriation

Tolstoy, Nikolai (1979). *Victims of Yalta*. London: Corgi Books. 640 pp. [Revised and updated edition]
This is a detailed historical study of the forced repatriation of Soviet citizens *and others* into Soviet hands by the Allies as World War II came to an end and after. Some 5,500,000 people were repatriated, among whom (based on statistics Tolstoy gives) perhaps 825,000 to 1,100,000 were killed (pp. 515-16), many within hours of being repatriated.

Treatment of Occupied or Absorbed Nations

Gross, Jan T. (1988). *Revolution from Abroad: The Soviet Conquest of Poland's Western Ukraine and Western Belorussia*. Princeton, N. J.: Princeton University Press. 334 pp.
A description of the Soviet rape of Poland from 1939 to 1940, mass murder of Poles, and the deportation of 1,250,000 others (p. 146) to inhospitable parts of the Soviet Union; through September 1941, 300,000 Poles died from deportation and in concentration camps (p. 229).

Misiunas, Romuald J., and Taagepera, Rein (1983). *The Baltic States: Years of Dependence 1940-1980*. Berkeley, CA : University of California Press. 333 pp.
An excellent history of the Soviet occupation of the Baltic states. Gives a statistical appendix, which includes figures on war and occupation deaths 1940-1945 (with a "very approximate 'questimate'" of 550,000 dead). Also presents information on the deportation of Balts in which many died, perhaps over 100,000 in 1949 and after (p. 100).

Conquest, Robert (1970). *The Nation Killers: The Soviet Deportation of Nationalities.* London: Macmillan. 222 pp. [Revision of the 1960 ed. published under the title: *The Soviet Deportation of Nationalities*]
    This is a balanced description of the deportation of Soviet national and ethnic groups during World War II, including a conservative analysis of the numbers deported and their deaths. In total, 1,850,000 people from eight national/ethnic groups were deported (pp. 65-66), with a likely 530,000 dying as a result (p. 162).

COMMUNIST CHINA

General

In the magnitude of its killing, communist China is only second to the Soviet Union. Since they formerly seized power in 1949 and up to 1987, the Chinese communists killed 5,999,000 to 102,671,000 people, most likely 35,236,000 (not counting the toll of the great famine of 1959 to 1961, nor the 3,466,000 killed by the communists before they assumed total control). The following works particularly help understand this democide and provide supporting statistics.

Chow Ching-wen (1960). *Ten Years of Storm: The True Story of the Communist Regime in China.* New York: Holt, Rinehart and Winston. 323 pp. [Translated and edited by Lai Ming. Foreword by Lin Yutang]

Chu, Valentin (1963). *Ta Ta, Tan Tan: The Inside Story of Communist China.* New York: W. W. Norton. 320 pp.[Ta ta, tan tan means fight fight, talk talk]

Garside, Roger (1981). *Coming Alive: China After Mao.* New York: McGraw-Hill. 458 pp.

Guillermaz, Jacques (1976). *The Chinese Communist Party in Power 1949-1976.* Boulder, CO: Westview Press. 614 pp. [Translated by Anne Destenay]

Hunter, Edward (1958). *The Black Book on China: the Continuing Revolt.* New York: The Bookmailer. 136 pp.
    Hunter believes the communist democide to be closer to 50,000,000 than to 30,000,000 (p. 137).

Labin, Suzanne (1960). *The Anthill: The Human Condition in Communist China.* New York: Praeger. 442 pp. [Translated by Edward Fitzgerald]

Tang, Peter S. H., and Maloney, Joan M. (1967). *Communist China: The Domestic Scene 1949-1967.* South Orange, NJ: Seton Hall University Press. 606 pp. [Introduction by John B. Tsu]

Calculations of Overall Democide

Li Cheng-Chung (1979). *The Question of Human Rights on China Mainland.* Republic of China: World Anti-Communist League, China Chapter. 180 pp.
    A description of the various ways in which the communist have violated human rights. Based on statistics from the Republic of China, the author calculates the

democide as 78,860,000 people for 1949 to 1968, not counting the Korean War and guerrilla dead (p. 153).

Shalom, Stephen Rosskamm (1984). *Deaths in China Due to Communism: Propaganda Versus Reality.* Tempe, AZ: Center for Asian Studies, Arizona State University. 234 pp. [Occasional Paper No. 15]
A must study for anyone interested in China's overall democide. This is a careful and detailed line by line critique of Walker's democide statistics (see below), which Shalom concludes are far too high. Rather, he calculates that 3,000,000 to 4,000,000 were killed from 1949 to 1970 (p. 111).

Walker, Richard L. (1971) *The Human Cost of Communism in China.* Washington, DC: United States Senate, Committee on the Judiciary, U.S. Government Printing Office. 28 pp.
He outlines the nature of communist Chinese democide and also gives a widely quoted table of democide organized by type, which adds up to a total (ignoring Korean War dead) of 31,750,000 to 58,500,000 killed between 1949 to 1970 (p. 16).

Rummel, R.J. (1991). *China's Bloody Century: Genocide and Mass Murder Since 1900.* New Brunswick, NJ: Transaction Publishers. 333 pp.
Presents an historical and statistical analysis of communist democide from 1928 to 1987. Finds that the democide by the People's Republic of China probably amounted to 35,236,000 killed.

Mao Tse-tung

Mao Tse-tung (1967). *Selected Works of Mao Tse-tung, 4 vols.*, Peking, China: Foreign Languages Press. [In English]
This collection contains many selections that are essential reading for understanding the background of Mao's later policies and the underlying rationale for the associated democide.

Paloczi-Horvath, George (1963). *Mao Tse-Tung: Emperor of the Blue Ants.* NY: Doubleday. 393 pp.

Gulag

From 1949 to 1987, possibly as many as 15,720,000 Chinese died in the Chinese forced labor camps. Unlike for the Soviet gulag, there are few works on the Chinese camps system. Following are a some of the most relevant.

Bao Ruo-Wang (Jean Pasqualini), and Chelminski, Rudolph (1973). *Prisoner of Mao.* New York: Coward, McCann and Geoghegan.

White Book on Forced Labour and Concentration Camps in the People's Republic of China I: The Hearings. (1956 circa) Paris: Commission Internationale Contre Le Régime Concentrationnaire.

White Book on Forced Labour and Concentration Camps in the People's Republic of China: II: The Record. (1959 circa) Paris: Commission Internationale Contre Le Regime Concentrationnaire.

Whyte, Martin King (1973). Corrective labor camps in China. *Asian Survey*, 13 (3), 253-269.

Cultural Revolution

From 1964 to 1968, during the height of the killing associated with the violent cultural revolution, some 1,000,000 Chinese were murdered or otherwise killed. Few social revolutions have been as violent. The following works provide analysis and background for appreciating this democide and associated events.

Domes, Jürgen (1973). *The Internal Politics of China 1949-1972*. New York: Praeger. 258 pp. [Translated by Rüdiger Machetzki]
    An informative analysis of the events and debate among the top leaders that led to and comprised the Cultural Revolution.

Liu Guokai (1987). *A Brief Analysis of the Cultural Revolution*. New York: M. E. Sharpe. 151 pp. [guest editor Anita Chan]
    An abridged translated version of the author's essay published in China, this is a first rate analysis of the revolution by a participant.

Thurston, Anne F. (1987). *Enemies of the People*. New York: Alfred A. Knopf.

NAZI GERMANY

Stacks of volumes on Nazi Germany are available, many of them concerned with its history, diplomacy, politics, aggression, repression, and the Holocaust. Very few of them, however, consider the democide against other than the Jews. Yet, from 1933 to 1945 the Nazis probably killed in cold blood some 15,003,000 to 31,595,000 people, probably 20,946,000 overall, including 5,291,000 Jews. Only those works providing the most relevant statistics are noted below.

General

Berenbaum, Michael (Ed.) (1990). *A Mosaic of Victims: Non-Jews Persecuted and Murdered by the Nazis*. New York: New York University Press. 244 pp.
    This is an especially important collection of articles that cover topics and provide information not easily available in other works. For example, there are chapters on Nazi policies in Ukraine, the U.S.S.R. proper, Poland, Belgium and France, as well as on the Slavs, the Nazi euthanasia program, forced labor, pacifists, and Croatia.

Hirschfeld, Gerhard, (Ed.) (1986). *The Policies of Genocide: Jews and Soviet Prisoners of War in Nazi Germany*. London: Allen & Unwin. 172 pp. [Introduction by Wolfgang J. Mommsen]

Kogon, Eugen (1960). *The Theory and Practice of Hell: The German Concentration Camps and the System Behind Them*. New York: The Berkley Publishing Co. 328 pp. [Translated by Heinz Norden]
    Although relatively short in treatment, this gives a useful history and accounting of

the Nazi concentration-death camp system. Kogon has a chapter on the "statistics of mortality" that gives a yearly breakdown of the concentration camp population and calculates the overall concentration/death camp death toll as 7,125,000 people (p. 251).

Calculations of Democide

Rummel, R. J. (1992). *Democide: Nazi Genocides and Mass Murder.* New Brunswick, NJ: Transaction Publishers.150 pp.
An attempt to outline and explain Nazi democide and collect available statistics to calculate the overall toll, including that in occupied countries. Finds that 20,946,000 people probably were murdered by the Nazis, including Jews, Gypsies, Poles, Russians, Yugoslavs, Frenchmen, and many others. The author argues that along with the democide of the Soviet Union and People's Republic of China, this is another example that absolute ideology coupled with an absolute power of the state is deadly to human life.

Wytwycky, Bohdan (1980). *The Other Holocaust: Many Circles of Hell.* Washington, D. C.: The Novak Report on the New Ethnicity. 93 pp.
Tries to explain and calculate the overall Nazi democide, especially focused on the Slavs. Wytwycky concludes that 15,450,000 to 16,300,000 Jews, Gypsies, Soviet POWs, Ukrainians, Poles, and Byelorussians were murdered (pp. 91-2).

Holocaust: Genocide of the Jews

Among the many works on the Holocaust, the following have been selected for the detail and excellence of their treatment, the understanding they provide to a non-Holocaust scholar, and the usefulness of their calculations of the total genocide.

Reitlinger, Gerald (1968). *The Final Solution: The Attempt to Exterminate the Jews of Europe 1939-1945.* London: Vallentine, Mitchell, and Co. 668 pp. [Second revised and augmented edition]
Gives in Appendix I a country-by-country statistical summary and analysis of the genocide. "Conjectures" that 4,204,400 to 4,575,400 Jews were thus murdered (p. 546), the lowest count by any reputable study.

Bauer, Yehuda (1982). *A History of the Holocaust.* New York: Franklin Watts. 398 pp. [With the assistance of Nili Keren]
Presents a through history of the Holocaust and related events, with pertinent statistical tables; touches also on other genocides. Gives a country breakdown of the Holocaust, which Bauer totals to 5,820,960 Jews murdered (p. 335).

Dawidowicz, Lucy S. (1975). *The War Against the Jews 1933-1945.* New York: Holt, Rinehart and Winston. 460 pp.
In addition to a general analysis and history of the genocide, Dawidowicz also gives an Appendix providing a brief account for each country of what happened to the Jews and their toll, which overall sums to 5,933,900 murdered (p. 403).

Fein, Helen (1979). *Accounting for Genocide: National Responses and Jewish Victimization During the Holocaust.* New York: The Free Press. 468 pp.

A unique and careful social science and statistical attempt (including the use of multiple regression) to explain the Holocaust. There is much important information of value given in its various tables, themselves well worth separate study. Fein calculates that 4,610,000 Jews were lost (p. 21), not counting the U.S.S.R. (p. 21).

Fein, Helen (1981). Reviewing the toll: Jewish dead, losses and victims of the Holocaust. *Shoah, 2* (2), 20-26.
Compares a variety of estimates of the Holocaust's toll and tries to account for their differences. Concludes that "all sources suggest the likelihood that competent estimates will fall... between five and six million" (p. 23).

Fleming, Gerald (1984). *Hitler and the Final Solution*. Berkeley, CA: University of California Press. 219 pp. [Introduction by Saul Friedlander]
Gives a country breakdown of the genocide toll, which he sums to 4,975,477 murdered (p. 193).

Gilbert, Martin (1982). *The Macmillan Atlas of the Holocaust*. New York: Macmillan, 256 pp.
An excellent collection of maps on a variety of aspects of the genocide, including where anti-Jewish pogroms and persecutions have occurred, Poland's major Jewish communities, the destruction of the Jews of Croatia, deportations and revolt, death camps, and the Jews of Bessarabia. Many of the maps also give statistics, and one in particular maps the toll by each country which totals slightly over 5,750,000 (pp. 244-45).

Hilberg, Raul (1985). *The Destruction of the European Jews*. New York: Holmes & Meier. 1273 pp. [Revised and definitive edition]
Deservedly, perhaps the most quoted work on the genocide. Historically and statistically thorough. In Appendix III, Hilberg tabulates a statistical recapitulation by killing operation and country, totalling 5,100,000 Jews murdered.

Gutman, Israel, and Rozett, Robert (1990). Estimated Jewish losses in the Holocaust. In Gutman, Israel (Ed.), *Encyclopedia of the Holocaust, Volume 4*. New York: Macmillan, pp. 1797-1802.
Gutman, who is editor-in-chief of the Encyclopedia, analyzes the Jewish losses by country and totals them up to 5,596,029 to 5,860,129 (p. 1799).

Slavs

Dallin, Alexander (1981). *German Rule in Russia 1941-1945: A Study of Occupation Policies*. New York: Macmillan. 707 pp. [2nd revised edition]
Must reading for an understanding of Nazi democide in the Soviet Union. The book is historically and analytically thorough.

Gross, Jan Tomasz (1979). *Polish Society Under German Occupation: The General gouvernement, 1939-1944*. Princeton, NJ: University Press. 343 pp.

Kamenetsky, Ihor (1961). *Secret Nazi Plans for Eastern Europe: A Study of Lebensraum Policies*. New Haven, CT : College and University Press. 263 pp.

Gypsies

Kenrick, Donald, and Puxon, Grattan (1972). *The Destiny of Europe's Gypsies*. New York: Basic Books. 256 pp.
This is a major and rare work on the Nazi genocide of the Gypsies. The author's give the overall toll as 219,700 Gypsies murdered (p. 184).

Tyrnauer, Gabrielle (1989). *Gypsies and the Holocaust: A Bibliography and Introductory Essay*. Montreal: Interuniversity Center for European Studies and the Montreal Institute for Genocide Studies. 51 pp.

Homosexuals

Rector, Frank (1981). *The Nazi Extermination of Homosexuals*. New York: Stein and Day. 189 pp.
One of the few major works in English on the Nazi treatment of homosexuals, which amounted to genocide. He concludes that at least 500,000 homosexuals were murdered (p. 116).

Porter, Jack Nusan (1991). *Sexual Politics In the Third Reich: The Persecution of the Homosexuals During the Holocaust: A Bibliography and Introductory Essay*. Newton, MA: The Spencer Press, April 1991, 35pp.
An annotated bibliography of German and English language works on sex, homosexuality, and the Nazis.

MILITARIST JAPAN

No major general works on genocide and mass murder discuss the massacres and atrocities of militarized and totalitarian Japan. Yet, just considering World War II and the Sino-Japanese War (1937 to 1945), the Japanese democide probably amounted to 3,017,000 to 9,488,000 people, most likely 5,890,000. This is surely the forgotten democide.

General

Dower, John W. (1986). *War Without Mercy: Race and Power in the Pacific War*. New York: Pantheon Books. 398 pp.
This is an exellent and comprehensive non-military work on the Pacific War. It not only includes much material relevant to various Japanese democides, as in China and Indonesia, but also includes an extensive discussion of the American side of the war and their atrocities. He argues that this was a racial war for Americans.

James, David H. (1951). *The Rise and Fall of the Japanese Empire*. London: George Allen & Unwin. 409 pp.
A most helpful analytical description and analysis of the Japanese empire and particularly of the Japanese treatment of Western POWs by a scholar who was such a prisoner himself.

Kerr, E. Bartlett (1985). *Surrender and Survival: The Experience of American POWs in the Pacific 1941-1945*. New York: William Morrow and Co. 356 pp.

Pritchard, R. John, and Zaide, Sonia Magbanua (Eds.) (1981). *The Tokyo War Crimes Trial, 22 volumes*. New York: Garland Publishing. The complete transcripts of the proceedings of the International Military Tribunal for the Far East.
　　A first source for serious study of Japanese democide, it is an excellent collection of testimony and facts on Japanese democide. Included is an excellent index, that contains items on massacres and atrocities.

Williams, Peter, and Wallace, David (1989). *Unit 731: The Japanese Army's Secret of Secrets*. London: Hodder & Stoughton. 366 pp.
　　An account of the Japanese development of bacteriological weapons, from their testing stage to actual field testing in China. Gives limited information on numbers killed, but essential information on the how and why.

Sino-Japanese War

Most of Japan's democide was against the Chinese during the 1937-1945 Sino-Japanese War. The Japanese murdered a conservatively estimated 3,949,000 Chinese. There are no works on this democide per se, although the following and the above volumes provide some understanding of it.

Dorn, Frank (1974). *The Sino-Japanese War, 1937-41: From Marco Polo Bridge to Pearl Harbor*. New York: Macmillan. 477 pp.

Timperley, H. J. (1938). *Japanese Terror in China*. New York: Modern Age Books. 220 pp.

KHMER ROUGE CAMBODIA

It is now well known that the communist Khmer Rouge committed an incredible democide in Cambodia once they grabbed power in 1975. Most published collections on genocide now include a chapter on Cambodia. Considering the various estimates of the toll, from 600,000 to 3,000,000 were murdered during their reign, probably 2,000,000 Cambodians overall - close to a third of the population. The following are the best of the studies giving a foundation for understanding this incredible figure.

Becker, Elizabeth (1986). *When the War Was Over: Cambodia's Revolution and the Voices of Its People*. New York: Simon & Shuster. 501 pp.
　　This is an excellent starting point on the Khmer Rouge period by a reporter who covered the war in Cambodia for the Washington Post. Becker claims that 2,000,000 died from the Khmer Rouge (pp. 19-20).

Jackson, Karl D. (Ed.) (1989). *Cambodia 1975-1978: Rendezvous with Death*. Princeton: New Jersey: Princeton University Press, 334 pp.
　　A collection of first-rate articles by experts on the Khmer Rouge period, particularly focusing on the context for understanding the Khmer Rouge, the dynamics of power among them, and the nature and consequences of their economic politics. Contains translations of importatant Khmer Rouge documents.

Kampuchean Inquiry Commission (1982). *Kampuchea in the Seventies: Report of a Finnish Inquiry Commission.* Helsinki, Finland, 114 pp.
   A detailed investigation into conditions under the Khmer Rouge. Gives the toll as nearly 1,000,000 (p. 35).

Kiernan, Ben, and Boua, Chanthou (1982). *Peasants and Politics in Kampuchea, 1942-1981.* London: Zed Press. 401 pp.
   This has become a classic collection of relevant, in depth scholarly studies that provide a helpful background for understanding the Khmer Rouge and their rule. It is particularly helpful in understanding the material and social conditions of the peasantry and the communist movement and Pol Pot's role in it. Also useful for perspective and context are the large number of testimonies from Cambodians who lived under the Khmer Rouge.

Barron, John, and Paul, Anthony (1977). *Peace With Horror: The Untold Story of Communist Genocide in Cambodia.* London: Hodder and Stoughton. 234 pp. [American edition titled *Murder of a Gentle Land.* New York: Reader's Digest Press-Thomas Y. Crowell]
   Based on refugee reports, this was among the first and most influential reports of the horror and mass killing under the Khmer Rouge in its first year-and-a-half. It is detailed and close to the experience of the average Cambodian. Barron and Paul estimate the democide toll as 1,200,000 in the first twenty-one months (p. 206), which they subsequently believed much too low.

Ponchaud, François (1977). *Cambodia Year Zero.* New York: Holt, Rinehart and Winston. 212 pp. [Translated by Nancy Amphoux]
   A report on what happened under the Khmer Rouge in its first year or so by a Frenchman who had lived among Cambodian peasants and is fluent in the language. This independently complements the above work by Barron and Paul. Ponchaud estimates the early democide toll as "certainly" over 1,000,000 (p. 71).

Democide

U.S. Central Intelligence Agency (1980). *Kampuchea: A Demographic Catastrophe.* Washington, DC, 14 pp. [A January research paper of the National Foreign Assessment Center]
   This is a widely quoted attempt by the CIA to determine from demographic statistics the extent of the toll under the Khmer Rouge. They calculate the absolute population decline under the Khmer Rouge as 1,200,000 to 1,800,000 (p. 5).

Vickery, Michael (1982). Democratic Kampuchea - CIA to the rescue. *Bulletin of Concerned Asian Scholars, 14* (October-December), 45-54.
   This is a hostile but important critique of the above CIA report. Vickery calculates that the CIA estimate of 1,300,000 dead should be reduced to about 290,000 to 425,000 (p. 54), figures he subsequently admits are much too low.

Kiernan, Ben (1988). Orphans of genocide: The Cham Muslims of Kampuchea under Pol Pot. *Bulletin of Concerned Asian Scholars*, 20 (4), 2-33.
   This is a scholarly and detailed account of the Khmer Rouge genocide against the Chams by a first rate scholar on Cambodia. Out of some 250,000 Chams in 1975 (p. 6), Kiernan estimates that 90,000 were killed (p. 30).

Kiernan, Ben (1990). The genocide in Cambodia, 1975-79. *Bulletin of Concerned Asian Scholars*, 22 (2), 35-40.
> Responding to Michael Vickery's critique of the above article, Kiernan provides more calculations on the Cham genocide, and then outlines the genocide against other groups in Cambodia and presents statistics on the overall democide. He estimates this as 1,500,000 (p. 38).

COMMUNIST VIETNAM

The mass murder and country-wide killing by the Vietnamese communists from 1945 through the 1980s has been totally ignored among students of genocide, doubtlessly in part because of the confusion of much of this killing with the Vietnam War, not to mention the controversies engendered by that war. However, the major part of this democide took place before and after the war. In any case, from 1945 to 1987 the North Vietnamese (which controlled all Vietnam after April 1975) murdered from 715,000 to 3,657,000, probably 1,659,000 people.

General

Canh, Nguyen Van (1983). *Vietnam Under Communism, 1975-1982*. Stanford, CA: Hoover Institution Press. 312 pp. [With Earle Cooper. Foreword by Robert A. Scalapino]
> By a Vietnamese and former law professor, this is an important description and analysis of life in Vietnam after the North Vietnamese takeover of the South. Must reading for an assessment of this period and its democide.

Chi, Hoang Van (1964). *From Colonialism to Communism: A Case History of North Vietnam*. New York: Frederick A. Praeger. 252 pp.
> Based on personal experience and extensive research, the work by a Vietnamese nationalist gives a detailed account of the communist suppression of the nationalist movement and consolidation of power in the North after 1945, and the subsequent land reform and purges of the party. This is essential reading for understanding the associated democide. The author believes that just in the Land Reform Campaign of 1953 to 1956 500,000 Vietnamese were "sacrificed" (pp. 72, 205).

Lewy, Guenter (1978). *America in Vietnam*. New York: Oxford University Press. 540 pp.

> Among the best and most balanced works on the Vietnam War, Lewy also provides information on communist democide in the South during the war and judiciously weighs allegations of extensive American massacres and atrocities.

Democide

Desbarats, Jacqueline (1990). Repression in the Socialist Republic of Vietnam: executions and population relocation. In Moore, John Norton (Ed.), *The Vietnam Debate: A Fresh Look at the Arguments*. New York: University Press of America, pp. 193-201.
> Based on extensive interviews of Vietnamese refugees, Desbarats reports her discovery and surprise at the extent of executions in Vietnam after the Vietnam War. Concludes that over 100,000 people must have been executed (p. 197).

United States Senate, 92d Congress, 2d Session, Committee on the Judiciary, (1972). *The

Human Cost of Communism in Vietnam. Washington, DC: U.S. Government Printing Office, 119 pp.
This compiles excerpts of publications that describe North Vietnamese democide and present relevant analyses. The aim is to predict the bloodbath that would occur in case of the North's victory in the Vietnam War.

Hosmer, Stephen (1970). *Viet Cong Repression and Its Implications for the Future.* Lexington, Massachusetts: D.C. Heath and Company. 176 pp. [a Rand Corporation report]
This is a study of the communist use of terror and repression as a method of revolutionary warfare. It helps to understand why democide was seen as a legitimate tool, and the extent and variety of its uses during the Vietnam War.

Wiesner, Louis (1988). *Victims and Survivors: Displaced Persons and Other War Victims in Viet-Nam, 1954-1975.* Westport, CT: Greenwood Press. 448 pp. [Foreword by Phan Quang Dan]
This work by an internationally recognized expert on refugees gives the best overall view of the refugee problem during the Vietnam War. It is full of statistics and facts, and contains diverse information on the democide in the South by the North Vietnamese such as attacks on refugee movements or camps.

Boat People

Since 1975, perhaps as many as 1,500,000 Vietnamese have fled Vietnam, many in rickety boats, risking storms and pirates in order to reach an uncertain haven. Many thus died at sea, perhaps 500,000 of them. This constitutes democide by Vietnam for those who thus died while fleeing for their lives. Virtually all that has been written on the so-called boat people is in newspapers or popular magazines. The following are among the few more serious discussions of their flight and plight.

Cerquone, Joseph (1987 October). Uncertain harbors: the plight of Vietnamese boat people. *Issue Paper of the U.S. Committee for Refugees.* Washington, DC: American Council for Nationalities Service. 39 pp.

Hugo, Graeme (1987). Postwar refugee migration in Southeast Asia: Patterns, problems, and policies. In Rigge, John R. (Ed.), *Refugees: A Third World Dilemma.* Totowa, NJ: Rowman, & Littlefield, pp. 237-252.

OTHER TOTALITARIAN DEMOCIDE

Little has been written in English on the democide in other totalitarian states. Attempts to determine the how, when, and why of democide in, say, communist North Korea, Afghanistan, Cuba, Ethiopia, Laos or Eastern Europe, or Fascist Italy, fundamentalist Moslem Iran, and elsewhere is a matter of digging out of conventional histories and political studies bits and pieces or digging into relevant newspaper and news magazine articles and specialized pieces. In North Korea, for example, possibly 1,000,000 to 2,000,000 Koreans have been murdered since 1948, but even partially related studies of this in English are generally unavailable. Following are a few publications that do focus on democide in Yugoslavia.

Paris, Edmond (1961). *Genocide in Satellite Croatia, 1941-1945: A Record of Racial and Religious Persecutions and Massacres*. Chicago: American Institute for Balkan Affairs. 322 pp. [Translated by Lois Perkins]

This gives analysis, facts, and personal testimonials on the genocide of Serbians by Croatia under totalitarian Ustashi rule during the Second World War. While the book ignores the counterpart genocide of the Croatians carried out by the Serbs when the war was ending and afterward (see Prcela and Guldescu below), it establishes in horrible detail the extent of this mass murder. Paris claims that 750,000 were killed, almost all Serbs (pp. 4, 9, 211).

Prcela, John, and Guldescu, Stanko (Eds.) (1970). *Operation Slaughterhouse: Eyewitness Accounts of Postwar Massacres in Yugoslavia*. Philadelphia: Dorrance & Co. 557 pp.

This describes much of the democide of Croatians and others by Tito's communist (partisan) forces as World War II ended in their victory, and gives testimonials of eyewitnesses, often survivors of particular massacres. The book ignores the genocide of the Serbs by the Croatians described in the above work. Prcela and a colleague calculated that 600,000 Croats were murdered by the Tito regime (p. 121).

PART II
Religion and Genocide

2

Religion and Genocide

Leonard B. Glick

INTRODUCTION

The people known as Apa Tanis live in a cluster of villages in the mountainous Subansiri district of northern Assam, just south of the Chinese border. Their world has changed dramatically over the past two or three decades, but until quite recently they were living much as their ancestors had lived for generations. The anthropologist Christoph von Fürer-Haimendorf conducted ethnographic studies among them in 1944-45 and several times thereafter through 1978, and his accounts of their culture (1962, 1980) provide an appropriate point of entry into the subject of how religious beliefs and practices connect with sentiments and dispositions that may lead to genocide. We begin with them not because traditional Apa Tani culture was exceptionally violent or otherwise distinctive in this regard, but simply because they may be taken as representative of innumerable peoples living in small-scale ("tribal") societies throughout the world.

The Apa Tanis are agriculturalists, dependent on their rice and other crops for subsistence. Each year in March, just prior to the planting season, they perform a communal ritual, called Mloko, when priests representing the various Apa Tani clans perform sacrifices and recite chants intended not just for their own group but for "the general welfare of the people". These events serve "to give ritual expression to the unity of the tribe," "to cement friendly relations across village boundaries and to counteract tensions and jealousies between the inhabitants of different villages" (1962, pp. 141, 143; 1980, p. 162). In short, applying terms familiar to our own experience we may say that the ritual affirms and maintains ethnic solidarity. To participate is to acknowledge that one experiences personal identity as an Apa Tani, and that one's individual welfare and that of the entire community are inseparable.

Consistent with this intense and virtually exclusive identification with their own tightly defined social world, traditional Apa Tanis defined morality solely in terms of that world. "All relations with members of other societies," we are told, stood "outside the sphere of morally prescribed action," and people were able to "conceive of right or wrong conduct" only in connection with the values and expectations of their own immediate social environment (1962, p. 150).

As one might expect, Apa Tani religion is congruent with this moral perspective. The local deities divide into three main categories, one of which comprises deities associated with warfare and raiding. In past years, when such activities were still an integral part of their lives, Apa Tani men invoked the blessing and protection of their deities before setting off on raids against ethnically alien neighbors (1980, pp. 169-171; 1962, p. 136). The raids were not of a sort that would earn a rating on our scale of atrocities, but in the very small world of the Apa Tanis and their neighbors these were devastating assaults with significant numbers of casualties. Fürer-Haimendorf describes one raid conducted by a man he knew, a clan leader and "a balanced and reasonable person insofar as the conduct of affairs inside the Apa Tani valley was concerned." This man "once led a raid on the Dafla village of Dodum which resulted in the killing of thirteen men and the sale into slavery of seventeen captive women and children" (1962, p. 129).

LOCALIZED RELIGIONS AND
THE ROOTS OF ETHNOCENTRISM

I have focused briefly on these aspects of traditional Apa Tani life not because they seem especially unusual or remarkable but for just the opposite reason: because they may tell us something fundamental about all human culture and behavior. The first and perhaps most obvious point is that for these people, as for people everywhere who adhere to their own local religions, the distinction between "religion" and "culture" is essentially meaningless. What we identify as religious beliefs and rituals are inseparable components of a total way of life, symbolic expressions of the recognition that a people, their land, and their culture are ineffably linked. I call religions of this kind "localized," because sacred places, sacred times and sacred beings must find realization in the lives of particular people living in particular locations. Conversion to a localized religion is possible only by becoming one of the people; obviously one could not convert to the Apa Tani religion without becoming part of that small community.

Ethnocentrism - broadly defined as preference for one's own sociocultural group and conviction that it is superior to all others - is an intrinsic feature of localized religions. As we have seen for the Apa Tanis, rituals have as one of their foremost (if unstated) purposes the affirmation of internal bonds and celebration of collective identity. By their very performance rituals enhance the conviction that the gods look upon one's own people with particular favor - and implicitly, that they care less or not at all about outsiders. To put this somewhat differently, the message of localized religions is love not for humanity but for one's own people exclusively. Caring only as they do for the welfare and survival of the local community, the deities are readily enlisted in battles against outsiders, and they are not given to making fine-tuned judgments about the fairness or morality of particular military decisions. In conflicts with alien peoples, whether defensive or offensive, it is entirely logical to expect that the deities, if properly supplicated, will bless the local community with a bloody victory. After all, why should they not be pleased by the destruction of those who serve strange gods?

Behavior of this sort is often called "warfare," but obviously it does not compare in scale or duration with what we ordinarily understand by that term; rather, we are talking about episodic raiding with what I shall call *proto-genocidal intent*. Typically, the goal in such raids is to destroy an entire village or settlement, the common intention being to kill everyone, perhaps excepting a few of the younger women and children who are carried off for incorporation into the home group. Actions of this sort have been recorded well into the twentieth century in parts of the Amazon, New Guinea, the Philippines and elsewhere. (See, e.g., Harner, 1972, pp. 182-187, on the Jivaro of eastern Ecuador; Godelier, 1986, pp. 103-104, on the Baruya of Papua New Guinea.)

But lest I be misunderstood to be trying to create an unflattering portrait only of people unenlightened by the world's great religions, let me now extend our perspective. It may come as a surprise to say that perhaps the most familiar of all localized religions is Judaism, but a moment's thought will reveal that this is the case. Conversion to Judaism is impossible, a contradiction in terms, without entry into Jewish ethnic identity, and the "Gentile" who converts to Judaism literally becomes a Jew. Judaism is the religion of the Jewish people; it celebrates their history, their identity, their covenantal relation with a God who is conceived to be at one and the same time the creator of the universe and the particular deity of a single people - a theological problem that need not detain us. The ancient Hebrews were distinguished from their contemporaries by their conviction that there was only one God; but like their contemporaries, all of whom adhered to localized religions of their own, they were certain that their God, ineffably alone though He might be, was attached to them, and only to them, in the kind of firm contractual relationship that one finds in localized religions everywhere. He was well prepared, of course, to support them in war as in peace, and indeed He looked with favor on what we may fairly call their proto-genocidal destructiveness. The Book of Joshua provides us with one of the earliest texts in which a deity quite plainly promotes the destruction of a people. As the Hebrews, under Joshua's leadership, undertake the conquest of Canaan, they massacre everyone who stands in their way. Here, in a representative passage, we learn what happened immediately after the complete destruction of Lachish and Eglon:

> From Eglon Joshua and all the Israelites advanced to Hebron and attacked it. They captured it and put its king to the sword together with every living thing in it and in all its villages; as at Eglon, he left no survivor, destroying it and every living thing in it. Then Joshua and all the Israelites wheeled round towards Debir and attacked it. They captured the city with its king, and all its villages, put them to the sword and destroyed every living thing; they left no survivor. They dealt with Debir and its king as they had dealt with Hebron and with Libnah and its king. So Joshua massacred the population of the whole region - the hill-country, the Negeb, the Shephelah, the watersheds - and all their kings. He left no survivor, destroying everything that drew breath, as the Lord the God of Israel had commanded. Joshua carried the slaughter from Kadesh-barnea to Gaza, over the whole land of Goshen and as far as Gibeon. All these kings he captured at the same time, and their country with them, for the Lord the God of Israel fought for Israel. (Joshua 10: 36-42; New English Bible: Old Testament, 1970, p. 301)

It is instructive (and distressing) to note that contemporary Jewish ultra-nationalists in Israel root their politics in the Book of Joshua and equate their territorial aspirations with the will of God. Here, for example, is Shlomo Aviner, a prominent theorist for the Gush Emunim ("Bloc of the Faithful") movement in a 1982 article entitled "The Moral Problem of Possessing the Land": "From the point of view of mankind's humanistic morality we were in the wrong in (taking the land) from the Canaanites. There is only one catch. The command of God ordered us to be the people of the Land of Israel." Others have identified the Palestinians as "Canaanites" who are engaged in a "suicidal" struggle opposing God's own intentions; hence the Jewish people must be prepared to destroy them if they persist in pursuing their collective "death-wish" (Lustick, 1988, pp. 76-78).

We can only speculate about how deeply such patterns of thought and behavior are embedded in the human psyche, but there is good reason to surmise that everything I have discussed so far - *ritual affirmation of communal unity and ethnocentric sentiments, belief in deities that belong exclusively to the home group, proto-genocidal attacks on neighboring groups identified as alien or "other," conviction that one's own deities approve of such attacks and promote their success* - have been intrinsic components of the human condition since the emergence of our species, late in the Pleistocene epoch, some fifty thousand or more years ago.

Judging from what has been learned in recent decades about human evolution, individuals in the earliest human societies must have been subjected to powerful selective pressures for intelligence, cooperativeness, effectiveness as communicators, and capacity for coordinated action and interaction with members of the home community. In line with this went pressures for the development of qualities conducive to group survival: people who were capable of understanding and promoting collectively created behavioral rules and expectations, shared values and goals, sentiments and beliefs congruent with communal survival. The unfit - those who were too unintelligent, aggressive, greedy, or otherwise unqualified to contribute to the collective welfare - must have been rigorously eliminated, either by murder, expulsion, or, at very least, ostracism.

The inescapable corollary of the favored disposition was readiness to defend the group against all its enemies, animal or human, and even to undertake expeditions of conquest to gain fresh territory and resources. In short, not just the capacity but the inclination to behave in a manner that we now label "ethnocentric," even to the point of proto-genocidal conquest, and to believe that such behavior is sanctioned as much by the gods as by one's more visible companions, must be an essential element in the human evolutionary inheritance (Alexander, 1979; Eibl-Eibesfeldt, 1979, Chapters 5 & 6; Reynolds et al., 1986; Wilson, 1978, Chapters 5 & 7).

UNIVERSALIST RELIGIONS

I have characterized *localized* religions as those in which religious expression is deeply rooted in ethnic or communal identity, such that conversion to the religion without incorporation into the ethnic community is a logical impossibility. In contrast, the two religions that qualify least ambiguously for the label "world religions," Christianity and Islam, are manifestly *universalist*: first, because they explicitly reject ethnic limitations in their claims to having originated in revelations that utterly transcended all historical and geographical boundaries; second, because propagation of the faith and conversion of the unredeemed are among their definitive purposes. Adherence to such a belief system requires an inescapably paradoxical stance on ethnocentrism. On the one hand, ethnic identity is presumably of no real significance, since the universal truths of the religion transcend such worldly categories; on the other hand, possession of such truths not only justifies but indeed requires extraordinary effort to convert others - even though that may entail the undermining of their individual societies and cultures, and even though it may lead to their individual deaths.

Localized religions characteristically define moral behavior in terms of local norms, values, and purposes: moral behavior is that which sustains the group and promotes its welfare. Universalist religions appear on first acquaintance to present a loftier definition of morality, one that emphasizes adherence to relatively abstract standards of love and fellowship. In striking contrast to the pragmatic ethnocentrism of localized morality, universalist morality declares that human beings should be benignly disposed toward others, and that selfish or aggressive behavior is a manifestation of wickedness or evil. In effect, it endeavors to repress, perhaps even to deny, the undeniable: the sinister aspect of human nature that finds expression in readiness to oppress those who are defined as Other (cf. Charny, 1982, pp. 188-191; Staub, 1989, pp. 58-62). But the histories of Christianity and Islam are of course replete with evidence that those who profess universalist doctrines are ready and willing to engage in egregious crimes of genocidal or near-genocidal dimensions, not only against people whose religions differ radically from their own but also against anyone perceived as posing a challenge or threat to orthodoxy.

CHRISTIAN PERSECUTION OF THE JEWS

Nowhere has this been more evident than in the history of Christian persecution of the Jews. The subject has been examined over the years by so many writers that one hesitates to add yet more commentary, but the matter is too central to our subject to be overlooked. Obviously the problem is complex, but its foundations can be laid out in a few words. In the Christian world view, Judaism is not just another erroneous religion, and Jews are not just another people in need of revelation and conversion. To the contrary, Judaism has always been *the* other religion, the one from which Christianity had to disengage itself, and against which Christianity had to define itself, in order to come into being and to endure. Likewise, Jews have always been *the* other people, those against whom Christians positioned themselves, and in contrast to whom they identified themselves. For Christianity was a revolutionary religion, a departure of immense proportions from the world of localized religions, a reinterpretation of Judaism so radical that the two could not possibly co-exist peacefully as equally "correct" interpretations of human history and destiny. Most importantly, the Jewish messiah, envisioned by Jews as a fully human descendant of King David who would restore them to the glory of the Davidic past, was wholly transformed into a divine redeemer who accepted suffering and death for the salvation of all humanity. And of course Jews were the descendants of the very people among whom the redeemer had appeared and preached, only to be scorned and condemned to death (Ruether, 1974; Davies, 1979).

Considering the magnitude of their crime, why had Jews been spared at all? Why had God not willed complete destruction as their only appropriate punishment? Pondering this question in his *City of God*, Augustine explained that although the Jews were spared, they were dispersed, not only to punish them but also so that they might fulfill their destined purpose as "testimony," or "witness," to Christian truth:

> They were dispersed all over the world - for indeed there is no part of the earth where they are not to be found - and thus by the evidence of their own Scriptures they bear witness for us that we have not fabricated the prophecies about Christ... for we recognize that it is in order to give this testimony, which, in spite of themselves, they supply for our benefit by their possession and preservation of those books, that they themselves are dispersed among all nations, in whatever direction the Christian Church spreads... For if they lived with that testimony of the Scriptures only in their own land, and not everywhere, the obvious result would be that the Church, which is everywhere, would not have them available among all nations as witnesses to the prophecies which were given beforehand concerning Christ. (Bettenson, 1972, pp. 827-828)

Thus does Augustine explain why a people with a localized religion came to be located everywhere in the known world!

This statement provided foundations for papal policy toward Jews right up to our own time: they were to be restrained, as befitted their deplorably rebellious and intractable nature; but they were to be tolerated, in accordance with God's will that they be permitted to live as "testimony" until He would reveal to them the light of Christian truth and restore them to favor.

But subtle theological arguments and papal pronouncements were of no concern to the people who perpetrated crimes against Jews throughout the later medieval period, often in the name of Christian zeal. Beginning in the late eleventh century, the emergence of a new class of Christian merchants and steady increase in Christian clerical influence created an ideological climate that was increasingly unfavorable to Jews, and that led first to their relegation to the role of despised moneylenders, then to their being identified as embodiments of evil, literally the devil's own people, appropriate objects for extortion, persecution, and destruction (Chazan, 1973; Hsia, 1988; Jordan, 1989; Little, 1978, Chap. 3; Parkes, 1976; Trachtenberg, 1943). The harbinger of all that was to follow came in 1096, when armies participating in the First Crusade made their way to the Rhineland cities of Speyer, Mainz, Worms, and Cologne, where they perpetrated a series of massacres that resonate in Jewish memory to this very day. Jonathan Riley-Smith, an authority on the crusades, challenges the customary view of these armies as "undisciplined hordes of peasants" under the command of incompetent or irresponsible leaders. To the contrary, he argues, they were well organized, well-equipped units commanded by "experienced knights" of noble birth who knew quite well what they intended to accomplish. Thus, he concludes, it is no longer possible "to adhere to the comforting view that the massacres were perpetrated by gangs of peasants" (Riley-Smith, 1984, pp. 54-56; 1986, pp. 51-52). Moreover, he continues, although crusading armies were chronically impoverished, and given to extortion and pillage whenever opportunity presented, this is not an adequate explanation for the Rhineland massacres; rather, the crusaders were motivated primarily by religious fervor. They wanted to avenge the Crucifixion: sometimes by forcibly converting Jews and killing those who resisted; more often, perhaps, by killing them outright. Many crusaders were probably unable even to distinguish between Moslems and Jews, "and could not understand why, if they were called upon to take up arms against the former, they should not also persecute the latter" (Riley-Smith, 1984, pp. 67-69; 1986, pp. 54-55).

The deepest irony in this story attaches to the relationship between Jews and bishops. In the most complete contemporary account of the massacres, the *Chronicle of Solomon bar Simson*, we read of Jews turning repeatedly to these foremost representatives of the Church, and we learn that these men consistently did their best to defend and protect Jews, even when this meant not inconsiderable danger for themselves (Eidelberg, 1977, pp. 21-72; Chazan, 1987, 90-95). We envision Jews huddling terrified in cathedral courtyards, crowding for days on end in rooms of an archbishop's palace (surely a place they had never expected to see from the inside), racing for their lives into a cathedral sacristy filled with priestly robes and crucifixes. We see them bringing their wealth and valuables for safekeeping to a cathedral treasury, and on at least one occasion bringing even Torah scrolls to the bishop's palace to save them from the mob. The bishops themselves behave for the most part with commendable, even astonishing, sympathy and generosity. True, they often urge conversion as the only way out, but under the circumstances one must conclude that the advice was reasonable. (With benefit of hindsight it can be said that had more Jews been willing to go through the motions of conversion, they would have lived to return to Judaism within a year, for that was explicitly permitted by a decree of Emperor Henry IV.) To put this in contemporary terms, considerations of social class and economic welfare seem to have outweighed religious differences when a bishop was acting in his role as a political authority. For in the final analysis most Jews were respectable people, industrious merchants who contributed substantially to the local economy; and despite all religious obligations, the bishop's overarching priority was to maintain "law and order" and to protect people of this kind - even Jews steeped in blindness. That they failed for the most part was not due to want of effort.

Although medieval popes were intent on degrading Judaism and Jews at every opportunity, they adhered nevertheless to the principle that Jews, provided they conducted themselves with appropriate humility, were not to be subjected to inordinate oppression or physical harm (Grayzel, 1966, 1989; Stow, 1988). Interestingly enough, it was not Jews but heretical Christians against whom medieval popes were prepared to direct violence of genocidal proportions; as witness the Albigensian Crusade of the early thirteenth century, in which a French army, assembled in response to a call from Pope Innocent III, invaded the southern French territory of Languedoc to destroy the dualist heresy known as Catharism or Albigensianism. The historian Walter Wakefield explains why medieval Christians viewed heretics with such loathing:

> Heresy could not be a casual matter when religion was so vital an element in life. It had to be regarded as the most grievous sin and crime into which man could fall, for by denying the magistracy of the church which Christ had established, over which His vicar in Rome presided, the heretic became a traitor to God himself. Moreover, he imperilled others by his words and example; medieval writers were fond of likening heresy to a loathsome and contagious disease... So noxious was the crime that unless it were resolutely dealt with many other souls might be gravely endangered. Secular officials put heretics to death in the conviction that one faith in one church was the indispensable cement of Christian society. (Wakefield, 1974, pp. 16-17)

The Cathars viewed the world as a battleground between a spiritual domain created by God and a material domain created by Satan. In defiance of the Nicene Creed they taught that Jesus did not share in God's divine nature but was His spiritual emissary, a spirit in the form of man who had never assumed a truly material body. The essential elements of Christian sacraments - communal wafers, wine, baptismal water - were nothing more than evil matter, they maintained; even the sacrament of marriage should be condemned, because it led to the entrapment of spiritual souls in material bodies subject to sin and wickedness.

Catharism found widespread acceptance in much of western Europe, but especially in northern Italy and southern France, where it had attracted adherents from every social class and encouraged widespread defections from the Church. The town of Albi was among the first places where Cathars were identified and condemned as heretics - hence the name Albigensians for adherents in Languedoc (*ibid.*, pp. 30-33).

In 1208 a papal legate in southern France was murdered. Blame naturally fell on the Albigensians, and with this as the ostensible provocation, Innocent preached a crusade to liberate the region from heresy. In 1209 a vast army assembled at Lyon and made its way southward, killing heretics and faithful Christians alike; the record of brutality matches that for the Rhineland in 1096. The most dreadful massacre occurred in Béziers, a town near the Mediterranean coast southwest of Montpellier. Having forced their way into the town, the troops "cut the inhabitants down mercilessly." A local church, crowded with terrified townspeople (many no doubt with no connection to Catharism) was burned, as were many other buildings, all this accompanied by the usual pillage. A gratified archbishop, one of the crusade leaders, reported (probably with exaggeration) that his army had killed some fifteen thousand people, "showing mercy neither to order nor age nor sex," and characterized the victory as "miraculous." The miracle had its desired effect: "A shock of horror," says Wakefield, "spread across Languedoc," and eventually Catharism disappeared as a challenge to the Church (*ibid.*, p. 102).

CHRISTIANS IN THE NEW WORLD

Since the onset of the colonial era in the fifteenth century, missionizing has been so intimately connected with colonizing that one cannot readily separate their adverse effects on non-European peoples - and at times those effects have reached proportions that qualify readily as genocidal. Perhaps the grimmest example is the Spanish invasion of Mexico, in which colonists espousing Christian sentiments but motivated primarily by lust for gold were accompanied by missionary friars whose foremost purpose was to win savage souls for Christ. To the friars, says the historian Charles Gibson,

> America offered a larger and more challenging stage than Europe. The non-Christian peoples of America were not simply to be converted. They were to be civilized, taught, humanized, purified, and reformed. To the humanist friars, America appeared as Christian obligation writ large. Its vast populations were to be set on new paths of Christian virtue and godliness. (Gibson, 1966, pp. 71-72)

That most of these missionaries had essentially benign intentions can hardly be doubted, but the harsh reality was that an inescapable corollary of their efforts was relentless destruction of Mexican Indian religions and cultures - a process that went hand in hand with the more explicitly oppressive practices of the colonists. Conversion often meant little more than the most superficial formalities - two Franciscan friars are said to have baptized fifteen thousand Indians in one day (Hanke, 1970, p. 20) - but even that was enough to promote the cultural dissolution that was already under way. In the eyes of the missionaries Indians were either childlike innocents or degenerate savages, but in either case it was axiomatic that their only hope for eternal life lay in Christian enlightenment and conversion. Unfortunately for the vast majority of Indians, eternal life was the only kind remaining to them. Massive disease epidemics, exhaustion from forced labor and other forms of egregious mistreatment, despair over the disappearance of traditional community life and culture - all these combined to produce a demographic decline of awesome proportions: from an original native Mesoamerican population of some twenty-five million to about one and one-half million by 1650 (Wachtel, 1984, pp. 212-213; Wolf, 1982, p. 134).

Among the Spanish clergy were some who questioned the legitimacy of forcefully subduing people for the ostensible purpose of bringing them into the Christian fold. The outstanding spokesman in this regard was Bartolomé de las Casas (1474-1566), the Dominican friar whose *History of the Indies*, based on his own observations and reflections, is renowned as one of the earliest indictments of colonial oppression. In 1550 Las Casas participated in an event that may be said to have epitomized both aspects of the relationship between religion and genocide in the Americas: on the one hand, an appeal to human decency as the foundation of virtue; on the other, insistence that the demands of revealed religious truth override all other considerations. The occasion was a public disputation staged in Valladolid, Spain, before a council of theologians and public officials. The contestants were Las Casas and Juan Ginés de Sepúlveda (1490-1573), a prominent humanist scholar whose reputation rested in particular on a distinguished translation of Aristotle's *Politics*. The two men were to address their arguments to a single question: "Is it lawful for the king of Spain to wage war on the Indians before preaching the faith to them in order to subject them to his rule, so that afterwards they may be more easily instructed in the faith?" Sepúlveda defended the affirmative, grounding his position in the Aristotelian doctrine of natural slavery (*Politics*, Book 1, Chap. 5), and arguing that subjugation of Indians was both necessary and just: necessary in order to spread the Christian faith, and just because Indians were a sinful and idolatrous people. Las Casas replied that, to the contrary, warfare and subjugation were "iniquitous, and contrary to our Christian religion," and argued that nothing justified decimation of a people and complete destruction of their way of life (Hanke, 1970, pp. 38-41 and passim). Not surprisingly, no clear decision or resolution emerged from the learned council members; nor, we may safely assume, did ordinary Spanish colonists or missionaries much concern themselves with the intricacies of philosophical reasoning over the justice or injustice of their way of life. In effect, Spanish colonialism in the Americas had arisen on foundations of pious religiosity coupled with unbridled greed, and their ultimate product was genocide.

THE ARMENIAN GENOCIDE

But Christians have certainly not been the only perpetrators of genocide, and indeed they themselves have been subject to severe oppression. The suffering of early Christians under Roman persecution is common knowledge. The most infamous case in modern times is undoubtedly the Armenian genocide of 1915-1917, an atrocity that only recently has begun to receive the attention it deserves (Hovannisian, 1967, 1986; Housepian, 1966; Charny, 1984; Walker, 1980; Lang and Walker, 1987; Institut für Armenische

Fragen, 1987; Kuper, 1981). Since the subject has been covered authoritatively in the first volume of this series (Hovannisian, 1988), it will not be considered in detail here, but it merits our attention for several reasons. First, the sheer magnitude and extensiveness of the mass murder was exceeded in our time only by the destruction of the Jews of Europe. Second, it was initiated not by religious fanatics or narrowly educated reactionaries but by the so-called Young Turks, whose emergence to power in 1908-09 might have been expected to herald a new era of acceptance and integration for the beleaguered Armenian minority. Ironically, the result was precisely the opposite. "One of the most unanticipated and for the Armenians most tragic developments in modern history," observes Richard Hovannisian, "was the process from 1908 to 1914 in which the seemingly liberal, egalitarian Young Turks became transformed into xenophobic nationalists bent on creating a new order and eliminating the Armenian Question by eliminating the Armenian people" (1988, p. 94).

Third, it is not without significance that the Armenians, like the Jews of Europe, the Chinese of Southeast Asia, the Tamils of Sri Lanka, and to some extent the Ibo of Nigeria, differed not only religiously from the surrounding population but also occupationally, being prominent as merchants, shopkeepers, and office workers in predominantly agricultural societies (Dadrian, 1975; Tambiah, 1986, p. 38; Kuper, 1981, pp. 74-75).

Should the Armenian genocide be attributed primarily to religiously based antagonism, or would it be more accurate to say that the Christian identity of the victims was incidental to their situation? The answer returns us to the propositions on religion, culture and identity introduced at the beginning of this paper. No matter what their personal religious convictions may have been, the Turkish perpetrators looked upon Islam as an integral element in their collective identity; likewise, Christianity was an equally definitive element in the identity of their victims, who could have "become Turks" (if ever) only by converting to Islam. It is instructive to note that apologists for the Turks cited the need for "Turkification and Moslemization" as an essential precondition for establishment of a modern republic (Hovannisian, 1986, p. 124). Thus, the "Armenian question" was an irreducible compound of ethnic and religious identity; and the Armenian genocide was an effort - successful, in the final analysis - to purge a people whose crime was ethnic and religious distinctiveness.

NEAR-GENOCIDAL ETHNIC-RELIGIOUS CONFLICTS

During the past several decades religious differences have been salient in a number of ethnic conflicts that have reached near-genocidal dimensions. In some cases the antagonists, although at times unequally matched, generated enough violence on each side to suggest that we should characterize the conflicts as ethnic warfare but not genocide. I have in mind such situations as the civil war in the Sudan between Islamic Arabs living mainly in the northern part of the country and black Africans in the southern provinces who adhere either to traditional religions or to Christianity (Johnson, 1988; Morrison, 1973; Young, 1976, pp. 489-501); the Algerian War, which pitted an indigenous Muslim population against French Christian colonial settlers (Horne, 1977); the Catholic-Protestant conflict in Northern Ireland (Carroll, 1977); and the Chinese campaign against Tibetan Buddhist monasteries and monks. (The last named is perhaps the most subject to debate about its nature and severity; see especially Mullin and Wangyal, 1983.)

These are all "plural societies," that is, societies characterized not just by the presence of diverse ethnic groups but by "persistent and pervasive cleavages," often in conditions of social-economic stratification and political inequality (Kuper, 1981, pp. 57-59); thus, the ethnic-religious identities of the contestants have been inseparable in effect from the political and economic contexts of their conflicts.

The most dramatic of such situations in recent times, and almost certainly the most destructive of human life and property, were the violent conflicts associated first with the separation of Pakistan from India and later with the separation of Bangladesh from Pakistan. In 1947, when independence for India and Pakistan was accompanied by massive ethnic warfare, the slaughter and destruction were especially severe in the Punjab, the northwestern province of India that was home not only to a thoroughly mixed population of Hindus and Moslems but also to millions of Sikhs, for whom partition of the region into Indian and Pakistani segments meant political dismemberment of their homeland. Hindus and Sikhs were pitted against Muslims in vicious fighting that reached levels of unspeakable brutality on both sides. The intentions of the combatants clearly qualify as genocidal, but they were well enough matched in numbers and destructive capacity to inflict immense suffering in both directions (Kuper, 1981, pp. 63-68; Collins and Lapierre, 1975, Chapter 13).

This was not the case in 1971, when East Pakistan seceded from West Pakistan and became Bangladesh; there the contestants were not equally matched, and it was only the intervention of the Indian army that enabled the Bengalis to gain their independence. East Pakistan had a 1970 population of about seventy-five million, the great majority of whom were Muslims; but the population included some eleven million Hindus and more than a million Muslim immigrants from India, known as Biharis. The independence movement created complex alignments that do not correlate well with religious groupings. The response by West Pakistan was a sickeningly brutal military reprisal that caused probably two million or more deaths and left the country in a shambles. The murder, torture, and rapine were not limited to any segment of the Bengali population, and the fact that their victims were fellow Muslims seems to have made no difference to Pakistani troops on the rampage. There is evidence, however, that Hindus suffered disproportionately, having been regularly singled out by West Pakistanis and at times assaulted also by Bengali Muslims and Biharis (Mascarenhas, 1971, pp. 116-117). Bengali militants, probably both Muslim and Hindu, retaliated when they could against West Pakistanis, and against Biharis who were accused of collaborating with the invaders, in crimes of essentially equal cruelty (Aziz, 1974; Levak, 1974, p. 219), but the genocidal balance sheet appears to be tilted heavily in the other direction (Kuper, 1981, pp. 76-80; 1988, p. 166; Mascarenhas, 1971, Chapter 9).

More recently in Bangladesh, Muslim Bengalis have been responsible for oppression of near-genocidal dimensions perpetrated against predominantly Buddhist hill-dwelling peoples of the Chittagong district, in the isolated southeastern corner of the country. These people differ from the rest of the population not only in religion; they resemble Burmese physically and possess distinctive cultures and languages with Southeast Asian affinities. Those who are not Buddhist are mostly either Hindu or Christian, or adhere to their own localized religions. Bengalis have been moving into their region in ever-greater numbers for the past several decades; by 1980 immigrants numbered about 225,000 in a total population of 815,000, and they were increasingly disposed to force their way into territory occupied by the hill peoples. A local resistance movement formed in the 1970's, and the Bangladesh government responded with military intervention, mass arrests, destruction of villages and forced resettlements. In March 1980, soon after a conflict with resistance fighters in which some soldiers were killed, two to three hundred Chittagong people were massacred by troops joined by armed Bengali civilians. Following an initial assault, the violence spread: people were forcibly converted to Islam; Buddhist temples were attacked, "monks and nuns were mercilessly killed or wounded," and villages were burned (Anti-Slavery Society, 1984, p. 75). Further attacks involving even worse massacres, rape, torture and destruction took place repeatedly during the 1980's (Amnesty International, 1986; Anti-Slavery Society, 1984., p. 77); and the situation has continued to deteriorate into what one writer has called a "programme of systematic extermination of indigenous nationalities of the Chittagong Hill Tracts because they are ethnically, religiously, and culturally different from the Muslim Bengalis" (cited in Kuper, 1988, p. 166).

An especially grim situation has also developed during the past decade in Sri Lanka, where a Tamil independence movement, accompanied by considerable violence, has evoked severe retaliation by the Sinhalese majority. Murderous riots and vendetta killings have almost destroyed the frail social fabric of a nation that had experienced premonitory outbreaks of ethnic conflict ever since independence. The Tamils are largely Hindu; the

Sinhalese are Theravada Buddhists, and the more militant among them declare this to be central not only to their personal identity but to Sri Lankan national identity. In a penetrating study of the historical background and contemporary socioeconomic context of the conflict, the anthropologist Stanley Tambiah points out that religious rituals and cults derived from syncretic blending of Buddhist and Hindu elements are now gaining great popularity as expressions of doctrinaire Sinhalese Buddhist nationalism that is militantly anti-Tamil and anti-Hindu (1986, pp. 57-63). Ironically, forms of religious expression that owe their existence to cultural pluralism are now being invoked in support of monocultural nationalism.

CLERGY AND GENOCIDE: CHRISTIAN CLERGY AND THE HOLOCAUST

We have reviewed a number of situations in which atrocities of genocidal proportions were generated, at least in part, by religious motives or religiously sanctioned antagonism. But have religious leaders, particularly of the universalist religions, demonstrated any capacity beyond the ordinary to oppose actions leading toward genocide? Have they pointed the way toward a pan-human consciousness that might counteract parochialism, chauvinism, and ethnic antagonism?

The answer seems to be that with rather few exceptions they have not. Nor should that surprise us. People who achieve positions of religious leadership may be precisely those who are certain that they possess absolute Truth. That such individuals can be exceedingly dangerous is evident when one considers the actions of contemporary religious fundamentalists in such places as Iran, Israel, and Northern Ireland.

But most religious leaders are not "true believers" of the sort who are prepared to sweep away all obstacles from the path to redemption; they are intelligent people who want orderly, purposeful lives for themselves and for others. How do such individuals respond when confronted with prospects of imminent destruction, not of their own people but of another? Are they able to transcend religious parochialism? Do they take a stand on behalf of those who differ, or do they follow the more expedient path of looking out for one's own and accommodating to the world as it is?

Probably the best documented answers to such questions are to be found in the many studies of the responses of German clergymen, Protestant and Catholic, to the persecution and massacre of the Jews of Europe between 1933 and 1945. The Holocaust was indisputably the pre-eminent genocide of our time, but the subject has already been accorded detailed consideration in the first volume of this series (Berger, 1988). Here we shall consider only studies of how the clergy responded to Nazi persecution of German Jews in the 1930's and later to information that massacres of genocidal proportions were probably taking place in Eastern Europe. (See especially Conway, 1968, 1980; Ericksen, 1985; Gutteridge, 1976; Helmreich, 1979; Hunt, 1984; Kulka and Mendes-Flohr, 1987; Lewy, 1964; Littell and Locke, 1974; Zahn, 1962; Zerner, 1983.) Their conclusions are quite consistent: although a significant minority of German clergymen resisted what they perceived as a threat to fundamental Christian values, most adopted attitudes ranging from passive acceptance (characteristic of the great majority) to enthusiastic endorsement of the Nazi regime and its policies, including aggressive chauvinism and expansionism. Moreover, clerical resistance and protests, such as they were, focused almost entirely on issues connected directly with the welfare and survival of the churches, not the persecution of Jews or other victims of the Nazi regime.

Most instructive in this regard was their response to the so-called Aryan Clause, issued by a Protestant synod in Berlin, in September 1933, ordering that pastors of Jewish descent, or married to Jewish women, be dismissed; a number of clergymen protested, although most adopted the more prudent course of saying nothing. In addition, many clergymen and Christian laity made an effort, sometimes at serious risk to themselves, to assist and encourage "non-Aryan" converts to Christianity, acting in the conviction that faith was the sole determinant of status as a Christian; but of course, as they saw it they were supporting Christians, not Jews.

When it came to persecution of Jews as such, far fewer clergy - only a deservedly remembered handful - spoke out, and even they sometimes qualified their statements with references to Jews as people burdened with an inescapable curse. A statement issued in 1936 by the Bishop of Baden was representative of a view expressed time and again, by Protestants and Catholics alike:

> When the Jews crucified Jesus, they crucified themselves, their revelation and their history. Thus the curse came upon them. Since then that curse works itself out from one generation to another. This people has, therefore, become a fearful and divinely ordained scourge for all nations, leading to hatred and persecution. (Gutteridge, 1976, p. 71)

Even the two pastors most often cited as opponents of Nazism, Dietrich Bonhoeffer and Martin Niemöller, both accepted publicly the dictum that the Jews were destined to suffer as punishment for the Crucifixion (Zerner, 1983, pp. 63-64; Gutteridge, 1976, pp. 103-104).

Perhaps the most outspoken and least ambivalent public statement was issued in October 1943 by a Prussian synod of liberal Protestant pastors. Taking note of all victims of the regime, including "the people of Israel," the synod took a firm (if obviously belated) stand against mass murder: "Concepts such as 'elimination,' 'liquidation,' and 'unworthy life' are not known to the divine order. Extermination of people solely because they are related to a criminal, or old or mentally disturbed, or because they belong to an alien race, is not a sword granted by God to be wielded by the state" (Translation modified from Helmreich, 1979, p. 336 and Bracher, 1970, p. 385).

Such statements were the exception, and we know how much effect they had. But in fairness to those clergymen who might have resisted had they dared, we must remember that overt resistance to a fascist dictatorship meant, at best, exposure to ostracism and public condemnation, at worst, incarceration in a concentration camp or assassination. The well documented life of Dietrich Bonhoeffer is a case in point (Bethge, 1970), as is the fate of the brave priest Bernard Lichtenberg, who prayed publicly in Berlin for the Jews (Hilberg, 1961, pp. 299-300; Lewy, 1964, p. 293). In November 1938, a Lutheran pastor, Julius von Jan, preached a sermon condemning the infamous *Kristallnacht* attacks on Jews; he was beaten nearly to death by a mob, then carried off to prison (Conway, 1968, pp. 375-376). As the historian Karl Dietrich Bracher has observed, "the decision to resist was reached in terrible loneliness in the midst of a mass society," and retrospective judgments of the German clergy (as of all ordinary Germans) should be tempered with appreciation of the price of resistance (1970, p. 379). One may feel less charitably disposed, however, when it is remembered that many clergymen moved well beyond necessity in expressing support for the Nazi regime and its policies.

Although the Catholic clergy, generally speaking, were somewhat less overtly chauvinistic, their overall record was essentially like that of their Protestant counterparts. Guenter Lewy's definitive study of the subject shows that although Catholic priests also tried to protect converts, they paralleled the Protestant clergy in passive acquiescence, taking no significant stand on behalf of Jews (1964, Chapter 10). Gordon Zahn supports this conclusion in his study of the Catholic clergy: "at no time was the individual German Catholic led to believe that the regime was an evil unworthy of his support" (1969, p. 73). Commenting specifically on the Catholic clergy's response to the realization that persecution had reached the stage of genocide, Lewy says:

> The word that would have forbidden the faithful, on pain of excommunication, to go on participating in the massacre of the Jews was never spoken. And so Catholics went on participating conscientiously, along with other Germans. (1964, p. 293)

Lewy and others have pointed to instructive contrasts with France, Italy, Belgium, Holland and elsewhere in Western Europe, where many Christian clergy hid and otherwise assisted Jews on a scale quite beyond anything reported for Germany. It would appear that most clergy everywhere followed in the path of general public sentiment and were not significantly affected one way or the other by their religious professions; when it came to the difficult decisions, being German or French mattered more than being Christian (Lewy, 1964, pp. 293-294; Marrus and Paxton, 1981, pp. 270-279; Zuccotti, 1987, pp. 207-217).

With regard to the much-discussed question of papal actions during the Holocaust, it seems evident that although the two popes, Pius XI (1922-1939) and Pius XII (1939-1958) adhered to the traditional papal principle that Jews were not to be physically oppressed, they followed the path of political expediency, recognizing that some 40% of the German population was Catholic and not wanting to risk placing them in danger with the Nazi regime. Moreover, Hitler's touted determination to destroy Bolshevism resonated with the Church's deepest political aspirations. Thus, Pius XI's 1936 encyclical *Mit brennender Sorge* (With Profound Concern) rejected racist ideology as contrary to Christian doctrine but said nothing about antisemitism as such and did not mention the persecution of Jews. And when the Germans evacuated the Jews of Rome in October 1943, obviously for the purpose of despatching them to extermination centers, Pius XII said nothing publicly, although he appears to have given tacit approval to Italian priests and nuns who assisted Jews (Lewy, 1964, pp. 295-308; Zuccotti, 1987, pp. 128-135).

The conduct of Christian clergy and their congregations in the United States is tersely summed up by David Wyman in his study of American responses to the Holocaust: "At the heart of Christianity is the commitment to help the helpless. Yet, for the most part, America's Christian churches looked away while the European Jews perished" (1984, p. 320). Wyman provides a few pages of well documented commentary on the indifference and ineffectiveness of all but a handful of Christian clergy during the critical years. A "Day of Compassion" sponsored in May 1943 by the Federal Council of Churches (with substantial Jewish support) was supposed to raise awareness through appropriate sermons and services, but despite heavy publicity very few churches paid any attention. "Perhaps more significant in retrospect than the slight impact of the Day of Compassion," observes Wyman, "is the fact that this modest effort turned out to be the Christian church's main attempt during the entire war to arouse an American response to the Holocaust. And even it came only after months of prodding by Jewish friends of the Federal Council's leaders" (*ibid.*, p. 102).

Writing after the war, Martin Niemöller's brother Wilhelm, "an assiduous apologist in nearly all respects" for the liberal wing of German Protestantism, passed judgment on his church in terms that might well have been extended to others, and we may leave the final word on this subject to him:

The picture as a whole is dismal. One of the most glorious opportunities to make proof of Christian profession through Christian action was, taken as a whole, missed and unexercised. (Gutteridge, 1976, p. 267)

CONCLUSION

Western thought has been shaped by Christianity, a universalist religion that has always aimed to transcend ethnic or national boundaries; Christianity is understood to be a revelation that can be adopted by any people anywhere. Hence, we are inclined to distinguish "religion" from the totality implied by such terms as culture and ethnicity. But for many people, including Christians, religious beliefs and practices are an integral element of identity and experience, and every ethnic group - with all the bonds of shared history, physical type, language, and values that the term entails - possesses a religion as an essential feature of its identity. In a sense, then, it is something of a pointless academic exercise to try to disentangle religious motives and sanctions from the totality of considerations that may impel people of one ethnic group to perpetrate genocidal crimes against another. Did Turks massacre Armenians solely for "religious" reasons? Did the armies of West Pakistan clearly distinguish between Bengali Hindus and Muslims? I have suggested that we face here a complex problem, centering, unfortunately, on what appear to be universal human dispositions, rooted in our evolutionary heritage, to dislike, to mistrust, and, with relatively little provocation, to attack people perceived to differ from one's own reference group; and more often than not, religious differences are part of a larger picture .

If we accept this to be the case, it comes as no surprise and no disappointment to learn that religious leaders, whether they be shamans, priests, pastors, mullahs or rabbis, appear on the average to demonstrate neither more nor less compassion for aliens than anyone else. If a few men and women of strong religious faith and moral fiber have indeed taken a stand against genocidal oppression, so have an equal number of people with no particular attachment to religious or "spiritual" concerns. It appears that if we are ever to reach the point where genocidal massacres will have become a thing of the past, it will not be owing to religions: they are part of the problem.

BIBLIOGRAPHY

Anthropology, Psychology, and General Studies of Ethnic Conflict

Alexander, Richard D. (1979). *Darwinism and Human Affairs*. Seattle, WA and London: University of Washington Press. 317 pp.
  A modern evolutionary perspective on human behavior. See especially pp. 126-128, "Is Xenophobia Learned?"

Charny, Israel W. (1982). *How Can We Commit the Unthinkable?: Genocide, The Human Cancer*. Boulder, CO: Westview Press. 430 pp.
  A comprehensive analysis from a psychological perspective, arguing that the disposition to commit genocide must be viewed as pathology.

Charny, Israel W. (Ed.) (1988). *Genocide: A Critical Bibliographic Review*. London: Mansell Publishing Co.; and New York: Facts on File. 273 pp.

Charny, Israel W. (Ed.) (1991). *Genocide: A Critical Bibliographic Review, Volume 2*. London: Mansell Publishing Co.; and New York: Facts on File. 432 pp.
  The two volumes include essential bibliographic essays on the Holocaust, the Armenian genocide, the U.S.S.R., Cambodia, educating about genocide, and other topics relevant to the subject of this paper.

Eibl-Eibesfeldt, Irenäus (1979). *The Biology of Peace and War*. New York: Viking Press. 294 pp.
  A prominent ethologist discusses aggression and violence within and between groups, and offers biological perspectives on conflict resolution. Substantial bibliography, pp. 265-285.

Fürer-Haimendorf, Christoph von (1962). *The Apa Tanis and Their Neighbors*. London: Routledge and Kegan Paul; and New York: Free Press of Glencoe. 166 pp.

Fürer-Haimendorf, Christoph von (1980). *A Himalayan Tribe: From Cattle to Cash*. Berkeley and Los Angeles: University of California Press. 224 pp.
  Ethnographic studies of a representative people, neither more nor less violent than most. Both include discussions of connections between religion, group solidarity and antagonism toward outsiders.

Godelier, Maurice (1986). *The Making of Great Men: Male Domination and Power Among the New Guinea Baruya*. Cambridge and New York: Cambridge University Press. 251 pp.
  One study among many of people of the New Guinea Highlands, a region where until recently proto-genocidal raiding was endemic.

Harner, Michael J. (1972). *The Jivaro: People of the Sacred Waterfalls*. Garden City, NY: Natural History Press. 233 pp.
  Ethnographic study of a people of the Ecuadorian Amazon. See especially Chapters 4 and 5 on religion and warfare.

Kuper, Leo (1981). *Genocide: Its Political Use in the Twentieth Century*. New Haven, CT, and London: Yale University Press. 255 pp.

An essential reference; includes discussions of the Armenian genocide, India and Pakistan, Bangladesh, and much more.

Kuper, Leo (1988). Other selected cases of genocide and genocidal massacres: types of genocide. In Charny, Israel W. (Ed.), *Genocide: A Critical Bibliographic Review*. New York: Facts on File, pp. 155-171.

Kuper, Leo (1990). Theological warrants for genocide: Judaism, Islam and Christianity. *Terrorism and Political Violence*, 1990, 2(3), 351-379.
"This article concentrates on one aspect of religious differentiation, the theological warrants for genocide in the sacred texts in the interrelated religions of Judaism, Islam and Christianity. The influence of these texts is analyzed in historical perspective, with emphasis on the broad societal context, and the power to engage in genocidal action. The contemporary spread of religious fundamentalism enhances the significance of these texts, as notably in Israel and its occupied territories, where the clash of religious fundamentalisms introduces a particularly threatening extremist element in the ongoing conflict" (p. 351).

Reynolds, Vernon, et al. (Eds.) (1986). *The Sociobiology of Ethnocentrism: Evolutionary Dimensions of Xenophobia, Discrimination, Racism and Nationalism*. London: Croom Helm; and Athens, GA: University of Georgia Press. 327 pp.
The subtitle describes the contents of this useful collection of papers by biologists and social scientists, all exploring aspects of what may be an inherent disposition toward ethnic conflict.

Staub, Ervin (1989). *The Roots of Evil: The Origins of Genocide and Other Group Violence*. Cambridge and New York: Cambridge University Press. 336 pp.
A comprehensive study by a social psychologist whose research has focused on possibilities for encouraging development of "prosocial" behavior. Includes chapters on the Armenian genocide, the Holocaust, Cambodia and Argentina.

Wilson, Edward O. (1978). *On Human Nature*. Cambridge, MA, and London: Harvard University Press. 260 pp.
A prominent student of animal behavior extends his "sociobiological" perspective to humans. See especially the chapters on religion and aggression.

European Jews, Cathars, and Crusades

Bettenson, Henry, trans. (1972). Augustine, *The City of God Against the Pagans*. Harmondsworth: Penguin.

Chazan, Robert (1973). *Medieval Jewry in Northern France: A Political and Social History*. Baltimore: Johns Hopkins University Press. 283 pp.
History of a major segment of Ashkenazic Jewry in the later medieval period, including the persecutions of the 12th and 13th centuries which culminated in the expulsion of 1306.

Chazan, Robert (1987). *European Jewry and the First Crusade*. Berkeley and Los Angeles: University of California Press. 380 pp.
Detailed study of the attacks on the Rhineland communities; appendix containing translated texts of documents also in Eidelberg (1977).

Davies, Alan (Ed.) (1979). *Antisemitism and the Foundations of Christianity*. New York: Paulist Press. 258 pp.
Important collection of essays responding to Rosemary Ruether (1974).

Eidelberg, Shlomo (Ed. and trans.) (1977). *The Jews and the Crusaders: The Hebrew Chronicles of the First and Second Crusades*. Madison: University of Wisconsin Press. 186 pp.
Indispensable primary sources for the murderous assaults on the Jewish communities of the Rhineland as described by Jewish contemporaries.

Grayzel, Solomon (1966). *The Church and the Jews in the XIIIth Century*. Revised ed. New York: Hermon Press. 378 pp.
Texts with facing translations of papal letters and other documents, preceded by a long introductory essay. A standard volume, originally published in 1933 and still very valuable.

Grayzel, Solomon (1989). *The Church and the Jews in the XIIIth Century. Volume II: 1254-1314*. Stow, Kenneth R. (Ed.). New York: Jewish Theological Seminary; and Detroit: Wayne State University Press. 357 pp.
Continuation of Grayzel (1966) but with texts summarized and partly translated. Includes a reprinted essay by Grayzel on papal policies toward Jews in the medieval period.

Hsia, R. Po-chia (1988). *The Myth of Ritual Murder: Jews and Magic in Reformation Germany*. New Haven, CT and London: Yale University Press. 248 pp.
Describes persecution of Jews accused of ritual murder of Christian children. Includes chapters on Regensburg and Worms, both sites of crusader assaults on Jews centuries earlier.

Jordan, William Chester (1989). *The French Monarchy and the Jews: From Philip Augustus to the Last Capetians*. Philadelphia: University of Pennsylvania Press. 369 pp.
Describes policies of French kings toward Jews: people whom they could "confront, humiliate, and exploit for moral, political, and financial purposes" (p. 256).

Little, Lester (1978). *Religious Poverty and the Profit Economy in Medieval Europe*. Ithaca, NY: Cornell University Press. 267 pp.
Contains an excellent chapter on "The Jews in Christian Europe," showing how 12th century economic developments led to sharply escalating persecution.

Parkes, James (1976). *The Jew in the Medieval Community*, 2nd ed. New York: Hermon Press. 440 pp.
A standard history with much information on connections between legal and economic status of the Jews and their vulnerability to oppression.

Riley-Smith, Jonathan (1984). The First Crusade and the persecution of the Jews. *Studies in Church History*, 21, 51-72.

Riley-Smith, Jonathan (1986). *The First Crusade and the Idea of Crusading*. Philadelphia: University of Pennsylvania Press. 227 pp.
A leading historian of the crusades concludes that vengeance for the Crucifixion was the primary motive for the Rhineland massacres of 1096. The discussion in this book repeats the argument of the 1984 article cited just above.

Ruether, Rosemary (1974). *Faith and Fratricide: The Theological Roots of Anti-Semitism.* New York: Seabury Press. 294 pp.
A provocative, widely read study arguing that anti-Jewish doctrine has been a basic element in Christianity from the beginning.

Stow, Kenneth R. (1988). Hatred of the Jews or love of the Church: Papal policy toward the Jews in the Middle Ages. In Almog, Shmuel (Ed.), *Antisemitism Through the Ages.* Oxford and London: Pergamon Press, pp. 71-89.
Jews were to be tolerated as long as they accepted their inferior status and behaved with appropriate humility.

Trachtenberg, Joshua (1943). *The Devil and the Jews: The Medieval Conception of the Jew and its Relation to Modern Antisemitism.* New Haven, CT: Yale University Press, 1943. 279 pp.
A classic study of medieval beliefs about Jews as demonic beings and sorcerers in league with the devil.

Wakefield, Walter L. (1974). *Heresy, Crusade and Inquisition in Southern France, 1100-1250.* Berkeley and Los Angeles: University of California Press. 288 pp.
The standard source on the persecution of the Cathars and other heretics.

Spanish Conquest of Mexico

Gibson, Charles (1966). *Spain in America.* New York: Harper & Row. 239 pp.
A standard history. See especially Chapter 4, "Church" and Chapter 7, "Spaniards and Indians."

Hanke, Lewis (1959). *Aristotle and the American Indians: A Study of Race Prejudice in the Modern World.* Bloomington, IN: Indiana University Press. 164 pp.
On the debate between Las Casas and Sepúlveda concerning whether Indians were naturally born to be slaves.

Wachtel, Nathan (1984). The Indian and the Spanish Conquest. In Bethell, Leslie (Ed.), *The Cambridge History of Latin America. Volume I: Colonial Latin America.* Cambridge and New York: Cambridge University Press, pp. 207-248.
Describes the process of "destructuration" - i.e., demographic decline and sociocultural disintegration - during the first forty years after the conquest in Mexico and elsewhere.

Wolf, Eric R. (1982). *Europe and the People Without History.* Berkeley and Los Angeles: University of California Press. 503 pp.
See in particular the section on "The Great Dying," pp. 133-135.

The Armenian Genocide

Charny, Israel W. (Ed.) (1984). *Toward the Understanding and Prevention of Genocide.* Boulder, CO, and London: Westview Press. 396 pp.
Includes papers by Richard Hovannisian and Marjorie Housepian Dobkin on the problem of denial.

Dadrian, Vahakn N. (1975). The common features of the Armenian and Jewish cases of genocide: A comparative victimological perspective. In Drapkin, Israel, and Viano, Emilio (Eds.), *Victimology: A New Focus. Vol. IV: Violence and Its Victims*, pp. 99-120. Lexington, MA: D.C. Heath.
    Points out that both groups were vulnerable and were defined as sources of threat by regimes that had the power to undertake genocidal policies with ease.

Guroian, Vigen. (1991). Armenian genocide and Christian existence. *Cross Currents*, 41(3), pp. 322-342.
    Theological and ethical reflections on the question of whether Armenians can or should accept the Christian injunction to forgive enemies. "There is a deep aversion to the heart of the Christian gospel among Armenians, and the church has not the courage to face that aversion..."

Housepian, Marjorie (1966). The unremembered genocide. *Commentary*, 42, pp. 55-61.
    A pioneering article that aroused considerable attention.

Hovannisian, Richard G. (1967). *Armenia on the Road to Independence*. Berkeley and Los Angeles: University of California Press. 364 pp.
    A study by an outstanding scholar, discussing the historical background, the genocide, and its aftermath.

Hovannisian, Richard G. (Ed.) (1986). *The Armenian Genocide in Perspective*. New Brunswick, NJ: Transaction Books. 215 pp.
    An important collection of articles by the editor, Leo Kuper and others on the history of the genocide, and on how it has been described and interpreted by perpetrators and victims.

Hovannisian, Richard G. (1988). The Armenian genocide. In Charny, Israel W. (Ed.), *Genocide: A Critical Bibliographic Review*. New York: Facts on File, pp. 89-115.
    A comprehensive bibliographic essay.

Institut für Armenische Fragen (1987). *The Armenian Genocide: Documentation*. Two volumes. Munich. Vol. 1: 654 pp. Vol. 2: 495 pp.
    Documents in several languages on all aspects of the genocide, including historical background dating back to the nineteenth century.

Lang, David Marshall, and Walker, Christopher J. (1987). *The Armenians*. London: Minority Rights Group, Report No. 32. 20 pp.
    An informative summary including discussion of the situation of Armenians today in various parts of the world.

Walker, Christopher J. (1980). *Armenia: The Survival of a Nation*. New York: St. Martin's Press. 446 pp.
    A well written history. Chapter 5 describes massacres in the 1890's; Chapter 7 describes the genocide of 1915.

India, Pakistan and Bangladesh

Amnesty International (1986). *Bangladesh: Unlawful Killings and Torture in the Chittagong Hill Tracts*. London: Amnesty International. 38 pp.

A measured and carefully documented report with recommendations to the Bangladesh government.

Anti-Slavery Society (1984). *The Chittagong Hill Tracts: Militarization, Oppression and the Hill Tribes.* Indigenous Peoples and Development Series, Report No. 2. London: Anti-Slavery Society. 92 pp.
   Provides substantial historical background and also documents the killings and destruction in this region. One appendix is a statement by a member of the Bangladesh parliament describing a massacre in March 1980.

Aziz, Qutubuddin (1974). *Blood and Tears.* Karachi: United Press of Pakistan. 232 pp.
   Aziz, a Pakistani journalist, documents atrocities committed in East Pakistan by Awami League militants against West Pakistanis and other non-Bengalis.

Chaudhuri, Kalyan (1972). *Genocide in Bangladesh.* Bombay: Orient Longman. 228 pp.
   The author, a Bengali journalist, presents a painfully detailed account of atrocities committed by Pakistani troops against helpless civilians.

Collins, Larry, and Lapierre, Dominique (1975). *Freedom at Midnight.* New York: Simon & Schuster. 572 pp.
   Chapter 13 describes in detail the massacres on both sides in the Punjab during August and September 1947.

Kuper, Leo (1981). *Genocide: Its Political Use in the Twentieth Century.* New Haven and London: Yale University Press. 255 pp.
   Includes discussions of India in 1947 (pp. 63-68) and Bangladesh in 1971 (pp. 76-80).

Levak, Albert E. (1974). Provincial conflict and nation-building in Pakistan. In Bell, Wendell, and Freeman, Walter E. (Eds.) *Ethnicity and Nation-Building.* Beverly Hills, CA, and London: Sage Publications, pp. 203-221.

Mascarenhas, Anthony (1971). *The Rape of Bangla Desh.* Delhi: Vikas Publications. 168 pp.
   An eyewitness journalistic account. See particularly Chapter 9, "Genocide."

Mey, Wolfgang (Ed.) (1984). *They Are Now Burning Village After Village; Genocide in the Chittagong Hill Tracts, Bangladesh.* International Work Group for Indigenous Affairs, Document No. 51. 190 pp.

Survival International (1983). Genocide in Bangladesh. *Survival International Review,* 43. 135 pp.
   This report and a 1985 followup are summarized by Leo Kuper in Israel W. Charny (Ed.) (1988), *Genocide: A Critical Bibliographic Review,* p. 166.

Other Ethnic Conflicts: Algeria, Israel, Northern Ireland, Sri Lanka, Sudan, Tibet

Amunugama, Sarath. (1991). Buddhaputra and Bhumiputra? Dilemmas of modern Sinhala Buddhist monks in relation to ethnic and political conflict. *Religion,* 21(2), pp. 115-139.
   How Sinhala Buddhist monks in Sri Lanka resolve conflicts between ethnic loyalties and Buddhist principles. They rationalize violence as defense of Buddhism: Tamil rebels often attack monks or worshippers, hence must be resisted.

Carroll, Terrance G. (1977). Northern Ireland. In Suhrke, Astri, and Noble, Lela G. (Eds.), *Ethnic Conflict in International Relations*. New York and London: Praeger, pp. 21-42.

Deng, Francis Madding (1990). War of visions for the nation. *Middle East Journal*, 44, pp. 596-609.
   Argues that the traditionally accepted distinctions in Sudan between the Islamic North and Christian or "animist" South oversimplifies a complex social mosaic, and that there are still possibilities for unity based on a variety of social and cultural linkages: "a more dynamic process of realignments."

Horne, Alistair (1977). *A Savage War of Peace: Algeria 1954-1962*. London: Macmillan; and Harmondsworth: Penguin Books, 1985. 604 pp.
   The best available history; readable and vivid.

Johnson, Douglas H. (1988). *The Southern Sudan*. London: Minority Rights Group, Report No. 78. 11 pp.

Lustick, Ian S. (1988). *For the Land and the Lord: Jewish Fundamentalism in Israel*. New York: Council on Foreign Relations. 244 pp.
   A capably researched study of ultra-nationalists who believe that they are divinely commanded to occupy all territory defined as the Land of Israel.

Morrison, Godfrey (1972). The Southern Sudan and Eritrea. In Whitaker, Ben (Ed.), *The Fourth World: Victims of Group Oppression*. London: Sidgwick & Jackson; New York: Schocken, pp.73-116.

Mullin, Chris, and Wangyal, Phuntsog (1983). *The Tibetans: Two Perspectives on Tibetan-Chinese Relations*. London: Minority Rights Group. 27 pp.
   Two opposed views on Chinese persecutions of Tibetan Buddhists. Mullin argues that this was a civil war against reactionary and oppressive elements in Tibetan society. Wangyal interprets the conflict as a genocidal assault.

Tambiah, S.J. (1986). *Sri Lanka: Ethnic Fratricide and the Dismantling of Democracy*. Chicago and London: University of Chicago Press. 198 pp.
   A prominent anthropologist of Sri Lankan birth interprets the conflict as the product of social and economic stress that has developed since independence.

Young, Crawford (1976). *The Politics of Cultural Pluralism*. Madison: University of Wisconsin Press. 560 pp.
   An instructive, well written book; includes sections on India, Bangladesh, Biafra, Southern Sudan, and much more.

Christian Clergy and the Holocaust

Barnett, Victoria (1992). *For the Soul of the People: Protestant Protest Against Hitler*. London and New York: Oxford University Press. 358 pp.
   Citing oral histories and archival records, the author discusses how Protestant clergy responded to and protested against state policies regarding the church and racist oppression of Jews.

Berger, Alan L. (1988). The Holocaust: the ultimate and archetypal genocide. In Charny, Israel W. (Ed.), *Genocide: A Critical Bibliographic Review*. New York: Facts on File Publications, pp. 59-88.
Extensive bibliographic coverage.

Bethge, Eberhard (1970). Dietrich Bonhoeffer, Man of Vision, Man of Courage. Eric Mosbacher et al., trans.; Edwin Robertson, ed. New York and Evanston: Harper & Row. 867 pp.
The standard biography of the German clergyman who was executed for resistance to the Nazi regime.

Boyens, Armin (1980). The ecumenical community and the Holocaust. *Annals of the American Academy of Political and Social Science*, pp. 140-152.

Bracher, Karl Dietrich (1970). *The German Dictatorship*. Jean Steinberg, trans. New York: Praeger. 553 pp.
The section on "Churches and Resistance," pp. 379-390, provides an informative overview.

Cochrane, Arthur C. (1962). *The Church's Confession Under Hitler*. Philadelphia: Westminster Press. 317 pp.
Focuses on the "resistance synods" held by the Confessing Church (liberal Protestants), especially the 1934 Barmen synod, which did not mention the predicament of the Jews. See pp. 126-127 for contrasting responses of two theological faculties to the "Aryan paragraph" concerning ministers of Jewish descent.

Conway, John S. (1980). The Churches. In Friedlander, Henry and Milton, Sybil (Eds.), *The Holocaust: Ideology, Bureaucracy, and Genocide*. Milwood, NY: Kraus International Publications, pp. 199-206.
A brief summary by one of the foremost scholars of the subject.

Conway, John S. (1968). *The Nazi Persecution of the Churches, 1933-1945*. New York: Basic Books. 474 pp.
An indispensable study that includes considerable information on responses to the fate of the Jews. Recognizing that the clergy presented very little resistance to Nazism, the author concludes that political passivity and conservatism were characteristic of the great majority.

Conzemius, Victor (1969). *Églises chrétiennes et totalitarisme national-socialiste. Un bilan historiographique*. Louvain: Bibliotèque de la Revue d'Histoire Ecclésiastique.

Die Evangelische Kirche in Deutschland und die Judenfrage: Ausgewahlte Dokumente aus den Jahren 1933 bis 1943. Geneva: Verlag Oikumene, 1945.

Ericksen. Robert P. (1985). *Theologians Under Hitler: Gerhard Kittel, Paul Althaus, and Emanuel Hirsch*. New Haven and London: Yale University Press. 245 pp.
An excellent study of three prominent theologians who endorsed Nazi ideology and policies.

Falconi, Carlos (1970). *The Silence of Pius XII*. Bernard Wall, trans. London: Faber & Faber; and Boston: Little, Brown. 430 pp.
Author believes that the pope fully understood the situation but chose not to act

because his foremost goal was to ensure that the Church would survive as an influential element in European politics after the war. Includes a detailed analysis of responses to events in Poland and Croatia.

Faulhaber, Cardinal (1934). *Judaism, Christianity and Germany.* George D. Smith, trans. New York: Macmillan. 116 pp.

Four sermons delivered in Munich in 1933, defending the Old Testament against Nazi invective but presenting the conventional image of Jews as "unfulfilled" people whose religion requires "completion" by the New Testament.

Fein, Helen (1979). *Accounting for Genocide: National Responses and Jewish Victimization During the Holocaust.* New York: Free Press, 1979. 468 pp.

An innovative study with important conclusions about why people do or do not cooperate in genocidal actions. Chapter 4, on responses of Christian churches to threats against Jews, describes the role of church and clergy in Croatia, Slovakia, Hungary, and elsewhere.

Fleischner, Eva (Ed.) (1977). *Auschwitz: Beginning of a New Era?: Reflections on the Holocaust.* New York: KTAV. 469 pp.

Includes a number of provocative essays by Jewish and Christian scholars, including Irving Greenberg, Rosemary Ruether, Yosef Hayim Yerushalmi and Alan Davies. One major theme is the problem of religious faith after the Holocaust.

Friedlander, Saul (1966). *Pius XII and the Third Reich: A Documentation.* New York: Knopf. 238 pp.

An analysis of diplomatic documents from the German Foreign Office. The accusing tone of this study should be compared with the interpretation of Beate Ruhm von Oppen in the volume edited by Littell and Locke (1974).

Friedman, Philip (1978). *Their Brothers' Keepers.* Updated edition. New York: Holocaust Library. 232 pp.

A pioneering study by an outstanding scholar; includes accounts of unselfish assistance to Jews by churches, convents, monasteries, and individual clergymen.

Gallin, Mary Alice (1961). *German Resistance to Hitler: Ethical and Religious Factors.* Washington, DC: Catholic University of America Press. 250 pp.

Maintains that aside from "the small group of fanatical Nazis, the German people were not in favor of persecuting the Jews," but says almost nothing about the matter thereafter.

Gutteridge, Richard (1976). *Open Thy Mouth for the Dumb!: The German Evangelical Church and the Jews, 1879-1950.* Oxford: Blackwell. New York: Barnes & Noble. 374 pp.

An essential source on German Protestant responses to the persecution of the Jews. "Select Bibliography," pp. 358-370.

Haas, Peter J. (1988). *Morality After Auschwitz: The Radical Challenge of the Nazi Ethic.* Philadelphia: Fortress Press. 257 pp.

A challenging study arguing that the Nazis did not violate any accepted ethical principles: they defined Jews as demonic enemies of the people and then dealt with them in accordance with accepted standards for responding to such a threat.

Hallie, Philip P. (1979). *Lest Innocent Blood Be Shed.* New York: Harper & Row. 303 pp.
    Describes the rescue of thousands of Jews by the citizens and clergy of a small town in southern France. The people were Protestants, sensitive to their Huguenot legacy.

Helmreich, Ernst Christian (1979). *The German Churches Under Hitler: Background, Struggle, and Epilogue.* Detroit: Wayne State University Press. 616 pp.
    A detailed history of the Catholic and Protestant churches; extensive bibliography, largely in German, pp. 577-600. The tone is scholarly and non-judgmental, but the evidence for clerical passivity is there.

Hilberg, Raul (1961). *The Destruction of the European Jews.* Chicago: Quadrangle. 788 pp.

Hunt, Chester L. (1984). A critical evaluation of the resistance of German Protestantism to the Holocaust. In Charny, Israel W. (Ed.), *Toward the Understanding and Prevention of Genocide.* Boulder, CO, and London: Westview Press, pp. 241-254.
    The author agrees that resistance was minimal but reminds us that the "essential question" is "why all parts of German society succumbed to the forces which produced the Holocaust."

Kershaw, Ian (1987). *The 'Hitler Myth': Image and Reality in the Third Reich.* Oxford and New York: Oxford University Press. 297 pp.
    An innovative study by a prominent historian showing how Nazi propaganda created an image of Hitler bearing little resemblance to the real man. Chapter 4 shows how religious imagery was employed to encourage clerical cooperation and to counter resistance from liberal clergy.

Koonz, Claudia (1987). *Mothers in the Fatherland: Women, the Family, and Nazi Politics.* New York: St. Martin's Press. 556 pp.
    Chapters on Protestant and Catholic women's organizations show that their responses paralleled those of men: overall accommodation occasionally modified by cautious resistance when basic religious institutions were threatened.

Kulka, Otto Dov, and Mendes-Flohr, Paul R. (Eds.) (1987). *Judaism and Christianity Under the Impact of National Socialism.* Jerusalem: Historical Society of Israel. 558 pp.
    An indispensable collection of papers, covering historical background, including several essays on the Weimar period; responses of churches in Germany and in a number of other countries, including France, Holland, Austria, Poland, Hungary, etc.; and theological issues. See the review of this volume by Ian Kershaw in *Yad Vashem Studies,* Vol. 19, 1988, pp. 427-437.

Lang, Berel (1990). *Act and Idea in the Nazi Genocide.* Chicago and London: University of Chicago Press. 328 pp.
    Discusses moral and ethical questions raised by the Holocaust.

Lewy, Guenter (1964). *The Catholic Church and Nazi Germany.* New York: McGraw-Hill. 416 pp.
    This remains the most informative book on the subject. See especially Chapter 9, on the Church's response to the "euthanasia" program, and Chapter 10, on the response to the persecution of the Jews. The author's essential conclusion is that the Church as an institution did next to nothing in response to the Holocaust.

Lifton, Robert Jay (1986). *The Nazi Doctors: Medical Killing and the Psychology of Genocide.* New York: Basic Books. 561 pp.
A very important study of how and why physicians participated extensively in genocide. Discusses clerical resistance to the "euthanasia" program on pp. 90-95.

Littell, Franklin H., and Locke, Hubert G. (Eds.) (1974). *The German Church Struggle and the Holocaust.* Detroit: Wayne State University Press. 327 pp.
Sixteen papers delivered at a conference in 1970. See especially the papers by Bonkovsky, Conway, Littell, Ruhm von Oppen and Zahn.

Marrus, Michael R., and Paxton, Robert O. (1981). *Vichy France and the Jews.* New York: Basic Books. 432 pp.
The authors show that the Catholic clergy protested against deportations of Jews to a degree never present in Germany, but that they also expressed support for the Vichy regime and were careful not to agitate beyond accepted limits. See especially pp. 270-279. See also Marrus' article in Kulka and Mendes-Flohr (1987).

Matheson, Peter (1981). *The Third Reich and the Christian Churches.* Grand Rapids, MI: Eerdmans. 103 pp.
Documents translated from German.

Morley, John F. (1980). *Vatican Diplomacy and the Jews During the Holocaust, 1933-1943.* New York: KTAV. 327 pp.
The Vatican was well informed about the Holocaust but pursued cautious policies aimed at preserving political relationships. No serious effort to aid Jews. Includes discussions of Germany, France, Slovakia, Poland, etc.

Neshamit, Sarah (1977). Rescue in Lithuania during the Nazi occupation. In Gutman, Yisrael, and Zuroff, Efraim (Eds.), *Rescue Attempts During the Holocaust.* Jerusalem: Yad Vashem. pp. 289-331.
Section on the Catholic Church, pp. 312-316, describes extensive collaboration by Catholic clergy but notes that some assisted Jews at great risk to themselves.

Poliakov, Leon (1979). *Harvest of Hate: The Nazi Program for the Destruction of the Jews of Europe.* Revised ed. New York: Holocaust Library. 350 pp.
See "The Christian Churches: Dogma and Reality," pp. 293-301.

Ross, Robert (1980). *So It Was True: The American Protestant Press and the Nazi Persecution of the Jews.* Minneapolis: University of Minnesota Press. 374 pp.
Argues that Protestant periodicals provided adequate information but it was ignored. In a perceptive critique, David Wyman shows that Ross actually demonstrated that the periodicals paid very little attention to the Holocaust (1984, pp. 412-413).

Rubenstein, Richard L., and Roth, John K. (1987). *Approaches to Auschwitz: The Holocaust and Its Legacy.* Atlanta: John Knox Press. 422 pp.
Chapter 7, "Their Brothers' Keepers? Christians, Churches, and Jews" provides a useful summary of the most important literature. See also Rubenstein's essay, "Religion and the Origins of the Death Camps," in his *After Auschwitz* (1966).

Ruhm von Oppen, Beate (1971). *Religion and Resistance to Nazism.* Princeton University, Center of International Studies, Research Monograph No. 35. 74 pp.
A critical counterpoint to the work of Lewy and others, emphasizing the

non-Christian nature and anti-Christian stance of Nazism. See also her paper in Littell and Locke (1974).

Sereny, Gita (1974). *Into That Darkness: From Mercy Killing to Mass Murder*. London: Andre Deutsch. 380 pp.
Explores extent to which clergy aided escaping Nazis and whether they adequately appreciated the nature of these men's actions. Also discusses assistance rendered to Jews and political considerations affecting papal policies. See pp. 289-323.

Snoek, Johan M. (1970). *The Grey Book: A Collection of Protests Against Anti-Semitism and the Persecution of Jews Issued by Non-Roman Catholic Churches and Church Leaders during Hitler's Rule*. New York: Humanities Press. 315 pp.
The title represents the author's conclusion that the dark side of the historical record must be balanced by recognition that a few people did express concern and did protest.

Tal, Uriel (1975). *Christians and Jews in Germany: Religion, Politics, and Ideology in the Second Reich, 1870-1914*. Ithaca and London: Cornell University Press. 359 pp.
Provides essential background for understanding responses of Christian clergy to anti-Jewish policies under the Nazi regime.

Tec, Nechama (1986). *When Light Pierced the Darkness: Christian Rescue of Jews in Nazi-Occupied Poland*. Oxford and New York: Oxford University Press. 262 pp.
See especially Chapter 9, "Religion."

Wright, J.R.C. (1974). *"Above Parties": The Political Attitudes of the German Protestant Church Leadership,. 1918-1933*. Oxford: Oxford University Press. 197 pp.
Agrees that Protestant church was for the most part "monarchist, nationalist, and authoritarian," but shows that it was accommodating to Weimar Republic and recognized danger in Nazi program to control churches.

Wyman, David S. (1984). *The Abandonment of the Jews: America and the Holocaust, 1941-1945*. New York: Pantheon. 444 pp.
The most recent and most thoroughly researched study of the subject, including responses of American clergy.

Zahn, Gordon C. (1962). *German Catholics and Hitler's Wars: A Study in Social Control*. London: Sheed & Ward; New York: E. P. Dutton. 232 pp.
A sociologist shows that most Catholic clergy warmly supported the German war effort and expressed opposition only to policies deemed antagonistic to welfare of Church. Author says almost nothing about reactions to persecutions of Jews.

Zerner, Ruth (1983). German Protestant responses to Nazi persecution of the Jews. In Braham, Randolph H. (Ed.), *Perspectives on the Holocaust*. Boston and The Hague: Kluwer-Nijhoff, pp. 57-68.
Their "primary concerns" were "institutional self-preservation and ultimately survival."

Zuccotti, Susan (1987). *The Italians and the Holocaust*. New York: Basic Books. 334 pp.
See pp. 207-217 on the pope's response to evacuation of Jews from Rome.

Zuccotti, Susan (1993). *The Holocaust, the French, and the Jews.* New York: Basic Books. 383 pp.

A penetrating study comparing the fate of native-born and foreign-born Jews in France. Includes considerable discussion of the behavior of Christian clergy, much but not all on the positive side. See especially the chapters on "Racial Laws" and "Attitudes toward the Jews."

PART III

**Compelling Confirmations
of the Armenian Genocide
in German & Austrian Sources**

3

Documentation of the Armenian Genocide in German and Austrian Sources

Vahakn N. Dadrian

PART I. THE IMPORT OF THE DOCUMENTS

Introduction

The documentation of a case of genocide that is subject to persistent denials by the perpetrator camp is in many respects a critical task. First, such denials are almost always attended by a web of obstructions encumbering the performance of that task. Second, the vehicle of documentation has to be as compelling as possible if the power leverage of the deniers is to be effectively obviated. The task of documentation has a methodological primacy as well as a fundamental value in the overall picture of historical analysis. But documentation is an operational term; the results sought are dependent largely on the quality of the material at hand. In order for such documentation to be compelling the sources upon which the documentary edifice is anchored are to be unimpeachable.

For a number of reasons to be explained below, the German and Austrian sources utilized in this study are not only the best among all the constellations of existing and available sources, but intrinsically they are almost incontestable.

Since the bulk of these documents originates from the state archives of Germany and Austria, but especially Germany, a comment may be in order on another and similar documentary work compiled by the eminent German missionary and at the same time historian Johannes Lepsius.[1] This work encompasses 444 separate documents culled from the archives of the Political Department of the German Foreign Ministry presently located in Bonn. However, in two respects this volume is vulnerable to the test of historiographical scrutiny. It lacks archival identification indexes such as file and volume numbers as well as the entry numbers of individual documents through which they were registered in the entry journal of the ministry's archives covering the diplomatic correspondence. Most important, contrary to the assurance given in the Preface, not all the documents are faithfully reproduced. Quite a few of them suffer from the effects of such irregularities as paraphrasing, excisions and occasional deletions within given paragraphs.[2] In its general thrust the Lepsius tome is nevertheless a massive, powerful and authentic source documenting an instance of a carefully designed and implacably executed genocide.

The present study is even more selective and fragmentary in the presentation of evidence than the work of Lepsius as it consists largely of a collection of minuscule excerpts of documents. Theoretically, such a practice of truncations is bound to undermine the reliability of that evidence which appears not only as incomplete but also as disjointed. Yet, this very feature of excerpting constitutes the essence of the methodological design of the study. That design is geared to the main objective of the study which is to ascertain whether or not official German and Austrian data support the assertion that the World War I anti-Armenian measures were tantamount to an act of genocide - in the strictest sense of the word. In other words, when reduced to its barest and simplest form, the objective is the determination of the fact of the genocide on the basis of German and Austrian sources and data. All other considerations are either outside, or are subsidiary to the framework of the study.

Such a determination is justifiable when one proceeds to distill from long-winded official reports, conclusions, judgments and occasionally decrials by competent and responsible functionaries underscoring the reality of the genocide. In other words, the focus of attention and demonstration is not the process surrounding the genocide, but the summary judgments of diplomats and military observing these processes as contemporaries. The aim is to garner and sketch the emergence of these judgments.

Ordinarily, such a procedure would be a way of employing data that is "out of context." But what is extraordinary about the present case is the amplitude of testimonies concurring in the observation that the World War I anti-Armenian measures were not only carefully planned, but that they were intended to destroy the victim population. The convergence on this crucial point of so many diverse sources is of abiding significance. Indeed, the sheer quantity of concurrent judgments is so overwhelming as to dispel any lingering doubts about the veracity of these judgments and to impart a new quality to the concordance involved.

In brief, *one is not dealing here with isolated and handful testimonies but a vast array of documents unequivocally confirming the historical fact of the Armenian genocide.* The present study proposes to single out, detail and integrate these testimonies in a coherent frame of reference.

CATEGORIES OF DOCUMENTS

In the main there are two categories involved. Incoming reports were prepared by the representatives of the governments of Imperial Germany and Imperial Austria who were stationed in the territories of the Ottoman Empire during the war. Then there are outgoing instructions and a variety of other communications emanating from the top officials in Berlin and Vienna directing the foreign affairs of wartime Germany and Austria. The incoming reports as a rule originate either from the individual German and Austrian consuls, vice consuls or gerents serving in the provinces of Turkey, or from the German and Austrian ambassadors on duty in Constantinople (Istanbul), then the Ottoman capital. Frequently, copies of German consular reports sent to the ambassador in the Ottoman Capital are simultaneously sent to the German Chancellor as well. It goes without saying that the incoming reports constitute the majority of the documents at issue here. Equally important, these are all official pieces of communication.

Then there are some scattered reports from a variety of German and Austrian high ranking military serving as staff officers, field commanders, sanitation chiefs or advisors and attachés. In the case of the Germans, most of the officers were under the jurisdiction of the German Military Mission to Turkey to whose chief, General Liman von Sanders, they directed their reports. The Austrian officers were under the control of the Austrian Military Plenipotentiary, namely, Vice Marshal Pomiankowski, who was attached to the Ottoman General Headquarters throughout the war. Given this command and control setup, the reports issued by these high ranking officers had also an official character.

Below is a list of most of the diplomats and consuls whose reports are excerpted for the purposes of this study. They are identified by name, title, duration of office and the latter's location.

THE DIPLOMATIC PERSONNEL

Ambassadors and Those Temporarily Deputizing for Them

German

1. Hans Freiherr von Wangenheim, 1912- October 25, 1915.
2. Prince Ernst Wilhelm Hohenlohe - Langenburg, July 20 - October 2, 1915 (serving as

Special Ambassador while Wangenheim was on sick leave).
3. Embassy Councillor (*Botschaftsrat*) Konstantin Freiherr von Neurath, deputizing as Chargé, October 25 - November 15, 1915.
4. Count Paul von Wolff - Metternich, November 15, 1915 - October 3, 1916,
5. Legation Councillor (*Legationsrat*) Wilhelm von Radowitz, October 3 -November 16, 1916, deputizing as Chargé.
6. Dr. Richard von Kühlmann, November 16, 1916 - July 24, 1917.
   a. Privy Legation Councillor Dr. Otto Göppert, deputizing for Kühlmann who was on vacation December 26, 1916 - January 5, 1917.
   b. Embassy Councillor Heinrich Count Josef von Waldburg zu Wolfegg und Waldsee, deputizing for Kühlmann who was again on leave, June 26 - July 7, 1917.
7. Count Johann Heinrich Bernstorff, September 7, 1917 - October 27, 1918.
8. Embassy Councillor Waldburg deputizing as Chargé, October 27 - December 20, 1918.

Austrian (Hungarian)

1. Johann Markgraf Pallavicini, October 5, 1906 - November 30, 1918.
2. Chargé Karl Count zu Trautmannsdorff - Weinsberg, deputizing for Pallavicini in September, 1915 when the Ambassador was in Vienna on a leave.
3. Julius Baron von Szilassy und Pilis, Envoy and Gerent, Spring and Summer 1918.

Consuls, Vice Consuls and Gerents

German

1. Dr. Edgar Anders, Gerent, Erzurum Consulate, September 4, 1913 - end of July, 1914.
2. Dr. Heinrich Bergfeld, Consul, Trabizon, 1910 - March 8, 1916; and after the Consulate's move to Samsun, March 8, 1916 - January 27, 1917, and July - November, 1918.
3. Dr. Heinrich Brode, Consul, Jaffa, June - July 13, 1914; September 9, 1914 - August 1, 1915. Consul and Gerent, Damascus, June - end of September, 1918.
4. Dr. Eugen Büge, Consul, Adana, May 1910 - October 1918.
5. Hesse, Consul, Sivas, October 8, 1917 - August, 1918.
6. Walter Holstein, Vice Consul, Gerent, Mosul, 1911 - end of April, 1918; absent from office on inspection tours, leaves and holidays: November 1 - December 19, 1914, October 1915, July 22 - September 23, 1916.
7. Hermann Hoffmann, Vice Consul, Gerent, Alexandrette, May 10 - August 10, 1917.
8. Humbert, Consul, Smyrna (Izmir), 1910 - January 8, 1916.
9. Kuckhoff, Vice Consul, Samsun, 1905 - August 1917; Gerent August 1917 - January 7, 1918; Gerent, Trabizon, January 27 - August, 1917.
10. Dr. Julius Loytved-Hardegg, Consul, Damascus, June 13, 1915 - May 7, 1917; Gerent, Haifa, September 13 - October 2, 1915.
11. Mutius, Consul, Beirut, 1912 - end of September, 1918 (Consul General since April 15, 1916), with leaves and vacations June 15 - October 25 and July 1 - 29, 1917.
12. Dr. Max Erwin von Scheubner-Richter, Vice Consul, Erzurum, February 17 - August 6, 1915; Reserve Officer and Co-Commander with Ittihadist leader Ömer Naci of the Caucasus Expedition involving guerilla operations behind enemy lines, Fall and Winter 1915.

13. Prince Friedrich Werner von der Schulenburg, Consul, Erzurum, August 6, 1915 - end of February, 1916; Gerent, Beirut, July 1 - 29, 1917 and Damascus, August 10, 1917 - April, 1918.
14. Dr. Walter Rössler, Consul, Aleppo, 1910 - May 10, 1918.
15. Dr. Paul Schwartz, Consul, Gerent, Erzurum, September 29, 1914 - February 17, 1915.
16. Prince von Spee, Consul, Gerent, Smyrna, January 8, 1916 - January 19, 1917.
17. Dr. Weber, Consul, Gerent, Smyrna, January 19, 1917 - November, 1918.
18. Werth, Consular Secretary, Erzurum, Gerent, February 12, 1916 - end of war (officiating mostly in Sivas to which city the Consulate had moved in February, 1916).

Austrian (Hungarian)

As far as it is known, these consular functionaries mostly remained at their posts most of the time throughout the war.

1. Prince Alois de Sylva Dandini, Consul, Aleppo.
2. Ernst von Kwiatkowski, Consul-General, Trabizon, Samsun.
3. Dr. Arthur Chevalier de Nadamlenzki, Consul, Adrianople (Edirne).
4. Karl Nedwed, Vice Consul, Beirut.
5. Louis Prohaska, Consular Agent, Rodosto.
6. Vladimir Radimsky, Consul and Gerent, Smyrna (Izmir).
7. Dr. Karl Ranzi, Consul-General, Damascus.
8. Richard Stöckel, Vice Consul, Adana.
9. Ludwig Trano, Chancellery Councillor, Gerent, Bursa.
10. A. Torre, Gerent, Samsun.

THE MILITARY PERSONNEL

The vast majority of military officers assisting in the Turkish war effort were Germans operating under the jurisdiction of the German Military Mission to Turkey whose head, Marshal Liman von Sanders, was in turn responsible to the German Imperial Headquarters in Berlin, with direct access to Emperor Wilhelm II. The Military Attaché or Plenipotentiary, and his subalterns, were attached to the German Embassy and were responsible to the authority of the Ambassador; the same applied to the Naval Attaché. The German Commander-in-Chief of the Turkish Fleet, and the German Inspector-General of the Coastal Artillery and Mining Operations (as well as Supreme Commander of the Straits) were likewise independent from the control of the Embassy and the Military Mission, with a right to report directly to the Emperor.

Another category of German military officers attached to the Military Mission involved military physicians who performed sanitation and medical work in the Ottoman War Ministry, Turkish Lazarets, and Field Hospitals. Most of the other officers of higher rank were either field commanders, or chiefs of staff at divisional or army corps levels, with a rank which, as a rule, was one grade higher than their German rank. There was no comparable setup and network among Austrian officers serving in wartime Turkey.

In addition to their wartime official reports, some of the officers recorded their experiences in memoirs, whether published, or unpublished and deposited after the war at archives as Papers. Others are quoted from these publications or Papers only.

The German Military Hierarchy as a Source

1. Fritz Bronsart von Schellendorf, Major General, Chief of Staff, Ottoman General Headquarters (1914 - 1917)
2. Wilhelm Leopold Colmar Freiherr von der Goltz, Field Marshal, Commander-in-Chief of 1st and subsequently Ottoman VIth Army (1914 - 1916).
3. Hans Humann, Lieutenant Commander (*Korvettenkapitän*),Captain of the Ambassadorial Yacht Lorelei, Naval Attaché, a protegé of the German Admiral von Tirpitz whose intelligence service he cultivated, and a close friend and confidant of War Minister Enver (1914 - 1917).
4. Friedrich Freiherr Kress von Kressenstein, Major General, Chief of Operations at General Headquarters, Chief of Staff of Cemal Pasha's IVth Army, Commander-in-Chief, VIII th Ottoman Army, and Chief of the German Imperial Delegation in the Caucasus (1914 - 1918).
5. Otto von Lossow, Major General, Professor of Tactics, Turkish Military College (*Harbiye*), member of staff of Abdullah Pasha, Supreme Commander of Eastern Army, Balkan War, Military Attaché (Military Plenipotentiary), and German Representative in treaty negotiations in the Trans-Caucasus (1911- 1918).
6. Ernst Paraquin, Lieutenant Colonel, Chief of Staff to a number of Ottoman Army Corps, and Chief of General Staff of Halil Pasha, Commander-in-Chief,Army Group East (1916 -1918).
7. Otto Liman von Sanders, General (Marshal), head of the German Military Mission to Turkey, Inspector-General of the Turkish Army, Commander of the Ist and subsequently Vth Army in the Dardanelles and Commander of the Army Group F in Syria (1913 - 1918).
8. Max Schlee, Major General, head of Dept. V (Weapons and Munitions), Ottoman General Headquarters (1915 - 1918).
9. Hans von Seeckt, Lieutenant General, Chief of the Staff at Ottoman General Headquarters (December 1917 - October 1918).
10. Wilhelm Souchon, Rear Admiral, Chief of the German Mediterranean Fleet (*Mittelmeer-Division*) and the Commander-in-Chief of the Turkish Fleet (1914 - 1918).
11. Stange, Colonel, Commander of 8th Regiment, attached to Ottoman III rd Army's XI th Army Corps - operating as a Special Organization Detachment comprising ex-convicts (1915 -1916).

The Austrian Contingent

1. Joseph Pomiankowski, General (Vice Marshal), Military Plenipotentiary,attached to the Ottoman General Headquarters (1914 - 1918).
2. Wladimir Freiherr Giesl von Gieslinger, General, Military Attaché (Plenipotentiary), Representative of the Austrian Foreign Ministry at the Austrian Army High Command (1909 - 1915).

The Highest German Civilian and Military Authorities in Berlin as Ancillary Sources

1. Gottlieb von Jagow, Foreign Minister (1913 - 1916).
2. Arthur Zimmermann, Deputy Foreign Minister (Undersecretary) May 1911 - November 1916; Foreign Minister, November 22, 1916 - August 6, 1917.
3. Dr. Richard von Kühlmann, Foreign Minister, August 8, 1917 - July 9, 1918 (he was born in Istanbul where his father administered German-financed railroads).
4. Paul von Hindenburg, Field Marshal, Chief of the German High Command (1916 - 1918).
5. Erich Ludendorff, General, Chief of Staff (Quartermaster) German High Command (1916 - 1918).

THE RELEVANCE OF THE SOURCES AND DATA EMPLOYED

It is a historical fact that no genocide of any kind can occur without the existence of a substantial disparity of power relations obtaining between a potential perpetrator group and a potential victim group embroiled in an exigent and consequential conflict. Genocide emerges here as a type of exercise of power, and as such it is to be regarded as functional for the radical and violent resolution of the conflict.

It appears that this characteristic of functionality of power may extend to the conditions prevailing in the aftermath of the genocidal enactment involving such issues as the recognition of the fact of the crime of genocide, determination of guilt through prosecution and retributive justice, not to speak of indemnification.

When Nazi Germany suffered total defeat and lay prostrate at the end of World War II, she was in no position to deny the authorship of the Holocaust and, therefore, submitted to the will of the victors to prosecute the authors and to exact retributive justice. Similar, if not identical, circumstances were prevalent at the end of World War I when Turkey sued for armistice and was impelled to institute thereafter her own court-martial proceedings against the authors of the Armenian genocide. The dominant mood in the country at that time conveyed a sense of both expedient contrition and compliant apprehension regarding the inevitable necessity of punitive justice.

Unlike in the case of Germany, however, in the case of Turkey the victors were neither resolute in the pursuit of justice, nor united on the issue of remolding the post-war world, especially with respect to the disintegrating Ottoman Empire. Profiting amply from this condition of irresoluteness and disunity, which was compounded by a general war-weariness among the victorious Allies, the Turks launched a successful insurgency movement in the Asiatic provinces. As a result, a near-total defeat at the end of World War I was skillfully, and one might add, heroically, harnessed and ultimately converted into a near-total military victory in less than three years (1919-1922).

Consequently, there appeared on the scene a new Turkey which not only displaced and replaced the decaying Ottoman state system, but in the process virtually imposed its will upon the erstwhile victorious Allies in Lauzanne in 1923 thereby discarding the previously signed 1920 Sèvres Treaty which was intended, among others to punish Turkey and impart justice to the Armenians, their principal victims.

Such a drastic and dramatic transformation in status could naturally not fail to transform in turn the psyche of the Turkish nation as a whole, generating a whole set of new attitudes punctuated by belligerence and defiance. The necessity to mollify the Allies on the one hand, and to assuage the Armenians on the other through manifestations of acts of remorse and reparations vanished fast from the consciousness of the Turkish people who now began to display instead a spirit of implacable remorselessness. Accordingly, the wartime mass murder of the Armenians was dismissed as sheer propaganda.

Equally important, the operating courts-martial, investigating that mass murder with a view to ascertaining and punishing the perpetrators were denounced, the judges were branded as traitors, the verdicts declared null and void, and the courts-martial themselves summarily abolished; the latter's vast archives until today are nowhere to be found.

Thus, with a shift of the preponderance of advantage of power accruing to the party identified with the perpetrator camp, both the rationale to further investigate the crime judicially and the incentive to punish the guilty evaporated swiftly. Concomitantly, the need to categorically deny the crime became almost an inveterate urge. But then who was going to contest this negation? By what means? And with what prospects of success? In the convergence of the principles of power and culpability, all other things being equal, the latitudes for arbitrarily defining the issues of dispute can be quite far-reaching; such latitudes may even provide sufficient scope to even indulge in role reversals whereby the victims are reduced to portraits of heinous perpetrators and the actual perpetrators are lamented as wretched victims.

It may, therefore, be observed that superior power is not only a requisite instrument for the enactment of genocide but it can also become a convenient matrix for the development of a syndrome through which that genocide may be denied intransigently, and as long as that power advantage lasts, persistently.

In the light of this state of affairs, one is faced with a vexing and at the same time trying situation. In fact one is confronted with a condition which is not unlike a trial, a criminal trial, if you will, where not the *corpus delicti*, i.e., the virtual vanishing of an entire nation from its ancestral territories, is the central issue, but rather the credibility of the parties involved, namely, the plaintiffs, the Armenians, and the defendants, the Turks. In such situations, the standard procedure in the annals of traditional justice has been and continues to be the assigning of particular weight to the testimony of a third category of people: reliable and credible witnesses. These witnesses may appear either on behalf of the accused, the defense witnesses, or the plaintiffs, the prosecution witnesses.

The relevance of the material in this study, culled from the official (and unofficial) testimony of German and Austrian functionaries, derives from this essential judicial fact. Furthermore, the realization that these functionaries were in no way identified with Armenian interests, but if anything, had a definite stake in protecting the welfare and good reputation of the Turks whose staunch allies they then were, accents that attribute of relevance-a relevance which is exceeded only by its significance.

THE SIGNIFICANCE OF THE SOURCES AND DATA USED

The extraordinary significance of the testimony of German and Austrian officials whose attributes as witnesses are measured in terms of a body of facts is best characterized as *evidence-in-chief*. As noted above, the evidence encompassed in that testimony and presented here is used for a limited but fundamental purpose, namely, the ascertaining of the occurrence of the World War I genocide of the Armenians. The bulk of that evidence is contained in the official reports which were transmitted to Berlin and Vienna from the embassies of the Ottoman capital, Constantinople (Istanbul), and occasionally directly from the German and Austrian consulates in the provinces. This type of material is supplemented by two other types furnished by some of these same officials in the form of either Papers deposited in a variety of archives, or in the form of post-war published memoirs. As constituted, these ancillary data rarely, if ever, do contradict the observations made by them earlier in official reports, but rather confirm them.

This is of critical importance as it demonstrates evidence of internal consistency - despite the incidence of disparate circumstances and context in the matter of recording one's judgments about the nature of the disaster of the genocide. The input from the testimony of a number of other officials in the German Foreign Ministry, the Austrian Ministry of Defence, and some prominent German journalists, representing in wartime Turkey the major organs of the German press, is such as to reinforce the recognition of the value of internal consistency. Indeed, as will be seen later in this study, these adjunct sources all but corroborate the conclusions reached by the diplomatic and military personnel stationed in Turkey.

Notwithstanding, a handful high ranking German officers, in particular General Bronsart von Schellendorf, Lieutenant Commander and Naval Attaché Hans Humann, and Rear Admiral Wilhelm Souchon, in various forms of condemnation saw fit to blame the Armenians, "rebels" and "traitors," who brought on themselves their punishment through their "extermination" (*Ausrottung*). A few others approved of the decision of the central authorities to undertake the wholesale deportations as "a military necessity" but castigated the perpetration of the attendant massacres. Still, a few others strongly objected to the inclusion in these deportations of the multitudes of inoffensive women, children, the infirm, and old men, who comprised the bulk of the residual Armenian population in wartime Turkey - as most of the able-bodied menfolk were conscripted for military service.

THE ALLIANCE AS A WARRANT
FOR THE CREDIBILITY OF THE SOURCES

By opting to join the Central Powers at the rudimentary stages of World War I, Turkey evolved into a staunch ally of Austria, but especially Germany. The alliance had a dual character, political and military; as such it enveloped and permeated many domains of the Turkish state organization. Even more important, for the Young Turk Ittihadist leaders that alliance was to serve as a "shield" (*Schutz*) for their own overt and covert designs. In a report marked "very confidential" (*streng vertraulich*), the Austrian Ambassador on April 8, 1916, informed Burian, his Foreign Minister in Vienna, that the Turks were "exploiting" the alliance as a "prop" (*Stütze*) to "proceed in the severest manner" against the Armenians.[3] In a July 27, 1915, "confidential" report, Aleppo's German consul Rössler complained to his Chancellor in Berlin, Hollweg, that the Turks in fact were bent on "resolving the Armenian Question during the war as the government is utilizing the alliance with the Central Powers for this purpose". Accusing the Ittihadist power-wielders of the crime of "the ruination (*Untergang*) of hecatombs of innocent people" he declared them "unworthy" (*unwürdig*) of an alliance with Germany.[4]

Naturally, the center of gravity of that alliance, the actual powerhouse, was Germany, imposing herself and eclipsing in the process, the other partner, Austria. This fact was figuratively acknowledged by no less a figure than Ittihad party boss and at the time Interior Minister Talat who during an exchange with General von Lossow, the German Military Plenipotentiary at Constantinople, declared: "Germany is our father but Austria is a neighbor, just like the others. We made our alliance with Germany not with Austria."[5]

Given the flourishing of this type of relationship, the Germans were able to eventually dominate in several, but not necessarily all, respects the many layers of the Ottoman state organization, especially those mobilized for the

Turkish war effort. They reigned supreme in the Ottoman General Headquarters where close and in some cases powerful personal bonds were cemented between German generals, such as Bronsart von Schellendorf and Navy Attaché Humann, and Turkish War Minister Enver; the former as a result became life-long apologists for Turkey, with veteran German General and Turkish Field Marshal Goltz redoubling his elan in the service of Turkey until his death in 1916.

Similar attachments to the Turks and Turkey developed especially among those German officers who served in Turkey for extended periods of time. This fact prompted General Seeckt, the last Chief of General Staff at Ottoman General Headquarters, to complain in his diary about so many "Turkified" (*vertürkt*) German officers.[6]

There were, of course, many exceptions to this trend of fraternization, as deep and in some respects insurmountable cleavages separating German from Turkish culture inevitably kept producing a stream of daily frictions between the members of both nation-groups.[7] Yet, the mandates of military discipline seemingly served to obviate these frictions, paving the ground for overall close and sustained cooperation.

The need for coordination of the Turkish and German war effort, dictated by the requirements of the alliance, had a specific Armenian application prescribed by the highest German authority, Kaiser Wilhelm II. As disclosed in an October 2, 1919, personal letter by General Bronsart von Schellendorf, the German emperor enjoined a group of high ranking German officers, who were received in audience by him on the eve of their departure to Turkey as members of the German Military Mission to Turkey, "not to interfere in Turkey's internal affairs." General Bronsart added that this prohibition extended to "the Armenian Question."[8] Furthermore, Maximillian Harden, the noted publisher and editor of the German weekly *Die Zukunft*, in a scathing criticism of the Imperial German government for "tolerating and condoning this Turkish affront, this most infamous instance of vileness in history (through which) nearly 1.5 million Armenians were slaughtered," for his part made the following disclosure in an editorial: "I personally heard a minion of the Kaiser... (at a banquet) tell in a low voice the Director of the Bureau of Wartime Press 'I just came from the Supreme Headquarters where I had an audience with His Majesty. In accord with the High Command, it has been decided that nothing will be said in the press about the Armenian issue.'"[9]

This directive of the German emperor was adopted as a general rule by the Supreme Board of Censorship of the Wartime Press (*Obere Zensur-Stelle des Kriegspresseamtes*), an outfit comprising the representatives of the Foreign Ministry, the General Staff, the High Command, and the Prussian Ministry of Defence. In a press conference on October 7, 1915, the members of the German press were exhorted as follows: "Our friendly relations with

Turkey ought not only not to be endangered through an involvement in such administrative matters, but in the present, difficult moment even it ought not to be examined. Therefore, for the time being it is your duty to remain silent."[10] In another conference on December 23, 1915, the same press people were told: "It is better to remain silent over the Armenian Question. The conduct of the Turkish power-wielders in this Question is not particularly praiseworthy."[11]

However, the imposition of this type of constraint had some paradoxical effects. On the one hand, it triggered among many Germans, and indirectly Austrians, a surge of negative sentiments ranging from mere disapproval to subdued consternation. But, on the other hand, it allowed these very same people to win the confidence of their Turkish cohorts who apparently appreciated the mask of nonchalance of their comrades-in-arm complying with the directives of their superiors - in face of the mass murder in progress. As a result, a number of Turkish officials at some particular occasions felt sufficiently relaxed to confide to the latter tidbits of secrets or, depending on position or status, complete secrets. The revelations by Austrian Vice Marshal Pomiankowski, Colonel Stange, the German commander of a Turkish Special Organization brigade, and Scheubner-Richter, Reserve Captain of Cavalry, and a co-commander of a Turkish guerilla contingent, are cases in point.

Superseding in importance this category of sources is the one based on immediate, personal experiences, such as eyewitnessing, the most forceful category of source under any circumstances. Despite elaborate efforts of concealment by the authorities, there were instances affording such eyewitnessing by allied military personnel, especially Germans. The following account by Ludwig Schraundenbach, the commander of 14th Ottoman Infantry Division, epitomizes the case. It depicts the fate of Armenians who supposedly were being driven to Mesopotamia for purposes of temporary wartime "relocation". The German officer spent some time in Ras-ul-Ain, one of the principal sites of the serial bloodbaths inflicted upon the exhausted and emaciated survivors of the long and tortuous deportation treks. Located some 60 miles southeast of Diyarbekir and 200 miles east of Aleppo, that town had become a large communication and supply center, and the terminal leg of the Baghdad railway at that time, thus a vital junction for military operations.

When relating the personal experiences of the members of a 300 men strong German motorized column, led by Lieutenant Pfeifer, Schraudenbach provided the following testimony in his journal on January 28, 1917: "Turkish officers and gendarmes each evening were picking out dozens of Armenian men from the ranks of the deportees and were using them as targets for practice games (*auf sie ein Scheibenschiessen veranstaltete*)."[12] Another German, Heinrich Elz, an artillery officer in the *Asiencorps* deployed in the same area, likewise recorded his personal observation in his diary regarding the fate of the Diyarbekir Armenians who according to him "were massacred in the area itself" and not deported.[13]

The impulse to admit of the resolve to effectively liquidate the Armenians found its expression in a declaration by Talat indulging in a kind of twisted logic. During an exchange with German Ambassador Wangenheim he is reported as saying: "We are getting rid of the Armenians in order to become better allies for you inasmuch as thereby we will be overcoming our weakness that stems from the presence in our midst of an internal enemy."[14] The effort to make the extermination of the Armenians appear doubly expedient by invoking higher German interests of alliance, along with higher Turkish national interest, is revealing for the urgency of the Turkish need to coopt the Germans in their lethal undertaking. This pattern of indulgence in caustic and furtive admissions of culpability was even more pronounced in the case of other Turkish authorities interacting with the diplomatic and military representatives of the two European allies. The results of these interactions yielded sufficient material to probe into that material's significance for documentary value, specifically in terms of the criteria of accuracy and reliability.

DIPLOMATIC REPORTING AND THE PROBLEMS OF ACCURACY AND RELIABILITY

Diplomats, as a rule, are perceived as consummate craftsmen in the art of equivocation, evasiveness and occasional doubletalk when conducting official foreign policy affairs and when internationally interacting with each other for that purpose. Such a proclivity is considered to be a legitimate and time-honored talent for role performance.

That image is belied, however, by the persona one finds when observing these diplomats operate within a context where foreign policies are conceived, debated and framed, and where officials interact within a hierarchical set-up. The leeways of role playing, including play-acting, are supplanted here by the institutional constraints of straightforwardness and forthrightness in the discharge of official duties. The relationship of consuls and ambassadors to their superiors in the Foreign Ministry is circumscribed by this *modus operandi*. This is particularly true in times of war when the stakes can be quite high and one's aptitude for candid and thoughtful patriotism in helping forge a viable foreign policy is severely tested. Under such circumstances there can be no room for wearing masks, and there is but one avenue for role performance, especially for diplomats stationed abroad: accurate reporting based on information that is optimally reliable.

Presently, in order to achieve a high level of accuracy, the diplomats involved had to devise and secure ways and means to obtain reliable information. In other words, they needed to locate and then engage sources which were more or less unimpeachable. The bearings of the alliance and in particular Turkey's critical dependence upon Germany for sustaining her war effort on several fronts considerably facilitated the procurement of such sources. Whether serving in the provincial consulates or in the Embassy in the Ottoman capital, German officials, for instance, were able to secure for this purpose several Turks who in many reports are described as our *Gewährsmann*, a kind of a secret, information gathering and relaying agent. The following are typical illustrations in this regard.

German Aleppo Consul Rössler on May 10, 1915, told his Ambassador of his use of such a Gewährsmann.[15] In a report marked "Confidential" the same consul on July 27, 1915, informed Chancellor Hollweg in Berlin that through this agent he had learned of the names of certain Turks implicated in the atrocities.[16] Ambassador Metternich on December 7, 1915, informed the Chancellor that through the medium of "a reliable party" he had learned of the secret plans of Constantinople's Director of Police regarding the gradually to be implemented deportation of that Capital's Armenian population, with a request to "keep this information secret."[17] On August 29, 1916, Hoffmann, Alexandrette's Vice Consul, wrote to his Ambassador that he "underhandedly" (*unter der Hand eingezogen*) secured information regarding the Turkish disposal of Armenian orphans in his district.[18] Even more significant, General Limann von Sanders as a result of a bitter dispute with the German Ambassador, Wangenheim, provided to the Turkish police the names of the secret agents working for the Ambassador and the agents' Ittihadist contacts.[19]

There was a fundamentally ambivalent issue involved in this line of official duty, however. On the one hand, these diplomats were expected to be protective of the good reputation of Turkey, their principal ally, and on the other hand, they felt constrained to relay observations and facts that placed that ally in a patently disreputable light. Generally speaking, the solution to such an apparent dilemma is intrinsic to the very rationale of diplomatic record-keeping and reporting. The reports are prepared for internal purposes only, and are not meant for public consumption, at least not immediately. The function of diplomatic correspondence is indeed for the sole, if not exclusive, benefit of in-house desiderata.

This fact alone should be sufficient to establish the authenticity of the contents of the reports in question. As if to underscore the value of this distinct attribute, many of the reports were marked "confidential" (*vertraulich*), "very confidential" (*streng vertraulich*) or (*ganz vertraulich*), "secret (*geheim*), and "very secret"(*streng geheim*). Thus, within the confines of a system geared to an exclusively internal flow of communication, additional restrictions were introduced to control the use of that information.

The conditions of processing that information and harnessing it into official documents are of sufficient importance to deserve a brief description. After all, diplomacy is a profession requiring not only political acumen but also a craftsmanship in managing the functional aspects of that profession.

THE PROCEDURES IN THE PREPARATION AND OUTPUT OF THE DOCUMENTS

The study of a document is the consummation of an end product of a belabored material whose genesis, channelling and the modes of molding it into a final artifice are conditions that have a bearing on the determination of the value of that end product. Therefore, an examination of the circumstances under which the German and Austrian documents at issue came into being may be called for. Foremost important in this respect is the consideration of the tensions that existed between the political orientation of the embassies on the one hand, and that of the consulates in the interior of Turkey, on the other hand. There were several reasons for this gulf of which three stand out and need highlighting.

1. The embassies in the capital were the nerve centers of setups generating a steady flow of propaganda in support of the war effort and akin to psychological warfare; it was an effort to bolster the alliance by a policy of exalting Turkey as a formidable ally. Anything which portended to undermine that effort was certainly a threat to the alliance. The reports from the consulates in the provinces were not only a discordant note but posed serious dilemmas as well. How could a diplomat afford to berate, if not condemn, an ally and thereby join those in the enemy camp who were doing exactly that? The dilemma was compounded by an endemic hesitation to either silence or replace the consuls who matter-of-factly were purveying a stream of material on the ongoing atrocities.

2. In the course of performance of their duties in the Ottoman capital the ambassadors came often into close contacts with Turkish officials identified with central authorities. The mutual affinities that developed as a result in a sense encumbered the German need to get a handle on the explosive Armenian Question. A confrontation was out of question. Moreover, the diplomats at the initial stages of the unfolding genocide were conveniently quite receptive to the succession of denials by the Turkish authorities. At that juncture of events the ambassadors were virtual hostages to a pro-Turkish bias that one way or another was instilled in their minds.

3. The embassy people were critically removed from the scenes of the ongoing carnages. This fact of physical remoteness in no small way contributed to a lack of appreciation of the scope and intensity of the mass murder being enacted in the interior of the country. This diluted imagery of the ongoing cataclysm sharply contrasted with the acute experiences of the provincial consuls for whom the massacres were center-stage tragedies, with an immediacy of impact that was as unsettling as confounding. One may hazard the assertion that the vigor of the response of the German and Austrian diplomats in Constantinople to the atrocities was in inverse proportion to their distance to the scenes of the atrocities.

Nevertheless, the embassy-consulate cleavage subsided in due course of time, and it was eventually overcome. The emergence of the vast corpus of the documentary material being explored in this study does attest to that fact. The initially persuasive flair of the litany of Turkish claims and anti-Armenian charges attenuated itself in short order in the face of cumulative and incontrovertible evidence. The stories of widespread Armenian rebellion, of crippling blows by Armenian insurgents to the Turkish war effort, consequently of enormous Turkish losses, and of many cases of Armenian espionage and sabotage acts eventually lost their original hold on believability as well as feasibility. The story that mostly irked the ambassadors was the one which was deemed to be the ultimate affront, namely, the claim that the Turkish government in all its solicitousness, was providing protective care to the deportees, feeding them and transporting them to new quarters for purposes of temporary "relocation". Another instance of affront was the companion claim that the government was limiting its operations of deportation only to the zones of War sparing the rest of the Armenian population. These falsehoods and misrepresentations lasted only until the middle of June 1915, as far as the German and Austrian ambassadors were concerned.

In the second half of June 1915, the avalanche of reports from the consuls finally managed to jolt the ambassadors, jarring them loose from the grip of deceptive Turkish pronouncements. From then on the dispatch of data to Berlin and Vienna represents a prolonged ritual of accounting and recounting respecting the macabre saga of the Armenian genocide, a pathetic recitation, bearing the imprimatur of the governments of Imperial Germany and Imperial Austria, the allies of Imperial Ottoman Turkey.

As will be seen in the Bibliography of this study, many of these officials, in particular Ambassadors Wangenheim, Metternich, Pallavicini, and their deputies Hohenlohe and Trautmansdorff, as well as German Consuls Büge (Adana), Holstein (Mosul), Rössler (Aleppo) reacted rather sharply to what they considered to be the duplicity of the Turkish authorities and in no uncertain terms specifically denounced Talat for disseminating "blatant lies" (*krasse Lügen*). These consuls and their other colleagues, German as well as Austrian, emerge here as the valiant champions of truth, symbolizing the unflinching conscience of outraged humanity in utterly inhuman surroundings. By persisting, they succeeded in bringing about a role reversal in the behavior of their superiors in Constantinople through the application of what might be called dissuasive persuasion-at least in the realm of record keeping and reporting.

It is likewise noteworthy that except for a few minor cases, the contents of the reports of these consuls, identifying perpetrators and victims, and offering diagnostic insights on the nature of the Turkish measures against Armenians, proved quite accurate in the light of the data emerging since the end of the war. The legal material compiled by the Turkish Military Tribunal prosecuting the Ittihadist perpetrators in the 1919-1921 period is a case in point. Consisting largely of authenticated Turkish official documents, on the basis of which many of the accused were indicted, tried, convicted, and sentenced, this material is of quintessential value, for the findings it comprises were so astutely presaged by many consuls discussed here.

The German consuls too were beset by certain dilemmas torn as they were between their sense of fidelity to the Turks as allies, on the one hand, and the duty to ascertain facts and convey them, on the other. In a report to his Chancellor in Berlin Consul Rössler on November 16, 1915, not only articulated this dilemma but also indicated his preferred option to solve that dilemma: "I do not intend to frame my reports in such a way that I may be favoring one or the other party. Rather, I consider it my duty to present to you the description of things which have occurred in my district and which I consider to be the truth (*was ich für die Wahrheit halte*)."[20] Rössler was reacting to the broadcast of a Turkish charge that the Armenians had begun to massacre the Turkish population of the Turkish sections of a city after capturing them. He dismissed this accusation with one word: "invented" (*erfunden*).[21]

The practice of truthfulness under taxing conditions could not prevent Rössler, a seasoned and veteran consul by any definition, to have nervous breakdowns. In a report marked "very confidential", and addressed to German Undersecretary of Foreign Affairs, Zimmermann, the well-informed journalist Tyszka on September 22, 1915 wrote that the pain and torment that Rössler was enduring while observing and reporting on the sufferings of the Armenians in one of the epicenters of the genocide, the area of Aleppo with its environs, was overwhelming him; in that report the German journalist revealed that Rössler was seen "weeping bitterly" (*bitterlich geweint*).[22] The other consuls and ambassadors, especially Metternich and Pallavicini, channeled their emotions into expressions of outrage, thus departing from the established forms of diplomatic discourse. This fact in itself bespeaks of the dimensions of the inferno of the Armenian holocaust as confronted by these officials.

As will be seen below, these decrials were expansive enough to yield in the framing of the respective reports additional data related to the methods of organizing and implementing the genocide.

THE ORGANIZATION OF THE BIOGRAPHY TO FOLLOW

The confirmation of the crime that is being rather vehemently denied is consequential in more than one way. It not only validates the accusation attached to that crime but concomitantly exposes the criminal on several levels related to the culpability at hand. By establishing the fact of the Armenian genocide, for example, German and Austrian diplomats, as well as military, ended up divesting the Turkish authorities, past and present, of their credibility. The ramifications of this stroke are manifold. One of these is that in order to sustain the falsehood these people have been forced to resort to additional undertakings for purposes of deflection or cover-up.

Unwilling to face the verdicts of their wartime allies, and therewith, the verdict of history, the custodians of the perpetrator camp are continuing to compound the enormity of the capital crime by indulging in activities which are as suspect as nefarious.

One final point. The collateral data contained in the observations and judgments of German and Austrian sources are such as to lend themselves to the task of probing deeper into the fabric of the genocidal enterprise. They provide invaluable glimpses into the hidden relationships of major determinants of the Armenian genocide and the web of their interconnections. The configuration that emerges from this method of reconstruction cannot fail but enhance the overall value of the documentary edifice presented in this study. Accordingly, the bibliographic compilation below, along with certain annotations, will be organized around the following three problem-foci: 1. intent; 2. outcome; and 3. extension of genocide to Russian Armenia in 1918.

NOTES

1. Lepsius, Johannes (1919). *Deutschland und Armenien*. Potsdam-Berlin: Tempelverlag.
2. When visiting in Berlin in 1978, I raised this question with Ms. Gitta Lepsius, the daughter of the author who in the December 1918-April 1919 period served as the latter's secretary, being solely in charge of the task of typing the entire manuscript. She emphatically declared that she received no instructions whatsoever to modify in any way the material when typing it. She also stated that as far as she knew her father had not resorted to any deletions. It is conceivable that someone from the Foreign Ministry did intercept the manuscript before it was allowed to enter the final stage of production. Indeed, when carefully scrutinizing the originals, which presently are deposited at the

state archives at Bonn, one can notice the insertion of faintly penned brackets at the very spots where portions of sentences are in fact deleted. Of the three officials of the German Foreign Ministry, namely Foreign Minister Dr. Wilhelm Solf, Aleppo Consul Dr. Walter Rössler (1910-May 1918) and Dr. Otto Goppert, Privy Legation Councillor (*Geheimrat*), who were involved in the authorization, preparation and production of the Lepsius volume, the latter was on record for favoring the resort to certain deletions to protect certain groups of people or to cover up certain facts. German Foreign Ministry, (*G.F.M.-*Bonn), Göppert Papers (*Nachlass*) VI, 1, p.2 in Goppert's February 13, 1919, communication. Moreover, in a correspondence with Lepsius, Göppert revealed his main concerns in urging deletions. First and foremost, Germany must be exculpated from charges of complicity in the enactment of the genocide. Second, he said that he didn't want to overload "the Turkish record of atrocities" (*das Kapitel der türkischen Greuel*). His rationale for this refusal to supply Lepsius additional documents involving consular reports was that in any event such overloading would not help the cause of Germany. (*G.F.M.*-Bonn) Türkei 183/58, A.20906, Lepsius to Göppert, July 13, 1919, and *id.*, Göppert to Lepsius, July 26, 1919.

3. Austrian Foreign Ministry (A.F.M.- Vienna), Political Department (PA), XII (Turkey), File (*Karton*) 218, or, XII Türkei/210, No.28/P.A.
4. *GFM*, Türkei 183/38, A23991.
5. *Ibid.*, 158/15, A14/133.
6. German Military Archives (*GMA* - Freiburg i. Breisgau), BA/MA - N247, No,202/d, 6 June 1918 entry in Diary.
7. The very same day Seeckt in the same diary describes how he was bombarded with complaints from German officers inveighing against manifestations of "Turkish mentality"; the effects of culture conflict were clearly in evidence. *Ibid.*
8. *G.M.A.*, Göppert Papers, VI/1, p.3 of the General's 7-page letter to Dr. Karl Axenfeld, a leader in the German missionary movement.
9. Harden, Maximillian. Zwischen Ost und West. Armenien in Moabit. *Die Zukunft*, 29(37), (11 June, 1921). 300-301.
10. Mühsam, Kurt (1918). *Wie Wir Belogen Wurden: Die Amtliche Irreführung des deutschen Volkes* (How We Were Deceived: The Official Acts of Misleading the German People), Munich: A. Langen Publishers, p.76.
11. *Ibid.*, p.79.
12. Schraudenbach, Ludwig (1924). *Muharebe* (War). Berlin: Drei Masken Publishers, p.315. This form of atrocity was confirmed by a Turkish grocer who after the war had migrated and settled in Maine, Portland, U.S.A.. As recounted to his Irish-American friend, this is what he personally experienced during the World War I Armenian genocide. "As a young soldier in the Turkish army he was part of a unit escorting a large group of Armenians into the countryside where they were to be left to die of starvation. At a pause in the march, he told me, an officer in his company walked over to him and told him and his companions to go into the group and bayonet some of them for practice, since they were going to die anyway. 'God help me', he said almost in tears, 'I did.'" William J. McLaughlin, *Boston Globe*, 18 September, 1987. Schraudenbach's book of recollections is full of narrations of similar acts of atrocities which evoked in him images of "Dante's Inferno" he said. (p.345), Referring to Salihzeki, the governor of the district of Der Zor in the desert, who "greeted us very politely and was wearing elegant European clothes," the author states that "shocking atrocities" (*haarsträubende Greuel*) were perpetrated in that region, including "the tying of the Armenian children between wooden boards and setting them on fire" (pp.351-52). The author likewise confirms that he had received specific instructions not to discuss the case of the Armenians. "It was one of the very few instructions... the Armenian Question was to be treated as *noli me tangere*" (touch me not), (p.147).

13. Elz, Heinrich (1 January 1928) Mit der Batterie Heiligbrunner nach Mesopotamien. (To Mesopotamia with the Heiligbrunner Battery). *Der Asienkämpfer*, X(1), p.9.
14. Quoted by Humann, Hans, *G.M.A.*, Papers, BA/MA, RM 40/456, 15 June, 1915.
15. *G.F.M.*, Türkei 183/37, A17735.
16. *Ibid.*, 183/38, A23991.
17. *Ibid.*, 183/40, A36184.
18. *Ibid.*, 183/44, A25739.
19. Weber, Frank G. (1970). *Eagles on the Crescent. Germany, Austria, and the Diplomacy of the Turkish Alliance 1914-1918.*
    Ithaca: Cornell University Press, p.111.
20. *G.F.M.*, Türkei, 183/40, A35046.
21. *Ibid.*
22. *Ibid.*, 183/39, A29593. The report was actually relayed to Zimmermann on October 1, 1915, the date of Tyszka's cover letter.

PART II. BIBLIOGRAPHY.

Note

As noted in the text, the vast majority of the excerpts utilized for this study is culled from official documents that comprise the political and military state archives of Germany and Austria. The respective German archives are currently housed in Bonn and are described as *Politisches Archiv des Auswärtigen Amtes, Abteilung IA*, which may be abbreviated in English as German Foreign Ministry Archives or, GFM. A large subdivision of these holdings, titled *Türkei* or, Turkey, contains multitudes of documents pertaining to Turkey in general. For purposes of research and identification each citation has to be described by the class *Türkei*, followed by the *Aktenzeichen* or, the file number which in turn is followed by the number of the *Band* or, volume. Incoming documents and those originating in the Foreign Ministry were registered in an entry-journal. The entry numbers usually run consecutively for each year, and in the case of the Political Department, the one in question here, they are preceded by the letter A. Example: Türkei 183/49, A8751. Another department of the same archive comprises mainly the incoming consular reports and are subsumed under the class *Botschaft Konstantinopel*, cited here as simply K, followed by the number of the volume. Example : K160. Another depository of German political documents is located in Potsdam (outside Berlin, the capital of the former German Democratic Republic or, East Germany), the site of the *Deutsches Zentralarchiv*, DZA in abbreviated form. The respective documents are itemized under *Bestand* (file) *Reichskanzlei* or in abbreviated form BRK, bearing a number, followed by a page number, and preceded by the letters Bl, abbreviation for *Blatt*, page. Example : GFM, DZA, BRK, No.2458/9, Bl.242. The military archive of the German federal government is located in Freiburg i. Breisgau under the name *Bundesarchiv/Militararchiv*, cited as BA/MA. The files are described as *Bestandsbezeichnung* bearing the letters P or RM along with the file numbers, followed by volume numbers. Example : BA/MA, RM40/5. Then there are Papers (*Nachlass*) of many German diplomats, high ranking military officers, political operatives, journalists etc; they are as a rule identified in these archives with the letter N., followed by the author's name. Example : BA/MA, N. Seeckt 247/163. Documents related to Germans from Bavaria are usually housed in *Bayerisches Hauptstaatsarchiv/Kriegsarchiv* Munich, Bavaria (*Bayern*), hereafter cited as BH/KA. The pieces are indexed with letters MKr, meaning *Ministerium des Krieges* (Ministry of War). As they are not paginated, the documents have mostly "production" numbers. Example : BH/KA, MKr 13841, ad 27.

A smaller batch of documents used is from the depositories of Austrian Archives (AFM) described as *Staatskanzlei, Ministerium des Aussern, Österreichisches Staatsarchiv, Abteilung Haus-, Hof-,* and *Staatsarchiv*-Vienna. The documents are contained in multitudes of *Kartons* (boxes) which as files are distributed among many categories and designations in the classification system of the AFM archives. Those relating to this study are subsumed under *Politisches Archiv* or PA and the classes of XII Türkei, *Berichte* (Reports); X Russland (Petersburg), *Armenische Republik*; XXXVIII *Konsulate*; 1 *Allgemeines*; and 10 *Interne Konfidenten-Berichte*. Some of these documents additionally bear assigned cipher numbers. Citation example: 12 Türkei/463, No. 21/P.B. In order to avoid unnecessary redundancy, the use of the symbols for the archives of the German Foreign Ministry, i.e., GFM, and Austrian Foreign Ministry, i.e., AFM, is being dispensed with altogether. Thus, unless otherwise indicated, all documents used below issue from these two state archives. Likewise, to maintain overall uniformity in style, class, file and volume numbers are being presented in Arabic numerals.

A Constellation of the Verdicts of the Highest German Political and Military Authorities

Von Jagow. Foreign Minister

K171, No. 855. To German Ambassador Metternich. 12 September 1916.
"The awful treatment of the Armenians calls for lodging a protest to the Turkish government whose leadership should be admonished regarding the disastrous consequences which the Turkish Empire is bound to incur as a result of such a policy of extermination" (*Ausrottungspolitik*).

The authoritative value of this judgment is even more accented by the disclosure of the German Ambassador Metternich to the effect that the above was a second "decree"(*Erlass*) framed the same day by Jagow's superior, Chancellor Bethman Hollweg, but for purposes of protocol was signed by Foreign Minister Jagow. *Türkei 183/48, A25749, p.65 of Ambassador Metternich's 72pp report to Berlin on 18 September 1916.*

Zimmermann. Undersecretary of State

Türkei 183/44, A260071, 25 September 1916.
Relates to Ambassador Metternich a conversation he had with Halil, Turkish Foreign Minister, in the course of which he warned the latter that the German government could no longer defend the anti-Armenian Turkish measures as it did defend them earlier "with a semblance of legality"(*mit einem Schein des Rechts*). Zimmermann characterized these measures as such which "in no way could be justified or excused" (*in keiner Weise gerechtfertigt oder entschuldigt*).

Von dem Bussche. Second Undersecretary

Türkei 183/50, A11280, 19 March 1918.
In preparation for his appearance before the German Parliament (*Reichstag*) on March 21 and 22, 1918, to answer questions on the fate of the Armenians Bussche wrote the following in his position paper : "The application of the measures of relocation was such as to betray an intent to destroy the Armenian population" (*Vernichtung*).

Von Kühlmann. Foreign Minister

Türkei 183/51, A23533, No.1178, 3 June 1918.
Reporting on the outcome of a Conference in Berlin to the General Headquarters and to the German Ambassador to Turkey, Kühlmann declared: "In complete disregard of their promises the Turks are pursuing their objective of the annihilation (*Vernichtung*) of the Armenians in the Caucasus, or are allowing it to happen with passive approbation."

In line with these assessments the German Embassy in the Ottoman capital twice in one month took steps (*démarche*) to formally protest the ongoing mass murder. Here are excerpts from these two notes.

Türkei 183/37, A21257, 4 August 1915.
The German government expressed its dismay over "the massive and indiscriminate expulsions (of the Armenian population), especially in view of the fact that the expulsions are accompanied by acts of violence such as massacres and pillages."

Türkei 183/37, A24507, 9 August 1915.
Repeating his decrial of "pillages and massacres (which) couldn't be justified "Ambassador Hohenlohe continued, "In the face of these occurrences the German Embassy on orders of its government is compelled to remonstrate once more against these acts of horror."

Ludendorf, Erich. General

Ludendorf, Erich (1919). *Meine Kriegserinnerungen 1914-1918.* Berlin: Mittler und Shon. 522 pp.
p. 136. "The Turks always pursued an ill-fated policy towards their indigenous populations. They have gone on the principle of taking everything and giving nothing... Their inexcusable treatment of the Armenians" hurt Turkey very badly.
p. 500. "The violent massacres against the Armenians... were indeed a grave blunder and nothing could justify them. The Chancellor of the Reich denounced them disparagingly" (*abfällig*).

Hindenburg, Paul von. Field Marshal

Hindenburg, Paul von. (1934). *Aus Meinem Leben.* Leipzig: Hirzel. pp. 319.
p. 169. "The Turkish war effort revealed the darkest side of the Turkish domination, i.e., the Turkish conduct against the Armenian elements. The Armenian Question... involved panturkic as well as panislamic ideologies. In the attempt at solving it racial hatred and religious enmities entered the picture... Turkey initiated a policy of annihilation (*Vernichtungspolitik*) against the Armenians."

Mayer, Georg, Prof. Dr. *Oberstabsarzt* (Colonel, Medical Services).

Meyer was the highest ranking German officer in the Department of Health Care of the German Military Mission to Turkey. At the same time, he was Deputy Chief in the Medical Department of the Turkish War Ministry, and Deputy Chief in the Medical Services Branch of the Turkish Army. (*K136, No.1112, 9 October 1915*). Below is an excerpt from his report to the German Military Mission to Turkey.

BH/KA, MKr, 13841, ad 27. 2 March 1916.
"The decision *(Beschluss)* to expel the women, children, and old men, was the result of a hatred against the Armenians, and involved a wild objective on the part of the Turkish government to obliterate this race *(diesen Stamm austilgen)*... the massive arrests of the men were carried out not only in the near of the front but throughout the empire... and in the corridors of the Turkish Ministry of War one heard people tell with cynical grins *(mit zynischem Lächeln)* the story of how all these thousands died natural deaths or how they were victims of accidents - as registered in official medical records... The destruction *(Vernichtung)* of the Armenians stopped once more when Erzurum fell (to the Russians)."

ON GENOCIDAL INTENT

German Ambassadors

Wangenheim

After automatically adopting as truth Turkish claims and assertions about the reasons and nature of the anti-Armenian measures Wangenheim in his reports of 2 February, 15 April, 30 April, 8 May, and 31 May 1915, disparaged the victims and in a qualified way justified the Turks thereby defending them. But the deluge of German consular reports from the interior of the country helped erode Turkish credibility causing Wangenheim to launch a series of reports to Berlin in which the focus was on the barbaric methods with which the victim population was being systematically destroyed.

Türkei 183/27, A19744, 17 June 1915.
The Ambassador in this report for the first time addresses the issue of extermination through massacres being implemented under the cloak of deportation. Three points are salient in this communication. 1. "Clearly, deportations are not determined by military considerations only" *(nicht allein durch militärische Rücksichten)*. 2. The Armenians of Diyarbekir who were supposed to be deported to Mosul "were en route all slaughtered" *(abgeschlachtet)*. 3. Interior Minister Talat is quoted as having "point-blank" admitted to the head of Embassy's Armenian desk that he is taking advantage of the war to "thoroughly clear Turkey of her internal enemies, i.e., the Christians," and thereby preempting all future possibilities of intervention in Turkish affairs by the European Powers. In a subsequent cipher Wangenheim for the first time and definitively acknowledges the reality of mass murder.

Türkei 183/37, A21257, 7 July 1915.
After expressing again his dismay that the deportations are being carried out in areas in no way connected with military operations and far removed from the theater of war, he declared: "This circumstance plus the manner in which the matter of relocation is being handled demonstrate that the government is in fact pursuing the goal of annihilating the Armenian race in Turkey" *(die armenische Rasse... zu vernichten)*.

Türkei 183/37, A22210, 16 July 1916.
Even more significant, Wangenheim felt constrained to certify to his superiors in Berlin that the disclosures by Lepsius, relayed earlier to German authorities about the ongoing process of destruction, proved true with Wangenheim for his part confirming the Turkish

intent for wholesale extermination. "The facts and the allied observations communicated to us a month ago by Lepsius are being confirmed (*bestätigt*) through consular reports. By her policy of deportation and relocation the Turkish government is delivering up the Armenians to (the clutches of) a policy of destruction" (*Vernichtung*)

K169, No. (3876), 25 June 1915.
In this report the Ambassador alludes to the instrument of destruction. "The deportees are being suddenly set upon and butchered by highwaymen and reportedly even by escort personnel."

Türkei 183/37, A21483, 9 July 1915.
In this report is specified the typical instruments. "The massacres are being carried out by convicts released from the prisons" (*entlassene Sträflinge*).

K.169, n.(4184), folio 162, 12 July 1915.
The manner of massacre is described as follows: "The Armenians of the convoy from Mardin were let be slaughtered just like sheep" (*wie Hammel abschlachten lassen*).

In his last comment made ten days before he succumbed to a stroke Wangenheim not only reiterated his conclusion about the Turkish intent of destroying the Armenians but exposed the parallel Turkish propensity to deny that intent by denying the incidence of massacres, as Interior Minister Talat had done during an interpellation a while ago.

Türkei 183/39, A30634, 15 October 1915.
"This flat out denial leads to the inference that (the massacre) did in fact occur and that the Turkish government is resorting to a copout through denial" (*Dementi*).

Hohenlohe

K170, folio 33, 2 August 1915.
"The government is resolved (*Entschluss*) to eliminate the indigenous Christians." When forwarding a copy of the official Note of protest of 9 August 1915, mentioned above, Hohenlohe in the cover letter wrote the following:

Türkei 183/38, A24507, 12 August 1915.
"The systematic butchery of the uprooted and deported Armenians have assumed such a scope (*Umfang*)... it was not only tolerated but openly promoted by the government. It meant the extermination of the Armenians" (*die Ausrottung der Armenier*).

Türkei 183/39, A28578, 25 September 1915.
"Despite governmental assurances to the contrary, everything points to the goal of the destruction of the Armenian people" (*läuft alles auf Vernichtung des armenischen Volkes*).

Metternich

Even though the larger part of the destruction process was already completed when he took office Metternich, rather less diplomatically, resisted the unrelenting Turkish onslaught against the remnants of the victim nation. In his discussions with Turkish leaders he questioned the sincerity of their argument that exigencies of war justify repression, in light of the fact that "an entire race" (*ein ganzer Volksstamm*) is being cast into misery and death. Here are some samples.

Türkei 183/40, A36134, 7 December 1915.
Departing from the path of his predecessors, the Ambassador set out to berate his government and German media for pampering the Turks and unnecessarily inflating their egos. "Their successes are due to our work, to our officers, to our canons and to our money. Without our help, the inflated frog is bound to collapse" (...*der geblähte Frog fällt in sich zusammen*). In a summary verdict, he then designated Talat "as the soul of the Armenian persecutions." (*die Seele der Armenierverfolgungen*). (These portions are deleted from Lepsius Volume V.N.D.)

Türkei 183/40, A36483, 9 December 1915.
During his meeting with Grand Vizier Said Halim, Metternich told the latter that the Turkish measures against the Armenians can in no way be justified as "legitimate defense of a state" and that their application against hundreds of thousands of women, children and the elderly will remain "a dark page in Young Turk history" (*ein dunkles Blatt in der jungtürkischen Geschichte*).

Türkei 183/41, A8373, 27 March 1916.
Metternich signals the very last phases of destruction of "the remnants of the deportees" (*Vertilgung der letzten Reste...Überreste der Verschickten*), adding that the Turks seem to be in a hurry to possibly finish off with the Armenians before the advent of peace (*vor Friedensschluss nach Möglichkeit zu vernichten*).

Türkei 183/43, A17310 or A18548 (document bears two entry numbers), 10 July 1916.
Metternich summed up the picture: "In the implementation of its scheme to settle the Armenian Question through the annihilation of the Armenian race, the Turkish government did not allow itself to be distracted". (*Die türkische Regierung hat sich in der Durchführung ihres Programmes: Erledigung der armenischen Frage durch die Vernichtung der armenischen Rasse... (nicht) beirren lassen...*). In the end, Metternich proved too much for the Turks; he was derisively labelled as "the Ambassador of the Armenians." Sustained pressures exerted both in Constantinople and Berlin, resulted in his eventual recall.

Kühlmann

Like Wangenheim, Kühlmann initially had special sympathies for Turkish nationalism and tried to promote it. In that sense he too espoused the Turkish line of denials and explanations regarding the wholesale massacres of the Armenians.

Türkei 183/39, A30053, 14 October 1915.
In a letter to Count Bylandt in Holland he dismissed these massacres as "alleged atrocities" against the Armenians (*angebliche Armeniergreuel*).

Türkei 183/45, A32227, 25 November 1916.
He was willing to justify and excuse the actions of the Turkish Government as "basically a matter of internal politics" (*in Wesentlichen eine Frage der inneren Politik*).

Türkei 183/46, A2615, 20 January 1917.
Making a turnabout, however, Kühlmann for the first time feels constrained to make use of the word "extermination" (*Ausrottung*) as a goal "largely achieved" (*zum grossen Teil*

erreicht), a goal with which "the current Turkish powerwielders are completely identified" (*die heutigen türkischen Machthaber sich mit der Armenierpolitik vollkommen identifiziert haben*).

Türkei 183/46, A5919, 16 February 1917.
Finally, in a summary review of the evolution of a policy of extermination, as a means to the end for national unification, Kühlmann concedes the fact of genocide by characterizing it as "the achievement of the large scale destruction of the Armenians" (*Die in grossem Umfange durchgeführte Armeniervernichtung*)... This policy of extermination (*Ausrottungspolitik*) will for a long time stain the Turkish name."

Bernstorff, Count Johann von

This Ambassador too initially remained a partisan of Turkey and as such was easily swayed by Turkish assertions. Indeed, as German Ambassador in Washington, D.C., he had denounced press releases describing the ongoing massacres which he dismissed as "pure inventions", and as "alleged atrocities." (*Washington Post*, Sept. 28, 1915). However, in the course of serving as German Ambassador to Turkey in the last year of the war he relinquished that posture of denial as reports from territories occupied by the Turkish army in the Caucasus indicated a resumption of exterminatory measures against the Armenian population there.

Bernstorff, Count Johann von (1936). *Memoirs of Count Bernstorff.* New York: Random House. 383 pp.
    p. 176. "When I kept on pestering Talat on the Armenian Question, he once said with a smile 'What on earth do you want? The question is settled. There are no more Armenians.'"
    p. 374. "In Armenia... the Turks had been systematically trying to exterminate the Christian population."

Austrian Ambassadors

Pallavicini

Like his German colleague Wangenheim, this Ambassador readily lent himself to Turkish claims and explanations at the rudimentary stages of the enactment of the genocide. He issued several reports blaming the Armenians and justifying the Turks. But he too found out eventually that he was rush in his assessment.

12 Türkei/209, No.50/P.C, 27 June 1915.
"... the Armenian population which is being expelled from its homeland is not only being subjected to the greatest misery but also to a total extermination" (*einer gänzlichen Ausrottung*).

12 Türkei/209, No.51/P.E, 1 July 1915.
Reporting to Vienna, the Ambassador summarizes his exchange with the Turkish Grand Vizier and relates his admonition to him that "The manner in which the Armenians are being deported for resettlement purposes is tantamount to a death verdict (*Todesurteil*) for the affected people."

12 Türkei/209, No.66/P.B, 13 August 1915.
"Too many court-martial executions of the Armenians are being carried out in the entire empire... the time will come when Turkey will have to account for this policy of extermination" (*diese Politik der Exterminierung*).

12 Türkei/209, No.71/P.B, 31 August 1915.
After a confrontation with Interior Minister Talat the Ambassador informs Vienna that as a result of "the scandalous measures taken against the Armenians it is generally agreed upon that the Armenian Question to a certain extent has been solved (*erledigt*).

12 Türkei/463, No.92/P.C, 2 November 1915.
The Ambassador relates a conversation of an intermediary with Ittihadist leader who is quoted as saying that the ultimate destiny of all the Armenians of Turkey is Mesopotomia where they are doomed to suffer the fate of "total extermination" (*gänzliche Ausrottung*).

12 Türkei/463, No.93/P.B, 7 November 1915.
While vacationing in Austria the Ambassador was verbally instructed by his Foreign Minister Baron Burian to make representations to the Turkish government regarding the fate of the Armenians.
   "Foreign Minister Halil in his comments on the respective intentions of Talat spoke very candidly and admitted that his ministerial colleague is endeavoring to solve, while the war lasts, the Armenian Question in his own fashion and to create an accomplished fact for the Powers."

I. Allgemeines/944, No.93 A-E, 7 November 1915. Very Confidential (streng vertraulich)
"Grand Vizier disagrees with Talat's policy on Armenians, and does not condone the tendency to bring about a nation-state by way of destroying the alien elements" (*durch Vernichtung der fremden Elemente*).

12 Türkei/463, No.21/P.B, 10 March 1916.
When conceding the need for security measures against the Armenians, the Ambassador chastises the Turks for their method of "massacring the men, deporting the women" denouncing it as inexcusable, and which will remain "an abiding blot on the reputation of the Turkish government." In the same report Said Halim is quoted as saying that from the very inception, he had opposed the measures adopted against the Armenians by Talaat and Enver."

12 Türkei/463, No.6/P.B, 20 January 1917.
In accounting for the comprehensive deportations and massacres, the Ambassador reveals two aspects of them that appear to be key functions of the genocide at issue. One of them deals with motivation. "The ruthless and inhuman treatment of the Armenians found an approbation only among those people who either are fanatical Ittihadists, or through the liquidation of the properties of the deported and murdered Armenians have enriched themselves." The other refers to the concealment of the intent of genocide. "...in recent times secret orders (*geheime Befehle*) have always been the precursors of Armenian deportations and massacres."

Trautmansdorff

I Allgemeines/947, No.77, 22 September 1915.

In an exchange with Nabi Bey, ex-Ambassador to Rome, and Ottoman Foreign Minister in the Armistice (14 October - 10 November 1918), the Ambassador stated that "the mistake which the Turkish leaders committed in the Armenian Question could not be repaid" (*nicht gut zu machen*).

12 Türkei/463, No.75/P.D, 15 September 1917.
"The more the war is approaching its end the more obvious it is becoming how severely the Turkish government is suffering the impact and consequences of the atrocious acts (*Greueltaten*) committed against the Armenians. (This is) a mistake that cannot be repaid."

12 Türkei/209, 79/P.A, 30 September 1915.
"The reports on unheard of atrocities are being confirmed by returning German officers. It can no longer be denied that the Turks... have undertaken the extermination of the Armenian race and it appears that they have largely succeeded in it. With a certain air of gleefulness Talat recently told me that in Erzurum, for example, there should be remaining not a single Armenian... Turkey today is under a maniacal spell due to the realization that she carried out the extermination of the Armenian race with impunity" (*in dem Wahne lebt the Exterminierung... ungestraft durchgeführt zu haben*).

German Consuls

Some of them were veteran diplomats with a long service in Turkey, and schooled in the art of collecting and relaying to their government material that was pertinent as well as identified with more or less unimpeachable sources. Rössler (Aleppo) had, for example, ten-year service at his post; Büge (Adana) likewise; Kuckhoff (Samsun), twelve years.

Berfgeld (Trabizon)

This Consul was initially very trusting of Turkish governmental officials, denying genocidal intent and massacres altogether, at the same time blaming Armenians as traitors and rebels. But he too learned some lessons in this respect.

K169, No.7, folio 135 (4002), 29 June 1915.
"All my colleagues and I are of the opinion that the deportation of women and children amounts to mass murder" (*Massenmord*).

Türkei 183/37, A22559, 9 July 1915.
"All signs indicate that (the Turks are bent on) exterminating the Armenians in other places... My impression is that the Young Turk Committee (Ittihad Party) is hereby trying to solve the Armenian Question."

K170, No.20 949960, folio 102, 28 August 1915.
Appalled at the conduct of the perpetrators, the Consul rather naively suggests to his government that it should urge the court-martialing of Ittihadist leaders and their military cohorts in and around Trabizon.

Türkei 183/54, A38986, 1 September 1918.
"The assaults against the Armenians led to their virtually complete extermination in eastern Anatolia."

Büge (Adana)

K170, No.699, 13 August 1915.
"The desire to wipe out everything Armenian is characteristic of a government which six years earlier delivered a bloody proof of the existence of this mentality." the reference is, of course, to the 1909 Adana massacre.

Holstein (Mosul)

Türkei 183/376; also K169, No.48 (3547), 10 June 1915.
"614 prominent Armenian families from Diyarbekir, comprising men, women and children, were slaughtered during transport through raft. Corpses and severed limbs for days have been floating in the river. I expressed my deepest revulsion (*tiefste Abscheu*) to the governor who blamed the governor of Diyarbekir province."

K169, No.3 (3612), folio 56, 13 June 1915.
"The butchery in Diyarbekir province is day by day becoming more evident."

Hoffmann (Alexandrette)

K171, No.123 (5989), 18 October 1915.
"There is a consensus that all deportees are doomed to die... This mass murder was implicitly conceded by the Turkish political director of Aleppo province who made a reference to the 300,000 deportees being sent to Der Zor for 'resettlement' but who will all die.'"

Türkei 183/41, A2889, 8 November 1915.
After stating that the outcomes (*Endergebnisse*) of Turkish actions allow a judgment on Turkish intentions and decisions taken "behind the scenes" (*hinter den Kulissen*), Hoffmann concludes: "The deportation of the Armenians does not differ much from their extermination" (*Ausrottung*).

Türkei 183/44, A25739, 29 August, 1916.
"All deportees in the northern concentration camps of the desert have disappeared (*verschwunden*). Officially, they were moved to Mosul... yet, they were done to death (*umgebracht*) in the small valleys southeast of Der Zor."

Türkei 183/44, A26116, 5 September 1916.
"Upon the arrival of deportees in the Der Zor area, short work is being made of them" (*kurzen Prozess gemacht wird*).

Kuckhoff (Samsun)

Türkei 183/37, A22101, 4 July 1915.
"...nothing less than the destruction (*Vernichtung*) of an entire people is at issue... the eradication (*Ausmerzung*) of one of the oldest and unhappiest peoples of this earth... the disappearance (*das Verschwinden*) of the populations driven from entire cities."

Rössler (Aleppo)

Türkei 183/37, A17735, 10 May 1915.
"Government's anti-Armenian measures are intended for the destruction (*Vernichtung*) of Armenians in whole districts."

K169, No.4, folio 54, 12 June 1915.
"Government's measures far exceeded the boundaries of preventive initiatives... an important segment of the population (in Cilicia) has already been destroyed" (*vernichtet*).

Türkei 183/38, A23991, 27 July 1915.
"The Turkish government has obligated the [provincial] authorities to implement the deportation measures in the most severe and harsh manner against women and children also, measures which date back to ancient times and which aim at the destruction of as many segments of the Armenian people as possible."

K170, No.(4683), folio 65, 12 August 1915.
"There are grave indications that the method of killing off (*umbringen*) the deportees en route will be applied in the districts of Aleppo and Marash also... Ittihad is preparing for it."

K170, No.60, folio 68 (4740), 15 August 1915.
"According to informations which keep coming in, the Armenians of eastern Turkey for all practical purposes have been completely destroyed" (*völlig vernichtet*).

Türkei 183/41, A2888, 3 January 1916. Enclosure No.2.
Referring to "very reliable" and "heart wrenching" (*erschütternd*) reports from a German source, a Baghdad Railway employee, Rössler describes how the Turks employed the method of zig-zagging in order to exhaust and decimate a convoy of deportees who were forced to march back and forth as follows:

> From Urfa to Telabiad
> From Telabiad to Rakka (500 km by ground)
> From Rakka back to Telabiad
> From Telabiad back to Rakka.

Even more significant, the Director of Deportations, Shükrü (Kaya) is quoted as having told the German source that "The end result of the Turkish measures must be the eradication (*Ausrottung*) of the Armenian race. It is the perpetual fight between Muslims and Armenians which must be decisively fought to the end. The weaker must vanish" (*Der Schwächere muss verschwinden*).

Türkei 183/42, A12911, 27 April 1916.
He reports, "again massacre at Ras ul Ain" and underscores the procedure followed in that part of the desert : "300 to 500 deportees are taken out of the concentration camp each day and butchered (*niedergemacht*) at a distance of 10 km. from Ras ul Ain. The corpses are then thrown in the river."

Türkei 183/44, A21969, 29 July 1916.

"Just received communication from Der Zor, dated 16 July, indicating that the last remnants, the survivors of the long deportation treks, are being wiped out (*vertilgt*)."

Scheubner-Richter (Erzurum)

Filled with premonitions about the fate awaiting the deportee convoys from Erzurum, the Consul in his three reports below hints at the probability of impending massacres.

K168, No.2843, 9 May 1915.
"One cannot rule out that the deportees will be murdered en route" (*Es ist nicht ausgeschlossen dass sie unterwegs ermordet werden*).

K169, No.47, folio 110 (3922), June 26, 1915.
"The order of Kâmil Pasha (Commander-in-Chief of the IIId Army) to deport all Armenians from Erzurum is not legitimate from a military point of view and in my opinion is founded on racial hatred."

K170, No. (4674), 28 July 1915.
"The partisans of Ittihad are unabashedly conceding that their ultimate aim (*Endziel*) is the total annihilation (*gänzliche Ausrottung*) of the Armenians of Turkey, adding, 'After the war we no longer will have any Armenians in Turkey'."

Türkei 183/39, A28584, 5 August 1915.
"The deportation and resettlement scheme was transformed into a crusade of revenge, destruction and plunder."

Türkei 183/39, A28584, 10 August 1915. Enclosure No.1.
"The Armenian Question, which for centuries engaged the attention of European diplomacy, is supposed to be finally solved in the course of this war... the governmental measures are being carried out in such a way that they amount to an absolute annihilation of the Armenians (*einer absoluten Ausrottung... gleichkam*). Also, I don't believe that a culture which is older and much more elevated than that of the Turks could be successfully destroyed in any other way... Only a violent eradication policy, a violent annihilation of the entire people, could enable the Turkish government thereby to achieve the desired goal: the 'solution' of the Armenian Question."

Türkei 183/45, A33457, 4 December 1916.
In this his final report, the German Consul summarizes his observations and concludes as follows: "I have conducted a series of conversations with competent and influential Turkish personages, and these are my impressions: A large segment of the Ittihadist party maintains the viewpoint that the Turkish empire should be based only on the principle of Islam and Pan-Turkism. Its non-Muslim and non-Turkish inhabitants should either be forcibly islamized, or otherwise they ought to be destroyed. These gentlemen believe that the time is propitious for the realization of this plan. The first item on this agenda concerns the liquidation of the Armenians. Ittihad will dangle before the eyes of the allies the specter of an alleged revolution prepared by the Armenian Dashnak party. Moreover, local incidents of social unrest and acts of Armenian self-defense will deliberately be provoked and inflated and will be used as pretexts to effect the deportations. Once en route, however, the convoys will be attacked and exterminated by Kurdish and Turkish brigands, and in part by gendarmes, who will be instigated for that purpose by Ittihad."

AUSTRIAN CONSULS

Kwiatkowski

12 Türkei/209, No.50 C/P, 27 June 1915.
"... these measures obviously are intended to entail the death of the majority of the deportees, including many women and children... the expulsions to Mosul are tantamount to a death verdict and on this my colleagues [the other consuls] agree" (*teilen meine Ansicht*).

38 Konsulate/368, No.44/P., 28 July 1915.
"After the unhindered elimination of the Armenians (*Unschädlichmachung*) the Turkish self-image underwent a mighty aggrandizement" (*eine mächtige Steigerung*).

38 Konsulate/368, No.46/P., 31 July 1915, Trabizon.
"On the basis of concordant pieces of information there can be no doubt that a large number of the local Armenians (Samsun) is being killed en route, others, women and children, are being loaded into barges, taken to the high seas and drowned there".

38 Konsulate/368, Zl.54/P., 4 September 1915.
"As expected, multitudes of Armenians are being killed off in the course of the implementation of the deportation orders. According to the information of a Turkish officer, 132 Armenians, who were enrolled in labor battalions, were executed near Hamziköy, 52 kms from Trabizon, in the first days of July. All information coming from Turkish sources uniformly tell that in the months of July and August a few hundred local Armenian women, children and old men were transported to the high seas on barges and were drowned there. Similar tragic news were contained in the consular report of 11 August 1915, from Giresun. Another report from Samsun's Vice Consulate mentions the murder of about 1,200 Armenians in Merzifun und about 1,600 in Amasya. Georgian members of Ittihad describe the limitless misery of thousands of Armenian deportees... and relate the open admission of Turkish military officers and officials that the Armenians are being exterminated (*ausgerottet werden*)... for Turkey the Armenian Question appears to be solved thanks to the present circumstances that are favorable to her."

12 Türkei/380, Zl.17/pol., 13 March 1918.
"And so came to pass a type of chastisement (*Strafgericht*)... which one seldom encounters in history and which hardly could be justified as an emphatic defense against Turkey's internal foes. It exceeds all sound measures of emergency self-defense ever undertaken by a state. It involved atrocities... without thereby accomplishing anything more than the near complete extermination of the Armenians" (*die fast gänzliche Ausrottung der Armenier*).

Nadamlenzki (Adrianople, Edirne)

12 Türkei/463, Z.95/P, 29 October 1915. Enclosure to No. 93/P.B. of 7 November 1915 by Pallavicini.
"It is depressing to watch this medieval conduct without being able to come to the assistance of the victims. The scenes... defy description. No pity is shown towards helpless and innocent people, only raw brutality and barbaric injustice are applied here."

12 Türkei/463, Z:97/Politisch, 2 November 1915. Enclosure to No.93B/P of 7 November 1915.
"I can assure you Excellency that only through a cruellest and most cynical phantasy can one imagine the heinousness of the events here, the incredible brutality of the leading circles... Just to illustrate the point; the Ittihadists arranged for pupils of the local school to witness for educational purposes the departure of the people who were wailing and were half crazed. The Director of the school openly declared that the purpose was to make future Ittihadists of them. Two Armenians who were not yet deported in the meantime have lost their senses, became crazy"(*wahnsinnig geworden*).

12 Türkei/463, Z:98/Pol., 6 November 1915.
A Procés-Verbal. A statement of facts in French, co-authored by Gourko Seraphimoff, the Bulgarian Consul at Adrianople.
"What is occurring is clearly the implementation of carefully premeditated plan (*d'un programme mûrement réfléchi*) which aims at the annihilation of the Christian elements in Turkey. It is of such gravity that the undersigned feel obligated to call it to the attention of the Powers. The scene, cannot be described. The issue is not just expulsion but the extermination of an entire race (*l'extermination d'une race entière*). The occurrences are conceivable only to a mind which is completely depraved (*tout à fait dépravé*) and to a soul that is barbaric and brutal. Involved are the secret designs concerning the internal policy of the Young Turk Committee... representing a premeditated plan" (*d'un programme fixé d'avance*).

Radimsky (Smyrna, Izmir)

38 Konsulate/368, No.69/P, 30 August 1915.
After quoting Grand Vizier Said Halim to the effect that the Armenians are the friends of Turkey's enemies, that as the Armenians separate themselves from the Turks so the Turks shall separate themselves from them, the Consul states: "The Turks are serious about exterminating the Armenian element."

Ranzi (Damascus)

12 Türkei/463, No.75/P, 7 November 1915.
"The expression 'relocation' is certainly not the right one... one may well assume that these 'settlers' are mostly doomed to destruction" (*dem Untergange geweiht*).

German Military Officers (not covered in the text)

Seeckt. Lieut.- General, Chief of Staff, Ottoman Armed Forces

In an extensive report analyzing the demise of Turkey, the German general in the wake of the Armistice agreement touches on the fate of the Armenians. The report is incorporated in his Papers deposited in the German military archives, BA/MA. N-247/202c. "Die Gründe des Zusammenbruchs der Türkei" (The Causes of the Turkish Collapse), 4 November 1918.
When discussing "the unhappy Armenian Question" in connection with manifestations of "rabid Turkish nationalism," Seeckt refers to the Turkish command and control system "Openly conveyed orders upholding official Turkish policy were followed

by secret instructions (*geheime Weisungen*) or by intimations (*Andeutungen*) that their execution was being discounted" (*auf ihre Ausführung nicht gerechnet wurde*).

This is a covert admission of the known existence of a two-track communication system whereby the formal orders for mere deportation, for example, were cancelled by informal orders for actual destruction of the deportees. However, Seeckt elsewhere appears to have condoned the Turkish plan of destruction as attested to in the following statement attributed to him.

Meier-Welcker, Hans (1967). *Seeckt*. Frankfurt am Main: Verlag für Wehrwesen, Bernard und Graefe. pp. 216.

   p. 154. "Any Christian sentiment and political consideration towards the Armenians had to disappear on account of the exigencies of the war" (*der Kriegsnotwendigkeit halber verschwinden*).

Stange. Colonel. "Special Organization" Commander, 8th Infantry Regiment, and in charge of a Turkish *Teshkilati Mahsusa* Detachment, of regimental strength, operating on the Russian border area.

Stange was involved in Turkish sabotage and guerilla activities organized and financed by the German Foreign Office. As such, he was not only an eyewitness but had valuable access to the representatives of the Turkish War Office and the top delegates of the Young Turk Ittihad party in connection with the mission of that secret organization, and with the command and control of the operations of his Detachment. Equally, if not more importantly, a large contingent of this outfit consisted of ex-convicts, released from prisons by the Directorate of the Ittihad party with which the conception, design and execution of the genocide is identified. The most crucial part of Stange's testimony refers to the employment of the convicts (*Sträflinge*) in the enactment of the genocide. They were part of "The Special Organization" (*Teshkilati Mahsusa*) which, after their more or less abortive guerilla campaign against Russia, were transferred to the command of the killer squads in the campaign of the extermination of the bulk of the Armenians of the eastern provinces. The principal architects of that extermination program during the December 1914 -April 1915 period were associated with his high command, and after February 15, 1915, were under his direct command. They were: Dr. Behaeddin Shakir, his deputy Hilmi, retired artillery major and Central Committee member Yusuf Riza, and Trabizon Responsible Secretary of Ittihad, Nail.

His rather lengthy report, the only one available, is most remarkable for candor, factual grounding, specificity, and broad perspective. In it, Stange offers in his own military style the operative contours of a syndrome of genocide in which ingredients of opportunism, premeditation, decision making, supervision, types of atrocities, and scale and agents of destruction, seem to configure in a fitting web of relationships. The report, marked "secret" (*geheim*), and issued from Erzurum, is dated 23 August, 1915, and is addressed to "The German Military Mission," headed by Marshall Liman von Sanders.

It is perhaps most significant that Stange prefaced his report with a declaration, underscoring the main reason for preparing that report. He referred to "The endeavor of the Turkish government to conceal or tone down the occurrences", (*zu verheimlichen oder abzuschwächen*), adding: "The situation is as follows," (*Die Lage ist folgendermassen*).

   Opportunity. "Military reasons were of secondary importance for the deportation of the Armenians. Mainly, (*hauptsächlich*), an intervention from the outside was not expected" (*diese günstige Gelegenheit, wo von aussen her*

Einspruch nicht zu erwarten war, zu benutzen). "The military considerations and insurgent tendencies in certain parts of the country afforded welcome pretexts *(willkommenen Vorwand).*

Premeditation. The Turks did have "a plan conceived long time ago." *(Einen lang gehegten Plan).*

Decision making (Intent). "The deportation and destruction of the Armenians was decided upon by the Young Turk Committee in Constantinople." *(Die Austreibung und Vernichtung der Armenier war vom jungtürkischen Komitee in Konstantinople beschlossen...)*

Organization and Supervision. "...well organized...members of that committee are on location for that purpose: Hilmi, Shakir, Deputy for Erzurum Seyfullah...and Commander-in-Chief (IIIrd Army) Kâmil..."

Agents of Destruction. They were essentially of two kinds.

a. The military: "With the condoning, even with the assistance of the military escorts" *(Unter Duldung der militärischen Begleitung, sogar mit deren Mithilfe),* and "with the help of the army". *(mit Hilfe von Angehörigen des Heeres)* was the annihilation of the Armenians effected.

b. "The scum" category. *(Gesindel),* involving "so-called çetes." Focusing on a specific case, "as conceded by the governor" *(Der Wali gab diese Tatsachen zu),* Stange declares: "It is absolutely established *(einwandfrei fest)* that practically without exception the Armenians were murdered in the area of Tercan" by these types.

Types and Techniques of Destruction.

a. "The manner in which the deportation *(Ausweisung)* was carried out by the government, the police officials and their organs, was a typical example *(Musterbeispiel)* of beastly brutality *(tierische Roheit)* on the part of all the participating Turks... they did everything to amplify the torments of the Armenians" *(die Quälereien der Armenier vermehren).*

b. "In Trabizon men were marched off to a mountain site and slaughtered" *(abgeschlachtet).* Again in the same city, "the Armenians were taken on board of vessels and dumped overboard in the sea." *(Auf's Meer hinausgefahren und dann über Bord geworfen).*

Kressenstein, Friedrich Freiherr von. Major General

Kressenstein, Friedrich Freiherr von (1938). *Mit den Türken zum Suezkanal* (To the Suez Canal with the Turks). Berlin: Vorhut Verlag. 308 pp.
   p. 171. "We Germans, soldiers and civilians, were condemned to see and watch the dreadful spectacle *(das grausige Schauspiel).* We found it incomprehensible and were outraged that the German government and German public opinion...did not withdraw from [partnership with] the Turks *(abrückten)* but rather through their silence they made us, Germans, to some extent moral accomplices" *(moralische Mitschuldigen).*

Von der Goltz. Generalfeldmarschall

Von der Goltz, Generalfeldmarschall Colmar Freiherr (1929). *Denkwürdigkeiten* (Memorable Events). Berlin: Mittler und Sohn. 510 pp.

> **p. 428.** Private letter to his wife, dated 22 November 1915, in which the marshal is summarizing his personal observations regarding the condition of the deportees being driven to the deserts: "immense wretchedness. A frightful national tragedy" (*grenzenloses Elend. Eine fürchterliche Völkertragödie*).

Schlee Pasha. General

General Schlee Pasha (1931). "Die Eisenbahnen der asiatischen Türkei während des Krieges" (The Railroads in Asiatic Turkey during the War), *Mitteilungen des Bundes der Asienkämpfer* 13(5), (1 May 1931).

> p. 54. In a series of articles, dealing with the railroads in Asiatic Turkey during the War, he discusses the devastating effects upon the work of completion of the Baghdad Railway of "the extinction of the Armenian laborers and craftsmen."

Guhr, Hans. Major General

Guhr, Hans, (1937). *Als türkischer Divisionskommandeur in Kleinasien und Palästina* (As Turkish Divisional Commander in Anatolia and Palestine). Berlin: Mars, 311 pp. He commanded the 1st Division of the 3rd Army Corps.

> **p. 138.** The Turkish solution of the Armenian Question was "devious" (*abwegig*); it consisted of "the violent extermination of the Armenians themselves" (*die gewaltsame Ausrottung der Armenier*).

Endres, Franz Karl. Major in the Turkish army

Die Türkei (1918). Munich: C.H. Beck. 301 pp.
> Endres served three years in that army and in 1915 as a member of the German Military Mission to Turkey served as Chief of General Staff of General Liman von Sanders. Describing himself as "a particular friend of the Turkish people," Endres in the 4th edition of his book laments the fate of the Armenians as follows: "Surely, no people on earth suffered as much during the World War I as the Armenian. Over 1.2 million Armenians perished."

Mühlmann, Carl, Dr. Major Adjutant to the Chief of German Military Mission to Turkey; later chief of staff officer

Mühlmann, Carl (1940). *Das Deutsch-Türkische Waffenbündnis im Weltkriege* (The German-Turkish Military Alliance in World War I). Leipzig: Koehler und Ameling. 317 pp.
> Having almost exclusive access to some very secret material, he is viewed as one of the most authoritative military historians.

> **p. 276** "It is a fact that a large part of the Armenian people perished through 'evacuation'. (*durch die "Aussiedlung" zugrunde gegangen ist*). It is likewise uncontestable that Turkish outrages considerably increased the number of victims."

A Foreign Military Commander in German Service.

Reference is made to a "Soldier of Fortune," a native of Venezuela, who joined the Turkish Army as a volunteer through German channels. The most remarkable aspect of his role is that he took active part in the abortive Turkish effort to overwhelm the Armenian defendants of Van by way of directing the massive artillery fire against them. In that capacity, he proved to be perhaps the only foreign officer personally witnessing scenes of butchery, overhearing conversations among Turkish officials and military officers (he knew Turkish enough to understand) relating to plans and details of massacres, and thus ultimately becoming a paramount liability for the Turks. In one of his books he cites specific instances where military and civilian authorities repeatedly tried to trap or to ambush him and thereby eliminate a dangerous "infidel" witness. Here is his account.

Nogales, Rafael. Major, Chief of Staff, Van Gendarmerie Division, May 1915; Commander of the Military Zone of Ramleh, Syrian front. Fall, 1916; Instructor and Deputy Commander of the 1st Regiment of Lancers, July, 1918

Nogales, Rafael (1926) *Four Years Beneath the Crescent.* New York: Scribner's. 416pp. (German edition in 1925. 255 pp.)

> **p. 135.** After stating that on-the-spot massacres were carried out in the provinces of Van, Diyarbekir and parts of Harput, he points out that "the deportations" from the rest of Turkey"...effected almost the same result as the massacres...[they] cost 3/4 of their number along the way, and on some occasions perhaps even 90 and 95%, through starvation and typhus...frequently the gendarmes of their own escort, ...tired after a while of contending with the unfortunate creatures, cut them down or obliged them by bullets to swim across swift rivers which sucked down whole caravans of walking skeletons, sinking never to rise again...*There can be no doubt that the massacres and deportations took place in accordance with a carefully laid-out plan for which the responsibility lay with the retrograde party, headed by the Grand Vizier Talaat pasha and the civil authorities under his orders. they aimed to make an end first of the Armenians, then the other minorities."* (Emphasis added. German original is on p.98).
>
> **p. 146.** He repeats this charge on the authoritative and decisive role of Talat, as confirmed to him personally by Dr. Reshid, the governor of the province of Diyarbekir.
>
> **p. 135.** Describes a scene of burning alive in Mush district (Bitlis province) where "women and children were penned and burned alive while others found their doom in the waters of Euphrates."
>
> **p. 124.** Contains a rare and an authentic description of a massacre scene near Siirt, south of Bitlis: "The ghastly slope was crowned by thousands of half-nude and still bleeding corpses, lying in heaps, or interlaced in death's final embrace. Fathers, brothers, sons, and grandsons lay there as they had fallen beneath the bullets and yataghans of the assassins. From more than one slashed throat the life gushed forth in mouthfuls of warm blood. Flocks of vultures were perched upon the mound, pecking at the eyes of dead and dying, whose rigid gaze seemed still to mirror the horrors of unspeakable agony; while the scavenger dogs struck sharp teeth into the entrails of beings still palpitating with the breath of life."

German Military Physicians

Stoffels, H. Staff physician with the Persian Expeditionary Corps.

AFM. 12 Türkei/380, folio 909, 26 May 1917.
He reported to the Austrian Consul in Trabizon that in the Fall of 1915 on his way to Mosul, he came across, in Mush and Siirt, "a large number of formerly Armenian localities in the churches and houses of which he saw charred and decomposed corpses of women and children." (*in einer grossen Anzahl früher armenischer Ortschaften in Kirchen und Häusern verkohlte und verweste Frauen-und Kinderleichen gesehen habe*).

Schacht. Major (*Oberstabsarzt*)

Türkei 183/40, A35070. Enclosure in Consul Rössler's 16 November 1915 report.
He was sent to Der Zor on official business "not in any way connected with the Armenian Question." When reporting to Consul Rössler on what he saw there, he stated: "No language and exchange of ideas can even approximately describe the reality of this human wretchedness; the occurrences there are so indescribable" (*kein sprachlicher Gedankenaustausch vermag auch nur annähernd die Wirklichkeit dieses menschlichen Elends zu schildern, so unbeschreiblich sind dort die Vorkommnisse*).

Schilling, Prof. Dr. Major. December 1915-June 1916 staff physician with the Persian Expeditionary Force. August 1916-February 1917, Sanitation Officer in the IV Army; later attached to the I Ottoman Army.

Türkei 158/19, A18911, 27 April 1918.
In his eight page report of April 27, 1918, he describes: "The planned destruction of the Armenians" (*Die planmässige Vernichtung der Armenier*).

Steuber, Dr. Major General (*Obergeneralarzt*)

Dr. Steuber *Jildirim. Deutsche Streiter auf heiligem Boden* (Thunderbolt. German Fighters on Holy Ground) 2d. ed. Oldenburg i.O. Gerhard Stalling Verlag. 174 pp.
   pp. 59-60. He explains "the extermination of the industrious Armenians" (*die Ausrottung, der fleissigen Armenier*) as having resulted from "the discharge of accumulated hatred" against them by the Turks who, seizing the opportunity of "isolated acts of violence" and on "suspicion of secret ties with Russia" on the part of the Armenians, unleashed "the atrocities (*Greuel*) against them, that led to "a general massacre" (*eine allgemeine Metzelei*). Referring to Urfa, he describes "the slaughter" on the outskirts of the city of several hundred men (*abgeschlachtet*), and the disappearance in harems of women and children.

Gaspar, Andreas, Dr.

Gaspar, Andreas (1930). *Sittengeschichte des Weltkrieges* (The History of Morals of World War I). 2 vols. Leipzig: Magnus Hirschfield. Vol.2, 326 pp.
   p. 263 He describes the collective rape in the Mesopotamian desert of Armenian girls and women who comprised the caravans located near the tents of the German

contingent of soldiers and officers.

p. 283 "At night, hellish noises were heard. The German officers and soldiers could not sleep that night on account of the heartrending cries and screams of the women and girls being violated...Next morning, a terrible spectacle was witnessed...the throats of all the victims were found slashed." He characterizes "the deportations" as an act of "outrageous bestiality" (*haarsträubender Bestialität*), and as

p. 290 "unquestionably the greatest crime of World War I, with its 1.2 million civilian victims, and at the same time being in world history a singular accumulation of acts of plunder and sex-murders, theft, rape, procuring and white slave traffic."

Austrian Military Officers

Pomiankowski, Joseph. Divisional General and Vice Marshal. Military Attaché and Military Plenipotentiary to Turkey, 1909-1918

Pomiankowski, Joseph (1928). *Der Zusammenbruch des Ottomanischen Reiches* (The Collapse of the Ottoman Empire). Vienna: n.p., 444 pp.

Pomiankowski's testimony has foremost significance on account of two facts. During the war he spent most of his time at the Ottoman General Headquarters to which he was attached by duty. Equally important, all Austrian military units, serving in Turkey, were subject to his authority with respect to matters of economy, education, administration, and discipline.

His statements and descriptions include a number of revelations reflecting the benefit of his access to the highest authorities of wartime Turkey, military and civilian. Some of these revelations involve personal and intimate exchanges with top Ittihadist leaders. Closely associated with War Minister and de facto Supreme Commander Enver, Pomiankowski accompanied him on eight separate inspection trips to the interior as well as the military operational zones of Turkey in 1916 and 1917. His testimony acquires further significance on account of his assertion that:

p. 13. "Since the year 1909 up to the end of the war...I had ample opportunity to get to know the land and people of Turkey. During the war, however, I was from start to finish eyewitness of practically all the decisions and activities of the Turkish government..." His accounts may be itemized and classified as follows:

p. 162. *Premeditation.* Turkish leaders attributed the decadence and decline of the Ottoman Empire "exclusively...to the overabundant humanity of the earlier Sultans who either ought to have had the conquered people forcibly embrace Islam, or ought to have exterminated them...In this sense there is no doubt that the Young Turk government already before the war had decided to utilize the next suitable opportunity for rectifying this mistake at least in part... It is also very probable that this consideration, i.e., intent, had a very important influence upon the decisions of the Ottoman government regarding joining the Central Powers and upon the determination of the exact time of their intervening in the war."

p. 158. *Preemption.* The specter of the rise of a future Greater Armenia haunted the Ittihadist leaders. "The Young Turk barbarians, who didn't recoil before any crime, recognized in the destruction (*Vernichtung*) of the Armenian people the means to preempt forever such an eventuality."

p. 158. *The Opportunity factor.* "The Turkish government not only resorted to all the means in order to protect itself against dangerous internal tendencies but also in order to take as much advantage as possible of the vulnerable situation of its Christian citizens."

p. 159. *Vulnerability due to lack of external deterrence.* "Compared to the Greeks, the Armenians were treated much more horribly by the Young Turks as they had no immediate backer outside Turkey, and the Turkish government did not have to fear a change in the war-political situation."

p. 160. *Deportation meant destruction.* "The implementation of this barbaric order in fact amounted to the annihilation (*Ausrottung*) of the Armenian nation in Asia Minor...on the road the men were all together murdered, attractive women were led into Turkish harems and the rest was wiped out through deprivations and debilitation, and only pitiful remnants arrived at the Euphrates river only to perish there in the shortest period of time."

p. 161. *Total annihilation - the end result.* "In the course of summer 1915 the Turkish government with inexorable consequence brought its bloody task of the extermination of an entire nation to an end."

p. 165. "The gruesome destruction of the Armenian nation in Asia Minor by the Ittihadist government was an act which was barbaric and which to the highest degree outraged all human senses... "Pomiankowski went even so far to suggest that this act of

p. 164. "Extermination (*Ausrottung*) of a Christian nation offended the sentiments and moral principles of humanity certainly to a much higher degree than the unlimited submarine warfare."

p. 163. *Ittihadist arch responsibility.* "The secret decisions of the Young Turk Committee determined the manner with which the national-Turkish and fundamental questions involving the overall policies of the empire were solved."

p. 160. *Defensive uprising.* "The Van uprising certainly was an act of desperation (*Verzweifelung*). The local Armenians realized that general massacres against the Armenians had started and they would be the next target."

Other German Sources

Rosenberg, Frederic Hans, Dr. Privy Councillor, Extraordinary Ambassador and Plenipotentiary Minister and Director of the Near East Department in the Foreign Office. After the war, he became Ambassador to Turkey, and died there. Throughout the war, he played a major role in the formulation of German policy concerning Turco-Armenian relations in general, and the Turkish genocide in particular.

Türkei 183/39, 1 October 1915.
In an exchange with the Turkish Chargé of the Turkish Embassy, Edhem, he remonstrated to him regarding "the persecution and destruction of the Armenian people" (*Verfolgung und Vernichtung*), as described in his *démarche* of 1 October 1915.

Von Tyszka. Reporter with access to "official, secret sources" (*geheime, amtliche Quellen*), according to Ambassador Wangenheim (*Türkei 159, No.2/12, A12586, 20 June 1913*). His report, used here is one of three he wrote.

Türkei 183/39, A29593, 30 September 1915.
Referring to the large scale deportations of the Armenians, he claimed that "The Turkish plan...is old standing" (*ist alten Datums*) and the evacuations are taking place from zones that are distant and have no relationship to military operations. He then underscores the widespread role of *çetes* (a mixed group of "volunteers", irregulars, and convicts) in "the massacres" taking place in zones such as Sivas, Angora, Malatya, Trabizon, Bayburt, etc., and their being "incited and led" by the Young Turks (*angestiftet und geführt*). "We

are dealing presently with such kinds of victims as Turkish history, in truth not lacking on instances of violence, does not yet know. This is a shocking truth." (*Es handelt sich heute um Opfer wie sie die an Gewaltakten wahrlich nich arme türkische Geschichte noch nicht kennt. Das ist eine erschütternde Wahrheit*).

Erzberger, Matthias. Reichstag Deputy. Director of Intelligence in Foreign Office, Foreign Secretary and Minister, 1918; Minister of Finance, 1920

Visited Turkey during the war and met Talat and Enver. In a Memorandum (*Denkschrift*) intended to reveal the complicity of these two wartime leaders and submitted to Baron von Rosenberg at the Armenian Desk of the Foreign Office, Erzberger in a nutshell explains the relationship between deportation and destruction.

Türkei 183/41, A5914, 3 March 1916.
"One might surmise that deportation is milder form of retribution than killing off. In reality, however, the former is not much different from the latter. (*Tatsächlich unterscheidet sich aber erstere nicht viel von letzterer*).

Türkei 183/49, A8751, 23 February 1918.
Erzberger relayed an Anonymous Report dated February 17, 1918 which he identified as coming from "a reliable source" (*zuverlässige Seite*) *in which for the first time the Turkish measures against the Armenians were described as "genocide"* (*Völkermord*).

Spieker, W. Baghdad Railway Employee.

Aleppo Consul Rössler describes him as "a most trustworthy eyewitness source". His report is based on observations he made during a trip in the area, July 28-August 20, 1915.

Türkei 183/38, A28019, 2 September 1915. Enclosure in Consul Rössler's 3 September 1915 report.
The 2800 deportees from Gurun, a town located about halfway between Sivas and Marash, "were deliberately dragged through detours and dangerous roads, instead of leading them through direct, four day route via Marash; they have been en route for a month." This method was to effect decimation.

In a related report in the same file, Spieker describes the condition of corpses floating upstream as "tied together on their backs by twos," and "five to eight tied together on their arms." He quotes a German captain of cavallerie describing "countless corpses lying unburied on the road from Diyarbekir to Urfa, lots of young men with their throats cut through. They must be those conscripts assigned to street construction labor" (*lauter junge Männer mit durchschinettenen Halsen. Es werden die zum Heeresdienste eingezogenen Strassenarbeiter*). "What I am writing is but a fraction of all the atrocities being perpetrated here in the last two months...I can anytime supply the dates and names of the eyewitnesses involved." He adds that Kader Pasha [a Kurdish chieftain] told him, "All Armenian men in the IIId Army zone have been killed."

Stürmer. Harry, Dr. Correspondent in Constantinople of the German daily *Kölnische Zeitung*, 1915-1916.

According to a file in the German Archives, Dr. Stürmer "knowingly immersed himself up to his neck with the most secret stuff" (*mit Wissen über die geheimsten Dinge bis an den Hals vollgesogen*. (Türkei 158/21, A53590). Though his extensive testimony is incorporated in two long reports filed at the German Foreign Ministry Archives, namely, Türkei 183/38, A30432, 5 September 1915, and Türkei 183/38, A28887, 6 September 1915, his published accounts are, however, free from the wartime constraints imposed by German press censorship and alliance obligations. The following are excerpts from the book.

Stürmer, Harry (1917), *Zwei Kriegsjahre in Konstantinopel* (Skizzen Deutsch-Jungtürkischer Moral and Politik). Lausanne: Payot. 262 pp. (English translation by E. Allen : *Two War Years in Constantinople*. New York : G.H. Doran. 292 pp.).

> **p. 36.** "From the very start the persecution extended to hundreds of thousands of inhabitants including women and children...who became victims of mass murder" (*Massenmord*). The whole enterprise was "a well thought out political-administrative arrangement." (*eine genau durchdachte staatsmännische Massregel*).
>
> **p. 43.** Equally significant is Stürmer's admission that he took his assignment as a Turkophile (*Türkenfreundlichkeit*) harboring
>
> **p. 38.** "My love to Turkey of today" (*meine Liebe zur heutigen Türkei*). He describes his sources as "personal" and as coming "from a trustworthy mouth" (*aus glaubwürdigem Munde*), including
>
> **p. 39.** "However in isolated cases, even Turks" (*Türke selbst, wenn auch nur vereinzelt*). "I could name names but I do not wish to expose these Turkish informants to danger." (*Gewährsmänner*).
>
> **p. 40.** He details types of atrocities including "casting children into the sea" (*ins Meerwerfen der Kinder*);
>
> **p. 41.** "Ambushing caravans of deportees through gangs of criminals and brigands engaged for that purpose" (*Überfälle...durch bestellte Räuber und Verbrecherbanden*);
>
> **p. 50.** "Resettlement" in notoriously malaria infested, in foodless, sandy and mountainous areas;
>
> **p. 53.** The indulgence in wild erotica involving children and pretty girls; "in brief, methods of extermination that are at once brutal, beastly and coldbloodedly refined." (*kurz, tierisch verrohte und kaltblutig raffinierte Ausrottungsmassregeln*).

Weitz, Paul. Permanent correspondent in Constantinople of the German daily *Frankfurter Zeitung*.

An "intelligence agent," an "unofficial diplomat" in the German Embassy, and as such "very well informed on all the secrets of German politic" (see Pomiankowski above, p. 115). With the assistance of the Turkish War Office, he participated in an inspection trip of the eastern provinces, April 14-May 14, 1918. He was to observe evidence of revenge acts by Armenian volunteers retreating to the Caucasus. This enabled him to visit the sites of the Turkish atrocities of 1915 and 1916, particularly in Erzincan.

Türkei 183/52, A27194, 20 June 1918. A 20 pp. report.

> **p. 13.** He refers to "the bands organized from Constantinople" as the instruments of "the extermination of the Armenians" (*Ausrottung*). He relates the gleeful narration

of that process of destruction by Kurdish notables, gendarmes, the district governor of Gümüshane, and the latter's
p. 8. Military Commander (*mit seltenem Freimut die grausamsten Einzelheiten von den Massakers erzählt*). During a trip to a bridge on the Euphrates river, he was told how the Armenian population of Erzincan, with their bishop at the head of the caravan, was taken to the river, pushed into it and drowned. "They showed us the spots where the
p. 11. victims of this ghastly inhumanity were driven into the waves, practically naked. We likewise inspected the giant barracks nearby where 1500 Armenians were literally slaughtered at the same time" (*buchstäblich abgeschlachtet*), with one of the gendarmes telling him, Weitz, that he killed 50, as another gendarme boasted of having killed 27, all of these killed, "with their own
p. 12. hands" (*eigenhändig getötet*). "They were telling us this and bragging of it as a heroic deed, without being taken to task." (*Das erzählten uns diese Leute prahlerisch als Ruhmestat, ohne danach gefragt zu werden*). As to
p. 18. those who took refuge in the great Armenian Cathedral, "they were all hacked by the sword" (*samt und sonders niedergemetzelt*).

Anders, Edgar, Dr. Ex-Consul, Ex-officer in Turkey.

Joined Weitz in the inspection described above, wearing his military uniform.

Gr. Hauptquartier, 191/6, No.41, his 16 May 1918 report.
He focuses on the atrocities in the Black Sea port city Trabizon. "The Armenians were loaded on board of barges (*mavuna*) and instead of being taken to Samsun, their port of destination, went down on the high seas with every soul on board" (*Mit Mann und Maus auf hoher See untergegangen sind*).

Outcome: The Scope of Destruction

The demographic uncertainties, due to inadequate and questionable Ottoman-Turkish standards of census-taking, make it very difficult to compute the exact figure on Armenian losses; the number of survivors needs to be related to the pre-genocide total Armenian population figure to obtain a reliable figure of genocide victims. In assessing the extent of Armenian casualties German officials and experts had no choice but to rely on estimates they reached on the basis of German data and computations available to them.

ESTIMATES ON PRE-GENOCIDE ARMENIAN POPULATION

Türkei 183/40, A25749, 18 September 1916.
The most authoritative figure in this respect is provided by Ambassador Metternich. Its unusual significance lies in the fact that it involved massive research and it is part of the most comprehensive report ever written by any Ambassador or any other Foreign Office authority on the Armenian problem during World War I. That significance is even more enhanced by virtue of the associated fact that Metternich was directed by Zimmermann, then the Minister of Foreign Affairs, to compose his 72 pp. report with a view to defending the German posture of no interference in Turkish internal affairs in the forthcoming Reichstag debate.
pp. 46-47 "Before World War I the number of Armenians in Turkey amounted to two million souls." In this connection the Ambassador underscores the fact that "a

large number" of Armenians have been embracing Islam to escape massacres, and that the Turks are providing this alternative not as an act of "religious fanaticism." Rather, for the Turks the aim is "the killing off of Armenian national sentiments" (*Abtötung des armenischen Nationalgefühls*), and for the Armenians, it is survival. "Reliable sources" (*zuverlässige Berichte*) indicate that this conversion practice is being indulged in "an abundance of cases" (*in sehr zahlreichen Fällen*).

Türkei 183/41, A2889, 18 November 1915, 25 pp. report.
Alexandrette's (Iskenderun) Consul Hoffmann too estimated the Armenian population to be two million, at the same time pointing out that the majority of them are artisans, skilled laborers, farmers and peasants in the provinces.

Türkei 183/44, A27493, 4 October 1916.
Chargé Radowitz is more specific with his 1,924,000 figure.

Türkei 183/40, A468, 20 December 1915.
Consul Rössler provides the estimate of 2.5 million.

Grothe, Hugo

Grothe, Hugo (1913). Die asiatische Türkei und die deutschen Interessen (Asiatic Turkey and German Interests). *Der Neue Orient*, Issue No.5.
   p. 15. While the massacres were in progress this famous pro-Turkish author, who was instrumental in founding and promoting in Germany German-Turkish associations, estimated the Armenian population of the 5 eastern provinces, i.e., Erzurum, Van, Bitlis, Diyarbekir and Harput, alone as 1.5 million.

Roth, Karl, Dr.

Roth, Karl (1915). *Armenien und Deutschland*. Leipzig: Veit and Co. Issue No.10. The author's military background includes the rank of captain, and commander of a company. In this essay, he offers some demographic computations.
   p. 6. "The total head count of the Armenians in Turkey should be in the 2-2.5 million range."

A German Portrayal of Turkish Miscounting of Armenian Victims

Türkei 183/39, A28584, 5 August 1915.
Erzurum Consul Scheubner-Richter provides the following examples of discrepancies between data available to him and data admitted by Turkish authorities.
   Of the first caravan of about 500 deportees of Erzurum that was en route in the direction of Harput-Urfa on June 16, 1915, the Turkish Government admitted only 14 men killed. According to the sources of the German Consul, however, nearly all the men were killed. In another instance, the large caravan in which converged subsequent waves of deportees from Erzurum and the villages of Passin Plain and which altogether was destroyed through a massive massacre, entailed a very large magnitude of victims. Scheubner-Richter estimates it to be between 10-20,000 (*dürfte zwischen 10-20,000*

betragen). The Government, however, admits only to 3-4000. Thus, with reference to this particular case, the Government is depicted as underestimating or underreporting the scale of Armenian victims by a ratio of 4 to 1.

Estimates on Total Armenian Victims

Türkei 183/40, A468, 20 December 1915.
Aleppo Consul Rössler estimated that 4/5 of the total Armenian population of Turkey had been deported; from the six eastern provinces, with a heavy concentration of Armenians, this ratio amounted to 1.2 million deportees, reckoned the consul. As far as the eastern provinces were concerned, he said, the casualty rates had "possibly" reached 75%.

Türkei 183/44, A27493, 4 October 1916.
The German Interim Ambassador Radowitz made a computation from a detailed list of 4056 Armenian orphans under German care in Aleppo, by way of establishing a ratio between the surviving orphans and their dead family members. Through extrapolation, he estimated the number of Armenian victims then to be 1.5 million dead and 425,000 survivors.

Türkei 183/42, A13959, also K172, A14024, 27 May 1916.
The German Deputy, Foreign Office Intelligence Director, and later Minister, Erzberger, with some access to Turkish leaders and sources, also made an estimate by referring to two "absolutely reliable" confidants (*Vertrauensmann*) or intermediaries, "one of which just arrived from Constantinople." He declared: "We estimate the loss of human lives...among the Christians to be 1.5 million."

Türkei 183/54, A44066, 18 October 1918. 20 pp. report.
Perhaps the most qualifying assessment is offered by the military chaplain of the German Embassy, Count von Lüttichau whom German Ambassador to Turkey, later Germany's Foreign Minister, Kühlmann extolled as "a symbol of the German Genius" (Kühlmann, Richard von (1948). *Erinnerungen* [Memoirs] Heidelberg: L. Schneider. 486 pp. from p.467). Lüttichau was acutely interested in gauging the yardsticks of the cataclysm. He undertook a three month trip to the southern provinces of Turkey, including Diyarbekir, Aleppo, etc. and compiled a 20 page detailed report on the Armenians. He claims his information came from both Armenians and Turkish notables, including former governors and religious figures, and that there is some consensus (*Übereinstimmung*) on major points which he proposes to enumerate. Arguing that "the proportional" losses in certain zones are far more important to understand than the total number of such losses, which are difficult to grasp (*sich schwer kontrollieren lässt*), the Count gives this picture of specifics in that report. Speaking of the eastern provinces 98% of the male
p. 2. population of the 80-90% of the total population "is no longer alive" (*nicht mehr am Leben*). "These figures lend themselves to verification locality by locality" (*Diese Ziffern...lassen sich Ort für Ort nachprüfen*). His conclusion: when discounting cities such as Constantinople and Smyrna that were mostly, but not entirely, exempted from deportation, "On the whole, at
p. 3. least 80% of the people have been destroyed" (*im ganzen, mindestens 80% des Volkes sind vernichtet*).

Endres, Franz Karl, cited in the section on German Military Officers, and, according to his prefatory statement, "a special friend of the Turkish people," concluded in the 4th edition of his book on Turkey

> **p. 161.** that "1.2 million Armenians perished in Turkey during the war" (*zugrunde gegangen*).

DeNogales. A Venezuelan officer

DeNogales who eyewitnessed actual massacres and served as Turkish commander of artillery in the assault against Van Armenians,

> **p. 137.** (p.98 in the German edition) lamented, "The martyrdom and slaughter of the million and one-half of Christians who perished during the massacres," of which 200,000 were Nestorians residing in the south-eastern border of Turkey.

Austrian Estimates on Total Armenian Victims

Reference may first be made to Vice Marshal Pomiankowski who was cited above also. According to his estimates, "approximately one million Armenians perished" p. 160.

AFM. 40. Interna 1848-1918; 270-275 Konfidenten-Berichte. Report in File 272. Confidential Report, 2 December 1915: "My secret source (*Gewährsmann*) informs me that about 1 million Armenians were exterminated (*ausgerottet*); this number is in accord (*in Übereinstimmung*) with other calculations" (*Berechnungen*).

12 Türkei/380, Zl.17/pol., 13 March 1918.
Consul Kwatkiowski reports from Samsun that "in round figure 1 million Armenians were with studied cruelty (*mit ausgesuchter Grausamkeit*) deported from the six eastern Anatoilian provinces as well as from Trabizon province and Samsun district. From these only a fraction could escape death..."

12 Türkei/463, Z.94/P, 29 October 1915.
Adrianople (Edirne) Consul Nadamlenzki provides a more complete picture on the total number of Armenian deportees from the entire realm of the empire, including the rest of Anatolia and European Turkey. According to his figures, by the above date "already 1.5 million Armenians were deported."

Extension of Genocide to Russian Armenia in 1918

Following the capture of sizeable chunks of territory in Russian Armenia in the spring and summer of 1918, the Turkish Army commanders embarked upon a campaign of demolition that aimed at the ruination of the remnants of the Armenian people. The methods included not only massacre but starvation through blockade and isolation. In other words, an attempt was made to extend the genocidal enactment against the Armenians of Turkey to the Armenians in the Transcaucasus. This is the gist of the testimonies of several German generals and their Austrian colleagues on duty in the Transcaucasus.

Von Lossow. Major General, Military attaché; and March 1916-September 1918, "German Military Plenipotentiary in Turkey"; German Representative at Batum Conference May, 1918. In Turkish military services, 1911-1914.

Türkei 183/51, A20698, 15 May 1918. His first report.
The Turks have embarked upon "the total extermination of the Armenians in Transcaucasia, also" (*Völlige Ausrottung der Armenier auch in Transkaukasien*).

Türkei 183/51, A21877, 23 May 1918.
"The aim of Turkish policy is, as I have always reiterated, the taking of possession of Armenian districts and the extermination of the Armenians." (*Ausrottung*).

DZA. BRK, No.2458/9 Bl.202, 3 June 1918. Report.
  p. 2. "Talat's government party wants to destroy all Armenians (*alle Armenier ausrotten will*), not only in Turkey, but also outside Turkey."

Türkei 183/53, A32123, 10 July 1918.
After"completely encircling" (*völlige Abschliessung*) the remnants of the Armenian nation in Transcaucasus "The Turkish intention (*Absicht*)...to starve off the entire Armenian nation, is evident" (*liegt klar zu tage*).

Türkei 183/53, A31345, 11 July 1918.
"on the basis of all the reports and news coming to me here in Tbilissi (Tiflis, Georgia) there hardly can be any doubt that the Turks systematically are aiming at the...extermination of the few hundred thousand Armenians whom they left alive until now." (*die Türken systematisch darauf ausgehen...auszurotten*).

Von Kressenstein, Kress. Major-General, July 1914. Chief of operations, Turkish General Headquarters; later Chief of Staff of Turkish IV th Army in Syria and Palestine; September 1917, Commander in Chief of 8th Army, Palestine; June 1918, Chief of the German Imperial Delegation in the Caucasus

Türkei 158/20, A31679, 13 July 1918.
"The Turkish policy of causing starvation is an all too obvious proof, if proof was still needed as to who is responsible for the massacre, for the Turkish resolve to destroy the Armenians" (*ein zu augenfälliger Beweis für den Vernichtungswillen der Türkei gegenüber dem armenischen Element...als dass noch Zweifel darüber bestehen konnten auf wen die Massakres zurückzuführen sind*).

DZA. BRK, No.2458/9 Bl.287, 31 July 1918.
"The Turkish intention is...quite obvious. Turkish General Esad with flimsy excuses refused relief. It is the urgent mandate of humanity to have the Central Powers exert the strongest pressure upon the Turks."

Türkei 183/54, A34707, 5 August 1918.
"The Turkish policy vis a vis the Armenians is clearly outlined (*zeichnet sich klar ab*). The Turks have by no means relinquished their intention to exterminate the Armenians (*ihre Absicht...auszurotten*). They merely changed their tactic. Wherever possible, the Armenians are being aroused, provoked in the hope of thereby securing a pretext for new assaults on them" (*Man reizt die Armenier, wo nur irgend möglich, man provoziert sie in der Hoffnung dadurch einen Vorwand zu neuen Angriffen...zu erhalten*). As to the

scenes of deportation he witnessed while travelling with Cemal Pasha, the Commander of the IVth Army of which he was the Chief of Staff, Ambassador Metternich describes his state of mind from a letter he received from him that the "the memories of the dreadful scenes of the Armenian Horrors" will probably remain with him as long as he lives (*die schauderhaften Bilder des Armenierelends ihn wohl sein Leben lang nicht verlassen würde*) (*Türkei 183/40, A36483*).

Türkei 183/54, A36001, 20 August 1918.
"The destruction of this old Christian people..." (*Vernichtung dieses alten christlichen Volkes*).

Türkei 183/54, A39244, 3 September 1918.
In this very comprehensive report General Kress underscores the Turkish resort to "unconscionable" methods of disinformation about the Armenians by Turkish civilian and military authorities reporting to their superiors in the Ottoman capital. He scorns the use of such clichés as "military necessity," "threat to our communication and supply lines," and "other similar pretexts," which are being advanced in order "to justify the murder of thousands of human beings." In an appended declaration, co-signed by the Austrian diplomat in the Caucasus, Georg Freiherr von Franckenstein, Turkish generals Esad, Shevki and War Minister Enver's brother Nuri, are taken to task for spreading "distorted information" (*entstellte Meldungen*) about Russian Armenia. "The perfidy (*Hinterhaltigkeit*) of General Esad was revealed when his explanations about Armenian refugees, without any danger of being slaughtered, being able to return, proved false" (*unwahr*).

Paraquin, Ernst. Lieut. Colonel, Chief of Staff of General Halil (Kut), Commander-in-Chief of Army Group East.
His Report on the September 1918 Baku Massacre:

Türkei 183/54, 26 September 1918. Report to General Seeckt, Chief of Staff, Ottoman General Headquarters.
According to Paraquin, Turkish General Mürsel, Commander of the 5th Division, and in charge of Baku City Fortifications, informed him of Tatar plans to massacre the Armenians of Baku as soon as it was captured by the Turkish Army. Only after three days of unrelenting butchery did the Turkish Commander and War Minister Enver's brother, Nuri, who had been forewarned about it by Paraquin, decree Martial Law. The Turkish Command indeed allowed the Tatars this opportunity of revenge. This view was openly and repeatedly suggested (*die vielfach offen ausgesprochene Ansicht*). "The Carnage (*Gemetzel*) was foretold weeks earlier and had no relationship whatsoever with the tactical phases" of the military operations (*ohne jeden Zusammerhang mit taktischen Vorgängen*). That carnage was confirmed by a Turkish major who upon returning from a tour of inspection on September 17, 1918, told the German Chief of Staff: "You are right. It has been terrible in the city. One cannot deny it" (*...ist es schrecklich zugegangen. Man kann es nich leugnen*). Paraquin was eventually relieved of his post by Halil for protesting against the Baku massacre.

Paraquin, Ernst (24 and 28 January 1920). Politik im Orient. *Berliner Tageblatt*. (*Türkei 158/24, A1373* has a summary of the contents of this two-part article).
Part I. "With hypocritical indignation (*geheuchelter Entrüstung*) the Turkish government denies all barbarous conduct against the Armenians. The evacuation of Anatolia by the Russians furnished the desired opportunity to clear out also the

Russian Armenians... The annihilation campaign against the Armenians proceeded...with inexorable ruthlessness."

Other Accounts

Kühlmann. Foreign Minister

Türkei 183/51, A28533, No.1178, 3 June 1918.
Following a high level conference in Berlin, Kühlmann issued the following report to General Headquarters and to Ambassador to Turkey. "The information supplied to us by our absolutely reliable agent...asserts that in violation of their promises the Turks systematically are pursuing their plan of annihilation of the Armenians in the Caucasus..." (*die Vernichtung planmässig betreiben*).

Ludendorf, Erich

Ludendorf, Erich (1922). *Urkunden der obersten Heeresleitung über ihre Tätigkeit. 1916-18 (Documents of the High Command on its Activities 1916-18*). Berlin: Mittler und Sohn. 626 pp.
p. 500. "Turkey plunged into a war of murder and looting (*Mord und Beutekrieg*) in the Caucasus."

Von Hindenburg. Generalfeldmarschall

Von Hindenburg, (1934). *Aus Meinem Leben*. Leipzig: S. Hirzel. 319 pp.
p. 168. "The atrocious events...which transpired in the entire domain of the Ottoman Empire and towards the end of the war occurred also in the Armenian part of the Transcaucasus... [they] were defined by the Turks as merely an internal affair..."

Austrian Testimony

10 Russland/155, No.61/P.A., 29 May 1918. Austrian Ambassador to Germany, Hohenlohe, to Austrian Foreign Minister Burian.

According to reports, "Turkey wants to annex the Caucasus entirely and exterminate the Armenians (*ausrotten*) with all means available; massacres and bloodbaths are the order of the day."

Vice Marshal Pomiankwski to the Chief of the Austrian General Staff. Kriegsarchiv, KM Präs.47-I/26-1917, 20 August 1918.

"In such a case we would be forced not only to protect the Armenians in the Caucasus against massacre but also against hunger..."

PART IV
Case Histories, Including Much-Avoided and Denied Major Events of Genocide

4

Genocide in Afghanistan
1978 - 1992

Rosanne Klass

WHAT HAPPENED AND WHAT IS KNOWN

On April 27-28, 1978, Afghan Communists under Soviet direction seized power in Afghanistan in a bloody coup. On April 22, 1992 the fourth Soviet-installed Communist regime in Kabul collapsed, following the dissolution of the U.S.S.R. which had sustained it.

During the intervening fourteen years of Communist rule, an estimated 1.5 to 2 million Afghan civilians were killed by Soviet forces and their proxies - the four Communist regimes in Kabul, and the East Germans, Bulgarians, Czechs, Cubans, Palestinians, Indians and others who assisted them.

These were not battle casualties or the unavoidable civilian victims of warfare. Soviet and local Communist forces seldom attacked the scattered guerrilla bands of the Afghan Resistance except, in a few strategic locales like the Panjsher valley. Instead they deliberately targeted the civilian population, primarily in the rural areas.

To a degree this was an uncoordinated terror campaign against any opposition, actual or potential, particularly during the period between the 1978 coup and the late December, 1979, Soviet invasion, when Soviet advisers had only partial control. But once the Soviets took direct control, operational patterns (particularly air attacks) indicated a systematic effort to depopulate selected areas on an ethnic basis - i.e., the overwhelmingly Pushtun-populated regions, stretching from the southwest to the eastern provinces - by killing hundreds of thousands and driving the rest into exile.

The Pushtuns[1] made up an estimated 40% - 50% or more of the prewar population. They are a fractious, independent people who have historically refused to be governed by any but themselves, and have dominated Afghanistan and given it its special character since the time of Alexander the Great. They have no ethnic ties north of the Oxus and were effectively indigestible. Moreover, the transfer of the Pushtun population in the form of millions of destitute refugees would also help to destabilize Pakistan, where a large Pushtun minority has long been the target of a Soviet-encouraged separatist movement backed by Kabul.

Although all parts of Afghanistan were brutalized to some degree, the treatment of civilian populations in Pushtun and non-Pushtun areas differed significantly. While military, punitive and terror operations were carried out elsewhere and several circumscribed non-Pushtun areas were depopulated to make them available for airbases, missile installations and other military uses, overall Soviet strategy focussed on emptying out the Pushtun areas and altering the ethnic makeup of Afghanistan in order to facilitate the integration of its strategically important territory into the Soviet system[2], possibly via eventual annexation to the Central Asian republics where Afghan Tajiks, Uzbeks and Turkomans have ethnic kinsmen.

According to figures of registered refugees provided by Pakistan and Iran, six million rural Afghans - most of them Pushtuns - were driven into exile in the makeshift refugee camps in these neighboring countries.

A variety of techniques were used to drive them out. Bombing reduced entire villages to rubble while helicopters slaughtered the fleeing inhabitants. Villages were singled out for gruesome massacres and other atrocities that impelled whole districts to flee. Crops were set afire at harvest time, orchards and vineyards were cut down, flocks and herds wiped out. Since it was not intended that those who fled should return, the irrigation systems on which Afghan agriculture depends were destroyed and the land turned to desert.

By the mid-1980s, Afghans made up half of all the refugees in the world, Afghanistan had been stripped of nearly one-half of its total population and the attacks continued, forcing the abandonment of the few remaining villages. The entire Pushtun south was all but abandoned.

Few concrete figures exist aside from those on registered refugees. Afghanistan has never been strong on statistics. No nationwide census has ever been taken of a population predominantly rural and widely scattered across a country the size of France, often in remote mountain villages and including a nomadic element. With illiteracy widespread, birth, deaths and other demographic data are seldom recorded. The U.N.'s prewar population estimate of 15 to 17 million was generally accepted, but extrapolations from a test census in Kabul in the mid-1970s suggested that the total population was in fact closer to 12 million and could not have been more than 15 million.[3] It is therefore impossible to develop precise figures on those killed between 1978 and 1992. In the towns, thousands were arrested and simply disappeared. In the countryside, the villagers usually buried their dead and fled.[4] Nevertheless, on the basis of a variety of sources, by the mid-1980s the U.S., and other governments had accepted the figure of 1.5 million deaths. As of 1992, United Nations estimates had reportedly raised that figure to 2 million.

Whichever prewar and casualty figures are used, it is clear that at least 10% and perhaps as much as 17% of the total prewar population was killed and an additional 35% - 50% or more were driven into exile. Altogether this amounted to a loss of half to two-thirds of Afghanistan's population.

But as regards the Pushtuns, who were singled out for "ethnic cleansing" and suffered the largest number of victims in both categories - deaths and exile - these numbers suggest that between 25% and 31% of the Pushtun population was killed. Since two-thirds to three-quarters of the victims in all categories were Pushtuns, when the numbers for deaths are combined with those for exiles, they add up to a loss of 80% - 93% of the Pushtun population. But for the post-1992 opportunity for refugees to return, this would have effectively erased the Pushtun presence and transformed the millennia-old character and identity of the region. Even if all refugees return, the irreversible losses by death will have a longterm effect.

Kandahar, for example - Afghanistan's second largest city, and overwhelmingly Pushtun - was reduced from about 250,000 to about 35,000. Whole regions were abandoned: Western observers who had seen still-functioning villages in the Logar Valley in 1985 found them totally abandoned in late 1986, following the most massive Soviet air raids of the entire war.[5]

Although the overwhelming majority of the refugees longed to return to their lands, they would never have been able to do so if the Communist regime in Kabul had not fallen as the result of the unexpected collapse of the U.S.S.R. and the loss of its massive military and economic support. It is clear that the Soviet policy makers did not intend for them to return. Thus, however the situation may develop in future, the judgment of genocide is not dependent on how many may eventually return under circumstances unforeseen by Soviet policy makers.

In the 13th century, Genghis Khan devastated and depopulated Afghanistan, slaughtering hundreds of thousands, wiping out flourishing cities and turning once-fertile areas into barren desert. The Mongols transformed what Arnold Toynbee identified as one of the key crossroads of ancient civilization into an underpopulated, impoverished backwater. Seven hundred years later Afghanistan had not yet fully recovered from the Mongol genocide. The Soviets recapitulated the Mongol devastation using the full arsenal of modern technology, including chemical contaminants. It remains to be seen how and when the Afghans will recover this time.

THE GENOCIDAL INTENTION

Before they seized power, members of the tiny, still obscure and clandestine Afghan communist party were wont to say, "We only need one million people to make the revolution. It doesn't matter what happens to the rest. We need the land, not the people." After the 1978 coup, the new communist leaders repeated this publicly, even on the radio - an open, almost casual declaration of genocidal intent.

As has too often happened elsewhere, most of those who heard them failed to take them seriously. But within hours of seizing power, the leadership of the Peoples Democratic Party of Afghanistan - Nur Mohammad Taraki, Babrak Karmal, Hafizullah Amin and others - moved to implement that policy.[6]

On the second day of the coup, President Mohammad Daoud and his entire family, including children, were murdered in the presidential palace. The entire cabinet was seized and imprisoned, as were other high level officials and former officials, including all former prime ministers, and military officers. Executions began immediately.

The unfinished Pul-i-Charkhi prison, designed to house six thousand common criminals, was immediately put into service as a political prison. Mass roundups of the educated classes began in Kabul. Over the next dozen years Pul-i-Charkhi was crammed with an estimated average of 20,000 prisoners (including women and children) at any given time. A military rifle range called "the Polygon" was transformed into an execution ground. Prisoners were routinely tortured, shot, drowned in cesspools, buried and burned alive en masse.

During the first two years, 150 - 300 prisoners were executed each night[7] at Pul-i-Charkhi alone as the regime moved to eliminate public figures, religious leaders, experienced officials, teachers, students, bureaucrats, businessmen, bankers, intellectuals, those educated abroad - in short, the whole of the small educated class that might offer any degree of opposition or potential leadership. One prominent religious family alone, the Mojadidis, lost 96 male members. No opposition was brooked: 300 Shi'ites in Kabul were slaughtered - half of them doused with kerosene and burned alive, the others buried alive in trenches by bulldozers (Barry, 1982).

A secret police - initially called by the acronym AGSA, then KAM, and finally KhAD - was rapidly established with the help of KGB and East German advisers and trainers. The basement of the Ministry of Interior and many private homes confiscated from those who had been imprisoned, murdered or fled were turned into interrogation and torture centers. Thousands simply disappeared; in many cases their fates still remain unknown.

In October 1979, the regime announced it would issue a list of those who had died at Pul-i-Charkhi (only). The first installment listing 12,000 names produced such public reaction that the remainder were not published. Extrapolating from these and other known figures, the Paris-based American scholar

Michael Barry has estimated the total killed at Pul-i-Charkhi alone in the first eighteen months at 32,000.[8]

The first refugee exodus - of the surviving urban educated class and their families - began. It eventually totalled an estimated 50-100,000, most of whom resettled in Europe and the U.S., Australia, and several Middle Eastern countries.

The Afghan communist leaders, who were not at that point fully controlled by Soviet advisers, were not political sophisticates; they had been trained only in crude, simplistic ideological slogans which they attempted now to implement in the clumsiest fashion.[9] In the provinces, where villagers rebelled at the introduction of the red flag, public denunciations of religion and other crude Marxist measures, mass atrocities began - punitive and random, unlike the systematic operations carried out after the invasion. Near Samangan, 1500 villagers were bound and thrown into the Oxus River to drown. In Kyrala (also known as Chagaserai) in Kunar province, hundreds of men and boys were called into the town square for a meeting and were then machine-gunned. As an object lesson to recalcitrant Laghman, 650 villagers were buried alive.[10]

The second exodus - of villagers - began. By August 1979, approximately 250,000 refugees were huddled in improvised camps in Pakistan.

PREVENTING INFORMATION FROM REACHING THE WORLD

Following the invasion, the systematic effort to drive the Pushtuns and others from territories the Soviets wanted strategically emptied began in earnest. Attacks throughout the southern and eastern provinces resulted in the mass exodus of millions and the creation of the empty zones desired. This policy reached its peak in the intensified bombing campaign of 1986, but all techniques were used in a campaign of terror and death against the rural civilian population: local atrocities, chemical weapons, weapons targeting children, destruction of crops, food and water supplies and animals, destruction of irrigation systems.

Stringent controls were imposed to prevent information from reaching the outer world. The Red Cross was ordered to leave the country. Attempts were made to interdict the small clandestine medical and humanitarian aid efforts mounted by Western NGOs (many of them ad hoc and most of them under-funded) and their personnel were hunted and attacked.

Only sympathetic leftwing journalists were granted visas. Those who entered clandestinely with Resistance guerrillas were openly threatened with death by Soviet officials, while millions of mines, the pervasive presence of KhAD agents and the mutual enmity of several resistance parties made their efforts extremely dangerous. Few press organizations were willing to assign reporters to take such risks and the war was covered largely by freelance journalists and humanitarian volunteers. Several journalists and French medical personnel were captured and imprisoned; several were killed. In addition, there was an intensive Soviet campaign to control and discredit those reports that did come out.

Meanwhile, in the cities Soviet and East European personnel took over all cultural institutions - schools, universities, radio, television and the press, the mosques and religious institutions, and began the process of social transformation - Sovietization.[11]

Large numbers of teenagers and adults were sent to the U.S.S.R. and Eastern Europe for visits of varying length or for training; teenagers were sent to Cuba's Isle of Pines to be trained as future cadres. When these efforts failed to produce the desired transformations, the Soviets turned to very young children, from infants to the age of ten. Some were sent to the U.S.S.R. for a year or less to be trained as spies and agents, and in 1984 Kabul announced that the Soviet Union had generously agreed to have two thousand children under the age of ten sent to the U.S.S.R. each year, there to remain for ten years or more of "education." Children were taken from school and sent off without their parents' permission or even knowledge.[12]

Since there has been no indication that this program was halted before the collapse of the Soviet Union and the Kabul regime, it can be assumed that approximately 16,000 young children were sent to the U.S.S.R. and apparently they still remain there: the interim Resistance government installed in May 1992 immediately demanded the return of the children but there has been no report of a response from Moscow.[13]

As in other cases, reports of genocide in Afghanistan initially met with disbelief. Subsequently they received only sporadic attention. In this case, there were more reasons than usual for the lack of attention. To the West, Afghanistan seems remote, exotic, unrelated to the course of world affairs and of little intrinsic interest to any but a handful of specialists: only the direct Soviet military involvement brought it to world attention.

But this Soviet involvement itself may have increased reluctance to confront events in Afghanistan. In Afghanistan, the Soviet army itself was acting. There was no client proxy interposed as in, say, Cuba, Cambodia or Ethiopia, to bear the guilt and deflect responsibility from Moscow itself. To face the reality of events in Afghanistan meant confronting the culpability of every Soviet leader from Brezhnev to Gorbachev.

The Soviet invasion of Afghanistan had derailed years of détentist hopes, and there was a widespread desire to re-establish the process and move toward friendlier relations with the U.S.S.R., especially after Mikhail Gorbachev took power.[14] The Afghan war was an impediment to the process - but public recognition that the Soviet Union, as a matter of policy, was systematically committing Nazi-style atrocities and even genocide would be an insuperable barrier. It is possible that, at least on a subconscious level, this was and perhaps even continues to impede attention, even among many of those ordinarily committed to human rights issues. (Churches of all denominations have remained almost totally silent on Afghanistan from 1978 to the present.)

In any case, for several years reports of atrocities that trickled out through the refugees pouring into Pakistan and the largely French medical personnel working inside Afghanistan were met with disbelief and often dismissed as propaganda. Except for a single article by Michael Kaufman in 1979 (Kaufman, 1979), the *New York Times* apparently gave no credence to atrocity reports, for none were published until early 1973. It was only over editorial protest that this writer was able to refer to them at all (see Klass, 1982).

In 1981, the book *Yellow Rain* (Seagrave, 1981) reported the Soviet use of chemical and biological weapons in Afghanistan and elsewhere and was soon followed by a U.S. State Department report on the use of CW and BW in Afghanistan, Laos and Cambodia. An energetic campaign to discredit their claims was mounted. The chief critic was Matthew Meselson of Harvard, who ridiculed the purported evidence of "yellow rain" as merely the excreta of a species of bee found in Laos; the testimony of witnesses and victims was dismissed as unreliable, the panic reaction of the uneducated. The acceptance of Meselson's analysis by the authoritative *New York Times* and several influential television newscasters effectively buried the issue.

In December 1981, ABC/TV showed an hour-long documentary report, "Rain of Terror," which provided considerable evidence supporting the accusation (including an interview with an Afghan victim). In 1984, William Kucewicz of *The Wall Street Journal* wrote an intensively-researched series of articles documenting Soviet use of both chemical and biological weapons. But these and extensive later documentation from a variety of sources and even film of a chemical attack in Afghanistan shown on public television in 1983 failed to revive the issue.[15]

By 1981, numerous reports were emerging of Soviet mines designed to target children - mines in the shape of dolls, toy trucks and other toys - and others disguised as wristwatches, snuffboxes, pens and other commonplace items. These mines carried just enough charge to blow off a hand or arm or foot, often leading to the slow death of a victim without access to medical care. These reports - which produced a burst of public outrage - were violently denounced by Moscow, and an intensive campaign was launched to discredit them, using as its chief argument the fact that no example had ever been produced. (Their explosiveness on contact made it nearly impossible to pick up and transport a sample intact.) Efforts were made to suggest that what Afghans called toys were in fact merely so-called "green birds": ordinary camouflaged butterfly mines, millions of which were scattered from the air, and which, although "children might mistake them for toys," were not designed for that purpose.

But French medical personnel reported seeing mines in the form of red plastic toy trucks (see Malhuret, 1983; also Livingstone and Halevy, 1990, and numerous interviews with French medical personnel in their own publications and the general press). Eventually the Kabul regime itself also produced the evidence when, after the New York-based Afghanistan Relief Committee published a full-page ad in the *New York Times* describing the lethal toys[16], an array of booby-trapped toys of the kinds described by witnesses and victims were displayed at a government press conference in Kabul as weapons provided to the Resistance by the United States.

The first extended research and reporting on atrocities in Afghanistan was done by Michael Barry (1980, 1982). Barry has been intimately associated with Afghanistan since childhood, is totally fluent in the major Afghan languages, and was moved by personal horror and moral outrage at the stories reaching him from his wide circle of Afghan acquaintances. His thoroughly researched articles in *Les Temps Modernes* (Barry, 1980) and *Commentary* (Barry, 1982) produced no significant reaction. Nevertheless he began working on the issue with intense dedication, using every avenue he could find and whatever support he could scrape up. Over the next decade he was to make numerous trips inside Afghanistan, often at great personal risk.

The field personnel of two Paris-based volunteer medical organizations - Médecins Sans Frontières (MSF/Doctors without Borders), which had rushed into action almost immediately after the invasion, and Aide Medicale International (AMI), which opened a clinic in Panjsher in 1981 - were also reporting in detail on horrendous atrocities. Volunteer groups to provide humanitarian aid to the Afghans had sprung up in many West European countries and the United States. Many of them had access to such information and were increasingly vocal on the issue.

In order to exercise damage control and control public opinion, Moscow moved to coopt such groups when possible and, if necessary, to set up competing organizations, usually working through local leftists and Afghan communists masquerading as refugees and resistance supporters. [See Bibliography: Dubious and Bad Sources] In 1981, the Tribunal des Peuples, set up by an Italian leftist as a reincarnation of the Bertrand Russell Tribunal and working closely with the Paris-based Bureau International Afghanistan, held a hearing in Stockholm at which it found the Soviet Union guilty of aggression in Afghanistan (but specifically not guilty of the use of chemical weapons) (1983).

In preparation for a second hearing to be held in Paris in December 1982, the B.I.A. sent a team headed by Barry into Afghanistan to investigate a specific atrocity, the burning alive of 105 men and boys in an irrigation tunnel in the village of Padkhwab-i-Shana in the Logar Valley. He returned with a group of eyewitnesses to this and other atrocities who presented dramatic testimony. The Tribunal found the Soviet Union guilty of "violation of the laws of war" (see Klass, January 24, 1983).

The press was not encouraged to cover the actual testimony, although it was highly dramatic and newsworthy; journalists were invited only to the brief press conference at which the judgement was announced. No interviews or other followup were scheduled for the Logar witnesses; the B.I.A./Tribunal told them to return to Pakistan immediately. However, this writer, who was present, immediately arranged for them instead to visit New York and Washington at the invitation of the Afghanistan Relief Committee for extensive press coverage there and official meetings. While they were still in Europe, the ARC arranged for them to meet with the political leaders of Britain and West Germany. This brought some press attention, and their trip to New York turned out to be a turning point in bringing the issue of human rights in Afghanistan to international attention.

Accompanied by Michael Barry, the Logar atrocity witnesses, along with a former justice of the Afghan High Court and an Afghan lawyer-turned-Resistance commander (Babrakzai, 1983), held a press conference at Freedom House in New York attended by more than one hundred journalists, including all major national press, wire services, television and radio networks. They received major attention - most notably from the *New York Times, Washington Post* and Associated Press. There followed a series of individual press interviews and meetings with community leaders and Congressional, State Department, Defense Department and White House officials in New York and Washington, culminating in a meeting with President Reagan.

The result was a sudden burst of press coverage worldwide which finally focussed international attention on the issue of human rights violations in Afghanistan.[17] From this time on, the press paid attention to atrocity reports coming from reliable sources, although seldom singling out the issue for attention.

Meanwhile, following a meeting with the author, in mid-1982 a concerned group in Oslo formed an ad hoc committee to conduct hearings on human rights violations in Afghanistan. They obtained the support of parliamentary leaders and called on this writer, Barry, Bahaouddin Majrooh and other experts to assist them in locating dozens of reliable witnesses. Unlike the B.I.A. in Paris, the Afghan Hearings Committee in Oslo sought maximum press attention for their hearing, which was held in March 1983. In the wake of the press events in New York a few weeks earlier, they were able to draw reporters from a number of countries.

All of the testimony was translated into English and published (Afghanistan Hearings Committee 1984). The sponsors took the nearly 300-page transcript to the Foreign Office, where they persuaded the Norwegian government to call for the appointment of a Special Rapporteur on Afghanistan by the United Nations Commission on Human Rights.

At that time, no Special Rapporteur had ever been appointed to inquire into violations in any Communist country. In late 1984, however, despite the vehement protests of the Kabul regime and the Soviet Union, the efforts of the Norwegians and other concerned governments culminated in the appointment of Professor Felix Ermacora of the University of Vienna as Special Rapporteur for Afghanistan, though with a carefully delimited mandate.

Meanwhile, Amnesty International's London headquarters had been noteworthy for its feeble efforts on Afghanistan (1978 et al.), but its U.S. representative for South Asian issues, Prof. Barnett R. Rubin of Yale, offered to work on Afghan issues if he could locate sources of reliable information. This writer, through the Afghanistan Relief Committee, arranged to bring to New York two of the witnesses who had testified in Oslo - one of them former police colonel Mohammad Ayub Asil who, while a member of the Resistance underground in Kabul, had been privy to KhAD and KGB operations. In April 1983, Col. Asil was introduced to Rubin, who then began what was to develop into a major inquiry over a period of several years.

A few months later, Jeri Laber, director of Helsinki Watch in New York, contacted Freedom House with a request for information about possible human rights violations in Afghanistan. She was provided with the materials then available and put in touch with Rubin, and they began a collaboration that led to five publications, the first of which appeared in 1984. (see Bibliography: entries for Laber, Rubin) These are among the most important documents available and are among the essential sources for any researcher.

Meanwhile, in late 1984, Ermacora began his research with the assistance of the computer facilities of the Bibliotheca Afghanica. Despite the limits of his mandate, which he meticulously observed, the niceties of diplomatic phraseology which he also meticulously observed, and the refusal of the Kabul regime to cooperate with him, his first report to the Commission on Human Rights in February 1985 was detailed, specific and damning. It received a good deal of press attention and triggered an extraordinary campaign of personal vilification against Ermacora. Nevertheless, he persisted, continuing to present his reports twice a year at least through 1993 and possibly later (see Bibliography).

During this same period - late 1984 - Senator Gordon J. Humphrey of New Hampshire established the joint Senate-House Task Force on Afghanistan in the U.S. Congress with Robert J. Lagomarsino of California as his co-chairman in the House of Representatives. In February 1985 the Task Force began holding hearings on many aspects of the Afghanistan issue, some of which heard detailed testimony relevant to human rights and genocide issues. In addition to those transcripts listed in the Bibliography (U.S. Congress, all), others may be available from Senate sources. Senator Humphrey (since retired from the Senate) became the point man on Afghanistan in the Congress, but he was also joined by Rep. Bill McCollum of Florida, Rep. Don Ritter of Pennsylvania, Rep. Charles Wilson of Texas, Sen. Robert Byrd and others. Some of the many statements entered in the Congressional Record from 1980 on are relevant to human rights issues.

The years 1983 to 1986 were the most active period on human rights issues relevant to the genocide in Afghanistan. However, these questions never came to dominate the Afghanistan issue as they did, for example, in Cambodia, and comparatively little has been done since.

When Gorbachev became the leader of the Soviet Union and began talking of reforms and hinting at the possibility of a withdrawal from Afghanistan, attention shifted to a possible diplomatic settlement and the withdrawal of Soviet troops. Following the signing of a U.N.-sponsored settlement on April 14, 1988, and the ostensible troop withdrawal that followed, Afghanistan all but dropped from public attention. What interest now survives appears to be limited to the power struggle emerging in the wake of the Communist regime's collapse.

In addition, from 1987 on, the Soviets expanded and upgraded their largely successful disinformation campaign whose primary element is the equating of Afghanistan and Vietnam - as mistakes stumbled into, regretted, but hard to disentangle from. Shortly before the U.S.S.R. collapsed, two books purporting to be objective reports by independent journalists were published in London and New York and received uncritical acceptance by reviewers (see in the Bibliography section, Unreliable Sources: Borovik, 1990, and Bocharov, 1990). Efforts to establish ties between Vietnam veterans in the U.S. and "Afghantsi" (veterans of the Afghan war) in the U.S.S.R. have made considerable headway. All of this ignores and falsifies long-term Soviet policy and systematic operations in Afghanistan, of course.

Given the human rights records of Marxist dictatorships, the fact that the Special Rapporteur on Afghanistan was the first to be appointed for any Communist country is in itself indicative of international reluctance to confront the Soviet Union and its clients and the actions of their leaders since Stalin. Since the collapse of the U.S.S.R., the desire to support its successor states, especially Russia, and to encourage their peaceful development has led to a widespread moratorium on discussion of their actions in their previous incarnations. But to fulfill the obligation to the historic record, it is at the least necessary to draw up an accurate moral balance sheet; the future must not equate the suffering of the Afghan (and other) victims with the political and economic problems of the executioners.

Nor should the sporadic brutalities of individual Afghans and Resistance groups be allowed to balance out the systematic horrors inflicted by the Soviets and their clients as policies. Finally, in order to reconstruct not only their country but their society, the Afghans will need an accurate assessment of what they have lost - as will the international community if it is to help the rebuilding.

CRITICAL ISSUES FACING
STUDIES OF THE AFGHAN GENOCIDE

The essential tasks of scholars of the genocide in Afghanistan are the following:

1. To collect, organize and analyze the widely-scattered published data, much of it ephemera in the general press and unpublished material from earlier researchers, journalists, medical and aid personnel. To date, the largest body

of published systematic research has been done by Michael Barry, Barnett Rubin, and Felix Ermacora. Much future understanding of this issue will undoubtedly be based on their work. But hundreds of journalists, freelancers and aid personnel spent time in various parts of Afghanistan between 1979 and 1992. Many published articles or were interviewed by a wide range of journals. Moreover, many individuals have important unpublished eyewitness material.

2. To gather the uncollected and unpublished data from survivors and witnesses and to gather physical evidence before it disappears.

3. To train Afghan researchers in reliable collecting and checking techniques to carry out the work of the above item (2).

4. To bring the evidence to international attention and at least establish the historic record.

5. It would be highly useful if copies of all research publications were deposited with the several appropriate special resource centers.

The most important problems are:
1. Lack of international interest.
2. A resulting lack of funding to support field research.
3. The unsettled situation inside Afghanistan.
4. Lack of written records.
5. An inadequate number of skilled Afghan researchers.

WHAT ARE THE REAL PROBABILITIES OF PROGRESS IN THIS FIELD?

As indicated above, the burst of interest in Soviet actions against the Afghan people was limited and soon faded; and both post-war Soviet and post-Soviet Russian efforts to erase their actions in Afghanistan from international memory have been largely successful. The chaotic power struggle in Kabul inclines the media to dismiss the Afghans as squabbling ruffians rather than the heroic victims of yore. Under the circumstances, it seems entirely likely that little further attention will be paid to this issue unless another crisis erupts.

Yet, precisely because so little work has been done on the issue of Afghanistan, the subject offers a wide range of possibilities for doctoral theses, scholarly papers and publishable articles in a number of fields. It offers many opportunities for original research.

This could make it an attractive research subject not only for specialists in South Asian, Central Asian and Near Eastern studies but also for doctoral candidates and scholars in such less specialized fields as history, sociology, political science, Soviet studies, journalism, economics, health services and military affairs (including weapons systems) - if they are made aware of it.

While some aspects require field work in Europe or South Asia, hence major funding, a great deal of the basic and essential research could be done using standard research resources. A few of the possible projects and subjects would include the following:

1. Compiling a comprehensive study of events as reported in the general press, using Lexus and Nexis data bases and library resources. Since so much of the data is scattered in the general press, this project is the essential basis for future studies. Even with the help of a computer, the task may be large enough to engage more than one scholar, especially if French-language sources are included. Individual scholars might focus on a time period, e.g., 1978-1983, 1984-1988, or analysis under various rubrics - e.g., geographic, ethnic, types of operations, etc.

2. Searching the field reports of personnel in the files of major French volunteer aid organizations - particularly MSF, Médecins du Monde, Afrane, Guilde du Raid (later Soliderités Afghanistan) and AMI, all in Paris - and compiling and analyzing the relevant data found there. The same could be done for selected German, Swedish, British and Dutch organizations.

3. Study of weapons targeting children, particularly those disguised as toys.

4. Study of children sent out of the country: what has happened to them, whether or not they return, and if so, what their role may be and the impact on their families.

5. Investigating the use of chemical and biological weapons (CW and BW).

6. Study of press coverage and international response (possibly comparative, e.g., with genocides in Biafra, Cambodia, Yugoslavia/1992).

7. A comparison of genocide in Afghanistan under Genghis Khan (1219-1223) and the Soviet Union (1979-1982). (The Soviet military routinely studies Genghis Khan's strategy and tactics, and Soviet strategists analyzed his Afghanistan campaign in planning their own.)

8. Analysis of population shifts and selective depopulation. (Sliwinski has revised some of his published figures upwards.[18])

9. Study of the social and economic impact of large numbers of the maimed in a pre-modern society. (An estimated 125,000 Afghans, many of them children, have lost one or more limbs to mines or other attacks; this estimate may be low. No estimates are yet available on the number blinded or deafened, but it is probably large, given the types of weaponry used.)

10. Study of the social and economic impact of thousands of widows in a traditional Muslim society.

11. Study of the social situation and impact of thousands of orphans, including some whose entire family has been wiped out, in a tribally-structured society based almost entirely on family and clan identities.

12. Study of international responses (both short- and long-term) to genocidal situations and their aftermath when they cease to be of geopolitical interest.

NOTES

1. Depending on the dialect spoken, they are also known as Pukhtuns. In Indian dialects (and in the West) they are known as Pathans. They were also originally known as Afghans and, as the dominant ethnic group, gave their name to the modern country when it was formed in 1747. Rulers were always Pushtuns - including the four Communist leaders: Nur Mohammad Taraki, Hafizullah Amin, Babrak Karmal and Najibullah. As of 1992, a Tajik resistance leader has been made president. "Afghan" is, however, used here only in its modern meaning of any citizen of Afghanistan, whatever his or her ethnic origin.

2. Krakowski (1987); Sliwinski (1988).

3. Personal communication from a former cabinet member. This lower projected estimate was reportedly not made public because it would have affected certain international aid programs funded on the basis of population.

4. In some cases, detailed information was obtained by Western observers in the area. See, inter alia: Klass, The new holocaust; Barry, all citations; Rubin, all citations; Sliwinski (1988); *Bulletins* of the Afghanistan Information Centre, edited by Majrooh; U.S. State Department reports listed.

5. Personal communications from Michael Barry and journalists. Also see: Bodansky (1983, 1987) for military data; Sliwinski (1988) for population changes.

6. See Klass (1987, 1990); Amstutz (1986); Barry (1982); Majrooh and Elmi (1988); Laber and Rubin (1984, 1985) and others among sources listed.

7. In describing what they saw and heard, former prisoners who were in Pul-i-Charkhi at that time have consistently used these figures in conversations with this writer since 1981. See also Barry (1982); Cate (1988); Majrooh and Elmi (1988); Elmi (1988); and others among the sources listed.

8. Barry, Michael (August 1982). Afghanistan - another Cambodia? *Commentary*, p. 30. Barry has repeated this figure elsewhere.

9. In 1965, for example, Babrak Karmal, who had by then been under KGB direction for at least a decade, was a leading figure in the secret Afghan Communist party (PDPA) and called himself a revolutionary, acknowledged that he had never heard of the French Revolution or indeed any historic revolution other than the Bolshevik revolution. Conversation with this writer, Kabul, 1965.

10. In 1983, the first Oslo hearings on human rights violations in Afghanistan were electrified when one of the witnesses testifying revealed that, as a soldier in the Afghan army on guard at the town bridge, he had witnessed the Kyrala/ Chagaserai massacre. He provided the first eyewitness confirmation of survivors' reports that a Soviet officer gave the order for the massacre (Oslo Hearings Committee, 1984, testimony of Abdul Azim, pp. 213-216).

11. Discussed in detail by Elmi (1988), B. Majrooh (In *Bulletin of the Afghanistan Centre*), A.R. Amin (1987), and also by Rubin and Laber (1984, 1985).

12. See Laber (1986). See also Rubin and Laber (1988).

13. Since 1992, a few representatives of Western humanitarian aid groups have reportedly made fruitless attempts to locate some of these children and arrange their return. No authoritative international agency has taken up the issue. This applies also to the older children known to have been sent to other East Bloc states-Poland, Czechoslovakia, and even Cuba. Personal communications to author from several East-European and scholarly sources.

14. As soon as Moscow announced that it had completed the withdrawal of its forces, the press and media interest in Afghanistan all but vanished. In fact, so great was the international desire to resume improved relations that the withdrawal was not even independently verified. Soviet claims were false: only overt ground forces were withdrawn. Other units remained and Soviet Central Asian KGB ground troops ethnically similar to Afghans were reintroduced clandestinely in Afghan uniforms. Some are still there at this writing, though it is unclear whether under the command of the Russian KGB or the successor Central Asian governments. Statements of President Zia-ul-Hag, 1989; wire service reports, published and unpublished; personal communications to author from Afghan sources, military analysts and field personnel.

15. The attack was witnessed and filmed at close range in 1981 by the Dutch freelancer Berndt de Bruin, who also photographed the blackened body of an injured companion who had had to be left behind an hour earlier when de Bruin's group heard the approaching aircraft and fled. De Bruin himself was slightly contaminated and was still suffering aftereffects more than a year later. Conversation, December 1982, with this writer, who viewed his film and brought it to the attention of Amagin, Inc., Erie, Pa., the PBS documentary maker.

16. *New York Times*. October 16, 1986.

17. See: Barry, *Toronto Star* (1983); Bernstein (1983); Tyler (1983); and other articles from the period January 28 - February 28, 1983. See also numerous other articles in major publications worldwide during that period.

18. Conversation with author, December 1989.

REFERENCES

Toynbee, Arnold (1961). *Between Oxus and Indus*. New York and London: Oxford University Press.
Toynbee describes a trip across Afghanistan, which he views in the perspective of its historic significance since prehistoric times.

Congressional Record.
The Congressional Record contains many statements on Afghanistan made over the entire decade of the war by many members of the House and Senate.

BIBLIOGRAPHY

Afghanistan Hearings Committee: *Final Report, International Afghanistan Hearings, Oslo*

13-16 March 1983 (1984). Introduction by Bjorn Stordrange, Chairman. Oslo: Afghanistan Hearings Committee. 274 pp.

A group of concerned Norwegians formed an ad hoc committee in late 1982 for the purpose of holding hearings on human rights violations in Afghanistan before an international panel of questioners. A number of Afghan victims and eyewitnesses were brought to Oslo to testify. For the first hearing (March 1983), the committee arranged an elaborate system to record, translate and transcribe all of the testimony. A limited number of copies of the English-language translation of the transcript were later distributed to scholars, participants and others concerned.

The sponsoring committee, which included representatives of every major Norwegian political party, presented the transcript to the Foreign Office, which led to a Norwegian initiative in the United Nations Commission on Human Rights that resulted in the appointment of a Special Rapporteur for Afghanistan.

The transcript contains detailed and often dramatic testimony by torture victims and eyewitnesses to atrocities. While it had no general distribution, it is available at some archival sources (including those listed below under Archival Resources) and possibly through the Norwegian Foreign Office. A second hearing was held in 1986; no transcript was distributed but it may have been filed with the Foreign Office.

Almqvist, Borje (1983). Eyewitnesses to Afghanistan at war. *World Affairs: Special Issue on Afghanistan*, 145 (3), Winter 1982-1983, 311-313. Translated from *Dagens Nyeter*, Stockholm, 12 September 1982.

In the summer of 1982, Almqvist, a Swedish journalist, visited 30 villages in the Logar valley soon after a major Soviet operation. He collected and reported many eyewitness accounts of Soviet atrocities against the civilian publication.

Amin, A. Rasul (1987). The sovietization of Afghanistan. In Klass, Rosanne (Ed.), *Afghanistan - The Great Game Revisited*. New York: Freedom House/ University Press of America, pp. 301-334.

Amin, a former professor at Kabul University, heads the Jihad Works Translation Center in Peshawar, a group of largely western-educated refugee intellectuals who translated relevant materials (e.g., Orwell) into Afghan languages and distributed them clandestinely inside occupied Afghanistan. He had access to a great deal of information.

Amstutz, J. Bruce (1986). *Afghanistan: The First Five Years of Soviet Occupation*. Washington, D.C.: National Defense University Press. 544 pp.

The author, an American diplomat, served in the U.S. embassy in Kabul 1977-1980 and took over as chargé d'affaires after the American ambassador was murdered in February 1979. See pp. 223-226, 263-322 for material relevant to human rights and genocide issues. Fully annotated; index. Bibliography includes lists of newspapers and periodicals that frequently reported on Afghanistan and some short-lived specialized publications, not listed here, which may be useful. Ambassador Dubs' death is not discussed.

Babrakzai, Omar, and Yussofzai, Ghafoor (1983). Atrocities and violations of human rights and international law in Afghanistan. *World Affairs: Special Issue on Afghanistan*, 145(3), Winter 1982-1983, pp. 299-314.

Statements made to the Committee on International Human Rights of the New York Bar Association in January 1983 by a Sorbonne-educated former justice of the High Court of Appeals in Kabul and an Afghan lawyer turned Resistance commander, detailing the destruction of all legal restraints and destruction of the entire legal system. Also includes eyewitness information about atrocities.

Barry, Michael (1984). *Le Royaume d'Insolence*. Paris: Flammarion. 305 pp. [Revised English edition reportedly planned as *Afghanistan: The Destruction of a Nation*. London: Collins.]
A scholar of Islamic studies involved with Afghanistan since childhood and totally fluent in Afghan languages, Barry was the first and remains one of the most important researchers on Afghan genocide. A meticulous scholarly investigator with an encyclopedic knowledge of Afghan society. His work is one of the essential sources.

Beaurecueil, Serge de (1983). *Mes Enfants de Kaboul*. Paris: J.-C. Lattes. 217 pp.
Father Beaurecueil, a Dominican orientalist and teacher, lived for many years in Kabul, where he provided a home for handicapped boys until they were seized as Western agents by the communist regime.

Beaurecueil, Serge de (n.d.; 1989?). *Chronique d'un Temoin Privilegie I: 1979: la Terreur. Lettres d'Afghanistan de Serge de Beaurecueil*. Paris: CEREDAF [Centre de Recherches et d'Etudes Documentaires sur l'Afghanistan] 124 pp.
Father Beaurecueil's day-by-day eyewitness chronicle of the first communist reign of terror, 1978-1979.

Beaurecueil, Serge de (1990). *Chronique d'un Temoin Privilegie II: 1980: Au bord du désespoir. Lettres d'Afghanistan de Serge de Beaurecueil*. Paris: CEREDAF. 206 pp.
A continuation of his eyewitness report: Kabul in the "atmosphere of death" following the Soviet invasion.

Bodansky, Yossef (1983). The bear on the chessboard: Soviet military gains in Afghanistan. *World Affairs Special Issue on Afghanistan*, 145(3), Winter 1982-3, pp. 284-286 and *passim*.
Details of the Soviet use of chemical weapons in Afghanistan, including identification of the specific chemicals used. Annotated.

Bodansky, Yossef (1987). Soviet military operations in Afghanistan. In Klass, Rosanne (Ed.), *Afghanistan - The Great Game Revisited*, pp. 259-260 and *passim*.
Specifics of chemical weapons used in Afghanistan and anti-civilian genocidal strategies and tactics by one of the leading international experts on Soviet military operations in Afghanistan. Annotated.

Bonner, Arthur (1987). *Among the Afghans*. Durham, NC, and London: Duke University Press. 366 pp.
A report on the war, including mass atrocities against civilians, by a veteran journalist who travelled in many parts of Afghanistan for two years (1985-87) for the *New York Times*. Includes reports on atrocities, attacks on civilians, depopulation, etc.

Broxup, Marie (Ed.) (1988). Afghanistan according to Soviet sources, 1980-1985. *Central Asian Survey, Special Issue on Afghanistan*, 197 - 204. Papers from the CEREDAF Conference, Paris, November 1986.
Broxup assesses Soviet attitudes toward Afghanistan and finds traditional Russian contempt for Central Asians combined with a unique ruthlessness and tensions. Several other papers, including the several tributes to Bahaouddin Majrooh, contain references to Afghan genocide.

Cate, Curtis (Ed.) (1988). *Afghanistan: The Terrible Decade, 1978-1988*. New York: American Foundation for Resistance International. 84 pp.
A useful chronology of events, which includes specific information - dates, locations,

numbers killed - on several large-scale massacres and other atrocities, plus a summary of data on numbers killed, villages destroyed, etc., and useful maps. Contributors include Michael Barry, Alexandre Bennigsen, Sidney Hook, Rosanne Klass, Chantal Lobato and others. [This appeared earlier in a slightly different French-language edition: *Afghanistan: dix années terribles, 1977-1987* (1987). Paris: Internationale de la Résistance. 82 pp.]

Elmi, [S.M.] Yusuf (Ed.) (1988). *Afghanistan: A Decade of Sovietization.* Peshawar, Pakistan: Afghan Jehad Works Translation Center. 375 pp. [GPO Box 417, Peshawar]
Distinguished Afghan scholars in exile provide details of cultural genocide and more. Uneven but contains some important information. This is Part 2 of a work Elmi undertook with Bahaouddin Majrooh (see Majrooh, below) and completed after Majrooh's murder. Elmi's center enables Afghan intellectuals in exile to address their country's situation. Elmi himself was severely deafened by torture, hence is more isolated from Western contacts and less widely known internationally than was Majrooh, but is highly respected.

Fullerton, John (n.d., 1983?). *The Soviet Occupation of Afghanistan.* Hong Kong: South China Morning Post. 205 pp.
Fullerton covered the early years of the war for *The Telegraph* (London), *Far Eastern Economic Review*, and Reuters and was one of the first to report on atrocities against civilian population and the Soviet strategy of depopulating large areas. Historical data is flawed but firsthand reporting is excellent.

Girardet, Edward R. (1985). *Afghanistan: The Soviet War.* New York: St. Martin's Press. 259 pp.
Girardet, correspondent for *The Christian Science Monitor*, made many trips into Afghanistan from 1979 on, and wrote extensively on genocide issues. Chapters on repression and Sovietization, pp. 107-161. See also Girardet's reports in *Christian Science Monitor*, 1979-1988.

Goodwin, Jan (1987). *Caught in the Crossfire.* New York: E.P. Dutton. 330 pp.[no index]
A former women's magazine editor especially concerned with Afghan women and children, Goodwin spent several months travelling widely inside Afghanistan in 1984-1985 and later became a field administrator for Save the Children Foundation's Afghan program. Her first person narrative includes atrocity reports.

Klass, Rosanne (Ed.) (1983). Introduction and comments. In *World Affairs: Special Issue on Afghanistan*, 145 (3), Winter 1982-3. (97 pp.), pp. 220-224, 299-300.
This was the first American publication to provide data calling into question the initial assessments of the Afghan crisis, its causes and its possible outcome. The introduction outlines the significance of the analyses and calls attention to several genocidal aspects of Soviet and Afghan communist policies.

Klass, Rosanne (Ed.) (1987). *Afghanistan - The Great Game Revisited.* New York: Freedom House/University Press of America. 1987; enlarged second edition 1990. 565 pp. Index, bibliography and substantive as well as source notes.
This is the standard comprehensive reference resource on the Soviet-Afghan war. For material relevant to genocide, see in particular individual chapters listed below (Amin, Bodansky, Klass, Krakowski, Roberts, Rubin) and *passim* references in other chapters.

Klass, Rosanne (1987). The great game revisited. In Klass, Rosanne (Ed.), *Afghanistan - The Great Game Revisited, ibid.*, pp. 17-22.
Introductory chapter, completely different from 1979 article with the same title. Criticizes international silence in the face of Soviet conduct of genocide and cultural destruction in Afghanistan.

Klass, Rosanne (1990). The Geneva Accords. In Klass, Rosanne (Ed.), *Afghanistan - The Great Game Revisited*, 2nd edition, 1990, *op. cit.*, pp. 377-378, 380-381, 384.
Discusses the 1989 settlement negotiated by the United Nations and guaranteed by the United States and the Soviet Union. Critical assessment of its potential consequences, including effects related to aspects of genocide. Had the U.S.S.R. not collapsed, leading to the collapse of its puppet regime in Kabul, this settlement would have consolidated depopulation and cultural genocide.

Krakowski, Elie (1987). Afghanistan and Soviet global interests. In Klass, Rosanne (Ed.), *Afghanistan - The Great Game Revisited*, op. cit., pp.161-185.
See pp. 176-183 for discussion of Soviet plans to depopulate selected areas and expel selected ethnic groups in order to integrate parts of Afghanistan directly into the Soviet system. Dr. Krakowski served as director of the Office of Regional Defense in the Policy Section of the U.S. Defense Department in the 1980s.

Laber, Jeri, and Rubin, Barnett R. (1988). *"A Nation Is Dying."* Evanston, Ill.: Northwestern University Press. 179 pp.
A condensation of the two 1984 -1985 Helsinki Watch reports (see below: Laber, Rubin) plus additional material. Source notes, notes on methodology, and bibliography.

Laber, Jeri, and Rubin, Barnett R. (1984). *Tears, Blood and Cries: Human Rights in Afghanistan Since the Invasion, 1979-1984.* New York: Helsinki Watch. 210 pp. [A Russian language edition, *Pogibayet Tselii Narod* (1984), was smuggled into the U.S.S.R.]
The first of five publications prepared and/or issued by Helsinki Watch which form the single most comprehensive published source on genocide-related issues in Afghanistan. Carefully researched by experienced investigators, highly detailed, based on taped interviews with hundreds of eyewitnesses, victims, survivors and defectors in Pakistan, Europe and the U.S. Annotated.

Livingstone, Neil C., & Halevy, David (1990). *Inside the PLO.* NY: William Morrow.
Photograph of booby-trapped explosive doll facing p. 224. This is the only published photograph of a doll of the type widely reported to have been used, with other explosive toys, against Afghan children.

Majrooh, Bahaouddin, and Elmi, S.M.Y [usuf] (1988). *The Sovietization of Afghanistan.* Peshawar, Pakistan: Afghan Jehad Works Translation Centre. 195 pp.
Study by two distinguished Afghan scholars in exile. Chapters by various authors are uneven in quality; several by Majrooh and others are excellent and contain important data, including statistics, not available elsewhere. Majrooh, head of the Afghanistan Information Centre (see below), was internationally regarded as the most authoritative Afghan scholar working on the issue.

Malhuret, Claude (1983). Report from Afghanistan. *Foreign Affairs*, 62(2), 426-435.
Dr. Malhuret, then executive director of Médecins Sans Frontières, later became France's first Secretary of State for Human Rights. His sophisticated account of Soviet policies, based on observations by MSF doctors, was a significant factor in

persuading the press of their reality. Condensed in *Reader's Digest*, May 1984 (U.S. edition; later overseas).

Reshtia, Sayed Qassem. (1984) *The Price of Liberty: The Tragedy of Afghanistan*. Rome: Bardi Editore. 141 pp. [In English]
 A survey by a respected Afghan diplomat and historian living in exile in Switzerland, using personal experiences and contacts inside his homeland. Includes a full chapter on human rights violations; other references passim.

Roberts, Guy B. (1987). Selected treaties and international law relevant to human rights issues in Afghanistan. In Klass, Rosanne (Ed.), *Afghanistan - The Great Game Revisited, op. cit.*, Appendix I, pp. 359-368 in 1st edition (pp. 393-401, 2nd edition).
 Summaries of relevant principles of international law, basic treaty principles and applicable treaties to which the U.S.S.R., Afghanistan or both are parties, including the 1907 Hague Convention IV, the 1925 Geneva Protocol prohibiting chemical weapons, the 1945 United Nations Convention on the Prevention of Genocide, the four 1949 Geneva conventions, the 1972 Biological Weapons convention and the 1980 Conventional Weapons convention. Sources of full texts are given.

Rubin, Barnett R. (1987). Human rights in Afghanistan. In Klass, Rosanne (Ed.), *Afghanistan - The Great Game Revisited, op. cit.*, pp. 335-358.
 Includes additional information and updating of Rubin's Helsinki Watch reports, plus overall assessments.

Rubin, Barnett R. (1985). *To Die in Afghanistan*. New York: Helsinki Watch. 106 pp.
 The second carefully researched, highly detailed report on Afghanistan issued by Helsinki Watch. Supplement to Laber and Rubin's *Tears, Blood and Cries*. Annotated. One of the essential documents.

Schultheis, Rob (1992). *Night Letters: Inside Wartime Afghanistan*. New York: Orion Books. 155 pp.
 Schultheis, a freelance journalist who had visited Afghanistan several times in the 1970s, made repeated trips there from 1984 to 1989 to report on the war. This personal memoir describes atrocities.

Schwartzstein, Stuart J.D. (1983). Chemical warfare in Afghanistan. *World Affairs: Special Issue on Afghanistan*, 145(3), Winter 1982-3, 267-272.
 A former Foreign Service officer, Schwartzstein directed the Chemical/Biological Weapons Project of the Institute for Foreign Policy Analysis.

Seagrave, Sterling (1981). *Yellow Rain: A Journey Through the Terror of Chemical Warfare*. New York: M. Evans. 316 pp.
 The Soviets employed chemical and biological weapons widely in Afghanistan, often against civilian targets. Seagrave's ground-breaking study on mycotoxin weapons, which brought the issue of CW and BW to public attention and established the term "yellow rain," includes nearly 20 detailed entries on its use in Afghanistan. Also useful in connection with research on Cambodia, Laos, Ethiopia, Yemen, etc. Notes, bibliography, index.

Shabbir, Syed Hussein; Alvi, Abdul Hamid; Rizvi, Absar Hussain (1980). *Afghanistan Under Soviet Occupation*. Islamabad: World Affairs Publications. 208 pp.

By three well-known Pakistani journalists, includes detailed reports of atrocities under pre-invasion communist regimes.

Sikorski, Radek (1990). *Dust of the Saints: A Journey Through War-torn Afghanistan.* New York: Paragon House. 273 pp. [London: Chatto & Windus (1989)]
First-person journalistic narrative includes atrocity incidents and reports.

Official Reports and documents

United Kingdom, Foreign and Commonwealth Office, (November 1980). The Sovietization of Afghanistan and other reports. London: Background Brief Series.
This office issued several papers every year for more than a decade on various aspects of the war, many of which include useful information and serve to verify reports by others. In addition, the British Information Service issued excellent films each December; several contain material relevant to genocide.

U.S. Congress. Congressional Task Force on Afghanistan (February 25, 1985). *Hearing on Famine.* Humphrey, Sen. Gordon J.; Lagomarsino, Rep. Robert J.; Lord Cranborne, Robert; Crouan, Dr. Antoine; Haq, Abdul; Klass, Rosanne; Lohbeck, Kurt; Rubin, Barnett R.; and Wheeler, Jack. 50 pp. prepared statements. 134 pp. official transcript, question period. Available at specialized archives (see below) and possibly from the Senate Foreign Relations Committee.
Former Sen. Humphrey and Rep. Lagomarsino were co-chairmen of the Task Force. Lord Cranborne chaired AfghanAid, London; Crouan administered the Afghanistan program of Médecins Sans Frontières; Abdul Haq was a major Resistance commander for the Kabul region; Klass was director of the Afghanistan Information Center, Freedom House; Lohbeck was a freelance journalist; Rubin was human rights investigator for Helsinki Watch; Wheeler went into Afghanistan clandestinely as director of the Freedom Research Foundation.

U.S. Congress. Congressional Task Force on Afghanistan (March 4, 1985). *Hearing on Medical Conditions in Afghanistan.* Humphrey, Sen. Gordon J.; Symms, Sen. Steven; Lagomarsino, Rep. Robert J.; Fournot, Dr. Juliette; De Vecchi, Robert; Akram, Dr. Khalid; and Simon, Dr. Robert. 31 pp. prepared statements. 98 pp. official transcript, question period. Availability as above.
Fournot was field director of Médecins Sans Frontières' program in Afghanistan; De Vecchi was Deputy Director of the International Rescue Committee; Akram was an Afghan physician; Simon headed International Medical Corps. They testified to the suffering of the civilian population created by Soviet policies of decimation and depopulation.

German Federal Republic: Bundestag hearings.
In (former) West Germany Dr. Jürgen Todenhöfer, member of the Bundestag for CDF/CSU, was the leading spokesman for the Afghanistan issue in the FRG much as Sen. Gordon J. Humphrey was in the U.S. Congress. Following a clandestine trip inside Afghanistan he held hearings on Afghan genocide in the Bundestag in January 1985; some of these were broadcast on the radio. For information on testimony, transcripts and publications, contact Dr. Todenhöfer or the records offices of the Bundestag in Bonn.

Ermacora, Felix. *Report* [s] *on the Situation of Human Rights in Afghanistan Prepared by the Special Rapporteur, Mr. Felix Ermacora, in Accordance with Commission on Human*

Rights resolution 1985/88. Geneva and New York: United Nations Commission on Human Rights.

From 1985 on, the Special Rapporteur submitted two separate reports each year: one to the meeting of the Commission on Human Rights in Geneva, one to the General Assembly in New York. These are essential sources.

The first two are perhaps the strongest and most comprehensive. Dr. Ermacora was subjected to a campaign of vilification and at times even threats. Efforts were made to limit publication of his fourth and fifth reports, and were partly successful. Some observers feel that the reports from 1988 on were somewhat constrained.

Available in major research libraries or from United Nations Commission on Human Rights, Room 3660, United Nations, New York, NY 10017; or from Commission offices in Geneva. Some were published in both English and French, some in English only. When ordering, give document numbers and dates if possible and choice of language if applicable (reports 7, 10, 11 are available only in English). For document numbers of more recent reports, check with Commission offices.

Document No. E/CN.4/1985/21. 19 February 1985. 57 pp. [first report, English/French]

Document No. A/40/843. 5 November 1985. 43 pp. [second report, English/ French]

Document No. E/CN.4/1986/24. 17 February 1986. 28 pp. [third report, English/ French]

Document No. A/41/778. 9 January 1987. 25 pp. [fourth report, English/French] Originally issued 31 October 1986 but only in part; following widespread publicity, the full text was made public ten weeks later.

Document No. E/CN.4/1987/22. 19 January 1987. 12 pp.[fifth report, English/French] Four months after it was formally submitted to the Commission in Geneva, it had not yet been published. It was finally made available to the persistent.

Document No. E/ CN.4/ 1987/ 22. 19th February 1987. 12 pp. [sixth report, English/French]

Document No. A/42667/Corr.1. 10 November 1987. 31 pp. [seventh report, English only]

Document No. E/ CN.4/ 1988/25. 26 February 1988. 13 pp. [eighth report, English/French]

Document No. A/ 43/ 742. 24 October 1988. 37 pp. [ninth report, English/French]

Document No. E/ CN.4/ 1989/ 24. 16 February 1989. 17 pp. [tenth report, English only]

Document No. A/ 44/ 669. 30 October 1989. 23 pp. [eleventh report, English only]

U.S. Department of State. *Country Reports on Human Rights Practices for 19-- .* Washington: U.S. Government Printing Office. An annual publication. Usually 1400-1500 pp.

An annual compilation of reports on all countries in the world, submitted to the Committee on Foreign Relations of the U.S. Senate and the Committee on Foreign Affairs of the U.S. House of Representatives in accordance with sections of the Foreign Assistance Act of 1961 and other legislation, in order "to assist Members of Congress

in considering legislation in the area of foreign assistance."
For genocide in Afghanistan, see especially reports from 1978 on; for comparative purposes, see also those of 1964-73 (the constitutional period) and 1973-78 (following the Communist-aided coup that overthrew the liberal constitution and the monarchy and installed Prince Mohammad Daoud.)

U.S. Department of State.
In 1980-81, the U.S. State Department, faced with criticism of its accusations of Soviet use of chemical weapons, issued a number of supportive items, some of them mimeographed and undated and/or without formal identification of the author or the office issuing them. These included two massive documents: *Reports of the Use of Chemical Weapons in Afghanistan, Laos and Cambodia* (Summer 1980) and *Update to the Compendium on the Reports of the Use of Chemical Weapons* (March 1981). It may be possible to locate some of this material through the State Department; many items are in the archival resources listed below.

United States Information Agency/Service [USIA/USIS]. *Films and publications.*
USIA published many materials and released a number of excellent films available through USIS offices and libraries only outside of the United States; by law they cannot be distributed in the U.S. Congress approved a single exception to the law for the film, *Thanksgiving in Peshawar*, narrated by Kirk Douglas; it is available from USIA in Washington for viewing in the U.S. and contains material of value on atrocity survivors in the refugee camps, especially children.

Van Hollen, Eliza, et al. *Afghanistan: [...] Years of Soviet Occupation.* Annual series, December, 1980-1987. The number in the title changed each year to reflect the number of years of Soviet occupation [e.g., *Two Years of Soviet Occupation* (1981), *Three Years of Soviet Occupation* (1982)]. Title was changed in 1988/1989 to *Afghanistan: Soviet Occupation and Withdrawal.* Washington: Bureau of Public Affairs, U. S. Department of State. Usually 18-24 pp.
Prepared by the Bureau of Intelligence and Research of the U.S. State Department as part of a series of Special Reports on the situation in Afghanistan. These and other State Department publications on Afghanistan, including special reports and policy statements, are available from the Bureau of Public Affairs, Department of State.

Articles in Popular Publications

Barron, John (November 1985) "From Russia with hate." *Reader's Digest*, 127 (763).
Soviet use of booby-trapped toys and other disguised mines targeting Afghan children.

Barry, Michael (July-August 1980). Répression et guerre soviétiques. *Les Temps Modernes*, No. 408-409, 171-236.
Barry's first writing on the subject, and one of the first to appear anywhere. *Les Temps Modernes* devoted this entire issue to Afghanistan.

Barry, Michael (August 1982). Afghanistan - another Cambodia? *Commentary*, 74(2), 29-37.
A highly detailed report on mass political arrests, secret mass executions, use of napalm against civilians and other atrocities under the first two communist regimes (April 1978-December 1979) by one of the first and most important scholars to investigate. During this period an entire generation of educated Afghans, all established leadership

classes (political and religious) and all potential opposition leaders were systematically wiped out and the first mass slaughters occurred in the provinces. Eyewitness and victim testimony and detailed analysis of numbers of victims.

Barry, Michael (15 January 1983). The trail that led to a massacre. *Toronto Star.*
A report on Barry's on-site investigation of the massacre of 105 men and boys burned alive in an irrigation tunnel at the village of Padkhwab-i-Shahna in the Logar Valley by Soviet troops. Includes specifics of other atrocities as well. Two full pages,with photographs. Barry accompanied six eyewitnesses to Paris and New York as translator.

Bernstein, Richard (28 January 1983). Afghans, in New York, tell of a massacre by Russians. *New York Times.*
Detailed report on press conference held by the survivors of the Padkhwab-i-Shahna atrocity. When the BIA brought the witeses to Paris for the Tribunal des Peuples, it did not present them to the press. They were subsequently brought to the U.S. by the Afghanistan Relief Committee and brought to media attention at a major press conference. See also "U.S. reiterates support," brief item, same page: the State Department verified the Afghan survivors' account.

Brailsford, Guy (Spring 1989). Room for doubt. *Afghanistan: A Quarterly Magazine.* Issue No. 10, 17-19. London: AfghanAid
In exchange with Klass 1989, Brailsford argues that there is insufficient evidence to justify claim that U.S.S.R. used chemical weapons and boobytrapped toys.

General Press Reports about Afghanistan.
Aside from Helsinki Watch publications, U.N. Special Rapporteur reports, and Afghanistan Information Centre bulletins, the general press and wire services are the major source of ongoing information from about 1983 to date. After the New York press conference of atrocity survivors on January 27, 1983 [but not earlier; see Michael Kaufman, Richard Bernstein, Patrick E. Tyler et al.], specific articles about atrocities, famine, depopulation, etc., began to appear in general press. Even more often, brief references can be found in news stories about the fighting or the refugees.
The best general media sources are (roughly in order of usefulness): *Christian Science Monitor* [Edward Girardet reports]; *Telegraph* (London); *Washington Times; Washington Post; Economist; Far Eastern Economic Review; Associated Press, Reuters and Agence France Press bulletins; Los Angeles Times; Reader's Digest; New York Times,* including *Sunday Magazine Section; National Review; Time* [Edward Desmond's reports] and *Newsweek.* But reliability is uneven; some journals sometimes agreed to Kabul regime controls in order to get "exclusive" reports.
See also *Le Monde* and other French journals, Swedish press, and articles by J. A. Emerson Vermaat in the Netherlands. Because of the presence of many French medical and other aid personnel inside Afghanistan and the capture of several, the French press gave the issue more coverage than did others in Europe.

Gertz, Bill (20 January 1989). Biological weapons made in Soviet Union, report says. *Washington Times.*
Cites report prepared for National Security Council by U.S. intelligence agencies including confirmation of toxin weapons use in Afghanistan, Laos and Cambodia and transfer of technology to Iraq and Libya.

Girardet, Edward R. (1980-1989) Reports in *The Christian Science Monitor* 1980-1989.
Girardet provided the only consistent coverage in the American media, making many

trips inside Afghanistan with the Resistance and, in particular, repeatedly visiting the Panjsher Valley and the eastern provinces. He became actively involved in trying to bring atrocities to public attention, testifying at a number of hearings in Europe and the U.S.

Hyman, Anthony (February 1982). Afghan intelligentsia 1978-81. *Index on Censorship*, 11(1), 8-10.
Systematic repression and mass executions of the educated class during the first four years of communist rule reported by a British expert.

Kaufman, Michael (11 September 1979). Report on Afghan who said he saw soldiers blind and strangle children. *New York Times*.
This was the first report of atrocities to appear in any major American publication. The information was cautiously labeled as unconfirmed but Kaufman was clearly shaken by what he was told. Kaufman's account indicates the probable presence of Soviet personnel during this atrocity.
There was no follow-up and the *Times* gave no credence to atrocity stories until the witnesses to the Padkhwab-i-Shana atrocity came to New York in early 1983. See Barry, 15 January 1983, and Bernstein (above); Klass, 4 January 1982, and Tyler (below). Following the *Times'* lead, neither did any other major U.S. media. Dan Rather's attempt to report first-hand was widely ridiculed. Except for Girardet's reports in the *Christian Science Monitor* from 1980 on, no major news organization investigated human rights issues in Afghanistan until 1983.
GEO magazine sent Klass to Peshawar in August 1979 to report on the early resistance, but dismissed her report of mass executions at Pul-i-Charkhi and the Polygon in Kabul and massacres of civilians and chemical attacks in Kunar and other provinces as unbelievable and refused to print it. Reports of atrocities and genocidal policies consistently met with editorial disbelief at many publications and were dismissed as propaganda until 1983.

Klass, Rosanne (25 January 1980). Mr. Brezhnev's doctrine. National Review, XXXII(2), 99-100.
Early mention of mass attacks on civilians.

Klass, Rosanne (February 1980). The Afghans may win. *New York Times*, Op Ed page.
The first mention in the U.S. press of cultural genocide as Soviet policy.

Klass, Rosanne (March/April 1981). Missing in action: treasures of Afghanistan. *Asia*, 3(6), 26-35, 52.
Also: Letters, *Asia*, May/June 1981, 4(1), 5, 52-53.
The first and thus far the only report on looting and destruction of major Afghan art, particularly from the Kabul Museum. It is still unclear how much damage was done and how much of Afghanistan's major artistic heritage was stolen and destroyed. The Buddhist sites at Hadda were apparently deliberately destroyed by the radical Islamic Hezb-i-Islami party, but elsewhere objects were reportedly looted by Soviet and Afghan communist officials. Reports that the Soviets had looted and destroyed Afghan art were heatedly contested in an exchange of letters in the May/June issue.

Klass, Rosanne (4 January 1982). U.S., aid the Afghans. *New York Times*, Op Ed page.
The first assertion in the most influential American publication that Soviets were carrying out mass atrocities; this claim was judged dubious and excessive by editors who urged that it be omitted.

Klass, Rosanne (24 January 1982). Lifting the curtain on Afghanistan's horror. *Wall Street Journal*.
Report on the testimony of eyewitnesses and victims at the Paris hearings of Tribunal des Peuples [See below; also Bernstein, Tyler and general press.].

Klass, Rosanne (4 October 1985). The new holocaust. *National Review*, XXXVII(19), 28-29.
Discusses failure of the press to report on genocide in Afghanistan. Detailed reports of the systematic Soviet slaughter of 631 villagers in Baghlan province, December 1984, and nearly 800 in Laghman province, April 1985. Condensed and combined with article by Jean-Francois Revel in *Reader's Digest*, March 1986 (U.S. editions: later issues overseas).

Klass, Rosanne (24 December 1986). The Afghan holocaust: Year eight. *Wall Street Journal*.
Depopulation of selected regions, desertification, civilians as targets, lack of international concern.

Klass, Rosanne (March 1987). Letter. *Commentary*, 83(3), 18.
Letter discussing the silence of churches and human rights spokesmen about genocide in Afghanistan.

Klass, Rosanne (Spring 1989). Facing a terrible truth. *Afghanistan: A Quarterly Magazine*, Issue No. 10, 15-17. [London: Afghan Aid].
Evidence of chemical warfare and toy bombs in Afghanistan. Response to doubts expressed in review of *Afghanistan - The Great Game Revisited* in the previous issue. [See above: Brailsford; also Livingstone and Halevy]

Kucewicz, William (23 April-18 May 1984). Beyond "yellow rain." *Wall Street Journal*.
Eight-part series on Soviet chemical, biological and genetic weapons development. "Soviets search for eerie new weapon," 23 April; "The science of snake venom," 25 April; "Surveying the lethal literature,"27 April; "Lead scientist in a scourge search," 1 May; "Accident prone and asking for calamity," 3 May; "The gates slam shut on a microbiologist," 8 May; "A non-stop Russian response to WW II," 10 May; "The threat of Soviet genetic engineering," 18 May.
A carefully researched series that not only supported reports of the use of tricoth-ecene mycotoxins in Afghanistan, Southeast Asia and elsewhere by the U.S.S.R. and its proxies but pursued additional aspects of the CW/BW issue. The series implicitly rebutted and demolished the theory put forth by several academics that evidence of "yellow rain" was merely a misunderstood natural phenomenon, which nevertheless continued to be accepted by leading press and media. Relevant for Laos, Cambodia and Ethiopia as well as Afghanistan.[See Kucewicz below; also Meselson et al.]

Kucewicz, William (6 September 1985). The "bee feces" theory undone. *Wall Street Journal*.
An analysis of strenuous efforts by Matthew Meselson of Harvard, Thomas Seeley of Yale and their associates to dismiss U.S. State Department and other reports of the use of mycotoxin weapons as an uninformed misidentification of naturally occurring droppings of a bee species native to Laos, Cambodia and other parts of South East Asia.

Mackenzie, Richard (5 December 1988). The butchers of Kabul. *Insight*, 4(49), cover story: 8-17.
KhAD, the Afghan KGB, and its operations against the population. Mackenzie covered

the Afghanistan story for several years and continues to do so. See also Mackenzie's other reports on Afghanistan in *Insight* and *The Washington Times* from 1985/86 on. As of 1992, he continues to visit Afghanistan and report for various publications.

Majrooh, Bahaouddin (June 1985). Killing the fields: The other Afghan war. *Wall Street Journal*.
Systematic physical destruction of selected rural areas, including calculated desertification, to drive out particular ethnic groups, especially Pushtuns. (See Krakowski.)

New York Times, 6 June, 1984. 500,000 Afghans are reported to face starvation.
Report on press conference held by Lord Cranborne to announce the AfghanAid famine report (see D'Souza below).

Parry, John (March 14, 1985). U.N. rights unit assails Soviet abuses in Afghanistan. *Washington Post*.
Soviet efforts to discredit Prof. Felix Ermacora, Special Rapporteur of the U.N. Commission on Human Rights. See also other reports in the world press over several days in March 1985.

Revel, Jean-François (4 October 1985). The awful logic of genocide. *National Review*, XXXVII (19), 22-28.
Analysis of international silence on Soviet genocide in Afghanistan and the political implications of that silence. Includes detailed atrocity reports from French sources. Condensed in *Reader's Digest*, March 1986, pp. 106-109 (later issues overseas).

Rubin, Barnett R (25 May 1984). Afghans, beleaguered. *New York Times*, Op Ed page.
Describes systematic Soviet operations against the civilian population.

Schultheis, Rob (8 January 1989). The Soviets' ugly exit: Do atrocities belie Moscow's pr?" *Washington Post*.
Atrocities against civilians prepared and conducted by departing Soviet troops, including the booby-trapping of food supplies and beds, the use of lethal chemicals, mines disguised as toys, etc. See also Schultheis' numerous other reports from 1980 on in *Washington Post* and *Rolling Stone*.

Tyler, Patrick E., and Jacobson, Philip (13 February 1983). The horrors and rewards of the Soviet occupation of Afghanistan: Burning 105 villagers to death in a sacred underground stream. *Washington Post (Sunday edition)*, pp.C1 & C4 (two full pages).
Detailed report on the Padkhwab-i-Shana massacre, based on extended interviews with the eyewitnesses who came to New York and reproducing their diagramatic drawings of the Soviet operation.

Van Dyk, Jere (2 November 1984). M*A*S*H without laughter. *National Review*, IIIVI(21), 40-42.
Report on French medics inside Afghanistan and what they observed: anti-personnel mines targeting children, systematic destruction of food sources, bombing of marked medical facilities. Van Dyk was the first American journalist to report on the war from inside Afghanistan [*New York Times*, 6-part series, 17, 20, 21, 24, 31 December 1981 and 12 January 1982; also Sunday *New York Times Magazine*, 17 October 1982.] Although he did not focus specifically on atrocities, his sensitive reports are useful for research on events in the Kandahar region, where few reporters went, as is his subsequent book: Van Dyk, Jere (1983). *Afghanistan*. New York: Coward McCann.

Reuters (20 June 1986). U.S. may cite Soviets for genocide in Afghanistan. *New York City Tribune.*
> Senate Majority Leader Robert C. Byrd (D, W. Va.) threatened to have the United States invoke the U.N. Genocide Treaty for the first time on the issue of Soviet atrocities in Afghanistan.

Archival Resources

These are quasi-private collections which are accessible to serious researchers by arrangement. They contain rare materials otherwise difficult or even impossible to locate, including ad hoc publications of Afghan resistance parties, humanitarian aid organizations, etc., some of which no longer exist. Each has strengths not shared by the others. None has funding or facilities to provide photocopying, research or secretarial services.

Afghanistan Resource Center. Rosanne Klass, Director. As of 1993, access is limited, but arrangements are being made to establish a permanent home for this archive at a major university. For information, contact the director: 250 West 82nd Street, New York, N.Y. 10024-5423, U.S.A.
> Formerly the Afghanistan Information Center at Freedom House. Massive files of press reports, annotated Foreign Broadcast Information Service (FBIS) reports, Congressional testimony, resistance and NGO publications, unpublished materials, etc., on the war plus pre-war material and books. Begun as a private collection in the 1950s, greatly enlarged from 1978 on, to become the most extensive American collection on the war, with many items not available in the European collections. Predominantly but not entirely English-language. Much on human rights violations, atrocities, CW. The center was the leading nongovernmental information source in the U.S. and helped government and private offices, including Helsinki Watch, the U.N. Special Rapporteur, the Oslo Committee, the Congressional Task Force, journalists, researchers and others initiate and pursue their investigations, research and rapportage.

Bibliotheca Afghanica Foundation [Stiftung]. Benzburweg 5, CH-4410 Liestal, Switzerland. Paul Bucherer-Dietschi, Director.
> Founded as a private collection in the 1950s, it has received some Swiss government support since the 1980s. Publishes occasional monographs, usually in German. Massive and unique, it is perhaps the single most comprehensive such collection on Afghanistan anywhere, covering many aspects other than the war years: culture, art, etc. Especially strong on multi-lingual European materials but not on U.S. items. As a Swiss, Bucherer has been able to visit Kabul. The U.N. Special Rapporteur worked closely with this center, which computerized some of his research.

CEREDAF [Centre de Recherches et d'Etudes Documentaires sur l'Afghanistan]. c/o AFRANE, 12 rue de Cotte, 75012 Paris. Etienne Gille, Director.
> An adjunct to AFRANE [See *Les Nouvelles d'Afghanistan*]. As of 1993, CEREDAF continues to issue regular bimonthly bulletins and publishes occasional documents of significance, e.g., the letters of Father Beaurecueil (above), usually in French. Useful for important documentation and contacts with eyewitnesses and distinguished Afghan refugees now living in Europe.

Cultural Council of Afghan Resistance. House No. 886, St. No. 27, G/9-1, Islamabad,

Pakistan. Sabahuddin Kushkaki, Director.
This center has a vast, remarkably complete index of Resistance members and other individuals, including information on thousands of individual deaths.

Private collections on Afghanistan.
A number of the individuals mentioned elsewhere in this bibliography, including former Sen. Gordon J. Humphrey, Jürgen Todenhöfer, Felix Ermacora, and journalists who devoted extended attention to Afghanistan may have private collections of materials that have not been published. In addition, there are hours of film, much of it made by freelance television journalists. Most of the private humanitarian agencies working inside Afghanistan throughout the war received detailed reports from their personnel in the field and several of them - notably Médecins Sans Frontières, Médecins du Monde and the Swedish Committee [Svenska Afghanistankommitten] - maintain extensive files and records. Some of these sources might be willing to make materials available to serious researchers.

Monographs and Specialized Publications

Afghanistan: A Quarterly Magazine (1986-1989). Published by AfghanAid, London.
Since 1989, reduced to a newsletter, *AfghanAid News*. Articles of interest based on field observations of AfghanAid personnel.

Afghan Realities (1981-1987). Peshawar, Pakistan: Afghan Information and Documentation Centre. Monthly. Sayed Fazl Akbar, editor.
Less carefully edited and objective regarding political and military matters than Majrooh's *Bulletin of the Afghanistan Information Centre* (below), but a valuable source of information on human rights issues. Available in archival centers and many research libraries.

Amnesty International: *Annual Reports.* (1978 to date). London: Amnesty International Publications.
Amnesty showed only minor interest in Afghanistan; annual entries were relatively low-key and limited. See overall assessment of these and other Amnesty efforts below.

Amnesty International (September 1979). *Violations of Human Rights and Fundamental Freedoms in the Democratic Republic of Afghanistan.* London: Amnesty International Publications. 34 pp.
Report on widespread arrests, torture, disappearances and deaths in detention from the Communist coup of April 1978 to May 1979.

Amnesty International's Concerns in Afghanistan. (October 1980). London: Amnesty International Secretariat.

Amnesty International (11 October 1983). *Background Briefing on the Democratic Republic of Afghanistan.* Washington: Amnesty International USA. 19 pp.

Amnesty International (1984). *Torture in the Eighties. London: Amnesty International. 253 pp.*
A minimal report (pp. 180-182) that appears to be largely based on the first interviews done by Barnett Rubin with refugees in the U.S. No reference to the many more extensive reports that were emerging elsewhere by 1984.

Amnesty International (November 1984). *Summary of Amnesty International's Concerns in the Democratic Republic of Afghanistan*. London: Amnesty International Secretariat. 16 pp.

In dealing with Afghanistan, Amnesty continued to emphasize the context of its universal concern for the death penalty per se over specific atrocity policies being carried out there by the communist regime and Soviet occupiers.

Amnesty International's efforts regarding Afghanistan have on the whole been noticeably limited, almost perfunctory. Under pressure from scandalized European humanitarian organizations, the secretariat finally commissioned the 1986 report by Anthony Hyman (listed below under the author's name).

In its annual reports (which average 350 - 450 pages), on average about three pages were devoted to Afghanistan - about half the attention devoted to Pakistan or South Korea and in some years less than that devoted to Amnesty's concerns regarding the United States, although, as indicated above, by 1982-1983 journalists, aid workers and large numbers of refugees were providing information about atrocities of massive proportions to other investigating agencies.

In the annual report for 1980 (the first year after the invasion), which dealt with the period 1 May 1979 - 30 April 1980, the coverage of Afghanistan (pp. 176-183) was relatively strong. Amnesty had sent a delegation to Kabul in October 1978 (during the regime of Hafizullah Amin) and again in February 1980 (following the Soviet invasion) to inquire into reports of gross violations, including mass executions. Both times, it received assurances that violations would cease, but continued to receive reports of ongoing violations.

Some figures given in the 1980 report support Michael Barry's analyses. Subsequent reports focused increasingly on the issues of prisoners of conscience, trials of political prisoners that fell short of internationally recognized standards of fairness, the death penalty (which Amnesty opposes everywhere in principle) and, in less specific terms, torture, with little attention to mass executions and atrocities of various kinds carried out as policy. *[Editor's Note: In various communications with Amnesty in the 1980's, the Institute on the Holocaust and Genocide in Jerusalem, was told by Amnesty that it would not focus on large-scale events of genocide but only on specific prisoners. It is my understanding from conversations with the late Martin Ennals, the Founding Secretary-General of Amnesty, that this was the main reason for his leaving Amnesty to become Founding Secretary-General of International Alert. - Israel W. Charny]*

In 1982, Amnesty was still making formal inquiries about the fate of a former prime minister who was known to have been killed in 1978 and in its annual report, discussion of torture in Afghanistan was much less detailed and specific than discussion of the same issue in, for example, Chile or Pakistan despite the flood of victims who had by then fled and were available to testify. Indeed, in the spring of 1982, the regional director in the London office told this author that he considered Pakistan to have the most serious human rights problem in the region.

Subsequently, Amnesty joined others in taking up the cases of several individual prisoners of conscience, notably the historian, Dr. Hasan Kakar, and helped to obtain their release, but it never played a significant role regarding Afghanistan. Its publications are useful primarily as supplements to other sources on this issue.

Asian Lawyers Legal Inquiry Committee (1982). *Report on Afghanistan*. New Delhi: Lawyers Association for Democracy. 46 pp.

Report of a hearing held in New Delhi December 1-3, 1981, at which 16 eyewitnesses were examined in the context of the U.N. Genocide Convention, including testimony on the use of chemical weapons. Contains parts of the Afghan communist constitution as well as summaries of relevant international law. The Government of India, which was cooperating closely with the Soviet Union and the communist regime in Kabul, harassed the Lawyers Association over a period of years for this and other independent work; its chairman, P.N. Lekhi, was put under house arrest or jailed for long periods.

Barry, Michael; Lagerfelt, Johan; and Terrenoire, Marie-Odile (1986). *Mission to Afghanistan and Pakistan (September-November 1985)*. Central Asian Survey Incidental Paper No. 4. London: Society for Central Asian Studies. 41 pp.
> Text of report submitted to Felix Ermacora, Special Rapporteur of the U.N. Commission on Human Rights, following a mission for the International Humanitarian Inquiry Commission on Displaced Persons in Afghanistan sponsored by the BIA. Barry and Lagerfelt are reliable researchers; Terrenoire was on the BIA staff. (For BIA, see below: Dubious Sources.)

Brauner, Alfred; Brauner, Dr. Francoise Erna; and Majrooh, Bahaouddin. *Children in War: Drawings from the Afghan Refugee Camps*. (n.d., 1988?). Central Asian Survey Incidental Paper No. 5. London: Society for Central Asian Studies. 128 pp. 92 drawings: 29 color, 63 b&w.
> Drawings by refugee children in Pakistan collected by French sociologist and pediatric psychiatrist; commentary in English and French.

Bulletin du CEREDAF (1984-). Paris. Monthly newsletter since 1989. See above, Archival Resources: CEREDAF.

Bulletin of the Afghanistan Information Centre (1981-1989). Peshawar, Pakistan: Afghanistan Information Centre. Monthly, 1981-1989, irregularly thereafter. Founded and edited by Syed Bahaouddin Majrooh until his assassination in 1988; by his son Naim Majrooh thereafter.
> Almost every issue contains reports pertinent to genocide issues. Available in all archival centers and many major university and research libraries in the U.S., Europe and Australia. Established and directed by Bahaouddin Majrooh, French-educated former dean of the College of Letters at Kabul University, until he was murdered, probably by a joint team of KhAD/KGB agents in collaboration with his radical Islamist political opponents of the Hizb-i-Islami party. Not affiliated with any party, this center, its director and its publications were internationally recognized as the most reliable, independent, comprehensive and objective Afghan source of information and analysis on many aspects of the war and the Resistance. Journalists relied heavily on this source and Majrooh lectured widely in Europe and the U.S.

Central Asian Survey. London: Society for Central Asian Studies. Marie Broxup, Editor.
> There is relevant information in almost every issue since 1981.

CEREDAF (1988). *Central Asian Survey Special Issue on Afghanistan: The Last Thirty Years*, 7(23). 221 pp.
> Papers given by more than 30 European, Afghan and American experts at a CEREDAF conference held in Paris in November 1986. A number of them contain useful information. No index.

Committee on Media Accountability [COMA] (January 1989). *Media Massacres: Gaza and Afghanistan Coverage*. Santa Monica, California:
> Comparative analyses of major media reporting on alleged Israeli human rights violations in Gaza and Lebanon and those of the U.S.S.R. in Afghanistan. The results of a two-year study, 9-12 pages each, plus summary press announcements. Reports

assess coverage by *New York Times, Los Angeles Times* and weekly news magazines - number of articles, column inches, headlines, etc.

D'Souza, Frances (May 1984). *The Threat of Famine in Afghanistan: A Report on Current Economic and Nutritional Conditions.* London: AfghanAid. 57 pp. [Bibliography]
Results of a study conducted September-December 1983 among children in 30 Afghan provinces.

Dupaigne, Bernard (October 1985). *Les Nouvelles d'Afghanistan: Special Issue on Human Rights.* Paris: AFRANE.
Written and edited by deputy director of Musée de l'Homme and official of AFRANE who made many trips into Afghanistan during the war. In French. Valuable.

Fahimi, Fatima. (1986) *Women in Afghanistan/Frauen in Afghanistan.* Liestal, Switzerland: Stiftung Bibliotheca Afghanica. 111 pp.
By an Afghan woman journalist, originally published in Kabul in 1977, reissued with update by Nancy Hatch Dupree and annex on women as political prisoners since 1978. [English and German.]

Hyman, Anthony (1986). *Afghanistan: Torture of Political Prisoners.* New York: Amnesty International. 51 pp.
Under pressure from European organizations for its minimal attention to conditions in Afghanistan, Amnesty commissioned Hyman to do this report. Hyman, one of whose specialties is Afghanistan, did a good job within the limitations of his mandate (see comments on Amnesty International limitations above).

Johnson, Andrew, et al. (1985). *Report on the Status of Human Rights in Afghanistan: Submitted to the United Nations Human Rights Committee in conjunction with the First Periodic Review of the Initial Report of [sic] Afghanistan under Article 40 of the International Covenant on Civil and Political Rights.* New York: International League for Human Rights. June 1985. 35 pp.
Based primarily but not entirely on published sources.

Jones, Allen K. (January 1985). *Afghan Refugees: Five Years Later.* U.S. Committee for Refugees Issue Paper. New York: American Council for Nationalities Services. 24 pp.
Survey report on the conditions, circumstances, location, etc., of the five to six million Afghan refugees, primarily those in Pakistan.

Laber, Jeri (1986). *To Win the Children: Afghanistan's Other War.* New York: Helsinki Watch/Asia Watch. 21 pp.
Soviet efforts to indoctrinate Afghan children, including taking thousands of infants and young children to the Soviet Union for ten years or more. Largely synthesizes and focuses material scattered in earlier Helsinki Watch reports but contains some new material.

Les Nouvelles d'Afghanistan (1980-). Paris: AFRANE (acronym for Amité Franco-Afghane). Published quarterly (at times bi-monthly). French language.
Consistently the best analytical publication on Afghanistan issues. Heavy focus on human rights. Edited by Etienne Gille and Bernard Dupaigne, expert scholars with first-hand field experience before, during and since the war. Major attention to human rights issues. Every issue contains relevant material, notes and bibliographical information.

Médecins Sans Frontières. Publications, internal reports, 1980-1989. Paris: Médecins Sans Frontières.
This was the single most active volunteer medical group operating clandestinely throughout Afghanistan, and the most active and sophisticated in recording and bringing human rights issues to public attention. Often published excerpts from the reports of their field personnel. Also have documentary materials, films and files to which serious researchers might be given access.

Norchi, Charles, and Busuttil, James J. (18 November 1987). *Report of the Independent Counsel* [sic] *on International Human Rights on the Human Rights Situation in Afghanistan.* 29 pp. Washington: distributed by Committee for a Free Afghanistan.
The Independent Counsel was an ad hoc panel of distinguished European and American specialists in international law. The authors analyze events in relation to international law. Part G specifically considers the question of intentional destruction of the Afghan people under sections (a) to (e) of the Genocide Convention and concludes that there is significant evidence of genocide as defined by international law.

Rone, Jemera (1988). *By All Parties to the Conflict: Violations of the Laws of War in Afghanistan.* New York: Helsinki Watch/Asia Watch. 90 pp.
A survey of the applicable international law and its violation by the U.S.S.R., the Democratic Republic of Afghanistan and some Resistance organizations, with emphasis on the use of outlawed weapons, treatment of civilians and prisoners of war, refugee policies and the problems faced by the International Red Cross.

Russian Atrocities in Afghanistan. (1981) Franklin, Georgia: Solidarity Council of Afghan Freedom Organizations in America [SCAFOA]. 73 pp.
Largely extracts from world press reports, and useful as a guide to coverage.

Sliwinski, Marek (1988). *Afghanistan 1978-87: War, Demography and Society.* Central Asian Survey Incidental Paper Series No. 6. London: Society for Central Asian Studies. 24 pp.
Depopulation policies. Statistics, maps, graphs. Sliwinski, a political scientist at the University of Geneva, has subsequently revised some of his data and conclusions; he now thinks the population losses were even greater than his first estimates.

Thorne, Ludmilla (1986). *Soviet POWs in Afghanistan.* New York: Freedom House. 40 pp.
Interviews with Soviet defectors who later came to the United States. They describe atrocities they witnessed.

Dubious Sources to Be Used with Caution

Afghanistan People's Tribunal [Tribunal des Peuples], Stockholm 1981-Paris 1982, Selected minutes from the Tribunal's meetings: Special issue of The Letter from the B.I.A. (1983) Paris: Bureau International Afghanistan.
Contains some useful information but must be assessed cautiously in the context of the nature and purpose of the Tribunal des Peuples and the B.I.A. (see B.I.A. below).
The Bertrand Russell War Crimes Tribunal, established in the 1960s for the purpose of denouncing American involvement in Vietnam as a war crime, was reactivated as the "Permanent Tribunal des Peuples" c. 1974 by the Rome-based Lelio Basso Foundation, itself the creation of Muammar Qaddafi's Italian lawyer who, though

never openly a member of the CPI, was elected to the Italian Senate on the Communist Party list.

Many Tribunal members had well-established ties to Moscow and/or national Communist parties. Almost all Tribunal hearings are devoted to accusations against pro-Western governments and their allies, especially in the Third World. Following the Soviet invasion, the Tribunal in association with the BIA held two hearings on Afghanistan (Stockholm 1981; Paris 1982), possibly to establish its bona fides; they resulted in limited and apparently predetermined condemnations of Soviet actions.

These were designed (a) to validate the claim of the Tribunal and its associated organizations to "objectivity", enabling them to fulfill other disinformation functions; (b) to preempt and thereby limit the damage from an issue that had triggered massive international outrage; (c) to divert attention from genocidal *policies* to a limited number of individual atrocity incidents; and (d) to establish Tribunal/BIA affiliates as the authoritative spokesmen for the Afghan issue in Europe and elsewhere, thereby controlling information and public reaction. The 1981 Afghanistan hearing, for example, rejected evidence of Soviet use of chemical weapons as "inadequate." The Tribunal's most important associate for Afghanistan is the BIA, but all of the numerous local European groups using as part of their names *Comité... de Soutien du Peuple* [or, *das Volk*] are associated with this network and often also with FASA (see below). Their publications must be evaluated in this context.

Lettre du B.I.A., Defis, and other publications of the Bureau International Afghanistan. The BIA was established shortly after the Soviet invasion by former French Communist Party members who declared themselves disillusioned, but was reportedly funded by the French and Italian Communist parties. Establishing or infiltrating groups in every European country, BIA attempted to become coordinator and spokesman for all European groups supporting the Afghan cause. Its financial resources and moderate leftist stance enabled BIA to enlist a number of respected non-political experts, especially for important field research which served to legitimatize it. It has been quite successful in establishing itself as an aid agency in Pakistan/Afghanistan, as has its associate Solidarité Belgique. Publications - *Lettre de B.I.A.* and *Defis*, plus occasional monographs and reports - contain useful data but reservations indicated above re the closely associated Peoples Tribunal also apply to BIA. Contributions by independent scholars like Barry or Dupaigne are reliable and valuable; those by BIA staff and associates are subject to same reservations as the Tribunal, as are BIA affiliates.

Unreliable Sources

Afghanistan en Lutte
Published by MSRA [Mouvement de Soutien à la Résistance du Peuple Afghan], Paris. MSRA was established to co-opt opposition to Soviet policy in Afghanistan, but was less successful than the BIA in disguising its connections and attracting independent support; lost credibility and declined. See Peoples Tribunal and BIA (above). Same reservations apply.

Afghanistan Tribune.
A glossy disinformation magazine published in German and English by West German-based FASA [Federation of Afghan Students Abroad], an Afghan Maoist front organization with North Korean connections which posed as a resistance and humanitarian support group and propagandized and raised funds for its political/military

arm inside Afghanistan. Active efforts as far afield as Iceland and the U.S. Its offshoot ADAF (Aidez des Afghans en France) had its own publications.

Ahmad, Iqbal.
A longtime fellow of Washington's leftist Institute for Policy Studies and its European branch, the Transnational Institute in Amsterdam, Pakistan-born Ahmad published skilfully slanted articles in *The New Yorker* and other elite media. His selective use of data, omissions and distortions make his writings essentially disinformation.

Andronov, Yona.
Member of post-Soviet Russian parliament now voicing heartfelt concerns about fate of captured Soviet soldiers and other humanitarian issues re Afghanistan. Formerly correspondent for *Liturnya Gazeta* in New York where he was well known as a crude propagandist with KGB connections.

Borovik, Artyom (1990). *The Hidden War*. New York: Atlantic Monthly Press. 288 pp.
Bocharov, Gennady (1990). *Russian Roulette: Afghanistan Through Russian Eyes*. Harper Collins. 181 pp.
Two major entries in the Soviet disinformation campaign designed to deflect international attention from genocidal policies by acknowledging relatively minor individual incidents, acknowledging that Afghanistan invasion was a "mistake," equating it with Vietnam, and omitting damning data while purporting to be independent reports on the war by objective journalists. Bocharov is crude and clumsy but the much more sophisticated Borovik (whose father was a leading disinformation agent and whose uncle, Vladimir A. Kryuchkov, headed the KGB) was widely welcomed by the American media as a genuine reporter. His cleverly-written book has been widely accepted at face value - but it should not be.

Cockburn, Alexander.
On January 21, 1980, Cockburn (a member of the well-known family of leftist British journalists) wrote in New York's *Village Voice*, "If ever a country deserved rape it's Afghanistan." James Ridgeway and Andrew Kopkind published similar views there, but unlike them, Cockburn also writes widely for more respected publications like *Wall Street Journal* and *Vanity Fair* in which he is somewhat less obvious. He campaigned against reports of chemical and biological weapons, equating them with accusations of American use of germ warfare in Korea (now known to be false) and reports of flying saucers.

Evans, Grant (1983). The Yellow Rainmakers.
Australian sociologist recommended by Cockburn as an authority on chemical weapons.

Halliday, Fred.
Writings in various publications, and analyses for BBC. Journalist and University of London lecturer and, reportedly, a member of the IVth International. Steadfast apologist for Soviet actions and one of the few non-Soviet journalists admitted to Afghanistan by the Communist regimes.

Meselson, Matthew; Seeley, Thomas D.; Nowicke, Joan; Guillemin, Jeanne; and Akratanakul, Pong Thap (September 1985). Yellow rain. *Scientific American*, 253(30), 128-137. Also: letter, *Wall Street Journal*, 2 October 1985 (riposte to article by William Kucewicz, 6 September 1985).
Through writings and interviews, Harvard's Meselson and his associates argued that "yellow rain" is merely a natural phenomenon (droppings of a bee species native

to southeast Asia) - not tricothecene mycotoxins, not lethal, not man-made and not a weapon used by the U.S.S.R. and its proxies. They concentrated on evidence from Laos and Cambodia, consistently avoiding or dismissing that from Afghanistan, where a completely different climate, topography, ecology and fauna - e.g., bees - invalidated their theory. Their academic credentials and intensive efforts persuaded most American and international media to reject evidence of use of biological/chemical weapons in Afghanistan and elsewhere.

Vercellin, Giorgio (1985). *Crime de Silence et Crime de Tapage*. Naples: Universita degli studi di venezia instituto di iranistica.
    Vercellin, a prominent leftwing Venetian scholar, spearheaded sophisticated disinformation efforts in Italy.

5

Genocide of the Kurds

Martin van Bruinessen[1]

MASSACRES IN KURDISTAN

The Kurds number at present perhaps 18 to 20 million; their ancestral land, Kurdistan (which has never been a united independent state), has since the First World War been divided among Turkey, Syria, Iraq and Iran, with a few significant enclaves in the Transcaucasian republics of the former Soviet Union. In all these states the Kurds have at times been at the receiving end of violent government repression claiming numerous lives. In most cases, the military violence was in response to Kurdish separatist aspirations or actual rebellions; in some cases, it was preventive. In the course of the suppression or prevention of rebellions, numerous noncombatants were killed.

In at least some of the cases, more appears to have been involved than just overkill; there are indications of deliberate destruction of part of the Kurdish population. This was the case in Turkey following the rebellions of the 1920s and 1930s, especially in the suppression of the last great rebellion, in Dersim in 1937 and 1938. It has definitely also been the case in Iraq since the mid-1980s; the true scale of the killings and destruction is only gradually becoming apparent. It is also only recently that more information has become available on the deportations of Soviet Kurds under Stalin and on the large numbers of them that perished on the way to Central Asia. I shall not attempt to establish here whether all these cases fit the definition of the Genocide Convention, insofar as that definition hinges on the question of intent. There may remain differences of interpretation on the issue of intent in these cases (with the exception of the 1988 mass killings of Kurds in Iraq, which were clearly planned). However, in each of the cases mentioned, large numbers of Kurdish noncombatants were deliberately killed or left to perish and their Kurdish identity was the major reason for their plight.

Besides physical elimination, the Kurds have also been subject to policies of ethnocide, deliberate destruction of their ethnic identity. This has been most clearly so in Republican Turkey, which until very recently openly pursued a policy of forced assimilation. The Soviet Union appears also to have practiced forced assimilation of Kurds, although here the evidence is as yet less unambiguous. In Iraq, there was no overall policy of forced assimilation to the Arab majority, but there was rather the deliberate annihilation of traditional Kurdish rural life and its economic basis by the wholesale destruction of Kurdish villages and the deportation of their inhabitants (i.e., those that were not killed) to strategic villages, "new towns," or concentration camps.

So far, there has been no systematic collection and analysis of data for any of these cases; the published material yields only a fragmentary overview. Recent political changes have made much hitherto unknown documentary material available, and the prospects for a more adequate understanding of what happened are encouraging.

MASSACRES OF KURDS AND FORCED ASSIMILATION IN TURKEY

The Republic of Turkey, established in 1923, was soon confronted with large uprisings in the Kurdish provinces. The major ones took place in 1925, 1930 and 1937, and there were numerous rebellions of more modest scope in between. To some extent these rebellions reflected the reaction of a traditional society to interference by a modern bureaucratic state, but there was also a distinct nationalist dimension to them. The leaders of the uprisings, especially, were motivated by serious grievances over discrimination against the Kurds. The Turkish Army and Air Force suppressed the rebellions with great violence. Thousands may have been killed in combat in the 1925 rebellion alone; almost 50 leaders were hanged after a political trial. Besides these, there were apparently numerous extra-legal killings. Kurdish nationalist sources claim that over two hundred villages were destroyed and 15,000 men, women and children were killed in the course of Turkish reprisals (Chirguh, 1930, pp. 49-52).

Soon after the 1925 rebellion, the government set upon a course of mass deportations of Kurds to the western provinces, both as punishment and as a means of preventing future Kurdish risings. The large-scale 1930 rebellion provided a further impetus to the resettlement program, which assumed mass dimensions. The Turkish sociologist, Beşikçi, has presented evidence suggesting that a major objective of the policy of resettlement was the destruction of Kurdish ethnic identity (Beşikçi, 1977; cf. Bruinessen, in press). Contemporary Kurdish authors give improbably high estimates of the numbers deported: a half million deported within three years, of whom 200,000 are said to have perished (Chirguh, 1930, p. 33), or even a million deported or killed (Bedr Khan, 1927, p. 52-53). More credibly, Chirguh lists village by village how many houses were burned in the repression of the 1925 rebellion, how many persons were killed and how many survived. This adds up to 15,000 killed and 8,750 houses burned (Chirguh 1930, pp. 49-52). These figures are repeated by Rambout (1947) and in his track several other pro-Kurdish authors.

Official Turkish statistics on the deportations, let alone on numbers killed, have not yet come to light. An indication of their scale may be had from a few observations by foreign visitors. The British official, Edmonds, visited the region in May 1930 and reported that the population of Bitlis had been reduced from 40,000 to 5,000, that of Muş from 30,000 to 3,000 (Kutschera, 1979, p. 105). Both towns, it should be noted, used to have sizeable Armenian populations, and the reduction may owe as much to the Armenian deportations and massacres of 1915 as to the more recent disappearance of Kurds. The Norwegian geographer Frödin (1944), who visited Kurdistan in 1936 and again in 1939, confirms that entire villages were destroyed after the 1930 rebellion, and mentions mass executions: "*All Kurds who were found carrying arms were beheaded on the spot. This concerned tens of thousands. Large parts of the remaining Kurdish population were sent to concentration camps in the western provinces*" (p. 5). As a result, Frödin observed, the population of many districts had been reduced to a quarter of what it used to be. In the years 1936-1938, however, the deportees were allowed to return (Frödin, 1944, p. 5). The only author who speaks of genocide in connection with the Turkish punitive measures before 1937, although in a very loose sense, is Kutschera (1979, pp. 89-90). However, the government objectives and the measures that he refers to are more appropriately termed *ethnocide*. It was the Kurdish identity that was to be eliminated, not necessarily large numbers of Kurdish individuals.

A stronger claim that actual genocide took place can be made for the pacification of Dersim, a particularly unruly part of Kurdistan, in two extremely bloody military campaigns in 1937 and 1938. The people of Dersim were culturally distinct from the other Kurds, and by their fierce independent-mindedness they had come to epitomize in the Turkish bureaucratic mind reactionary obstacles in the way of progress. Official discourse, analyzed by Beşikçi (1990), was openly and aggressively racist. The Turkish position was that these "primitives" and "bandits" should give way to modern civilization, just like the American Indians had. This should be effected by their assimilation to the supposedly superior Turkish culture and the physical elimination of those who resisted. An uprising in 1937, which was at least in part provoked by the first pacifying measures, provided the occasion for brutal military campaigns, in which thousands of noncombatants were killed and a large proportion of the villages destroyed and the crops burned. The British consul at Trabzon, who probably was the nearest European observer, compared the brutal and indiscriminate violence with the Armenian massacres of 1915. *"Thousands of Kurds,"* he reported, *"including women and children, were slain; others, mostly children, were thrown into the Euphrates; while thousands of others in less hostile areas, who had first been deprived of their cattle and other belongings, were deported to [provinces] in Central Anatolia"* (italics by author of chapter).[2]

The Kurdish nationalist, Nuri Dersimi, has left a graphic and detailed description of the massacres (Dersimi, 1952). Most later pro-Kurdish accounts lean heavily on this source. There is some independent confirmation based on local oral sources in a more recent book by a local political activist (Şivan, 1975). More recently yet, two persons of Dersim extraction have published novels in which the Dersim rebellion and massacres play a central part and which were clearly meant to present a Kurdish view of what had happened (Cem, 1990; Işik, 1990). These novels complement two earlier ones by the Turkish author, Barbaros Baykara, that were considerably less sympathetic to the Kurds (Baykara, 1974, 1975). The Turkish sociologist, Beşikçi, published an important study on the Dersim massacres and their background (Beşikçi, 1990). His description of the actual killings is largely based on Dersimi and Şivan, but he adds an analysis of Turkish official discourse (parliamentary and academic debates, high officials' reports on the area, military despatches) to show that the massacres were not just an unfortunate accident. He accuses the Turkish government of genocide - a very courageous thing to do even now.

Most Turkish authors dealing with the events speak of resistance to modernization by reactionary tribal and feudal chieftains and mention their violent suppression by the Army, but neglect mentioning massacres. An early typical example is the book by the Ulug (1939), a journalist who had earlier written a booklet on "feudalism" in Dersim. A whole series of pro-state books on the Kurds and the Kurdish movement follow the same line; Kurdish rebels represent the dark Middle Ages, the Turkish Army the Age of Enlightenment. This was also the tone of the reports in the contemporary Turkish press, which even showed pride in the amount of violence expended in the suppression of the rebellion. The most remarkable Turkish source, however, is the official military history of the campaigns (Halli, 1972). This study has long been extremely hard to find, but a recent abbreviated reissue (Bulut, 1991a) has made this essential source material more easily accessible. It is an enlightening work, both because it graphically illustrates how the Turkish elite viewed the Kurds and because it gives a very blunt account of how many villages were burned and how many "bandits and their dependents" were exterminated. The book was not written for the general public, and there is no attempt to hide the brutal violence against women and children as well as against armed insurgents.

Prior to the massacres, the population of Dersim was estimated at 65,000 to 70,000 for Dersim proper (Tunceli) or 150,000 for the wider area sharing the same basic culture ("larger Dersim"). The body count in the military history of the campaign, which is not very detailed and does not include the hundreds of women who in despair jumped to their deaths or the families walled in the mountain caves into which they had fled, adds up to something between three and seven thousand. Dersimi gives figures that are several times higher, and later publications mention even higher numbers, such as 50,000 killed and 100,000 deported (Baran, 1989, p. 113; Felser, 1991, p. 45). If we stick to a conservative estimate, 5 to 10% of the Dersim population were killed, and the numbers deported must have been much higher (but no serious estimates have been published so far).

Dersim and persons of Dersimi extraction have continued to suffer discrimination. This may have contributed to the fact that both left-wing radicalism and Kurdish nationalism have found some of their strongest support bases precisely in Tunceli (the new name for Dersim proper). Incidental deportations of undesirable persons from Tunceli have regularly occurred; in the 1980s, the government announced new plans for large-scale resettlement, ostensibly on behalf of forest conservation. In 1988, it was reported that the population of Tunceli had declined from 200,000 to 162,000 during the previous decade (Laber and Whitman, 1988, p. 39). Most of the Dersim population live dispersed through Turkey and western Europe, and not much of their traditional culture is alive anymore.

The policy of forced assimilation of the Kurds reached its apogee in the late 1930s. With the general political liberalization since 1945 it gradually relaxed, to be temporarily revived after the military interventions of 1961, 1971 and 1980. The 1982 Constitution and several newly enacted laws provided the legal framework for a new concerted effort to destroy Kurdish culture. One of these laws, banning the use of the Kurdish language, is discussed by Rumpf (1989); various other aspects of the destruction of ethnic identity are referred to by Laber and Whitman (1988). Both are brief and fragmentary analyses; there exists as yet no comprehensive treatment of this last effort at forced assimilation. The policy was a dismal failure and created a strong Kurdish nationalist reaction and growing popular support for a small violent party, the Workers' Party of Kurdistan (PKK), that carried out a guerrilla war against the state (see Bruinessen, 1988; Gunter, 1990; Imset, 1992).

In early 1991, the Turkish government, under pressure from abroad, made an about-turn in Kurdish policy and recognized the existence of the Kurds, implicitly granting them cultural rights and allowing them a certain amount of political expression in Ankara and Istanbul. At the same time, repression in the Kurdish area increased. Death squads became active against prominent Kurdish personalities (Cowell, 1992; Amnesty International, 1991 and 1992). The PKK had meanwhile changed its tactics to *intifada*-type popular rebellions leading to violent military reaction and further polarization. The confrontation reached a climax on March 21, 1992 (the Kurdish "national" holiday, *Newroz*), when the military shot at peaceful demonstrations in several towns, reportedly killing some 80 and wounding much larger numbers (Helsinki Watch, 1992). It seems likely that increasingly grave massacres will keep occurring in Turkish Kurdistan.

DEPORTATIONS AND ASSIMILATION
OF KURDS IN THE SOVIET UNION

When the Georgian, Armenian and Azarbaijani republics joined the Soviet Union (1920-21), there were Kurdish villages scattered across all three republics. One district in western (Soviet) Azarbaijan, around the city of Lachin (lying between Nagorny Karabakh and the Armenian Republic), was almost entirely Kurdish, elsewhere they constituted small minorities. For a brief period, the Lachin district was made an autonomous region within the Republic of Azarbaijan. During the first years of the Union, Kurdish culture was allowed free expression and experienced a revival. Under Stalin, however, the autonomous region was abolished, Kurdish culture was suppressed and there was strong pressure on the Kurds to assimilate to Russian or other acceptable cultures. At one point, allegedly even the word "Kurd" was banned.

In the 1930s and 1940s, the Kurds, like a dozen other nationalities, suffered mass deportations. What precisely happened has long remained hidden, but due to *glasnost* some information is at last becoming available. Nadir K. Nadirov, a Kurdish member of the Kazakhstan Academy of Sciences (who as a child was deported himself) has recently gone public with accounts of the deportations (Laber, 1990; Nadirov, 1992). In 1937, Azarbaijan expelled large numbers of Kurds to Armenia, and in 1944, many of the Kurds of Georgia were deported to Central Asia.[3] Entire towns and villages were deported, the men first, and later the women and children. The communities were apparently broken up and dispersed over the Central Asian republics (Kazakhstan, Kirghizia, Uzbekistan, Tajikistan and Turkmenistan) as well as Siberia. It is claimed that as many as half of them died on the way (Laber, 1990). Unlike other ethnic groups, the deported Kurds were not allowed to return to their original homes after 1957.

According to the official Soviet censuses, the numbers of Kurds in the Azarbaijani Republic decreased from 41,000 to 6,000 between 1926 and

1939, and in 1959 only 1,500 Kurds were reported there (Vanly, 1992, p. 204). It is not possible to say how much of this decrease is due to deportations and how much to assimilation or deliberate under-reporting. Soviet Kurds claim that even the most recent census seriously under-reports their number; the official figure is 153,000 for all republics together, but Kurdish claims are at least three times that high (Laber, 1990; Vanly, 1992, p. 208).

The resurgence of nationalism in the former Soviet republics has resulted in a new wave of expulsions of Kurds. In 1987, ethnic rioting caused many Kurds to flee Kirghizia, Tajikistan and Uzbekistan. Most of them appear to have moved to Transcaucasia, to the Krasnodar area. Not much later, large numbers of Muslim Kurds (allegedly 18,000) were forced to leave Armenia.[4] They also sought recourse in Krasnodar, some of them later moving on to Azarbaijan. At the same time, Kurds from Azarbaijan were reported fleeing towards Armenia (Vanly, 1992, p. 207-208).

CHEMICAL WARFARE, MASS KILLINGS, AND WHOLESALE DESTRUCTION IN IRAQI KURDISTAN

In Iraq, guerrilla warfare between Kurdish nationalist organizations and the central government has been going on since 1961 with but few and brief interruptions. In the course of the conflict, the Iraqi Kurds have established close ties with the successive Iranian regimes. This provided the various Iraqi regimes with legitimation for violent measures that often went well beyond the mere suppression of rebellion and dissent. Cruel torture and summary executions have been the hallmark of the Iraqi Ba'ath regime, which has been in power in Baghdad since 1968. The bombing of civilian targets and other reprisals against innocent civilians (such as the arrest and execution of children in the town of Sulaimaniya in 1985) have been standard practice. Saddam Hussein's climb to the position of sole leader (completed in 1979) was marked by an increase in the overall level of violence (al-Khalil, 1989). Guerrilla warfare and army repression together resulted in a large flow of refugees into Iran (peaking in 1975, after the Shah had given up his support of the Iraqi Kurds in exchange for border concessions). Large parts of Iraqi Kurdistan along the state borders were deliberately laid waste, tens of thousands of villagers deported and large but still unknown numbers disappeared. Still, until the 1980s it may not be possible to speak of genocide in a strict formal definition. The Kurds may have suffered more altogether, but Arab citizens were treated with equal cruelty.

Things changed during the Iraq-Iran war (1980-88). A first important case to be mentioned is the disappearance of the Barzani Kurds. The Barzani "tribe" constitutes a culturally distinct group among the north Iraqi Kurds, which had long formed the core of the Kurdish movement. Mulla Mustafa Barzani (who died in 1979) was the legendary national leader of the Iraqi Kurds. About half of them had lived as refugees in Iran since 1975, the other half had surrendered to the Iraqi army and had been resettled in camps near Arbil, far from their tribal area. The villages of the Barzan area itself were razed. In August 1983, all men aged between 8 and 70 of this group, eight thousand in total, were rounded up in the camps and driven off in army lorries. None of them have been seen again. According to information confidentially leaked by Iraqi military sources, at least some of them were used in experiments with chemical arms; there is little hope that any of them are still alive (Zibari, 1989). The women and children remaining behind were subjected to cruel mistreatment and humiliation, apparently including systematic rape (Makiya, 1993, pp. 161-2). The abduction of the Barzanis apparently was a reprisal for the capture, a month earlier, of a strategic border post by the Iranian army, possibly aided by Iran-based Iraqi Kurds loyal to Barzani's sons. If it is true that all or many of them were killed, this constitutes an unambiguous case of genocide by the terms of the 1948 definition in the United Nations Convention on Genocide.

The Iraqi regime was probably the first government ever to use chemical weapons against its own citizens. In March 1988, in an apparent reprisal for its capture by Iranian military assisted by Kurdish guerrillas, the Kurdish town of Halabja, near the Iranian border, was bombed with chemical warheads. A large number of civilians were killed - 5,000 according to the most widely accepted estimate, and at least 3,200, for so many of them are known by name. Iraq had used chemical weapons before, both against the Iranian army and against its own Kurdish villages, but this was the first attack that drew world-wide attention, because foreign journalists were able to film and photograph the victims. It was only after Halabja that Kurdish reports of the earlier gas attacks were taken seriously. The first attacks, in April 1987, were against villages in or near guerrilla-held territory. Kurdish sources claimed three hundred dead. These attacks appear to have been experimental. The first chemical bombing was recorded on video. Surviving villagers who reached Erbil were not allowed treatment but were taken to an army hospital for observation; from there they disappeared and were not seen again. More gas attacks were reported in May, June and September 1987 (Kurdish Program, 1988, p. 4; Middle East Watch, 1990, p. 83; Makiya, 1993, pp. 164-5; Middle East Watch, 1993, pp. 59-73, 360).

Although the Halabja massacre created an outcry internationally, there was a surprising lack of international pressure on Iraq, and no sanctions - the Iraq-Iran war was still continuing and the Reagan administration in the U.S.A. strongly "tilted" towards Iraq. Appropriate pressure might conceivably have dissuaded Iraq from further use of chemical weapons against the Kurds. As it was, Iraq used war gases again on a wide scale between February and September 1988, in anti-Kurdish military campaigns of unprecedented brutality that were given the ominous code-name of *Anfal* ("Spoils"). Only the last of these offensives, which took place in August 1988, after Iraq had signed a ceasefire with Iran, received international attention at the time.

The attacks this time were concentrated in the Zakho-Duhok-Amadiya triangle near the Turkish border, a zone that had to some extent been under Kurdish guerrilla control. Kurdish sources claimed that 77 villages were bombed with chemical warheads and some 3,000 people killed. Most of the survivors fled in panic towards the Turkish border; some 65,000 crossed it in time before the Iraqi army blocked their way. Interviews with the eyewitnesses among these refugees are our chief source for these events. The major report based on such interviews was until recently that by U.S. Senate aides Galbraith and Van Hollen (1988); see also those by Tuşalp (1989), Middle East Watch (1990, pp. 75-85), and Saeedpour (1992). Important new testimonial and documentary evidence is presented in Middle East Watch, 1990, pp. 261-281. Initially, some observers refused to believe, in spite of the consistent testimonies of Kurdish eyewitnesses, that Iraq had actually used chemical weapons in this August offensive (Viorst, 1988). The testimonial evidence, however, is supported by the chemical analysis of various samples taken inside Iraq (Hay and Roberts, 1990; Middle East Watch and Physicians for Human Rights, 1993).

The use of poison gas against the Kurds is closely associated with the name of Ali Hassan al-Majid, a cousin of Saddam Hussein who was put in charge of northern Iraq, with unlimited powers, in March 1987. Al-Majid apparently saw it as his task to achieve a "final solution" to Iraq's Kurdish problem. Chemical arms constituted only one element in his approach, perhaps used chiefly for their psychological effect. Mass deportations and mass killings, and overall violence of unprecedented brutality even by Iraqi standards characterized al-Majid's tour of duty. The cordon sanitaire along the Iranian and Turkish borders was extended to a 30 kilometer wide security zone in which all villages and towns were razed to the ground, fruit trees cut and water-wells filled up with concrete.

The brutal series of *Anfal* offensives, beginning in February 1988, had the overt dual objective of destroying the Kurdish guerrilla resistance and of forcing the villagers out of settlements in the "security zone." In the process, numerous villages much further inland were destroyed as well. The inhabitants were driven off to camps in other parts of the country. What happened to them then remained for several years a well-kept secret. Many perished on the way; evidence that has come to light since 1991 indicates that many, many more were summarily executed and buried in mass graves.

The *Anfal* offensives, it is becoming increasingly clear, were not just ruthless campaigns to subdue pockets of guerrilla resistance and to remove the population on whom these depended. Secret official Iraqi documents captured by the Kurds during the March 1991 uprising contain explicit instructions, issued by al-Majid in June 1987 and remaining in force throughout that and the following year, to kill all adults arrested in the "security zone" (Middle East Watch, 1993, pp. 79-84). This concerned well over 1,000 inhabited villages, and the indications are that these instructions were carried out to the letter. In the words of the first author to see part of the said documents and to interview eyewitnesses, the *Anfal* involved the "bureaucratically organized, routinely administered mass killing of villagers for no reason other than that they happened to live in an area suddenly designated 'prohibited for security reasons'" (Makiya, 1992, p. 58).

Among the official documents seized by the Kurds is an audio recording of a meeting between Ali Hassan al-Majid and other high functionaries in January 1989. Al-Majid can be heard to boast how he took care of all those Kurds from the destroyed villages. *"Taking care of them means burying them with bulldozers. That's what taking care of them means... These people gave themselves up. Does that mean that I am going to leave them alive? Where shall I put these people, so many of them? So I began to distribute them across the provinces. And from there I had bulldozers going backward and forward"* (Makiya, 1992, p. 58; longer extracts of this recording, in a different translation, are given in Middle East Watch, 1993, pp. 351-2). This was not an empty boast. It was confirmed by one young boy who survived a mass execution of deportees, near the Saudi border. The people in his convoy, women and children, were driven into deep, bulldozer-dug pits and shot in the head (Middle East Watch and Physicians for Human Rights, 1992, pp. 23-25; Makiya, 1992, pp. 60-61). There are at least seven other survivors of mass executions. Their stories, highly consistent with each other, are told in the Middle East Watch report (1993, pp. 239-258, 326-333).

From their and other testimonies, confirmed by documentary evidence, planned and systematic mass murder can be reconstructed. The *"Anfal* villagers" - those who were not killed in the offensives and did not succeed in fleeing - were taken to collection points, where women and children were separated from the men. After interrogation and a rough screening procedure, the men were put into closed vehicles and driven to various destinations in the south of Iraq, where mass graves had already been dug for them. Women and children from certain districts were also executed, others were sent to prisons or prison camps and ultimately ended up in one of several "housing complexes" where displaced villagers were supposed to live and build their own houses, without any facilities provided.

The Kurdish parties, based on a rough count of evacuated villages, claim that 182,000 noncombatants disappeared in the process, and they fear that all were killed. Makiya estimates that "at least 100,000 noncombatant Kurds" were killed in the 1988 *Anfal* offensives (ibid., p. 61) and refers to a meeting in 1991 where al-Majid was heard to mention the same number. The most recent, painstakingly documented report by Middle East Watch concludes that the number killed in mass executions cannot have been less than 50,000 and may be twice that number (1993, p. 345). Over 1,200 villages were razed in the *Anfal* offensives alone, bringing the total of villages destroyed since 1968 to 4,000 out of an estimated 7,000 Kurdish villages, i.e., more than half (see the lists compiled in Rasool, 1990 and Resool, 1990).

After the final *Anfal* offensive, Iraq declared a general amnesty for the Kurds and invited refugees back. Mass executions, however, continued for some time, new arrests were made, further villages razed. Returning refugees and other survivors were resettled in "housing complexes." Members of the Christian and Yezidi religious minorities, however, were separated from among the Muslim Kurds and taken to an unknown destination. They have not been seen or heard of again (Middle East Watch, 1993, pp. 312-318).

There were new Kurdish massacres in the wake of operation "Desert Storm," the American-led international offensive that expelled the Iraqi occupying troops from Kuwait in February 1991. President Bush called upon the people of Iraq to overthrow Saddam Hussein; the Shiites in the south and the Kurds in the north rose up in spontaneous, badly prepared rebellions. Much more of the Iraqi armed forces had remained intact than was believed, and elite troops quelled both rebellions in blood. The Kurdish rebellion was far more massive than all previous ones; virtually the entire population took part, and all towns were in rebel hands. In late March the army attacked, with tanks and helicopter gunships, wreaking death and destruction and sending up to two million people to flight. As they tried to reach the Turkish or Iranian borders, many of these refugees were killed by Iraqi fire; many others died of fatigue, cold and hunger. The total number of Kurdish deaths in these few weeks has been estimated at 25,000 to 30,000 (Makiya, 1993, p. 203, citing the *Journal of American Medicine*, vol. 266, no. 5, August 7, 1991, p. 639). It is likely, incidentally, that the number of casualties among the Shiites in the south was even higher, but no reliable estimates are known.

CHALLENGES AND PROSPECTS FOR IMPROVING OUR UNDERSTANDING OF THE MASSACRES

Much of our information on the Kurdish massacres in Turkey in the 1920s and 1930s, and to a lesser extent that on the events in Iraq in the 1980s, derives from highly partisan sources. One is torn between sympathy and respect for victims' reports and the need for further corroborating information. There have been few if any independent eyewitnesses and few independent researchers working on more objective assessments of the evidence. The governments concerned are obviously not at all supportive of such research, preferring to have their official versions of the events canonized.

Language problems constitute another barrier; a researcher working on any of the cases mentioned above will have to have a command of Turkish or Arabic to read official communications as well as important secondary sources, and preferably of several Kurdish dialects if he or she wishes to make interviews. Galbraith and Van Hollen (1988) and van der Stoel (1992) have shown, however, that one can produce a good report just working with translators. Nevertheless, much relevant information will only be retrieved by one who has access to written material in Middle Eastern languages. Important relevant written material has recently become available in both Turkey and Iraq.

Turkey

The political liberalization of the late 1980s and early 1990s in Turkey has for the first time made the Kurdish problem publicly debatable. Censorship has been considerably relaxed, so that older books on the Kurds could be reissued. An important event was the publication of Beşikçi's (1990) study of the Dersim massacres. It was almost immediately banned, but those really interested, both in Turkey and abroad, will not find it hard to get access to a copy. Two other relevant books, long hard to find, were recently reissued (Dersimi, 1952; Bulut, 1991a, which is a reissue of Halli, 1972). Some relevant materials from various Turkish archives have incidentally found their way to Kurdish intellectual circles. Parts of this material have been published in various Kurdish journals appearing in Europe during the 1980s (see also Bulut, 1991b). It is likely that more is to follow if the relatively liberal political climate in Turkey continues.

One would, of course, wish to see all relevant Turkish archives opened to independent investigators. The official history of the suppression of rebellions (Halli, 1972) and the documents that were leaked so far suggest that there is a vast store of material to be uncovered: military reports and despatches, correspondence between the coordinating governor and local-level officials, instructions for deportation and records of its implementation, population statistics. A political decision at the highest level will be necessary to make even part of this material accessible; but one would hope that the possibility of such a decision is not so unrealistic now as it would have been only a decade ago.

Another approach that may now be taken is the systematic interviewing of survivors. For a long time this was virtually impossible for political reasons; people did not dare to speak out for fear of reprisals. The liberal wind blowing in Istanbul and Ankara has not yet reached Tunceli, where it is important to realize a reign of severe repression continues, but many of the survivors live elsewhere in Turkey now, or even in western Europe. Systematic interviewing has to be done before long, since the adolescents of 1937-38 are now in their seventies, and soon there will be no one alive who remembers. Some young intellectuals have in fact already been conducting such interviews, and Şilan (1990-92) used them in a new account of the Dersim rebellion published in a Kurdish magazine.

Iraq

A large part of Iraqi Kurdistan is at present withdrawn from central government surveillance. Under the protective umbrella of the American airforce, the Kurdish parties exercise control of the area. This has made it possible to compile lists of the disappeared and to systematically record oral testimony on the killings and other abuses. The economic situation of the area is so catastrophic that most Kurds have, understandably, other priorities. Nevertheless, a few Kurds, among whom the name of Shorsh Rasool stands out, have started doing this, and their research lies at the base of the first published accounts of the *Anfal* (Makiya, 1992, 1993; Middle East Watch and Physicians for Human Rights, 1992, 1993). Middle East Watch took the important step of sending a research team to Iraqi Kurdistan, that spent a total of six months there in 1992 and 1993, interviewing some 350 eyewitnesses. The testimonial evidence compiled so far makes a convincing reconstruction of the Kurdish genocide possible (Middle East Watch, 1993). Many things, however, still remain obscure, and the effort to systematically interview survivors should be continued.

The study of genocide in Saddam Hussein's Iraq will be facilitated by the regime's somewhat astonishing penchant for documentation of its own terror. During the popular rising of March 1991, the Kurdish organizations captured vast amounts of Iraqi secret police archives and other official documents. The collection contains a wide variety of documents, including video recordings of interrogation and torture, tape recordings of important meetings, military communications concerning the *Anfal* campaigns, informers' and spies' reports, intelligence files on hundreds of thousands of persons and, most importantly, the paperwork of Iraq's bureaucracy of terror. These documents will probably make a detailed reconstruction of the *Anfal* and the mass executions possible and give an insight in who were responsible for which acts. The first person to be shown some of these documents, to realize their importance, and to write about them was Makiya (1992). Fourteen tons of these documents have now been shipped to the

United States, where they are being analyzed under the supervision of Middle East Watch. An significant part of the evidence presented by this organization in its important report on the Iraqi Kurdish genocide (1993) is based on these documents, although so far only a small fraction has been systematically analyzed. Further important findings are likely to surface as the analysis continues.

Middle East Watch also cooperated with an other organization, Physicians for Human Rights, in carrying out a number of forensic investigations in Iraqi Kurdistan (1992, 1993). Careful exhumations of reported mass graves and chemical analysis of soil and other samples have corroborated testimonial evidence on mass executions and chemical attacks. The most important work of this kind will have to wait until the other parts of Iraq are open to investigation. The *Anfal* villagers were taken to the deep south of Iraq, close to the Saudi border, to be killed. There must lie, hidden in the desert sand, mass graves holding between 50,000 and 100,000 bodies from the 1988 killings alone; other mass graves, of earlier series of killings, may also be recovered.

The full story of the genocide will probably only be known when the archives of Baghdad can be investigated. The amount and quality of the documentation of massive human rights abuses that is already available to independent investigators, however, is virtually unprecedented. The Iraqi Kurdish massacres have thus become one of the best documented cases of genocide since the Holocaust. It is likely that a strong case can be made against the Iraqi regime on the basis of evidence contained in its own documents. The urgent question is, what to do next? Can the perpetrators be brought to trial (or should they be tried in absentia)? Which states would be willing to lodge a formal complaint against Iraq? Which court should adjudicate such a trial, or should a special court be set up as in Nuremberg? Are official Iraqi documents, acquired and exported without authorization, admissible as evidence in court? The political balance in the United Nations is at present against Iraq, making an international trial at least conceivable. Many states will, however, be hesitant to become actively involved for fear of creating a precedent. *It is precisely this possibility of establishing a precedent that makes the Kurdish case all the more important for those of us who are committed to human rights.*

NOTES

1. This chapter was written while I was living in Indonesia, far from any reference library. I wish to thank Professor Joyce Blau, Hamit Bozarslan and the Kurdish Institute of Paris, Vera Beaudin Saeedpour of New York, and Pieter Muller and Michiel Leezenberg of the Netherlands for their kindness in providing me with copies of important materials.

2.   Despatch from the British consul at Trabzon, dated 27 September 1938.   Enclosed in Foreign Office files, series FO 371, document 1938: E5961/69/44 (Public Record Office, London).

3.   These deportations have gone almost unnoticed. They are not even mentioned in Robert Conquest's (1970) well-known study, which deals in detail with the fate of other Transcaucasian peoples.

4.   A considerable proportion of the Kurds in Armenia are not Muslims but Yezidis, adherents of an Iranian religion that only survives among the Kurds. When the conflict between Christian Armenia and Muslim Azarbaijan turned violent, Muslim Kurds became targets of violent aggression, but the Yezidis apparently were left unharmed.

REFERENCES

Bruinessen, Martin van (1988). Between guerrilla war and political murder: The Workers' Party of Kurdistan. *MERIP Middle East Report* No. 153 (July-August), 14-27.

Conquest, Robert (1970). *The Nation Killers: The Soviet Deportation of Nationalities*. London: Macmillan.

Gunter, Michael M. (1990). *The Kurds in Turkey: A Political Dilemma*. Boulder, CO: Westview Press.

Hiro, Dilip (1989). *The Longest War: The Iran-Iraq Military Conflict*. London: Grafton Books.

Imset, Ismet G. (1992). *The PKK: A Report on Separatist Violence in Turkey (1973-1992)*. Ankara: Turkish Daily News Publications.

al-Khalil, Samir (1989). *Republic of Fear: The Politics of Modern Iraq*. Berkeley and Los Angeles: University of California Press.

Kreyenbroek, Philip G., and Sperl, Stefan (Eds.) (1992). *The Kurds: A Contemporary Overview*. London: Routledge.

BIBLIOGRAPHY

Massacres of Kurds, General

Bruinessen, Martin van (1993, in press). Genocide in Kurdistan? The suppression of the Dersim rebellion in Turkey (1937-38) and the chemical war against the Iraqi Kurds (1988). In Andreopoulos, George (Ed.), *The Conceptual and Historical Dimensions of Genocide*. Philadelphia: University of Pennsylvania Press.
    Reconstruction and analysis of the Dersim massacres and of Iraq's use of chemical arms against the Kurds in the late eighties. The available evidence is surveyed, and the events placed into the context of the states' overall policies towards the Kurds.

Felser, Gerd (1991). Die Kurden in diesem Jahrhundert: Leid und Verfolgung. In Zülch, Tilman (Ed.), *Völkermord an den Kurden. Eine Dokumentation der Gesellschaft für Bedrohte Völker.* Frankfurt am Main: Luchterhand, pp. 41-59.
A survey of massacres of Kurds during this century. Sympathy for the Kurdish cause is expressed in high estimates of numbers of victims and what appears to this author an overly uncritical repetition of Kurdish claims. Around 50,000 Kurds are said to have been murdered in the Dersim campaigns of 1937 and 1938 (p. 45); the Iraqi airforce is said in 1969 to have bombed Kurdish villages with napalm (pp. 47-49). The Iraqi regime is accused of having killed, between 1968 and 1990, 200,000 Kurds and 20,000 Assyrian Christians, most of them civilians; of having systematically destroyed 5,000 villages and deported 1.5 to 2 million people; of killing 13,000 Kurds and 2,000 Assyrian Christians with poison gas (p. 56).

Jwaideh, Wadie (1960). *The Kurdish Nationalist Movement: Its Origins and Development.* Ph.D. Dissertation, Syracuse University. 895 pp.
The best study of the early phases of the Kurdish national movement. Its discussion of the rebellions in Turkey (pp. 593-634) is based on published sources only but is judicious in its evaluation. The punitive measures by the government are mentioned in passing but not specially analyzed. The author mentions deportations, mass arrests and summary executions and cautiously refers to the high estimates given by contemporary Kurdish nationalist sources, alongside a few much lower estimates found in the European press.

Kutschera, Chris (1979). *Le mouvement national kurde.* Paris: Flammarion. 393 pp.
One of the best studies of the Kurdish national movement, especially good on the Iraqi Kurdish movement from 1961 to 1975. The author has frequently visited Kurdistan as a journalist and consulted French and British archives besides published accounts for the earlier period. In discussing the Turkish repression following the first great Kurdish rebellion, the author speaks of "genocide" (pp. 89-90); describing the prelude to the Dersim rebellion he mentions mass deportations and plans for "de-kurdification" of the region (pp. 104-105, 120-122).

McDowall, David (1992). *The Kurds: A Nation Denied.* London: Minority Rights Publications. 150 pp.
The most recent general survey of the situation of the Kurds in the various countries where they live. Briefly discusses the use of chemical weapons in Iraq in 1987-88 and the exodus of spring 1991 (based on secondary sources). Poses, and answers in the positive, the question of genocide.

Rambout, Lucien (1947). *Les Kurdes et le droit: Des textes, des faits.* Paris: Editions du Cerf. 160 pp.
A strongly pro-Kurdish overview of the situation of the Kurds under the various governments of Iran, Turkey and Iraq, written under pseudonym by Father Thomas Bois, a well-known authority on Kurdish culture. Uncritically repeats inflated Kurdish claims of numbers killed, etc., but is useful in identifying cases of deliberate mass killing, and contains some material not easily found elsewhere.

Zülch, Tilman (Ed.) (1991). *Völkermord an den Kurden. Eine Dokumentation der Gesellschaft für Bedrohte Völker.* Frankfurt am Main: Luchterhand. 135 pp.
Contains a compilation of press reports on the Kurdish rebellion and mass flight of spring 1991, with interviews with refugees (pp. 13-27), followed by a survey of earlier massacres of Kurds in the present century (see Felser, 1991) and a discussion of the repression of the Kurds under Ba'ath rule in Iraq. Other chapters deal with the

treatment of the Kurds in Syria, Iran and contemporary Turkey.

The Kurds in Turkey

DESTRUCTION OF KURDISH ETHNIC IDENTITY

Baran, Ute (1989). Deportations: Tunceli Kanunlari. In *Documentation of the International Conference on Human Rights in Kurdistan, 14-16. April 1989, Hochschule Bremen.* Bremen: The Initiative for Human Rights in Kurdistan, pp. 110-115.
Discusses Turkey's 1934 law on resettlement and its implementation, as well as deportations of Kurds as recently as 1986. Unsystematic and marred by mistranslations and other minor factual mistakes.

Bedr Khan, Emir Sureya (1927). *The Case of Kurdistan against Turkey.* Philadelphia: Kurdish Independence League (Hoyboon). 76 pp.
An angry indictment of the Turkish policy vis-a-vis the Kurds by a leading Kurdish nationalist. Claims that following the first great rebellion one million Kurds were murdered or deported. Three years later the same author, writing under the pseudonym of Dr. Bletch Chirguh, gave lower but more detailed figures.

Beşikçi, Ismail (1977), *Kürtlerin 'Mecburi Iskan'i* (The 'Forced Resettlement' of the Kurds). In Turkish. Ankara: Komal. 205 pp. [reprint Istanbul: Yurt Kitap-Yayin, 1992]
Beşikçi is a Turkish sociologist specializing in Kurdish studies who has devoted his life, at great personal cost, to the critical analysis and refutation of the official Turkish ideology and the documentation of the treatment of the Kurds. Most of his books, including this one, have been banned in Turkey, and he spent well over a decade in prison for his writings. The present book analyzes the 1934 law on forced resettlement which arranged for deportation of Kurds from large parts of Kurdistan and the settlement of Turkish-speaking groups in their stead. The author argues convincingly that the objective of the law was the destruction of Kurdish cultural identity.

Chirguh, Bletch (1930). *La question kurde, ses origines et ses causes.* Le Caire: Paul Barbey. 56 pp.
Another indictment of Turkey's Kurdish policies by leading nationalist Sureya Bedr Khan, this time writing under a pseudonym. Gives a proud account of the Kurdish struggle for independence and a gloomy picture of Turkish repression. Mentions hundreds of villages destroyed by Turkish troops, thousands of houses burned down, and over 15,000 unarmed men, women and children killed and presents tables with a regional breakdown of these figures. Claims that between 1925 and 1928 over 500,000 Kurds were deported and that 200,000 of them died or were killed in the process.

Frödin, Johan (1944). Neuere Kulturgeografische Wandlungen in der östlichen Türkei. *Zeitschrift der Gesellschaft für Erdkunde,* 79(1-2), 1-20.
The Norwegian geographer, Frödin, visited eastern Turkey in 1936 and 1939 and reports on recent changes in the cultural and demographic landscape. Not only have the Armenians disappeared, Frödin found Kurdish districts depopulated too, while many recent Turkish settlements had arisen. He attributes the depopulation to the bloody suppression of the Kurdish rebellions, especially that of 1930. The Turkish army killed tens of thousands, Frödin reports, and large parts of the surviving population were sent into concentration camps in Turkey's western provinces.

Hoyboun, Ligue Nationale Kurde (1928). *Les massacres kurdes en Turquie.* Le Caire: Paul Barbey. 41 pp.

Attempts to prove the existence, at least since the 1910s, of Turkish plans for destroying the Kurds as a nation by mass deportations and assimilation or extermination, on the model of the Armenian massacres. Mentions various cases of deportations and mass executions but is otherwise poorly documented. The only documentation concerns the trials of participants in the 1925 rebellion.

Kendal (1978). Le Kurdistan de Turquie. In Chaliand, Gérard (Ed.), *Les Kurdes et le Kurdistan. La question nationale kurde au Proche-Orient.* Paris: Maspéro, pp. 69-153. [English translation: Kurdistan in Turkey. In Chaliand, Gérard (Ed.), *People Without a Country.* London: Zed Books, 1982, pp. 47-106].

History of the relationship between the Kurds and the state in Republican Turkey by a leading Kurdish intellectual. Pays considerable attention to the rebellions and their suppression and to the policy of forced assimilation. No extravagant claims, well referenced.

Laber, Jeri, and Whitman, Lois (1988). *Destroying Ethnic Identity: The Kurds of Turkey. An Update.* New York: Helsinki Watch. 73 pp.

A human rights report containing much anecdotal material but no systematic analysis of the attempted destruction of Kurdish ethnic identity in Turkey. Besides much on torture of Kurdish political prisoners, the guerrilla activities of the PKK and the government reprisals, the booklet also reports on forced migration from Tunceli province, whose population declined from 200,000 to 162,000 in a decade, while elsewhere high growth rates were registered.

Rumpf, Christian (1989). The Turkish law prohibiting languages other than Turkish. In *Documentation of the International Conference on Human Rights in Kurdistan, 14-16 April 1989, Hochschule Bremen.* Bremen: The Initiative for Human Rights in Kurdistan, pp. 68-89.

Analysis of a law issued in 1983 that banned the use of the Kurdish language (and thereby was a means towards forced assimilation). The constitutional and legal context of the law is discussed, and it is argued that the law contravenes international treaties to which Turkey is a party. Debate on the law in Turkey is briefly summarized.

Saydam, Abubekir; Kesen, Nebi; and Kranefeld-Wied, Paul (Eds.) (1991). *Kurdistan zwischen Aufstand und Völkermord: Fakten - Hintergrunde - Analysen.* Frankfurt am Main: Medico International, and Köln: KOMKAR. 155 pp.

In spite of the title, none of the articles in this book explicitly addresses the question of genocide. All authors deal primarily with Turkish Kurdistan (KOMKAR is an association of Kurdish immigrant workers from Turkey). The first contribution (by Nebi Kesen) discusses forced deportations in Turkish Kurdistan since 1989, claiming that these concerned 100,000 people. Out of 37 villages in the district of Şirnak, 28 are said to have been destroyed. A detailed report on the deportations, prepared by Medico International, is appended (pp. 135-140). Another contribution (by Petra Wurzel, pp. 47-53) deals with the ban on the Kurdish language and its partial lifting.

THE DERSIM MASSACRES

Baykara, Barbaros (1974). *Dersim 1937.* In Turkish. Istanbul: Akyar. 289 pp.

Baykara, Barbaros (1975). *Tunceli 1938*. In Turkish. Istanbul: Akyar. 247 pp.
Two-volume "documentary novel" on the Dersim rebellion, based on contemporary Turkish newspaper reports, and reflecting the official Turkish view of the events. Paints an unflattering picture of Dersim society as pervaded with criminal violence but also mentions excesses of violence by Turkish troops.

Beşikçi, Ismail (1990). *Tunceli Kanunu (1935) ve Dersim Jenosidi* (The 1935 law regarding Tunceli and the genocide of Dersim). In Turkish. Istanbul: Belge Yayinlari. 185 pp.
In this book the author analyzes the massacres of Dersim in 1937-1938 and the government measures that constituted the prelude thereto. Central place is given to a law on the pacification and "reform" of this Kurdish district. The parliamentary debates on this law are analyzed to establish the perceptions and attitudes of the Ankara political elite regarding the Kurds. The official motivations of the law (pacification, suppression of banditry, development) are juxtaposed with documents that could be construed to indicate an intent to wipe out a considerable part of the population. In Beşikçi's view, the law served to legitimate genocide. This book, like the author's earlier work, brings much of the Turkish Kemalist discourse of the 1930's, with its barely hidden racism, back to the surface and documents the intent to destroy Kurdish ethnic identity. The description of the actual massacres depends on Kurdish sources (Dersimi, 1952; Şivan, 1975) and the official Turkish military history of the campaign (Halli, 1972).

Bulut, Faik (Ed.) (1991a). *Devletin Gözüyle Türkiye'de Kürt Isyanlari* (The Kurdish rebellions in Turkey from the viewpoint of the state). In Turkish. Istanbul: Yön. 319 pp. [Abbreviated reissue of Halli, 1972, with additional documents]

Bulut, Faik (Ed.) (1991b). *Belgelerle Dersim Raporlari* (Reports on Dersim in documents). In Turkish. Istanbul: Yon. 336 pp.
A collection of official letters and reports from the 1930's concerning Dersim, including lists of tribes and population statistics of individual villages.

Cem, Munzur (1990). *Gülümse ey Dersim* (Smile, o Dersim). In Turkish. Köln: Özgürlük Yolu Yayinlari. 356 pp.
Novel set at the time of the Dersim rebellion. The author appears to be from Dersim himself.

Dersimi, Vet. Dr. M. Nuri (1952). *Kürdistan Tarihinde Dersim* (Dersim in the history of Kurdistan). In Turkish. Aleppo: privately printed. 341 pp. [Various recent reissues: Istanbul: Eylem Yayinlari, 1979 (as *Dersim Tarihi*); Köln: KOMKAR, 1991; Diyarbakir: Dilan yayinlari, 1992.]
Dersimi was a Kurdish nationalist active in the Dersim area during the years preceding the 1937-38 massacres. He fled to Syria not long before the military operations started but remained in regular contact with the area. His book gives the most detailed account available of the massacres and appears on the whole reliable, although the numbers of victims mentioned may be inflated. Dersimi claims that the Turkish air force in 1938 bombed the district with poisonous gas (p. 319), a claim later often repeated by Kurdish nationalist authors but not confirmed by any other source. The discussion of the massacres is preceded by a useful sociological overview of the tribal situation and a history of the region.

Halli, Reşat (1972). *Türkiye Cumhuriyetinde Ayaklanmalar (1924-1938)* (Rebellions in the Republic of Turkey, 1924-1938). In Turkish. Ankara: T.C. Genelkurmay Başkanligi

Harp Tarihi Dairesi. Reissued in abbreviated form in Bulut, 1991a.
The official military history of the Kurdish and other rebellions, prepared by the War History Office of the Turkish General Staff, and based upon the Army's archives. It was printed in a very limited edition for restricted circulation, and even those few copies were withdrawn almost immediately upon publication. The recent re-edition has at last made this highly important material generally available.
This voluminous study gives very detailed accounts of the military operations against rebel movements. With bureaucratic precision, numbers of rebels (and their dependents) killed or captured are listed day by day, and villages destroyed and burned down are proudly enumerated. Relevant government memoranda and reports are also quoted.

Işik, Haydar (1990). *Dersimli Memik Aga* (Memik Agha of Dersim). In Turkish. Istanbul: Belge Yayinlari.
A novel set at the time of the Dersim rebellion and the Turkish punitive campaigns. The author is from Dersim himself, and the narrative of the large events is clearly based on local oral history.

Pamukçu, Ebubekir (1992). *Dersim Zaza Ayaklanmasinin Tarihsel Kökenleri* (Historical roots of the uprising of the Zazas of Dersim). In Turkish. Istanbul: Yön. 142 pp.
A study of the backgrounds of the Dersim rebellion of 1937 that emphasizes the distinct ethnic character of Dersim. (Most tribes there do not speak Kurdish proper but a related language called Zaza; the author is a spokesman for a nascent Zaza nationalism).

Şilan, B. (1990-92). Degişik Yönleriyle Dersim Ayaklanmasi (Various aspects of the Dersim Rebellion). In Turkish. *Deng* 1(3), pp. 22-31; 1(4), pp. 33-39; 3(20), pp. 26-36.
Description of the Dersim rebellion and its suppression, based largely on interviews with survivors besides the standard written accounts. *Deng* is a Kurdish political and cultural monthly published in Istanbul since 1990.

Şimsir, Bilal N. (1975). *Ingiliz Belgeleriyle Türkiye'de 'Kürt Sorunu' (1924-1938)* (The 'Kurdish Question' in Turkey, According to British Documents, 1924-1938). Ankara: Dişişleri Bakanligi.
Straightforward publication of documents from the Public Record Office concerning the Kurdish rebellions in Turkey. Contains comments by British diplomats on the massacres and deportations, but is not exhaustive.

Şivan, Dr. (1975). *Kürt Millet Hareketleri ve Irak'ta Kürdistan Ihtilali* (Kurdish national uprisings and the revolution of Kurdistan in Iraq). In Turkish. Stockholm: privately printed. [First published clandestinely in Turkey in 1970].
A history of the Kurdish movement. The author, whose real name was Sait Kirmizitoprak, was the chairman of the Democratic Party of Kurdistan in Turkey and wrote this book when living in exile under the protection of the Iraqi sister party, so that his information on Iraq in the late 1960s is first-hand. He was born in Dersim, and the section on the Dersim massacres of 1937 and 1938, apparently based on oral sources, constitutes one of the very few written Kurdish testimonies on the events.

Ulug, Naşit Hakki (1939). *Tunceli Medeniyete Açiliyor* (Tunceli is opened up for civilization). In Turkish. Istanbul: Cumhuriyet Matbaasi.
Jubilant account, by a committed Kemalist politician (member of parliament for Kütahya in western Turkey), of the progress brought to previously backward Tunceli (the new name for Dersim), thanks to the civilizing mission of the Turkish Army.

There is not a word about massacres. This book is important for understanding the mentality of Turkey's ruling circles of the time.

COUNTERINSURGENCY, DEATH SQUADS AND INDISCRIMINATE KILLINGS OF CIVILIANS IN THE 1990'S

Amnesty International (1991). *Southeast Turkey: Attacks on Human Rights Activists and Killings of Local Politicians*. AI Index: EUR 44/114/91. London: Amnesty International, International Secretariat.
   The year 1991 saw the beginning of a wave of death squad-type killings of Kurdish politicians and human rights activists, the first of which are documented in this report.

Amnesty International (1992). *Turkey: Torture, Extrajudicial Executions, "Disappearances"*. AI Index: EUR 44/39/92. London: Amnesty International, International Secretariat. 32 pp.
   Describes new legislation in Turkey under which "prisoners of conscience" were released and death sentences commuted, the continuation of systematic torture and the alarming rise in killings of prominent Kurds in eastern Turkey by what appear to be death squads linked with security forces. Targets of the killings are Kurds suspected of links with the separatist PKK as well as Kurdish legal politicians and human rights activists.

Cowell, Alan (1992). Turkey's effort to quell rebel Kurds raises alarm in Ankara and Europe. *New York Times* (March 27), p. 10.
   Reports on death squads in eastern Turkey and on the growing influence of the radical Kurdish nationalist party, the Workers' Party of Kurdistan (PKK).

Helsinki Watch (1992). *Kurds Massacred: Turkish Forces Kill Scores of Peaceful Demonstrators*. New York: Helsinki Watch. 15pp. [Reports series, Vol.4, Issue 9, June 1992]
   Report of a mission to Southeastern Turkey to investigate the killings of Kurdish civilians by security troops during the 1992 Newroz celebrations in Cizre and Nusaybin. Provides the most detailed and balanced account of these massacres available in English, based on interviews with eyewitnesses. Documents also other recent cases of state terror against the Kurds and of violence against civilians by the Kurdish guerrilla movement PKK. Concludes that the Newroz massacres were not an anomaly, and that the security forces in the area can kill and torture civilians with impunity.

The Kurds in Iraq in the 1980's

DESTRUCTION OF VILLAGES, CHEMICAL ATTACKS, MASS EXECUTIONS

Bonner, Raymond (1992). Always Remember. *The New Yorker* (September 28), pp. 46-51, 54-58, and 63-65.
   An overview of the Anfal campaigns. [Not seen by the present author]

Galbraith, Peter (1991). *Kurdistan in the Time of Saddam Hussein*. A Staff Report to the Committee on Foreign Relations of the U.S. Senate, November 1991. Washington, D.C.: U.S. Government Printing Office.
[Not seen by the present author]

Galbraith, Peter W., and Van Hollen, Christopher, Jr. (1988). *Chemical Weapons Use in Kurdistan: Iraq's Final Offensive*. A Staff Report to the Committee on Foreign Relations, United States Senate, October 1988. Washington, D.C.: U.S. Government Printing Office. 46 pp.
    A detailed report of Iraq's gas bombing of at least thirty Kurdish villages in August 1988, based on interviews with Iraqi Kurds who fled into Turkey. Quotes verbatim eyewitness accounts (pp. 14-27) and summarizes the physical evidence of the use of chemical weapons.

Hay, Alistair, and Roberts, Gwynne (1990). The use of poison gas against the Iraqi Kurds: Analysis of bomb fragments, soil and wool samples, *Journal of the American Medical Association*, 263(8), 1065-1066.
[Not seen by the present author]

Heyndrickx, A. (1989). Clinical toxologic reports and conclusions concerning the biological and environmental samples brought to the Department of Toxicology at the State University of Ghent for toxicologic investigation. In *Documentation of the International Conference on Human Rights in Kurdistan, 14.-16. April 1989, Hochschule Bremen*. Bremen: Initiative for Human Rights in Kurdistan, pp. 210-225.
    Presents the results of chemical analysis of hair, urine, blood, water, stone, and bombshell samples taken at Halabja a few weeks after the gas attack of March 1988. Concludes that at least three war gases were used in combination: mustard gas, an organic phosphate such as tabun or sarin, and cyanide or derivatives.

Insan Haklari Dernegi Istanbul Şubesi (1990). *Halepçe'den Kamplara... Kürtler...* (The Kurds... from Halabja to the Camps...). In Turkish. Istanbul: Alan-Belge. 87 pp.
    Report on the Iraqi Kurds who fled into Turkey after the August 1988 gas attacks, prepared by the Istanbul branch of Turkey's Association for Human Rights. Deals mostly with the less than hospitable treatment of the refugees in Turkey, but also summarily lists Iraq's various chemical offensives against the Kurds.

Kurdish Program, The (1988). The destruction of Iraqi Kurdistan. *Kurdish Times* 2(2), 1-6. [Published by the Kurdish Program, Cultural Survival, Inc., New York]
    Furnishes some detailed information on mass deportations of Iraqi Kurds, deliberate destruction of Kurdish villages, and the use of chemical arms against the Kurds by the Iraqi authorities. Source of this information is apparently the Kurdish leader Jalal Talabani, interviewed on the occasion of his visit to Washington in June 1988. Out of approximately five thousand villages existing in Iraqi Kurdistan in 1975, 3,479 are said to have been deliberately destroyed. The number of Iraqi Kurdish refugees in Iran is said to be 250,000, which includes 100,000 Fayli Kurds forcibly deported by the Iraqi authorities. Several cases of mass executions and mass disappearances are mentioned. Details are given on several chemical attacks preceding the bombing of Halabja. Surviving civilian casualties who sought medical treatment were arrested and reportedly executed. The international community has not responded in any way to Kurdish calls for protection.

Makiya, Kanan (1992). The Anfal: Uncovering an Iraqi campaign to exterminate the

Kurds. *Harper's* (May), 53-61.

Moving report of a visit to Iraqi Kurdistan in November 1991 and analysis of some of the official Iraqi documents that were captured by the Kurds in the spring of 1991. Makiya provides new details about the *Anfal* offensives of 1988 and a reasoned estimate that at least 100,000 noncombatant Kurds were murdered in the course of these campaigns. Kurdish spokesmen quoted by the author even claim a figure of 182,000 dead or disappeared - an extrapolation based on the number of destroyed villages. 1,276 villages were totally destroyed during these campaigns alone. The article contains long interviews with survivors of the first gas attacks of 1987 and of the mass murders of 1988. (The author, himself an Iraqi Arab, had earlier published, under the pseudonym of Samir al-Khalil, the most penetrating analysis of the Iraqi Ba'ath regime to date, *Republic of Fear*).

Makiya, Kanan (1993). *Cruelty and Silence: War, Tyranny, Uprising, and the Arab World*. London: Jonathan Cape. 367 pp. [also New York: W.W. Norton and Co. 256 pp.]

An essay on the violence and cruelty of the Iraqi Ba'ath regime and the failure of Arab intellectuals to speak out in a moral voice. The first part of the book deals with the occupation of Kuwait, the uprisings of the Shiites and the Kurds following Iraq's defeat, and the *Anfal* campaigns. Chapter 4 (pp. 135-150) focuses on the village of Goktapa, where around 150 persons died in a chemical attack in May 1988. Chapter 5 (pp. 151-199), organized around a long interview with a boy who miraculously survived a fire squad, deals extensively and in great detail with the mass killings of Kurdish civilians in these campaigns (part of this material was earlier published in Makiya, 1992).

Medico International (1990). Deportations in Iraqi Kurdistan and Kurdish refugees in Iran. In *Yearbook of the Kurdish Academy 1990*. Ratingen (Germany): The Kurdish Academy, pp. 59-77.

Report on a visit by German parliamentarians and medical relief workers to Iraqi Kurdistan in November 1989 and a separate visit to refugee camps in Iran. Eyewitness accounts of destruction and new strategic settlements; interviews with Iraqi officials and Kurdish refugees. Quotes calculations by one of the Kurdish parties, the Patriotic Union of Kurdistan, on numbers of villages destroyed and persons deported. At least 100,000 persons said to have been deported or disappeared in the *Anfal* offensives; another 100,000 Iraqi Kurds are said to live in Iran.

Middle East Watch (1990). *Human Rights in Iraq*. New Haven: Yale University Press. 164 pp.

The first chapters of this important report (researched by David A. Korn) explain the institutions of repression in Iraq, the legal setting, and actual forms of repression. Numerous examples of political killings (including the notorious thallium poisonings), disappearances and deportations are listed. In many, but by no means all of these cases, the victims were Kurds. Chapter 5 (pp. 69-96) deals especially with the "Kurdish minority," sketching the struggle for autonomy and government reprisals against the Kurds and describing in detail the use of chemical weapons in 1988 and the forced resettlement and depopulation of Kurdistan. Official denials of chemical warfare by Iraqi authorities are also quoted and it is shown that they do not stand up to scrutiny. Finally, the report investigates the case of food poisoning in a Kurdish refugee camp in Turkey in 1989, affecting 2,000 refugees. There are indications that they may have been victims of deliberate poisoning with a chemical warfare agent, but the evidence is inconclusive.

Middle East Watch (1993). *Genocide in Iraq. The Anfal Campaign Against the Kurds.* New York: Human Rights Watch. 370 pp. [Commercial edition to appear at Yale University Press].

The most complete report to date on Iraq's treatment of the Kurds: destruction of villages, deportations, chemical bombardments, mass executions. Based on 350 interviews with eyewitnesses (among whom eight survivors of mass executions), a preliminary study of Iraqi military and intelligence documents captured by the Kurds during the March 1991 uprising, and some forensic evidence. Gives a very detailed account of the eight separate *Anfal* campaigns carried out between February and September 1988 and of the procedure by which tens of thousands captured in these campaigns were collected, screened and despatched to firing squads or inhumane prisons. The total number of Kurds executed (not including those killed in the military campaigns themselves) "cannot conceivably be less than 50,000, and it may well be twice that number" (p. 345). The executions continued even after the Iraqi government had declared an amnesty (pp. 326-333). Two distinct minorities living in Kurdistan, Christians and Yezidis, were excluded from the amnesty, and fell victim to mass "disappearances" even after that date. The authors conclude that the Iraqi regime had intended to destroy the Iraqi Kurds in part and had done so, "resulting in the consummated crime of genocide" (20). They also analyze the role of the various state organs involved in the genocide and attempt to establish responsibility for the different aspects of this process.

Middle East Watch, and Physicians for Human Rights (1992). *Unquiet Graves: The Search for the Disappeared in Iraqi Kurdistan.* New York: Middle East Watch, and Physicians for Human Rights. 41 pp.

Report of a forensic team that visited Iraqi Kurdistan in December 1991 to investigate graves believed to contain the remains of victims of extra-legal killings. A number of graves near Sulaimaiyah were opened; bullet wounds in the skulls confirmed information from gravediggers and other local people that these were victims of summary executions. Some of the Iraqi secret police documents captured by the Kurds were inspected, including long lists of names of prisoners executed between 1985 and 1989. Although concentrating on the traces of extra-legal executions that could be established in Kurdistan, the report also mentions the much more numerous disappearances in the course of the Anfal campaign, quoting the Kurdish estimate of 180,000 persons. Few of the captured documents shed light on what happened to them, but one person interviewed had received official confirmation that his disappeared relatives were dead. Another interviewee was the sole survivor of a whole convoy of trucks loaded with women and children, who had been taken to southern Iraq, herded into bulldozer-dug pits and shot dead in 1988.

Middle East Watch, and Physicians for Human Rights (1993). *The Anfal Campaign in Iraqi Kurdistan: The Destruction of Koreme.* New York: Middle East Watch, and Physicians for Human Rights. 116 pp.

Report of a team of forensic investigators who carried out exhumations at three sites in Iraqi Kurdistan. A mass grave in the destroyed village of Koreme contained the remains of 26 men and boys, all of whom had died by gunfire at close range in a line indicating execution by firing squad. The circumstances of the execution are reconstructed on the basis of interviews with survivors. In the destroyed village of Birjinni, which had been bombed with chemical weapons, soil and other samples were taken; chemical analysis of the samples in a British military laboratory found degradation products of mustard gas and nerve agents. The report contains a detailed account of the chemical attack on Birjinni, based on interviews with survivors (pp. 31-44). The third exhumation was at a graveyard in Erbil, where survivors of the

Anfal offensive had been taken.

Miller, Judith (1993). Iraq accused: A case of genocide. *The New York Times Magazine* (January 3), pp. 12-17, 28, 31-33, 36.
Discusses the Anfal campaign and Middle East Watch's work on the official documents captured in Iraqi Kurdistan.

Physicians for Human Rights (1989). *Winds of Death: Iraq's Use of Poison Gas against its Kurdish Population.* Somerville, Massachusetts: Physicians for Human Rights.
[Not seen by the present author]

Rasool, Shorsh Mustafa (1990). *Forever Kurdish. Statistics of atrocities in Iraqi Kurdistan.* Utrecht: Kurdish Information Bureau (distributed by the PUK foreign representation).
A detailed survey, district by district, of Kurdish villages forcibly evacuated and destroyed since the mid-1970s.

Resool, Shorsh (1990). *Destruction of a Nation.* Privately published.
[Not seen by the present author; referred to in Middle East Watch, 1993. Appears to be largely identical with Rasool, 1990].

Saeedpour, Vera Beaudin (1992). Establishing state motives for genocide: Iraq and the Kurds. In Fein, Helen (Ed.) *Genocide Watch.* New Haven: Yale University Press, pp. 59-69.
Argues that "the poison gas attacks in August 1988 cannot be explained simply as a response to Kurdish rebellion or the Kurds' role in the Iran-Iraq war but are better explained as the final phase of a deliberate Iraqi plan to remove Kurds temporarily from their ancestral lands for economic and strategic reasons." The Kurdish region in Iraq has great strategic importance, which further increased when Iraq's access to the Gulf was virtually cut off during the war. The villages subjected to gas attack in August 1988 were all located in a zone close to the major road, railroad and pipeline connecting Iraq with Turkey. The author concludes that the depopulation of Iraqi Kurdistan was a deliberate policy, for which the Kurds' siding with Iran during the war was only a pretext. Deportations and earlier use of chemical weapons against the Kurds are briefly discussed, presenting largely the same data as given earlier in Kurdish Program (1988). (The author is the chairperson of The Kurdish Program).

Sherzad, A. (1992). The Kurdish movement in Iraq: 1975-88. In Kreyenbroek, Philip G., and Sperl, Stefan (Eds.), *The Kurds: A Contemporary Overview.* London: Routledge, pp. 134-142.
An analysis of changes in the social composition of the Kurdish movement in Iraq, with comments on the role of neighboring countries, Iraq's radical solution of its Kurdish problem (deportation, destruction of villages, chemical weapons), and demographic change in Iraqi Kurdistan.

Stoel, Max van der (1992). *Report on the Situation of Human Rights in Iraq, Prepared by Mr. Max van der Stoel, Special Rapporteur of the Commission on Human Rights, in Accordance with Commission Resolution 1991/74.* (E/CN.4/1992/31, 18 February 1992). United Nations Economic and Social Council, Commission on Human Rights. 86 pp.
A careful and well-documented survey of the human rights situation in Iraq, based on independent investigation, including confidential interviews with victims and eyewitnesses in Iraq, Iran and Saudi Arabia. Section II.B.1 (pp. 27-30) details violations affecting the Kurds and discusses evidence of mass executions and

atrocities committed by the Government which, the Rapporteur found, "go beyond the cruelty and brutality directed against the population at large" (p. 28). The *Anfal* and other operations "were indiscriminately aimed against the Kurds as such" (p. 29). The *Anfal* operations in particular "constituted genocide-type activities which did in fact result in the extermination of a part of this population and which continue to have an impact on the lives of the people as a whole" (p. 65).

Tuşalp, Erbil (1989). *Zehir Yüklü Bulutlar: Halepçe' den Hakkari'ye* (Clouds carrying poison: From Halabja to Hakkari). In Turkish. Ankara: Bilgi. 172 pp.
   The core of this journalistic book consists of interviews with Iraqi Kurds who fled into Turkey after the August 1988 gas attacks. These eyewitness accounts (pp. 53-61) are sandwiched between observations on the situation of the Kurds in Iraq and Turkey and critical remarks on the government policies towards the Kurds of both countries.

Viorst, Milton (1988). Poison gas and genocide: The shaky case against Iraq. *Washington Post* (October 5).
   Claims that the gas attacks of August 1988 were only against "rebel positions," and that the symptoms observed in refugees who reached Turkey could have been produced by "a powerful tear gas, a conventional weapon in today's warfare." The author asserts that there is no convincing evidence of genocide or chemical warfare by Iraq. (In order to reach this conclusion, Viorst had to ignore numerous eyewitness reports according to which civilians in villages were targeted, and which consistently described the effects of the poison gases).

Zibari, Hisyar (1989). The missing Barzani Kurds. In *Documentation of the International Conference on Human Rights in Kurdistan, 14.-16. April 1989, Hochschule Bremen*. Bremen: Initiative for Human Rights in Kurdistan, pp. 205-209.
   Documents the case of 8000 male members of the Barzani tribe, who have disappeared after having been taken from the resettlement camps where they were then living and driven off in military trucks in August 1983. Describes also a new project for the forced resettlement of a quarter million Kurds in strategic "new towns" and four internment camps containing around 85,000 people previously deported to other parts of the country.

The Kurds in the (Former) Soviet Union

Laber, Jeri (1990). Stalin's Dumping Ground. *New York Review of Books* (October 11), 50-53.
   Report of a visit by Helsinki Watch director Laber to Kazakhstan, containing an interview with Kurdish academician Nadirov on the deportations of Kurds in the Soviet Union. Nadirov claims that half of those deported perished on the way.

Nadirov, Nadir K. (1992). Population transfer: A scattered people seeks its nationhood. *Cultural Survival Quarterly* (Winter), pp. 38-40.
   Discusses deportations of Kurds in the Soviet Union in the 1930s and 1940s, with some statistics on dramatic decreases of the Kurdish population of what once was the Kurdish National District (Lachin). As elderly people remember, "all the adult males in a town would be gathered at night and sent off by train. No one knows where they went, and none of them returned. After the men, the women and children were packed into freight cars and also sent to unknown destinations" (p. 38). The scattering of the

Kurds hastened the loss of their culture and ethnic identity.

Vanly, Ismet Chériff (1992). The Kurds in the Soviet Union. In Kreyenbroek, Philip G., and Sperl, Stefan (Eds.), *The Kurds: A Contemporary Overview*. London: Routledge, pp. 193-218.

Brief historical survey from the late nineteenth century down to the recent present. Describes Stalin's shifting policies towards the Kurds, and mass deportations of Kurds from Armenia and Azerbaijan in 1937 and from Georgia in 1944. Of the last group, "most adult males were deported separately and their fate is at present still unknown" (p. 203). Reproduces and analyzes the available population statistics with their mysteriously declining numbers of Kurds.

6

The East Timor Genocide

James Dunn

The experience of East Timor, following the invasion of the Portuguese colony by Indonesia in 1975, possesses unique characteristics as a case of genocide in a contemporary setting, in the terms of Article II of the Convention.

The annexation of the former Portuguese colony by Indonesian armed forces resulted, in relative terms, in one of the heaviest losses of life in modern history. A significant part of the national group were killed, while tens of thousands more suffered "serious bodily or mental harm." Moreover, the policies devised by the Indonesian authorities to bring about total integration are threatening the very existence of Timorese culture as it has existed for centuries. This last-mentioned process is still continuing, and it presents a challenge to the international community to rise up to the obligations set out in international humanitarian instruments. The fact that genocide in Timor has not been an international issue in the formal sense reflects not on the seriousness of the problem itself, but on the inadequacies in effective prosecution of this gross violation of human rights.

As far as the Timorese are concerned there is another, historical dimension to their case. In 1942, the Timorese rallied to the Allied cause, and their generous assistance enabled an Australian commando force to contain thousands of Japanese troops at a time when invasion of Australia seemed imminent. However, when the Australians withdrew, the Japanese turned on their supporters, imposing a harsh occupation which cost the lives of more than 10% of the population.

Thus, for the second time within half a century the unfortunate people of

East Timor faced another ordeal of indiscriminate killing, torture and destruction of their villages. The regime may have been different, but many of its methods were similar, and the loss of life in East Timor has turned out to be even greater. This time the violation of their supposedly inalienable right to determine their own future has raised the possibility that their captive status may be forever. Furthermore, the military regime which committed the offenses in the worst years continues to rule the territory, and its determination to resist international pressures in favor of some kind of act of self-determination remains undiminished. Despite the acknowledged gravity of this case, it is yet to be seriously addressed by the international community. One of the most disturbing aspects of the case is that this act of annexation was not opposed by the Western powers with influence in Jakarta; on the contrary, this blatant act of annexation was virtually accommodated by them in what could only be described as indecent haste.

THE INVASION OF EAST TIMOR BY INDONESIA

East Timor is a very remote and little known territory, and in the international circumstances prevailing in 1975 the Indonesian invasion attracted very little attention from the world community. Nor did the international community take much interest in its aftermath of genocidal killing, which contributed to a loss of population of devastating proportions, massive social disruption, and what has turned out to be the restoration of a form of colonial rule, a form harsher than that endured by the Timorese people under Portuguese rule. In stark contrast to not dissimilar situations such as the British reaction to Argentina's attempt to annex the Falkland Islands, the United States-led response to Iraq's seizure of Kuwait and the struggle of the Baltic States, this gross violation of the rights of the Timorese people was virtually condoned.

Most notably, it was ignored by two nations, the United States and Australia - both of whom were later to participate in the Gulf Coalition, where the issues at stake were strikingly similar. Indeed, the Indonesian military action was virtually facilitated by their compliance, and their accommodating acceptance of the status quo thus helped seal the fate of East Timor, the only former colony to be denied the right to enjoy independence. While it may be true that the way the operation was carried out did not enjoy the approval of western governments, at no stage were their expressions of disapproval serious enough to cause Jakarta to halt a campaign which was to inflict horrendous loss of life on the indigenous population.

As in the case of Kuwait years later, when the invasion occurred East Timor's hopes rested largely on the western response, though for somewhat different reasons. East Timor was not important in the convergence of super-power relations; it was of no political, strategic or economic interest to the Soviet Union or China - or even to Vietnam, to include all of Washington's potential adversaries in the Southeast Asian area. Unlike Kuwait, at no stage was East Timor the subject of a formal territorial claim from the government which had sent in the invading force.

SOME BASIC BACKGROUND

The island of Timor lies at the southeastern extremity of the archipelago of Nusatenggara, which in Dutch times was called the Lesser Sundas. It is located at the opposite end of the island chain which begins with one of Asia's best-known tourist attractions, the island of Bali. The Portuguese colony of East Timor comprised the eastern half of the island. As the result of colonial expansion and rivalry, Timor was divided into two almost equal parts, a partition which began to take shape about the middle of the 17th century, in line with the attrition of Portugal's colonial presence in the East Indies. Boundary disputes between the two colonial powers persisted until the late 19th century, that is until the Lisbon Convention of 1893, and the subsequent signing of the *Sentenca Arbitral* in April 1913, which set the borders as they exist today.[1]

East Timor is a small country, but it is not insignificant by the standards of smallness among today's membership of the United Nations. On the eve of the Indonesian invasion in 1975, the colony had an area of about 19,000 square kilometers, and a population of about 680,000 people, with an annual growth rate of approximately 2%. This means that today there should be in excess of 950,000 Timorese in the territory, but based on a recent census the population of what is now designated Indonesia's 27th province is only 740,000 people, of whom more than 100,000 have in recent years moved into the territory from elsewhere in Indonesia. It means that, in effect, the population of East Timor indicates such a catastrophic decline, that more than 17 years since the invasion, it is still over 10% less than what it was in 1975.[2]

Prior to the invasion, the ethnic and cultural pattern of life in East Timor was exceedingly complex, but, aside from some special characteristics, it resembled the patterns in the nearby islands of Eastern Nusatenggara.[3] The population was essentially Austronesian in character, but with a noticeable Melanesian influence. It reflected a long procession of migrations from west, north and from the east. But it would be simplistic to describe the territory as culturally part of Indonesia if only because of the great ethnic and cultural diversity within the sprawling archipelago. To call a Timorese Indonesian is rather like calling a Kurd an Iraqi, or a Tibetan Chinese. In such cases the labels are both imprecise and resented. In fact the Timorese regarded visitors from elsewhere in the archipelago with some suspicion, but they were not really hostile towards them until after 1974, that is, until after Indonesia's designs on the colony became apparent.

While most Indonesians today might have a strong sense of nationality, it could be argued that their nation was created not by a natural historical evolution but by colonial circumstances, determined by imperial and commercial rivalry in distant Western Europe. The legitimacy of the Indonesian state, it could therefore be said, has its roots in Dutch colonialism rather than in the natural evolution of a national political culture. The notion of an East Timor nation also had its roots in the territory's experience of Portuguese colonialism, just as Malaysia, Singapore and the north Kalimantan states were shaped by British colonial policies and fortunes. As a political concept, the idea of a nation of East Timor is surely no less valid, even taking into account the arbitrary division of the island.

Portuguese navigators first reached Timor about twenty years after Columbus completed his epic trans-Atlantic crossing, and about fifty years later their colonial rule of the area began in earnest. Therefore, for some four centuries in East Timor, Portugal had been the dominant, almost exclusive, external influence - except for a brief Japanese interregnum, from January 1942 until the surrender in August 1945.

Until 1974, the status of East Timor was apparently a matter of little concern or interest to Indonesia. In the last seven years of Sukarno's presidency, Indonesia was to become one of the most aggressive anti-colonial states, vigorously asserting its own claim for the "return" of West Irian. And after that objective was secured, Indonesia embarked on a costly and futile confrontation of Malaysia, which Sukarno perceived as a British neo-colonial creation. However, at no stage did Indonesia seek to bring any real pressure to bear on the Portuguese in East Timor, although the Salazar regime was at that time the only colonial power in open defiance of the post-war decolonization process endorsed by the U.N., which by the early sixties was gathering momentum.

While Dutch colonialism in West New Guinea was denounced in vitriolic terms, the more traditional form of colonial rule then being conducted by the Portuguese in neighboring East Timor was rarely mentioned. True, in the early sixties, at about the time of Indonesia's Confrontation of Malaysia, there were occasional remarks by a few leading Indonesian political figures, who hinted that East Timor's future lay with its big neighbor, but these statements were not taken further by the Government of the time in Jakarta, never evolving into a formal claim or political campaign.[4] Even in the two years preceding Indonesia's military intervention, most official statements from Jakarta emphasized East Timor's right to self-determination.[5] At no stage, therefore, either under Sukarno or Suharto, was it ever officially argued that East Timor's destiny lay with Indonesia.

FROM PORTUGUESE RULE TO
INDONESIAN INTERVENTION

In the post-war years, most governments of the former European powers wilted before the gathering winds of decolonization, and parted with their colonies. However, the Portuguese government led by Dr. Antonio de Oliveira Salazar ignored these winds of change, in the early sixties designating the component parts of Portugal's rambling empire "overseas provinces," a device designed to counter the international political implications of the formal U.N. pronouncements on decolonization.[6] It was not until after the April coup in Lisbon in 1974 that these overseas territories were granted the right to self-determination.

Prior to the coup, while most of Portugal's African colonies were engaged in armed struggles in pursuit of independence, in East Timor a relative calm prevailed. However, the Timorese quickly organized themselves into political parties. Two major movements emerged - Fretilin,[7] a left-wing nationalist movement, and UDT,[8] a more conservative grouping, both of which by the following September had come out in favor of independence.

While few Timorese were attracted to the notion of joining with Indonesia, integration was not discounted by the Portuguese colonial administrators who, for more than two decades, had lived with the fear of an Indonesian claim, that is, after President Sukarno's aggressive campaign to acquire West Irian began in the early sixties. To the Timorese themselves, it must be stressed, at the very outset integration was an option with little appeal among the population at large. However, a very small party, called Apodeti,[9] was formed with integration as its objective. But Apodeti was little more than a political contrivance, reflecting not the aspirations of an identifiable minority, but rather the opportunistic concerns of a group of Timorese, among them the more conservative feudal chiefs, who had always been pillars of support for the Salazar regime. Independence would mean popular government and an end to the privileges they had enjoyed under the Portuguese.

But even with this support, Apodeti would not have existed without strong Indonesian financial and political backing, and without some support from the Portuguese administration. In 1974, some officials, especially those of the military who were anxious that Portugal should withdraw from Timor as soon as possible, assumed a responsibility to urge the Timorese to give careful consideration to integration as an option. Some also believed that the Indonesians would be more likely to accept the popular will, if the option of joining with them were openly and impartially presented to the Timorese community.[10] Nevertheless, integration with Indonesia was the very last thing the Timorese wanted, and that should have been apparent to all who cared to find out. Most preferred to continue as a Portuguese territory rather than become part of Indonesia. To integrate with Indonesia was, as one put it to the writer, not *de*colonization but *re*colonization, or colonial rule from Java.

At this juncture, it should be stressed that the independence movement in Timor was not antagonistic towards Indonesia in its early stages. The Timorese may have been apprehensive about Indonesia's attitude to them, but they were not hostile towards Indonesians as a people. In fact, a generous response by the then Foreign Minister, Adam Malik, in May 1974 deeply impressed the young Timorese leaders in the Fretilin movement.[11] At the time, one of the Fretilin leaders, Jose Ramos Horta, told the writer that if Malik's magnanimous response were to prevail in Jakarta, his independence movement would consider inviting Indonesia to be responsible for East Timor's foreign affairs and defence when the territory became independent.[12] The reality of the time, however, was that power in Indonesia was in the hands of the generals and Malik's magnanimous gesture was not to prevail.

At this point, let us turn to the international stage, to those outside forces whose actions sealed the fate of East Timor. In 1974, this distant Portuguese colony was well outside the pressures of Cold War politics. It was undeveloped, isolated and poor, a remote territory beyond the reach of the global network of commercial and tourist communications. It had no abundance of resources to entice the interest of outside powers. It possessed no apparent strategic value to East or West, Indonesia being the only nation at all interested in it as a territorial asset. Its status was therefore of little consequence, in perceptions of national interest, other than to Portugal, Indonesia and, to a lesser extent, Australia, and it was on the goodwill and responses of these states that the territory's future was to depend. By the end of 1974, the Portuguese themselves had turned to Europe and had become disinterested in a distant colony whose weak economy was more of a liability than an asset.

In the view of the Australian political establishment, East Timor was of negligible strategic and economic importance. This was not always the case; in the fifties the Australian Government held the view that Indonesian rule over East Timor was not in Australia's interests. But in 1962, with the Dutch agreement to transfer West New Guinea to Indonesia, there occurred a major policy shift in Canberra. And, significantly, by 1974 Australia's position had shifted further: Prime Minister Whitlam, who developed an easy relationship with President Suharto soon after taking office in December 1972, was strongly of the view that East Timor's integration with Indonesia was a preferred solution, to use the jargon of the time. His views on the subject were made known unequivocally to the Indonesian President when the two leaders met in Central Java in September of that year.

The Timorese, however, had a much more optimistic view of Australia's position. Prime Minister Whitlam was an energetic and inspiring reformer, and shortly after gaining office he declared his strong support for the right of self-determination. Moreover his government was one of the first Western states to recognize the independence of Guinea-Bissau, a decision which did not pass unnoticed in Dili. Furthermore, the idea that Australia owed a debt to East Timor because of the extensive support our forces received during their commando operation against the Japanese in 1942 [13] had created an unshakeable belief that Australia could be relied upon to support whatever option the Timorese people chose.

In the circumstances prevailing in 1974-75, Australia was one country in a position to head off Indonesia's designs on East Timor, and not only because of the rapport developed between Prime Minister Whitlam and President Suharto. The Indonesian leader was himself concerned at the impact military intervention in Timor might have on his personal standing as a leader free of the territorial ambitions that had, under Sukarno, threatened Indonesia with international isolation. Of all countries, Australia knew more about Indonesia's intentions. Its diplomatic and intelligence community were in a position to monitor the moves for military action against the Portuguese colony, even as they were taking shape. Thus Australian analysts, and through them, U.S. advisers, knew what the Indonesian military were up to, including the setting-up of an elaborate covert operation designed to bring integration, if necessary by military force.[14] The Australians became aware of the subsequent mobilizing of a sizeable task force for the assault on the Timorese capital, months before the operation was launched.

In the circumstances, the compliant Australian response, at high official levels, clearly had the effect of strengthening the hands of the generals bent on the annexation on East Timor. Indeed, it could be said that the viability of this operation was predicated on the assumption that Australia would go along with it. And if Australia did not protest, nor would Washington oppose the invasion.[15] Paradoxically, at that time the Australian Government was under a dynamic leader, who had declared strong support for the principle of self-determination, and who was on good terms with the Indonesian leader. In short, Australia was in a position to use its extensive influence with like-minded governments to persuade Indonesia not to intervene in East Timor.

INDONESIAN MOVES TOWARDS INTEGRATION

By the end of 1974 Indonesia was waging a propaganda war against the Timorese independence movement. As a party of the left, Fretilin became a central target. The Fretilin leaders were accused of being communist, and of being anti-Indonesian, and falsified accounts of links between the Fretilin leadership and Peking and Hanoi were circulated. In reaction to these propaganda outpourings, the Timorese themselves became increasingly hostile to the Indonesian authorities.

While in the first couple of months after April 1974 some Portuguese administration officers were contending privately that joining with Indonesia made sense for East Timor, the enormous popular enthusiasm for independence eventually convinced Lisbon that the Timorese were simply not disposed to accept integration. They saw themselves as being different, culturally, politically, linguistically and in terms of their religion.[16] The aggressive and clumsy attempt by the Indonesians, after August 1974, to intimidate the Timorese merely served to strengthen their national consciousness.

The Portuguese authorities commenced a decolonization program late in 1974, presenting the Timorese political elite with three options - that is, full independence, continuing with Portugal under some new and more democratic arrangement, or integration with Indonesia.

It soon became clear to the Timorese themselves that the magnanimity conveyed to Jose Ramos-Horta by Foreign Minister Adam Malik in mid-1974 was not in fact shared by Indonesia's most powerful military leaders, who had from the very outset different plans for East Timor's future. To be fair it was not so much a desire for additional territory that motivated them - East Timor was, in the days before the recent offshore oil discoveries anything but an economic prize. One of their main concerns was that an independent East Timor would stimulate separatist tendencies among discontented ethnic groups nearby, such as the West Timorese, the Irianese and the Ambonese. Also, in the aftermath of the Vietnam War, Indonesia's military leadership was obsessed with the risk of Communist infiltration and insurgency. To the military, therefore, integration was the only acceptable solution for East Timor.

As early as the end of 1974, a covert intelligence operation was launched by a group of Indonesian generals, among them, Lieutenant General Ali Murtopo, a trusted presidential adviser, Major General Benny Murdani, a senior intelligence officer also close to the President, and Lieutenant General Yoga Sugama, then head of the Intelligence services. The existence of this operation, code-named "Operasi Komodo"[17] became known to U.S. and Australian intelligence agencies before the year was out. Its aim was to bring about the integration of East Timor by military means if necessary. Its first activities included a propaganda campaign vilifying the independence movement, the encouragement of Apodeti, and the sending of agents into the Portuguese colony. Its subversive ventures were at first clumsy and had the effect not of dividing the two major parties, but of bringing them together into a coalition for independence. Thus it was largely in reaction to this heavy-handed meddling that, early in January, 1975, Fretilin and UDT formed a common front for independence.

The year 1975 proved to be a turbulent one for East Timor. Difficulties, especially with the decolonization program, were further complicated by the political turmoil in Portugal. The conflict in Lisbon demoralized the colonial power's overseas administration, in particular weakening communications between the colonial government and the central government in Portugal. East Timor's neighbor could have eased these problems, but Jakarta followed the opposite course of action. The deteriorating situation in the colonial power was subtly and subversively exploited by the generals heading Operasi Komodo.

Economic conditions in Timor were affected by the crisis in Portugal, but nevertheless conditions in the colony were not in dark and dismal contrast to the more developed Indonesian neighborhood, as apologists for the annexation frequently assert. There was free political expression and movement, and there was great enthusiasm as to the future prospects of the territory. There was no oppression, little violence, no torture and a general feeling that the lot of the indigenous Timorese vis-a-vis the rest of the community was on the verge of radical improvement.

Portuguese colonial practice was undeniably authoritarian in the time of Salazar, but its character had began to change even before 1974, and since the April coup the change had been radical. The economic situation, however, suffered from the deteriorating situation in Lisbon, and Timor's economic development ground to a halt in 1975. The Timorese leaders were nevertheless optimistic that an independent East Timor could become self-sufficient in food and could attract foreign investment, especially for tourism. In the international circumstances of the time, such an optimism was not unsoundly-based.

By mid-autumn of that year, however, differences had surfaced between the two major parties. In other conditions they would not have been insuperable, but they were quickly exploited by the agents of Operasi Komodo, guided by General Ali Murtopo himself. The propaganda offensive against Fretilin was intensified, while the UDT leaders were invited to Jakarta - and courted. They were lectured, sometimes by General Murtopo himself, on the dangers of communist subversion, and were sent on subsidized tours to anti-communist political centers in Asia - to South Korea, the Philippines and Taiwan. And fabricated evidence of links between the Fretilin leaders, on the one hand, and Peking and Hanoi, on the other, was passed on to them. At least three of these Timorese leaders, Lopes da Cruz, Jose Martins and Mousinho, were actually recruited by Bakin, the powerful Indonesian military intelligence agency.[18] By the middle of 1974, relations between the two Timorese parties had become so brittle that talks between them broke down completely. At this sensitive juncture rumors were circulated by Bakin agents that Fretilin was planning a coup, prompting anxiety among the UDT leadership.[19]

Early in August 1975, Murtopo himself advised UDT leaders, whom he had invited to visit Jakarta, that a Fretilin coup was imminent, and he urged them to take preemptive action[20]. Within days of their return to Dili, the UDT leaders, with what military support they could muster, launched a hasty coup in Dili. It was an abortive conspiracy, because in three weeks it was over, Fretilin proving much too strong for the UDT forces. The coup leaders and their followers had been overwhelmed, the remnants being forced to flee across the border into Indonesian Timor.

In this short but intense conflict,[21] the Portuguese, whose administrative apparatus had been reduced to a small number of officials and less than 100 combat troops, withdrew to the offshore island of Atauro.

The Indonesian authorities were taken aback when Fretilin swiftly gained control of the province, and took urgent steps to head off the establishing of an independent East Timor. As soon as the civil war was over, the Fretilin leaders made conciliatory overtures to Jakarta but these were ignored. To respond would have been tantamount to according a legitimacy to Fretilin as the de facto administration. Operasi Komodo's military commanders sought to persuade President Suharto to authorize direct military intervention, but the President was still reluctant to agree to a military assault. He continued to hold back until late in September when Generals Murtopo, Murdani and Yoga Sugama (the intelligence chief) were able to assure him that countries like the United States, Australia and Japan, not to speak of ASEAN, would not object if Indonesian troops moved into Timor. Two weeks later, Indonesia's first major military action, a covert operation, was launched: it began with an attack on the border village of Balibo, but among those killed on the day of the attack were two television teams from Australia.[22]

After its victory, Fretilin set up an interim administration, moved promptly move to assuage Indonesian fears, and its leaders invited the Portuguese to return and resume decolonization. But there was little response from the Portuguese whose government in Lisbon was at that time at the peak of its crisis. Indonesia's reaction was to ignore Fretilin's overture, and to launch attacks over the border from West Timor, attacks designed to create the impression that the unthinkable - a Fretilin victory - had not happened. The official news agency, Antara, informed the world that the "anti-Fretilin forces" were counterattacking. In the light of the diffident Portuguese response to their request to return and resume decolonization, with the Indonesians attacking from the west, and with the international community ignoring their plight, Fretilin's decision to declare their country an independent republic on 28 November was hardly surprising.

For some time it has been fashionable for officials and politicians, especially in Canberra and Jakarta, to blame the Portuguese for what transpired in East Timor, and in particular for the latter's untimely withdrawal from their colony at the end of August 1975. That the Government of the day in Lisbon had much to answer for is beyond doubt, but the arguments used against them are often spurious, and are merely designed to obscure the actions of the aggressors, and the responses of those who accommodated them. One year after the April coup in 1974, Portugal was in the grip of a severe political crisis, which had a demoralizing impact on its understaffed overseas administration. These circumstances were deliberately and cynically exploited by the Indonesian military.

The Portuguese appealed to Australia, in particular, to help out with the decolonization program. After all, long before the 1974 coup Australia had been quietly urging the Portuguese to decolonize. In the circumstances this was a compelling request and deserved a positive response from what should have been a concerned neighbor, but Canberra's reaction was negative and unsympathetic, even cynical. The Australian Government of the time was, it seemed, disinclined to do anything that would get in the way of Indonesia's moves against Timor. Indeed, Australia declined to support moves by Portugal to internationalize the Timor problem, by requesting U.N. involvement.

Between September and December 1975 the situation in East Timor was conducive to a settlement by negotiation and conciliation, if only influential outside powers had taken a responsible interest in the problem. Military intervention by Indonesia was totally unnecessary, unprovoked and unwarranted. It is easy to blame the Portuguese, as Australian politicians have been apt to do, but the main culprit was undoubtedly Indonesia. Largely because of chaotic political conditions in Lisbon, Portugal's attempts to decolonize East Timor were largely ineffective, exposing the Timorese to external manipulation. But it was the Indonesian military who sought actively to undermine the process of self-determination, using an entirely groundless fear of Communist subversion as a pretext. The objective of *Operasi Komodo* was to create disunity among the main political parties in the independence coalition, to fuel suspicions between them, and ultimately encourage armed conflict, evidently in the hope that the ensuing chaotic conditions would provide a justification for military intervention and ultimately forced integration. Yet this sinister operation could have been halted by Jakarta's Western friends. Indonesia may have been somewhat outside the Western alliance in 1975, but the Suharto regime was heavily dependent on the West for economic aid, and on the U.S. for the kind of military assistance which was needed, among other things, for the conduct of military aggression against East Timor.

THE INVASION AND ITS AFTERMATH

Using Fretilin's hasty decision to declare unilaterally East Timor independent as a pretext, the Indonesians lost no time in mounting a full-scale invasion, an amphibious attack on Dili. Resorting to excuses reminiscent of such past incidents as the Nazi invasion of Sudetenland and the Warsaw Pact invasion of Czechoslovakia, the Indonesian authorities masked the attack with the monstrous lie that the attacking force was made up of "volunteers" who were responding to appeals for help from representatives of the majority of the Timorese people who desired integration with Indonesia.

The status of East Timor was nevertheless changed abruptly on 7 December 1975,[23] when this combined military and naval force - codenamed Operasi Seroja - under the overall command of General Benny Murdani, moved in from the sea. From the evidence accumulated over the past 15 years, it is clear that the invasion and subjugation of East Timor, especially in the early stages, was carried out with extraordinary ruthlessness, and at huge cost of the lives and, of course, the rights of the Timorese people. While the invasion provoked the condemnation of the U.N., in the form of General Assembly and Security Council resolutions, it was an issue somewhat outside the sensitive area of East-West confrontation, and failed to excite sufficient concern in the international community for the initial outrage to be maintained.

While the invasion was condemned as a blatant violation of the U.N. Charter, it was more than a year before the humanitarian consequences of the invasion began to attract serious attention. According to Church reports, as many as 60,000 Timorese, almost 10% of the population, may have died in the first twelve months of the invasion, with mass killings similar to those carried out at Dili's Santa Cruz cemetery in November, 1991 a frequent occurrence.

In the very first days of the invasion, rampaging Indonesian troops engaged in an orgy of indiscriminate killing, rape and torture. In the capital, Dili, there were a number of large scale public executions - some of the victims women - which were clearly designed to intimidate the population into accepting the new order. In some villages - for example, in Liquica, Maubara, Suai and Aileu, whole communities were slaughtered, except for infants aged 4 and under.

Outraged by these atrocities, the small but determined Timorese army, the Falintil, under the leadership of Nicolau Lobato, bitterly contested the advance of the invading forces, inflicting heavy losses on the attackers, and until the early eighties denied them effective control outside the main towns and administrative centers. The retaliation of the invaders to this determined resistance was the imposition of a harsh and oppressive occupation regime. In the areas under Indonesian control, such human rights violations as summary killings, torture and rape were a daily occurrence, forcing tens of thousands of Timorese to flee the towns and seek refuge behind Fretilin lines.

The rugged mountainous interior of East Timor provided excellent conditions for the Falintil guerrilla campaign, but the limited resources of the resistance forces were heavily taxed with the task of providing refuge, food and medical support (there was not a single doctor in their area of control) for the large Timorese population behind their lines, who were regularly subjected to air attacks. Bombings and strafing intensified once the Indonesian Air Force acquired Bronco's (OV-10's) from the United States. For a period the Indonesians used napalm which had a devastating impact on villages largely constructed of highly-inflammable dried palm leaves (palapa).

Nevertheless, for more than two years, Fretilin managed to feed the people within the areas under their control by hastily developing the agricultural resources accessible to them in the rich mountain valleys, but, according to radio messages sent by the beleaguered resistance forces, even the farms were eventually to come under attack by AURI aircraft. According to reports, chemical substances were dropped on the crops, causing the plants to die. Reports on the grim situation in East Timor began to come out of the territory as early as the end of 1976. In that year a confidential report from Catholic Church sources depicted a nightmare of oppression and wanton killing. Its authors suggested that in the year since the invasion, as many as 60,000 Timorese might have lost their lives.[24]

By 1978, the Fretilin leaders began encouraging the Timorese to return to Indonesian-occupied areas, the resistance forces no longer being able to feed them, nor to provide the most basic of medical treatment. In the conditions of the time, tens of thousands of Timorese perished from starvation and disease. And during those first terrible years the Indonesians denied international humanitarian organizations, including the IRC, access to the territory.

When the Timorese began to return to areas under Indonesian control, the manner in which they were received was anything but conciliatory and humane. Suspected members of the Fretilin organization were often summarily executed, while others, including children, were beaten or tortured at the slightest provocation. These de facto "refugees" were forced into resettlement camps, based on U.S. military techniques in Vietnam, but in Timor these centers were provided with little food and medical facilities. In

1979, even in the areas under Jakarta's control, thousands of Timorese died needlessly in these camps from famine and disease. Needless to say, this harsh treatment ensured the continuation of the resistance by Fretilin forces in late 1978 and 1979, especially after the killing of their commander, Nicolau Lobato, and the surrender of other leaders. By the early 80's, however, their ranks had been reformed and armed resistance to Indonesian occupation continued at a reduced strength until relatively recently, when Indonesian troops captured Lobato's successor, Xanana Gusmao, and a few months later, his lieutenant, Mau Huno. Gusmao had followed a different strategy from that of Lobato. His force engaged mainly in defensive operations, largely because of the risk of reprisals, while he sought to encourage open-ended negotiations with local Indonesian commanders. The guerrilla force is reported to have declined as a threat in the past year, though there is persistent evidence that it continues to exist.

THE INTERNATIONAL REACTION

Was the international community aware of this very heavy loss of life and if so, how did it react? In fact, these early reports aroused very little international attention, partly because of an indifferent attitude to a small, remote and inconsequential territory. East Timor was no Falkland Islands or Kuwait: it was without any strategic or economic importance, even, it seemed at the time, to its administering colonial power, Portugal. In the late seventies, when the Portuguese political establishment was evidently suffering from post-colonial fatigue, few in Lisbon seemed prepared to address the situation in distant East Timor. In fairness to the Portuguese, they received no encouragement or support from states in Asia-Pacific region. As for the rest of the global community, their reaction was apathetic. In the order of priority on the agenda of world trouble spots, the remote Portuguese colony had virtually no standing.

In the four years following Indonesia's invasion, when East Timor was a killing field, the gravity of the humanitarian situation in this territory could easily have been accorded prominence on the international agenda by Western governments. Best placed to do this were the United States, Australia, Japan and the Netherlands whose close links with Indonesia enabled them to monitor the situation on the ground. After 1979, the International Red Cross was able to regain only limited access to East Timor, and in any case the IRC is restrained from making public reports on such situations. However, diplomats from Western missions in Jakarta made some visits to Timor, though these were limited in duration and scope, and nothing seemed to come out of them until three years after the invasion. In September, 1978, a group of ambassadors visited Timor and were reportedly shocked at the conditions they encountered. There observations led to the readmission of the IRC, and a limited presence by some other humanitarian agencies. However, there were no major public reports condemning Indonesia's occupation of the territory. The western response was for the most part obsequious in character. The occupying power was encouraged to give more attention to humanitarian issues; its right to be there was never seriously questioned.

If these governments had chosen to respond more responsibly and compassionately, the situation in East Timor might today have been radically different.[25] Most chose the opposite path, that is, they helped shield Indonesia from international criticism, initially playing down reports of a genocidal loss of population as being ill-founded and exaggerated, and later stressing Jakarta's readiness to cooperate in the supplying of humanitarian relief. It is inconceivable that the major foreign missions in Jakarta were unaware of the seriousness of the humanitarian situation. Perhaps some reported frankly to their governments, but such reports did not surface in the international media. In the case of missions representing Australia, Canada and the United States, diplomats in Jakarta were clearly inhibited by the tacit support their countries had given Indonesia before and after the invasion. A true statement of the political and humanitarian situation in East Timor would inevitably have discredited the policies of the governments concerned.

Some official public statements could not conceivably have been honestly arrived at. For example, early in 1977, one State Department official told a Congressional subcommittee that only 2000 Timorese had died as a result of the invasion (by that time the death toll, according to Church sources in Timor was over 60,000!). A few weeks later, another official, Robert Oakley, came up with a revised figure of 10,000, which yet another official source later qualified with the comment that many of these deaths had occurred in the civil war between Fretilin and UDT.[26] The implied suggestion that the Timorese had virtually killed themselves was an ugly facet in this protective shield of disinformation fashioned by Jakarta's friends.

Most Australian official responses were delivered in this vein, that is, in a manner evidently designed to diminish the seriousness of the situation on the ground in East Timor, to discredit reports suggesting that Indonesian troops were responsible for serious human rights violations and thus to deflect international concern. Indeed, early in 1978, a year in which tens of thousands of Timorese died as a consequence of a major military campaign, the Australian Government, then led by Prime Minister Fraser, took the extraordinary step of recognizing de-facto the annexation of the territory, which by that had been time designated Indonesia's 27th province.[27] Integration was legitimized by a contrived "act of free choice" in July 1976. A so-called Popular Assembly was formed, with many of its members being coerced into participation. With the building ringed by Indonesian troops, and with the organization in the hands of intelligence officials, a unanimous vote in favor of joining with Indonesia was hardly a surprising outcome. The process was rejected by the United Nations.

It has often been claimed that East Timor has benefited materially from integration, that is, from the extensive development of the province's infrastructure, from the improvements in health, education and housing. In looking at this question, we need first consider how the country might have appeared had Indonesian not intervened. Firstly, there would be many more Timorese around - that is, more than 950,000 of them instead of about 600,000. Secondly, presumably Timor would have gained its independence no later than the early eighties, and its subsequent economic advancement, in particular its ability to attract foreign capital, would have been enhanced by the alluring prospects of rich benefits from offshore oil exploration. The country's development would have been assisted by support from a number of outside sources, including Australia, the ADB, Japan, and, not least, Portugal and her E.C. partners. Perhaps, most important of all, the Timorese would be playing the leading role in the development of their country, and the character of their nation would reflect their own distinctive cultural identity.

The genocidal dimensions of the loss of life in East Timor emerged starkly in 1979-80 when Indonesian authorities finally allowed a small number of international aid workers to survey the humanitarian needs of the province. The human misery they encountered shocked these officials, whose estimates suggested that in the preceding four years Timor has lost between a tenth and a third of its population and that 200,000 of the remainder were in appalling conditions in "resettlement camps," which one official, who had previously been in Cambodia, described as among the worst he had seen.[28]

These revelations should then have shocked the world into demanding that Indonesia withdraw from the former Portuguese colony, but such a response was not forthcoming. Not one of the major powers who were later to be affronted by Iraq's treatment of the Kuwaitis, or Argentina's seizure of the Falkland Islands, were prepared to demand that Indonesia allow for an independently monitored act of self-determination. The best that Washington and Canberra could come up with was to urge Indonesia to admit international humanitarian relief organizations, including the IRC, into the territory. These requests, which elicited a qualified response from Indonesia, resulted in the readmission to the province of the International Red Cross, which had been forced to leave on the eve of the invasion, in the face of Indonesia's refusal to guarantee the necessary protection.

It was to be more than a decade after the invasion before Jakarta could claim to exercise administrative control over most of the island. Even today some armed resistance continues, despite successful operations by Indonesian forces, who have managed to capture Xanana Gusmao, the Fretilin leader, and his successor, Mau Huno. Thanks to the intervention of international agencies - and the work of some concerned Indonesians - conditions in Timor improved markedly during the eighties. However, serious human rights abuses, mostly perpetrated by the Indonesian military, continued to be reported annually by human rights monitoring agencies.

The annual reports of Amnesty International, and the U.S.-based Asia Watch have regularly accused the authorities of summary executions, "disappearances," torture and imprisonment on grounds of conscience.[29] Nearly all of these allegations are focused on the Indonesian Army (ABRI), which until recently maintained a force of about 10,000 troops. The most serious of these incidents in recent times was the massacre of more than 100 Timorese near Santa Cruz cemetery in November, 1991. Because of international pressure, for the first time the Indonesian government launched an inquiry, and some action was taken against senior officers of the Timor military command. The action was, however, cosmetic in character. Relatively light sentences were handed out to a few junior military personnel, none of whom was charged with killing Timorese. Most senior officers were simply moved to other posts. For the Timorese demonstrators, the outcome was markedly different. Those identified in what had been an unarmed and peaceful demonstration received stiff prison sentences, ranging from 6 years to life imprisonment. Yet many western official observers complimented the Indonesian Government on its positive response to the massacre. In reality, the response was the least Jakarta considered necessary in order to weather international criticism.

THE PRESENT SITUATION

The principal targets of the occupation authorities for elimination, if we accept the words of no less that General Benny Murdani[30] were, and apparently still are, not only the armed resistance, but all supporters of the idea of independence for East Timor. It may well be that Indonesian reports that Timorese guerrilla force has diminished to a very small size, but all reports from outside visits disclose that Timorese opposition to integration continues to be widespread, enjoying the support of more than 90% of the population.

In the circumstances, if the Indonesian military persists with the idea of eliminating support for independence - physically or by suppression - it follows that the majority of the population is at some risk. Certainly this risk remains undiminished while the Indonesian military continue to be the dominant force in East Timor, which does not hesitate to use its extensive powers in the elimination of all vestiges of opposition to "the integrity of the

Indonesian state." While the official report on the Santa Cruz massacre has led to some changes in the military, and perhaps some soul-searching in relation to its behavior, it contained no suggestion that the regime would in future be more tolerant of the desire of most Timorese to shape their own destiny.

While it obviously needs to be acknowledged that the conditions under which the Timorese live have improved markedly over the past ten years, appearances are very deceptive, especially in relation to the much-vaunted economic development of the province that has taken place. Clearly most of this development benefits only the small elite and the affluent of the province, who today are mostly Indonesian. The better roads are therefore largely for Indonesian use, not for the Timorese, few of whom own cars. Much of the improved housing is for the new ruling and commercial class, most of them drawn from the more than 100,000 Indonesians who have poured into the province in recent years (not to speak of the military who number about 10,000. As for the development of education its central thrust is to Indonesianize Timorese society, and to purge influences inimical to the process of integration.

The international reaction to the Santa Cruz massacre has not diverted Jakarta from its objective of the total integration of East Timor, which Indonesian officials contend is not open to negotiation. To achieve this means eradicating a desire which is held by the great majority of the people. The armed resistance by Fretilin guerrillas may no longer be a serious threat, but popular opposition to integration and the aspiration for some form of independence remains the dominant aspiration of the Timorese.

It has been kept alive not only by oppressive policies, especially from the military side, but also by the rather patronizing attitudes of most Indonesian officials, and by development policies that have had the effect of marginalising the indigenous population. But this bitterness which is held by most Timorese is rooted in the cruel history of the past 18 years. The majority of Timorese have suffered family loss or victimization. It could be said that the entire nation has become permanently scarred. Mixed with this hostility is a kind of optimism that sooner or later right will win, and international pressure will lead to the realization of their cherished dream of independence.

Some recent international developments, such as the liberating of the Baltic States and Kuwait, have given the Timorese encouragement, not least because the liberation of these states was accompanied by rhetoric about the unacceptability of aggression by a big power against its small neighbor, and the sacrosanct nature of that right to self-determination to which the Timorese were so cynically denied. Indonesia has officially rejected this comparison, but the parallel is inescapable, and is one that Jakarta, and those who have accommodated with this particular annexation, must face up to.

The war, the massive loss of life, the intrusion of outsiders, and Jakarta's efforts to undermine the cultural identity of the Timorese, have created a widespread feeling among the indigenous population that their very identity is, in the long term, at risk. Fifteen years ago, Timor was a world of tiny hamlets, which formed the nucleus of community life. Hundreds of these hamlets were destroyed, or their inhabitants simply forced by the Indonesian military into resettlements, based on the concept of strategic hamlets in Vietnam. The Timorese used to study their own language and cultures, but this has been displaced by a curriculum designed to promote a sense of Indonesianness. In the last years of rule from Lisbon many of the indigenous population spoke Portuguese, but the teaching of this language is now denied most of them.[31] The intricate cultural patterns of the past, which so fascinated anthropologists, are steadily being destroyed or eroded. East Timor was the least "Indonesian" of the communities of the archipelago, its people not having shared with Irian Jaya, for example, the linking experience of Dutch colonialism. Nor was it ever really administered by the Majapahit empire, in the period prior to the European intrusion.

Moreover, unless there is a radical change in the attitude of the Indonesian authorities, whose behavior bears a remarkable resemblance to that of the most repressive colonial powers, the special cultural identity of this former Portuguese colony could simply be eradicated.

Finally, the act of aggression which resulted in the annexation of this small territory was no less blatant and unjustified than Iraq's seizure and annexation of Kuwait. If those powers who have responded to the seizure of Kuwait had reacted in similar vein when the invasion of Timor was being contemplated, the Timorese today would be in a very different situation. Not least, their country would have a population approaching one million people.

The Santa Cruz incident was a reminder that 16 years on, the military authorities are still prepared to kill indiscriminately, if their rule is challenged. The Indonesian response to that incident has been designed to deflect attention from the real issues at stake in East Timor, rather than as an indication of reform. Unfortunately, governments in, for example, the U.S., Australia and Japan, have only too readily accorded a credibility to the conclusions of the commission of inquiry. Perhaps this report is more than a whitewash, as some critics have described it. On the other hand it simply does not address or even acknowledge the essential human rights issues at stake in East Timor.

The fact that the world community not only failed to rally to the side of the Timorese when their fundamental rights were being violated leaves us, at this point in our history, with some unfinished business. We cannot ignore the rape of East Timor, nor brush it away as "past history." We cannot be upholding the rights of East European minorities, the Palestinians or the people of Western Sahara, on the one hand, and dismiss the rights of the Timorese as being beyond redemption.

The annexation of East Timor was not just a violation of the U.N. Charter and the later U.N. resolutions and other instruments enshrining the right to self-determination: it resulted in such a catastrophic loss of life that it must stand as one of the worst cases of genocide in modern times, in the terms of the 1948 Convention. In a way it provides the ultimate test of the commitment of the international community to the upholding of human rights - our readiness to rally in support of the rights of the small, the weak and the vulnerable.

NOTES

1. As well as the eastern half of the island, the Portuguese territory included the enclave of Oe-cussi, on the northern coast of the western sector.

2. In fact, in October 1989 Governor Carrascalao, in a briefing to visiting journalists, gave a much lower total figure - 659,000 which, he said, was growing at 2.63% annually. If this figure was correct it gives an indication of the pace of immigration from elsewhere in Indonesia.

3. I have chosen deliberately to use the past tense, because the great upheaval caused by the invasion, especially the resettlement programs, has clearly had a significant impact on cultural and settlement patterns.

4. Curiously the strongest argument for such an outcome was advanced in 1966 by an American academic, Donald Weatherbee, who concluded that, "In a sense Portuguese Timor is a trust territory, the Portuguese holding it in trust for Indonesia" [Portuguese Timor: An Indonesian Dilemma, *Asian Survey*, December 1966].

5. In June 1974, in contrast to most of his colleagues (who studiously avoided uttering the word "independence"), Foreign Minister Adam Malik generously assured the Timorese of Indonesia's support for East Timor's independence. In a letter to Jose Ramos Horta, a Fretilin leader, Malik wrote, inter alia; "The independence of every country is the right of every nation, with no exception for the people in Timor."

6. For example, see the UNGA Resolution 1514(XV), adopted in December 1960 - *Declaration on the Granting of Independence to Colonial Countries and Peoples.*

7. Fretilin: Frente Revolutionaria de Timor-Leste Independente - the Revolutionary Front for an Independent East Timor.

8. UDT: Uniao Democratica Timorense - the Timorese Democratic Union.

9. Apodeti: Associacao Popular Democratica Timorense - the Timorese Popular Democratic Association.

10. Australia, too, encouraged the Portuguese to include integration as an option in the political context of decolonization.

11. For details of this letter see Dunn, James (1993). *Timor: A People Betrayed*. Brisbane: Jacaranda Press, pp. 108-109.

12. Conversation with the author shortly after Horta's return to Dili in June 1974.

13. Within weeks of Pearl Harbor, a contingent of Australian and some Dutch forces had landed in East Timor - then neutral territory - against Portuguese protests, a move which brought in large Japanese forces. The Timorese gave the Australians extraordinary support until the forces' withdrawal a year later, receiving many informal undertakings that Australia would return and help them out in the future. For the next three years, however, the Japanese retaliated by imposing a harsh occupation at great cost to the Timorese. In all, between 40,000 and 70,000 people died as the result of the Australian intervention.

14. Australia was not as important to Indonesia as the United States, Japan or the Netherlands, but a firm Australian stand on the rights of the Timorese, would have influenced the policies of the other states, and almost certainly caused Suharto to reject military intervention.

15. An account of the attitudes of key Australian and U.S. officials is contained in *Documents on Australian Defence and Foreign Policy, 1968-75* (Walsh & Munster, 1980) pp. 186-225.

16. East Timor is predominantly Roman Catholic.

17. Named after the dragon, or giant lizard, which is found on the nearby island of Alor.

18. Lopes da Cruz himself told me of the initial approach. His recruitment was mentioned by Mousinho later in the year, and in an interview in 1976, Jose Martins, who until his defection had been held in high trust by Indonesian intelligence officers, confirmed this information.

19. An example of the provocative disinformation role of Bakin at this point was the circulation of a story by Operasi Komodo agents, that a number of Vietnamese officers had been smuggled in to Timor, and were training a Fretilin military force (the author was told of this by two former UDT leaders). In reality, at no stage did the Vietnamese show any interest in intervening in East Timor.

20. In fact, at the time most Fretilin leaders were out of the country, so it was an unlikely eventuality.

21. The humanitarian consequences of this civil war were assessed by the International Red Cross and the ACFOA mission, of which I was the leader, with the former insisting that the total loss of life was about 1,500.

22. There is ample evidence that these newsmen were shot by Indonesian troops, at least three of them having been executed some time after the force entered the village. Although this quickly became known to the Whitlam Government, to Jakarta's astonishment no formal protest was made by Australia.

23. As an indication of western complicity, U.S. intelligence was informed in Jakarta by their Indonesian opposite numbers that the attack would take place on 6 December. However, the Americans were shocked to discover that President Ford and Dr. Kissinger

would be in Jakarta on that day, and their hosts obligingly delayed the attack 24 hours.

24. A copy of this report, *Notes on East Timor*, is held by the writer.

25. Of Indonesia's major trading and aid-donor partners, the U.S., Japan, West Germany, Australia and the Netherlands, only the last-mentioned displayed any serious concern at the government level.

26. Testimony of Robert Oakley in *Human Rights in East Timor and the Question of the Use of U.S. Equipment by the Indonesian Armed Forces*, before Subcommittees of the Committee on International Relations, House of Representatives, 95th Congress, 28 March 1977 and letter from Edward C Ingraham, Department of State, 13 May 1977.

27. Canberra waited only one year before according *de jure* status to its recognition.

28. The confidential report to which the author was given access stated that, of the 200,000, about 10% were in such bad shape that they could not be saved.

29. See in particular the annual reports published by *Amnesty International*, and also the publications of Asia *Watch*, especially *East Timor: Violations of Human Rights*, (Amnesty International Publications, London 1985).

30. In a speech to Timorese officials in Dili, in February 1990, Murdani warned that those who still sought to form a separate state *"will be crushed by ABRI. ABRI may fail the first time, so it will try for a second time, and for a third time."* In a reference to Fretilin and its sympathizers he said: *"We will crush them all... to safeguard the unity of Indonesian territory."*

31. It is argued that Portuguese was the language of the colonial past, but in most former colonies study of the language of the imperial power has been permitted, if not encouraged.

BIBLIOGRAPHY

Amnesty International (1985). *East Timor: Violations of Human Rights*. London. 92 pp.
The first major report on the subject by Amnesty. It contains accounts of extrajudicial executions, torture, and of the repressive methods of the Indonesian military in the territory.

Amnesty International (November 1991). *East Timor: After the Massacre*. London. 11 pp.
A report on the killings at Santa Cruz cemetery, near Dili.

Amnesty International (August 1991). *East Timor: Amnesty International Statement to the U.N. Special Committee on Decolonization.*
One of Amnesty's most recent and most comprehensive statements to the U.N. Decolonization Committee.

Asia Watch (December 1991). *East Timor: The November 12 Massacre and its Aftermath*. New York: Asia Watch. 28 pp.
A report on the Santa Cruz killings, and the Indonesian response.

Asia Watch (April 1993). Remembering history in East Timor: The trial of Xanana Gusmao and a follow-up to the Dili Massacre. *Asia Watch*, 5(8).
  While this report focuses on the trial of the captured Timorese leader, Xanana Gusmao, it also refers to specific cases of killings by Indonesian forces, for example, at Creras in 1983. It also supplies a list of those who "disappeared" after the Santa Cruz massacre in November 1991.

Australian Parliament (1983). *Official Report of the Australian Parliamentary Delegation to Indonesia*, led by the Hon. W.L. Morrison, M.P. Canberra: Australian Government Publishing Service. 214 pp.
  This report which includes a chapter on Timor (Chapter 8) was put together largely by the leader of the delegation, who was at the time Chairman of the Joint House Committee on Foreign Affairs and Defence. Morrison had served as Defence Minister in 1975, during the build up to Indonesia's armed action against East Timor, and the report is largely representative of the stand of those Australian political leaders who were prepared to accommodate the annexation of the colony. It is a highly slanted account which provoked Senator Macintosh, then Chairman of the Senate Foreign Affairs Committee, to submit a dissenting report (page 80). The observations contained in the main body of the report largely reflect the views of the delegation's leader, who was subsequently appointed Australia's Ambassador to Indonesia. While it had little impact overseas it helped influence the new Hawke Labor Government not to change Australia's Timor policy, and to confirm its *de jure* recognition of the territory as a province of Indonesia.

Australian Parliament, Senate Standing Committee on Foreign Affairs and Defence (1983). *The Human Rights and Conditions of the People of East Timor*. Canberra. 106 pp.
  The result of hearings, involving a wide range of witnesses, before the Committee over a lengthy period. The general thrust of the report reflects the commitment of the Committee's Chairman, Senator Gordon MacIntosh, whose concern was not shared by the Government of the time, nor by all of his Committee colleagues.

Australian Government Publishing Service (1992). *A Review of Australia's Efforts to Promote and Protect Human Rights*. Canberra.
  Of interest is the section on East Timor in Chapter 6, pp 69-76. The report reveals the continuing concern in the Australian Parliament, despite the fact that the formal recognition of the incorporation of East Timor by the Australian Government.

Budiardjo, Carmel, and Liem Soei Liong (1984). *The War Against East Timor*. London: Zed Books. pp. 253.
  This work is by two activists of Tapol (an acronym for Indonesian political prisoners), an organization which has monitored the human rights violations of the Suharto regime. One of authors - Carmel Budiardjo - was herself a political prisoner. Its focus is on Fretilin's struggle, and the strategies followed by Indonesian forces. It contains a considerable amount of detail, most of it acquired from Fretilin and Indonesian dissident sources. Chapters 4 - 6 deal with the impact of the occupation on the population at large.

Clark, R.S. (1981). Does the Genocide Convention go far enough?: Some thoughts on the nature of criminal genocide in the context of Indonesia's invasion of East Timor. *Ohio Northern University Law Review*, 8, 321-328.
  A sceptical look at the implications of the Convention by Roger Clark, Distinguished Professor of International Law, Rutgers University. See also, by the same author, *The decolonization of East Timor and the United Nations norms on self-determination and aggression*. *Yale Journal of World Public Order*, 1980 7(2).

Dunn, James (1974). *Portuguese Timor before and after the coup: Options for the future.* Legislative Research Service, Australian Parliament, August. 28 pp.
The paper contains the author's observations and recommendations, based on his earlier experience as Consul in the colony and also on his participation in a two-man fact-finding mission to East Timor in June and July. It pointed out that the Timorese were most likely to choose the option of independence, and recommended that Australia support that option.

Dunn, James (1977). *The East Timor Situation - Report on Talks with Timorese Refugees in Portugal.* Australian Parliament, Canberra. 17 pp.
This was an early report of atrocities carried out by Indonesian troops, following the invasion of Dili in December 1975. It was based on the testimonies of Timorese refugees who had been allowed to go to Portugal by the Indonesian authorities late in 1976. Most were fearful to testify, because of the risk of reprisals against friends and relatives still in Timor.

Dunn, James (1983). *Timor, A People Betrayed.* Brisbane: Jacaranda-Wiley Press. 402 pp.
A general study of how the Timor tragedy unfolded, including an analysis of the way a group of Indonesian generals were able to manipulate Cold War attitudes in the U.S. and Australia to gain accommodation of their seizure of a territory in the process of decolonization, against the wishes of its people. See Chapters 8 to 12 for accounts of the fighting in Timor, the behavior of the occupying forces, the Timorese response and the international reaction.

Gusmao, Jose Alexandro (also known as Xanana). May 1993. Untitled final address to Indonesian court at Dili. 28 pp.
In this address, which was subsequently smuggled out of Indonesia, the independence movement leader describes the sufferings of his people after Indonesian forces intervened. He refers to a loss of life of 200,000 people, resulting from the invasion. After two pages were read out, the Indonesian judges suppressed the remainder of the address, and then sentenced Gusmao to life imprisonment.

Hull, Geoffrey (1992). *East Timor: Just a political question?* Occasional Paper published by the Australian Catholic Social Justice Council, Sydney.
A brief Catholic analysis of the Timor saga, with some discussion of the genocide aspect.

Jolliffe, Jill (1978). *East Timor: Nationalism and Colonialism.* Brisbane: University of Queensland Press. 362 pp.
A detailed study of conditions immediately prior to the invasion, by a journalist who was in the colony for more than 2 months during the Fretilin interregnum.

Kohen, Arnold and Taylor John (1979). *An Act of Genocide: Indonesia's Invasion of East Timor.* London: Tapol Books.
An analysis of the situation by John Taylor, an English academic, and Arnold Kohen, a Congressional human rights lobbyist who, for some 15 years, has labored energetically on behalf of the Timorese right to self-determination.

Lemos Pires, Brigadier Mario (1991). *Decolonizacao de Timor: Missao Impossivel?* Circulo de leitores/Publicacoes Dom Quixote. Lisboa. 452 pp.
This work is an account of the last months of Portuguese rule, including the civil war and the beginnings of Indonesian military intervention, by the last Portuguese governor of East Timor. At the end of August 1975, when there was intense street-fighting between UDT and Fretilin troops, the Governor and his small military force, which amounted to less that

100 combatant troops, withdrew from Dili to the tiny offshore island of Atauro. Lemos Pires and his party remained on Atauru until December 7, 1975, when the Indonesians launched a large-scale combined assault on the capital.

Mubyarto, Prof. Dr., and Dr. Loekman Soetrisno, et al. (1991). *East Timor: The Impact of Integration. An Indonesian Anthropological Study.* Yogyakarta: Indonesian Resources and Information Program. 70 pp.
    A perceptive, through carefully restrained socio-anthropological study by a research team under the leadership of Professor Mubyarto, which was sent to East Timor by Gadyah Mada University in 1990. While much of its observations are less than frank, it provides some useful insights into the impact of integration on the Timorese population. It does not, however, delve into the impact of military rule on the population at large. To an extent, the study reflects the discomfort felt by many Indonesian academics at the lack of popular acceptance, but it does not challenge in any way the morality and legitimacy of the annexation. Such views, if they were genuinely held, would not have been publishable in Indonesia.

Permanent Peoples Tribunal - *Verdict of Session on East Timor, Lisbon (June 1981).* 45 pp.
    This hearing of the Tribunal set up by the Lelio Basso Foundation conducted a hearing in Lisbon in relation to charges of Indonesian aggression against East Timor. A great deal of evidence was heard by a panel of distinguished jurists. Although the witnesses were predominantly Timorese, or their supporters, Indonesia was invited to testify, but declined to do so. The jurists found in favor of the plaintiffs.

Sword, Kirsty, and Walsh, Pat (1991). *'Opening UP': Travellers' Impressions of East Timor, 1989-1991.* Melbourne: Australia-East Timor Association. 50 pp.
    This is a useful collection of observations by visitors to East Timor in the 1989-91 period, when the territory was opened up, to a limited extent, to foreign visitors. It contains some vivid impressions of the position of the Timorese, and of their attitudes, some 14 or so years after the invasion.

Taylor, John G. (1991). *Indonesia's Forgotten War: The Hidden History of East Timor.* Zed Books. London. 330 pp.
    A useful, detailed general study of the annexation. Chapters 6 to 11, in particular, provide useful accounts of the impact of the occupation on the population at large.

Turner, Michele (1992). *Telling: East Timor, Personal Testimonies 1942-1992.* New South Wales University Press. Sydney. 218 pp.
    A collection of Timorese accounts of conditions, first under the Japanese occupation and, three decades or so later, after the Indonesian invasion in 1975. Part 3 provides some graphic descriptions of the treatment of the Timorese by the occupying forces.

7

The Fate of the Gypsies in the Holocaust

Gabrielle Tyrnauer

PRESENT STATE OF KNOWLEDGE

In the vast literature on Nazi brutality and genocide, the annihilation of a large part of the Gypsy population of Europe constitutes barely a footnote. Yet only two ethnic groups were targeted for total annihilation by National Socialist ideology and its state apparatus - Gypsies and Jews.

While there are significant differences in the ideological justifications for the exterminations and the thoroughness with which they were carried out, no other groups became comparable targets of destruction based on biological definitions. Between a quarter and a half million Gypsies were murdered by the Nazis, approximately a fourth of all those living in pre-war Europe.[1]

Yet there were no prosecutions of the killers; nor were there any Gypsy witnesses to testify in Nuremberg or at other major war crimes trials,[2] though references to Nazi crimes against the Gypsies were scattered through the testimony of many other witnesses. A single book exists on the subject in English (Kenrick and Puxon, 1972) and that is out of print; barely half a dozen can be found in other languages of the world. A French book published in 1979, was aptly titled *l'holocauste oublié*.

Ever since the end of World War II and the identification of those tragic events which have come to be known collectively as "The Holocaust," a debate has raged among survivors and historians as to whether the Holocaust was an exclusively Jewish or more general human disaster. It was in the context of this debate that Elie Wiesel uttered his now famous words, "not all victims were Jews but all Jews were victims."

In the years since the U.S. Holocaust Memorial Council was established by an act of Congress in 1979, the debates about the definition and meaning of the Holocaust for various victim groups has been translated into intense political activity on the part of representatives of some of these groups. In the first few years of its existence, the Council was besieged by demands for representation on the part of those claiming a "share" in the Holocaust: Armenians, Ukrainians, American blacks, Amerindians and others who had experienced large scale persecutions and massacres. Only the one group, whose history and destiny under the Third Reich was more closely linked to that of the Jewish people than any other, remained silent.

The silence of the Gypsies was matched by that of the historians about them. It lasted for some forty years, punctuated now and then by occasional works of fiction (Kanfer, 1978; Lakatos, 1975); or by an article in an obscure journal.

However, in the late 1970s, Gypsies in many individual countries of Europe - as well as on the international scene - began to organize politically around the issue of the "forgotten Holocaust." For them the silence at last was broken by public speeches, writings, demonstrations. The silence of the historians, on the other hand, remained largely intact.

There were exceptions. Some of the early Holocaust historians, who were survivors themselves, did speak of the Gypsies, although they were still consumed with the tragedy of their own people. In his classic 1951 book, *Bréviaire de la haine* (Harvest of Hate), Leon Poliakov devoted only two pages to the extermination of the Gypsies, but he clearly designated the Nazi massacres as another "collective condemnation of an entire people" (Poliakov, p. 305).

Philip Friedman went further. He wrote an article about the Gypsy genocide, first in Yiddish (Friedman, 1950) called "A Strange Common Destiny: The Extermination of the Gypsies," and then in English (Friedman, 1951) in an article entitled, "Nazi Extermination of the Gypsies: A Nazi Genocide Operation against the 'Aryan People.'" Friedman (1980) has deplored the sparse documentation of the Gypsy genocide.

> There has been little study of the tragedy of the Gypsies under Nazi rule...Compared with the extensive documentation of the Jews and on the tribulations of other people under the Nazi yoke, the literature on the Gypsies is meager and full of gaps. (p. 383)

In the final section of the early post-war plan for future Holocaust Research, Friedman proposed to compare the fate of the Jews with that of two other persecuted groups, the Karaites and the Gypsies. Furthermore, he proposed to study cooperation between Jews and other persecuted groups (*ibid.*, p. 576). Unfortunately, these proposals were never implemented.

J. Tenenbaum, in his 1956 book on Nazi racial policies, *Race and Reich*, included an appendix about the extermination of the Gypsies. He called it "one of the major mysteries of Nazi racialism" (p. 399).

Miriam Novitch was a survivor of the Warsaw Ghetto uprising and a resident of Lohamei Haghettaoth, the ghetto fighters' kibbutz in Israel. She was a delegate and honored speaker at the 1981 World Congress of the Romani Union, the Gypsies' international organization, in Göttingen. At this first international meeting of Gypsies on German soil, Novitch expressed her deeply felt commitment to telling the story of the Gypsy genocide: "... not to tell about their slaughter would be to commit a second injustice against them..."

Selma Steinmetz was a political as well as "racial" target of Nazi persecution. She became a chronicler of the Gypsy story after the war, while working in the archives of the Center for Documentation of the Austrian Resistance, in Vienna. Here she found the data to piece together the history of Austrian Gypsies under Nazi rule (1966, 1979). The German Sinti organization paid her a warm tribute in the dedication of a book commemorating their first major political demonstration - in the former concentration camp of Bergen Belsen. "Since the end of the war," they wrote, "she was the only author in the German language to tell the story of the Gypsy genocide." Steinmetz died shortly before the demonstration in which she was thus honored. Like Friedman, Steinmetz (1979) called attention to the paucity of research about the Gypsy genocide, which she described as a "gap in contemporary historical research" (p. 122).

The first German book on the Gypsies under National Socialism appeared in 1964 as part of a criminology series. The author, Hans J. Döring, originally wrote the work as a doctoral dissertation. He planned his research - at his professor's suggestion - as a study of a particular "criminal population" (1964). Documenting the crimes of the state against this group was not one of the intentions of the author, his academic advisor, or the editor of the series in which it was published. Nevertheless, Döring's book contains the first detailed documentation of the bureaucratic paper work, the policy decisions and military actions which led from traditional harassment to genocide.

Kenrick and Puxon's ground-breaking book was published in 1972. A decade after its appearance, the English original was out of print, although it has been translated into several languages (including Romanes, the Gypsy language), and is used extensively by all who write on the subject, whether scholars or political activists.

While Kenrick and Puxon's extensively documented study has made some scholars aware of this strangely neglected area of Holocaust studies (e.g., Fein, 1979; Porter, 1982; and Chalk and Jonassohn, 1990), little has changed in the general knowledge about the Gypsy genocide. Most English language books on the Holocaust also mention the Gypsies only in passing and where they are unavoidably linked to the writer's subject matter, such as medical experimentation (e.g., International Auschwitz Committee, 1986; Lifton, 1986).

The first English language book on Genocide which devoted an entire section to the Gypsies was Jack Porter's (edited volume) *Genocide and Human Rights* (1982). While most of the articles are older reprints, there is one written specifically for this volume by Tyrnauer.

The state of knowledge in the English speaking world about this subject can be illustrated by an incident recorded by this author in a report, *The Fate of the Gypsies during the Holocaust* (1985), prepared for the U.S. Holocaust Memorial Council. This report was commissioned in response to the persistent campaign of a few American Romani (the preferred term to the more pejorative "Gypsy") activists and their supporters for recognition of their genocide as an integral part of Holocaust history.

One of the most remarkable of these Romani activists was the late John ("Lazo") Megel, son of a well-known New York Russian Gypsy leader. Steeped in his traditional culture, Lazo nevertheless was finely attuned to the outside world, the world of the *gajo*, or non-Gypsy. Like most American Gypsies, he had little formal schooling. As an adult, he had taught himself to read in order to discover what the *gajo* had written about his people.

Lazo had first encountered the Holocaust as a young man, during the Eichmann trial, when, like millions of others, he had watched the "man in the glass booth" give his grisly testimony on TV. He learned that the Nazi terror apparatus had also targeted his people for extermination. This triggered childhood memories of stories about the murder of Gypsies in Europe during World War II. He had not paid much attention at the time, because he learned at an early age that persecution was his people's legacy. "So Gypsies was being murdered," he recalled thinking, "What else is new?"

As the young Lazo listened to the trial testimony, he began to understand that here indeed was something new. In the years that followed - and particularly after the creation of the United States Holocaust Memorial Council - he worked tirelessly to have his people's tragedy recognized. He believed that genocide, once known, could not be ignored. But he was bitterly disappointed by the sparsity of literature he found on the subject of the Gypsy genocide. "How can it be?" he would ask, his big fists pounding the air, "a quarter of a million people murdered and only a few articles, one book for me to read. Why?" he would ask repeatedly, "can you tell me why?"

Lazo's anguished question is still awaiting an answer.

WHY THE POVERTY OF
INFORMATION ABOUT THE GYPSY GENOCIDE?

One cannot attribute the paucity of research on the Gypsy genocide to malevolent intent on the part of historians and survivors of the Holocaust, for, as noted above, most acknowledge the importance of the omission and express hopes that some day it will be remedied. Holocaust scholars generally are receptive to new information about this tragic period of European history. Undoubtedly, the events of the last few years in East Europe and the former Soviet Union, the turmoil accompanying the reunification of Germany and the scholarly controversies surrounding revisionist World War II history, have sparked a renewed interest in the fate of a minority once again undergoing large-scale persecution in central and eastern Europe.

Nor can the scarcity of information be attributed only to the reticence of Gypsy survivors to be heard, for in recent years they have come forward, reflecting in the sunset of their lives a need to bear witness as great as that of Jewish survivors. Like them, Gypsy survivors are terrified by the emergence of revisionist history and neo-Nazi movements in Germany and elsewhere. Many who remained silent for forty years are now driven to speak.

Certainly, historians lack the large body of diaries, memoirs and other writings that so greatly helped the documentation of the Jewish Holocaust. Why, we may ask, is the new historical tool of oral history not being applied systematically to the survivors who are prepared to tell their story and to the bystanders who were eye-witnesses? Gypsy survivors constitute another class of witnesses to Nazi persecution, deportation and mass murder as well as to the deadly medical experiments and "racial research" that accompanied them. No other non-Jewish survivors of that terrible era can document it as they can, in all its ghastly details. Why, then, have the Gypsies been so long ignored as victims and data sources?

A cynical but perhaps realistic answer is suggested by Bernadac's (1979) account of a conversation with an old French doctor. Of course they will be ignored, the old man said, for "everybody despises the Gypsies." If they are persecuted and murdered, "who will complain?" the old man asked, "who will avenge them? Who will bear witness? The Gypsies have no representation in the states in which they were born. They do not exist on the national or international level... we have witnessed the perfect crimes. Crimes without corpses. Who - even today - would claim a Gypsy?" (p. 8).

No voices were raised while the killings were going on because the Gypsies had none to speak for them before the conscience of the world and they were not organized to speak for themselves. Since there were no "corpses" in the French doctor's sense, there were, officially, no crimes, and thus no defendants or prosecutors to research and prepare cases. Since the Gypsies themselves produced no historians or journalists to study and expose, the case rested for some forty years.

In languages other than English, the situation is somewhat better. The largest amount of material on the subject exists in German. That this should be so in the case of archival material is hardly surprising. As with every aspect of the documentation of this forgotten genocide, political pressure from newly politicized members of the surviving group played a large role in preserving material that otherwise might have been lost or destroyed.

One of the most dramatic examples of this preservation took place in an archive of Tübingen University in 1981. The Verband deutscher Sinti, the umbrella organization of the German Sinti in the early 1980s, staged a "sit-in" at the university. The purpose of this protest was to bring about the transfer of some 20,000 documents of the wartime Racial Hygiene Research Center of the Ministry of Health - housed temporarily in the cellar of a university building, to the Federal Archives in Koblenz, where such documented belonged by law. At the time of the demonstration, the entire archive had been brought back to Tübingen from Mainz at the request of an emeritus faculty member, Dr. Sophie Erhardt, a veteran of the very racial research team that had created the archive during the Third Reich. It had been entrusted to her by an associate of Professor Dr. Robert Ritter, director of the research center, and other surviving members of the interdisciplinary research team. Erhardt had permitted it to be transferred to Mainz Univerity in the 1960s, for the convenience of a former American student of hers doing post-doctoral research there. Several years later, after he had returned to the U.S., wary of the controversy surrounding the data his former professor urged him to use, the entire archive was returned to Tübingen at her request. Sinti activists nicknamed it "the nomadic archive." The Tübingen action was successful: the entire archive was transferred to Koblenz the same night.

In the late 1970s and early 1980s, the political organization of the Sinti led to a spate of journalistic works and a renewed scholarly interest in the contemporary culture and social problems of the Gypsies. In these works, the Holocaust experiences were gingerly touched upon by German researchers, mainly because of continued Gypsy reticence and distrust. Joachim S. Hohmann (1981), a German historian sympathetic to the Sinti political movement, carefully documented the history of the Gypsy persecutions in Germany both before and during the Nazi period. Hohmann (1980) also wrote about the scholars who contributed to the genocide. Some of these - and, in the Sinti view, their spiritual heirs - continue working in the Federal Republic as "Gypsy experts" up to the present time.

HISTORICAL OVERVIEW

Origins

While the homeland of the Jews was well known to Christians and Muslims alike, the location of the original home of the Gypsies was a matter of considerable conjecture until the 18th century when a Hungarian theology student at Leyden noted the uncanny resemblance between the speech of some Indian fellow students and the Gypsies of his home district of Komora. Subsequent linguistic studies convinced most scholars of the Northwest Indian origins of Gypsies, though the precise place, the ethnic and social groups from which they derived, remained a matter of dispute. As they produced no written history of their own and had preserved no clear "origin myths" even in their oral traditions, the task of tracing their migration routes fell mainly to linguists.

When the Gypsies left India, presumably in several waves, they travelled through the Middle East and on to southeastern Europe where the earliest record indicating their presence on the continent was found in Corfu and Greece, early in the 14th century. Nomadic Gypsies were recorded in Crete in 1322, "stopping only thirty days in one place" (Kenrick and Puxon, 1972, pp. 14-15). The Greeks called them by the name of a heretical sect, *atsigani*, from which derived the word used to designate them in most languages of Europe, i.e., the German "Zigeuner," the Hungarian "Cigany," the Italian "Zingari," etc.

After a relatively long sojourn in Greece - judging by the number of Greek loan words in Romanes - the nomads moved to Hungary and the Balkans, perhaps on the heels of the Turkish invasion. In some of these areas, in fact, they become associated with the invaders. During the 16th and 17th centuries, legislation was enacted in German and Czech areas expelling Gypsies as Turkish spies. At the Nuremberg trials, these beliefs were revived by some defendants to account for the round-ups and deportations of Gypsies as "security risks" (Musmanno, 1961, p. 110). There are ironic echoes of this in the Germany of the 1990s as Gypsies are sometimes mistaken for Turkish migrants or asylum-seekers, a "no-win" situation for them.

Gypsies appeared near the North Sea in 1417 carrying a safe-conduct letter from the Pope and calling themselves "Lords of little Egypt" (hence the name "Gypsy"). They explained their wandering through a number of pious stories, the best known one being that they had refused sanctuary to the Holy family during its sojourn in Egypt and were thus obliged to perform a nomadic penance for a number of years. This tale is said not only to have won over the Pope but also impressed King Sigismund of Hungary sufficiently for him to grant them a letter of safe conduct through his lands.

By the late 15th century, there are accounts of the Gypsies in the chronicles of almost every European country. The early curiosity and good will of the settled people were replaced by hostility. The dark strangers were accused of witchcraft, thievery, kidnapping and murder. Both Church and State discriminated against them and devised a large repertory of punishments for real or imagined crimes. These ranged from banishment to whipping to execution; Gypsy slavery in the Rumanian lands was not abolished until 1856, In the 18th century there was a well-known cannibalism trial of Gypsies in Hungary; after the torture of almost 200 of the defendants and the execution of 41, the alleged victims were found alive and well (Kenrick and Puxon, 1972, Chap. 3). Gypsies were treated like wild game ("freiwild") and "open seasons" were declared. These popular traditions prepared the way for the Nazi Gypsy hunters.

Harassment and stronger forms of persecution alternated with attempts at forced assimilation. The persistent nomadism and the cultivation of an ethnic and cultural distinctiveness made the Gypsies visible, if moving, targets of the integrators as well as the persecutors. Maria Theresa of Austria and her successor, Joseph II, used both carrot and stick, giving Gypsies land and calling them "New Hungarians," while forbidding them the use of their language and taking away their children to be raised by peasant families.

In a parallel assimilation attempt, Carlos III of Spain issued a 44 article "pragmatica" for the Gitanos (Gypsies) of his country, whom - following the Austro-Hungarian lead - he renamed "nuevos castellanos" or "New Castillanos." He too forbade them the use of their language, traditional dress and occupations and encouraged sedentary work and life-styles (Vossen, 1983, p. 54). Various German princes also experimented with integration attempts in their territories during the 18th century. In the 19th century, an evangelical missionary, Wilhelm Blankenburg, attempted to establish a model Prussian-Protestant colony of Gypsies in Naumburg.

But neither persecution nor forced assimilation had the desired effect, and two hundred years later, Gypsies, like Jews in the face of similar threats to their collective existence, continued to observe their customs, speak their language and draw sharp boundaries between themselves and outsiders.

Europe's Response to Gypsies: Ambivalence

At the same time that Gypsies were being imprisoned, expelled and enslaved by the princes through whose territories they passed, they became an important part of the European cultural scene. Individual musicians and dancers, singers and circus performers acquired legendary reputations. Gypsies became part of the entourage of princes and czars. With the advent of the Romantic movement, their unfettered life-style became attractive to a restless young generation of poets and painters. These helped to create a stereotype of Gypsies tinged by envy and nostalgia, at the same time that legislators throughout Europe were making laws to combat the "Gypsy menace".

In Nazi Germany, the European ambivalence towards the Gypsies expressed itself in the most bizarre ways. German scholars were encouraged to search for the Gypsies' "Aryan" origins and language by German officials whose bureaucratic colleagues defined Gypsies as vermin. This ambivalence, in its most malignant form, could permit SS soldiers to listen with pleasure to a Gypsy orchestra hours before sending its members to their death.

As Hohmann points out, the story of the Nazi persecution and mass murder of the Gypsies cannot be fully understood without grasping the continuity of stereotypes or of the ambivalence which underlay them (1980, pp. 14-17). It is here that we find the link between the romantic operetta cliches of Gypsy Barons and the Gypsy violins of Auschwitz.

The "Gypsy Question" in Germany

The "Gypsy Question" (*Die Zigeunerfrage*) in Germany, as in other European countries, was only formulated at the time of national unification in the nineteenth century. In feudal times, Gypsies had a clear niche in society. They were itinerant artisans, traders, entertainers and practitioners of healing and occult arts, particularly fortune-telling. They may have been despised and persecuted as well as romanticized, but their existence was not called into question.

With the rise of the bourgeois nation-state and its central focus on national identity, the "Zigeunerfrage" was born, as was the "question" of other troublesome minorities, particularly the Jews. The older Gypsy image of heathen, swindler, song-bird and kidnapper gave way to a more sinister picture of the "inner enemy," disloyal to the state (the Turkish spy image), a criminal element in society, and worst of all, in the Nazi catalog of sins, a threat to racial purity.

Data collection on the Gypsies for "law enforcement" purposes began under the monarchy with the establishment in 1899 of a *Zigeunernachrichtsdienst* (Gypsy Information Service) in Munich. In 1905 the Government of Bavaria issued a *Zigeunerbuch* (Gypsy Book) in which acts and edicts related to Gypsies in the years 1816-1903 were compiled to serve as guidelines for the continuing battle against the *Zigeunerplage* (Gypsy Plague). By 1904, the industrious workers of the Gypsy Information Service had collected 3,340 protocols about Gypsy individuals and families. Methods were refined after World War I, when the practice of fingerprinting was introduced. Thus, through the united efforts of the police, scholars and bureaucrats, the Gypsies of Germany became the most researched and easily identified in Europe (Streck, 1979, pp. 69-72).

The legal situation of Gypsies did not improve   under the Weimar Republic. A variety of laws pertaining to "Gypsies, Travellers and Malingerers" (*Zigeuner, Landfahrer und Arbeitsscheue*) were passed. In 1926 a "Gypsy Conference" was held in Munich to bring uniformity to the legislation of the different provinces (*Länder*) of the Republic. Draconian laws against nomadism, lack of identification papers, etc., were introduced and centralization of technical innovations such as fingerprinting made them more effective. Streck (1979, p. 73) notes the irony that "the first democracy on German soil" left a legacy with respect to the Gypsies which permitted the Nazis to implement their policies for a number of years without changing a single law.

THE THIRD REICH AND THE GYPSIES

The Legal Basis

While the Weimar laws sufficed for the first few years of National Socialist rule, new legislation, consistent with Nazi racial ideology was required. The earliest discriminatory laws were not specific to Gypsies but were applied to them; for instance, a 1933 law which permitted sterilization of mental defectives later applied to Gypsies of mixed blood; a 1934 law which permitted the deportation of undesirable aliens was applied to foreign Gypsies. In 1935 the Nuremberg Race laws were passed. These were aimed primarily at Jews and banned intermarriage with Germans. Although the Gypsies were not mentioned in the original legislation, later commentaries referred to them explicitly. In the same year, a citizenship law was passed, which distinguished between first class (German or related blood) and second class (alien blood) citizens. The second class category applied to Jews and Gypsies.

The Nazi Ministry of the Interior indicated its strong support of the activities of the newly established (1936) Vienna-based International Center for the Fight Against the Gypsy Menace (*Internationale Zentralstelle zur Bekämpfung des Zigeunerunwesens*). After the annexation of Austria in 1938, anti-Gypsy legislation began there, including a deportation decree which permitted the dispatch of 400 Sinti and Roma to Dachau, and another law which forbade nomadism.

In 1936, Himmler - by then the supreme chief of the merged SS and security forces - took over the campaign against the "inner enemies". His first assault was the "asocial action" of 1937, which permitted arrest and preventive detention of all "asocials" (*asoziale*) among whom the Gypsies were considered foremost. In the same year a research center was established in the Ministry of Health, under Dr. Robert Ritter, a neurologist and pediatrician. The *Rassenhygienische und bevölkerungsbiologische Forschungstelle* (Racial Hygiene and Population Biology Research Center) was to play a decisive role in the definition, apprehension and annihilation of the Gypsy population of Germany and, later, of occupied Europe. The two-pronged attack on the Gypsy Question, one related to race, the other to criminality, was launched by the racial scientists. Under the personal patronage of Heinrich Himmler, they were to establish the relation between the two, primarily through the collection of genealogies, designed both to enrich knowledge and to facilitate the work of law enforcement officers.

These officers had admitted to considerable confusion about Gypsies during the first few years of the "Thousand Year Reich." Some sent perplexed memos to their superiors requesting clarification as to whether the Gypsies in their custody should be treated as Aryans or *Untermenschen* (sub-humans). An important assignment of the Racial Hygiene and Population Biology Research Institute was to resolve such doubts.

Genealogy and Genocide

Genealogical research was a favored activity in the Third Reich. Himmler himself was fascinated by it and was patron of the "Ahnenerbe," the organization which researched the Aryan ancestry for SS members and lesser mortals in Nazi Germany. As we have noted, the Gypsy Information Service, established under the Imperial Second Reich, had started the work of collecting genealogies for purely practical purposes, the better to keep track of what had become by definition, a "criminal element." The Gypsy Information Service's genealogies became the nucleus of the collection in Ritter's Berlin research center. They were expanded to include nearly every German Gypsy. The research was conducted by an interdisciplinary team of scholars, and the data they gathered - in addition to the genealogies - included fingerprints, ethnological descriptions and anatomical measurements.

Under Ritter, the collection of this data became at once a scholarly and patriotic mission, a matter of "preserving the purity of German blood." A member of Ritter's research team, Adolph Würth, wrote in 1938:

> The Gypsy Question is today in the first place a racial question. Just as the National Socialist State has solved the Jewish Question, so it will have to fundamentally regulate the Gypsy Question. A start has already been made. In the regulations for the implementation of the Nuremberg Laws for the protection of German blood, Gypsies have been placed on an equal level with Jews in regard to marriage prohibitions. In other words, they count neither as of German blood or related to it. (Hohmann, 1980, p. 201)

The well-known commentator on the Nuremberg laws, Hans Globke, (a member of Konrad Adenauer's cabinet in the post-war years), translated the "scientific" data into legal philosophy in 1937: of all European peoples, only Jews and Gypsies had alien (*artfremdes*) blood and thus represented a mortal threat to German racial purity (Hohmann, 1981, p. 102).

It remained for the members of Ritter's institute to determine who was the carrier of that blood and in what proportions. By 1941 his team had assembled nearly 20,000 protocols on individual Gypsies who had been examined by them. Through genealogies, fingerprints and anthropomorphic measurements, they attempted to establish the relationship between the two bases for discrimination and eventual extermination laid down by their rulers - racial inferiority and hereditary criminality".

As the racial scientists provided their data to the police and the SS, they also produced recommendations for sedentarization, sterilization and deportation. While they did not openly recommend extermination, their research paved the way for it so directly that it is hard not to agree with Miriam Novitch's assessment (1981) that "the central role played by the German 'scientists' and 'racial experts' must be understood, because they were as responsible for the genocide of the Gypsies as were the members of the Einsatzgruppen who murdered them with bullets or the SS men in the death camps who murdered them with gas." Eva Justin, Ritter's student and assistant, wrote a doctoral dissertation (published in 1944) in which she studied Gypsy children who had been brought up in a Catholic orphanage at Mulfingen. She concluded that Gypsies could not be changed or integrated; therefore, all attempts at education should cease. Furthermore, since "the German people do not need the multiplying weed of these immature primitives", all "educated Gypsies and part-Gypsies of predominantly Gypsy blood, whether socially assimilated or asocial and criminal, should, as a general rule, be sterilized. Socially integrated part-Gypsies with less than half Gypsy blood can be considered as Germans" (Kenrick & Puxon, 1972, p. 68).

The Nazi's ideological dilemma, stemming from the presumed "Aryan" origin of the Gypsies, was nowhere more clearly seen than in the conflicting recommendations made by "racial scientists" and those in authority. While Justin recommended sparing the more assimilated, those with "less than half Gypsy blood," others, including her "doctor father," Ritter, and his boss, Himmler, showed a marked preference for the nomadic "pure" Gypsies, and proposed special reserves for the approximately five to ten percent to be so identified - reserves where they could roam freely, speak their own language, preserve ancient "Aryan" customs and multiply for the study of future German scientists. Those who were at first exempted from deportation to Auschwitz included both the traditional, nomadic and racially "pure" Gypsies and the "socially adapted" sedentary ones. These exemptions derived from two conflicting models of "Zigeunerpolitik."

The distinctions and classifications worked out in the Berlin Racial Hygiene Research Center came to be identified as one more of Himmler's hare-brained schemes by his Nazi colleagues. Bormann wrote to Himmler on December 3, 1942:

> Such a special treatment would mean a fundamental deviation from the simultaneous measures for fighting the Gypsy menace and would not be understood by all the population and the lower leaders of the party. Also the Führer would not agree to giving one section of the Gypsies their old freedom. (Quoted by Kenrick & Puxon, 1972, p. 89)

Himmler apparently deferred to Bormann and a few weeks later signed the infamous Auschwitz Decree, sending all of Germany's nearly 30,000 Gypsies - regardless of group or status or degree of assimilation - to the death camp. Sinti were even demobilized from the Wehrmacht and sent to Auschwitz. Survivors recall seeing them arriving in uniform, greeting the SS guards with "Heil Hitler," and sometimes continuing to wear their military decorations in the camp. About 100 of these men were withdrawn from detachments at the front. One of them, Jozef Weiss, the Kapo at the camp's clothing store, boasted 18 decorations, some going back to World War I (International Auschwitz Committee, 1986, pp. 4-5).

THE ROAD TO EXTINCTION

The "roads to extinction" (Friedman, 1980) were approximately the same for Gypsies as for Jews. Beginning with a definition of the target group by ideologues and "racial scientists," what followed was the identification of individuals who fit the definition, then their social - and finally physical - isolation from the surrounding population. Through this process, Jews and Gypsies were placed outside the law and deprived of the protection of the state (Friedman, 1980, p. 215).

The legal status of Gypsies and Jews was determined "irrevocably" by an agreement between Justice Minister Thierack and Himmler of September 18, 1942, which removed both groups from the jurisdiction of any German court (Fein, 1979, p. 29). Jews, Gypsies and Russians under "protective arrest" would henceforth be delivered by the Ministry of Justice to the SS. In a letter dated October 13, 1942, Thierack elaborated:

> With the intention of liberating the German area from Poles, Russians, Jews and Gypsies... I envisage transferring all criminal proceedings concerning [these people] to Himmler. I do this because I realize that the courts can only feebly contribute to the extermination of these people...

> There is no point in keeping these people for years in prison...(Kenrick & Puxon, 1972, p. 87)

The implementation order for this accord made it clear that Gypsies, like Jews, stood not only outside German law, but could not hope to be recognized by international law - what remained of it. While foreign Jews, even those with enemy nationality, were temporarily preserved from deportation, Thierack's order stated: "Foreign Gypsies are not to be classed as foreign and therefore also to be handed over" (*ibid.*).

Being thus identified and isolated from their neighbors, the members of the target group have been effectively placed "outside the universe of obligations of the dominant group" (Fein, 1979, p. 9). Members of the dominant group, as well as representatives of the state, were at liberty to treat them as whims and ideology dictated. The rest followed: forced sterilization, deportation to concentration camps, victimization by medical experimenters and mass annihilation with bullets or gas.

The success of this process in any given society, as Fein points out, is correlated with the degree of popular prejudice and official cooperation (1979, pp. 64-68). Where there was strong resistance to Nazi measures on the part of officials and the dominant population, these stages would not follow in orderly sequence. Unfortunately for the Gypsies, there was little evidence of resistance in any country to measures against them. There were few "righteous Gentiles" who risked their lives to save Gypsies.

At the time the war broke out in 1939, there were approximately 22,000 Gypsies and 375,000 Jews still living in Germany (Hohmann, 1981, p. 143). Their legal status, or lack of it, was, for all practical purposes, almost identical by this time. Both had been stigmatized, classified and stripped of their former identities and possessions. Nomadism was outlawed for the Gypsies in 1939. Lack of a fixed address was enough to send them to a concentration camp. After the fall of Poland, the first deportations to the conquered Polish territory began for both Jews and Gypsies. The Lodz Ghetto was erected in April 1940. Some 5,000 Gypsies were incarcerated there and subsequently exterminated in Treblinka and Chelmno. In October of the same year, the order for the creation of the Warsaw Ghetto was issued, and many more were imprisoned there. As the eastern countries were overrun, one after the other, the dreaded Einsatzkommandos swept through them in the wake of the German army to "cleanse" the conquered lands of Jews, Gypsies and political commissars, often with the enthusiastic support of native fascist organizations. The orders given both to army commanders and to SS troops in the east for the elimination of Gypsies always contained elements of both racial ideology and security considerations.

Final Solution at Auschwitz

Auschwitz was the last stop on the Gypsies' tragic journey in Nazi Europe. After Himmler's decree was issued, they were rounded up from carnivals and concert stages, from Slovak villages and Wehrmacht barracks, from Jewish ghettoes, labor camps and detention centers. In Auschwitz, they were permitted to be with their families, wear their own clothes and keep a few musical instruments so as to feed the German "Zigeunerromantik," even while they were being prepared for annihilation. "They were my favorite prisoners," Auschwitz Commandant Höss wrote in a Polish prison (1958). He was particularly fond of the children, introduced a nursery school and built them a playground with a merry-go-round a few months before he ordered their liquidation. Mengele never failed to produce candy from his pocket when he visited the Gypsy camp to select experimental subjects. According to some accounts, there was a small Gypsy boy, his special pet and mascot, who would often be seen standing by him on the selection ramp, until at last, he too was liquidated. It was said that Mengele personally brought him to the gas chamber (Nomberg-Prztyk, 1985).

The Gypsies' last night in Auschwitz was never forgotten by Jewish survivor-witnesses, even amidst the daily horrors of the camp. Lucie Adelsberger, a Jewish doctor in the Gypsy camp, recorded her memories of that night under the title of *Zigeunernacht* (Gypsy Night), an ironic title which evokes romance and campfires to the German ear. In great detail, she described the events of the days which preceded and followed the "Gypsy Night":

> In July, 1944, the mood in the Gypsy camp was even more tense than usual. Of the 20,000 Gypsies who were incarcerated, ... only 6,000 remained. The able-bodied were selected from among these by the camp doctor (Mengele)...The camp commander, who otherwise appeared only sporadically, inspected our camp often and for long periods. Something was in the air... the camp doctor occupied himself more than usually with the patients... two big kettles of soup were added to rations of the orphans' block.
>
> On the 31 of July, 1944, a Monday, the... train with the Gypsies that had already been sent to Auschwitz (the main camp), returned to Birkenau, to the Gypsy camp. That was unusual enough. Then the SS, despite curfew, permitted the Gypsies to gather on the platform and talk to the prisoners. Nothing like this had happened in the history of the concentration camp. In the presence of the SS, people called over the barbed wire, ...threw packages and cigarettes over it, waved their farewells on the platform. The camp doctor was standing by quietly and let it all happen...he greeted two young Gypsy boys that were going along on the journey... Only after the train left, were the prisoners driven back to their blocks.
>
> At four o'clock, the doctor examined the children's block again for those able to work, who would be loaded with the twins and sent to

Auschwitz. Then the events followed blow by blow...The strictest curfew was imposed. Before I could hurry to my children in the orphans' block, the camp street was already closed off... I fled to my colleagues in the quarantine block with the feeling that if, indeed, it has come to this, I wanted to walk the last stretch together with them.

This block was the last one in the camp, next to the Sauna. It was locked and bolted. I took on the night duty of the departed nurses and two colleagues who worked in the deserted office, counted the cards of the inmates of the block. Seemingly calm, they leafed through the red index cards with trembling fingers, counting over and over... The patients also knew what was happening. Their calm was astounding. A few wept quietly, others prayed. In the distance cars drove up and disappeared into the silence... Around 10:30 they stopped in front of our block.. It was not for us but for the orphans opposite us. We heard the clipped orders of the SS, the crying of the children. I recognized the individual voices. The older ones defended themselves audibly.... In a few minutes the cars drove off, the cries faded into the night.

After half an hour, the trucks came back to our block... Who will they take first, the Gypsies or the Jewish doctors? The doors were torn open, the SS stormed in... People were torn from their beds,... driven outside...We stood watching helplessly. In a few minutes, the block was empty. Then it was locked up again and the SS drove off with their victims...

The next morning, the first of August, the Gypsy camp, which the previous day had 3,500 inhabitants, was empty and...silent.

NOTES

1. The figure derives from estimates of Donald Kenrick and Grattan Puxon (1972), recently revised downwards. Some scholars and Romani (Gypsy) political activists, on the basis of recent information, claim the true figures are much higher. Ian Hancock (1987) maintains the losses were over half a million (1987) and suggests that new data might make it closer to one million (personal correspondence and conversations). As with most figures relating to Gypsies, they involve largely induction and guess-work. The most "accurate" numbers were those kept by German bureaucrats, police officials and scholars involved in the persecution and genocide. Gypsies have nowhere voluntarily identified themselves to census officials or other representatives of Government bureaucracies.

2. There was one courtroom drama at the Nuremberg trials involving a Gypsy. The accounts of this vary. According to one source (Bernadac, 1979, p. 63), the Gypsy was a survivor of the Dachau medical experiments named Karl Holleinreiner, who was to testify against his tormentor, Dr. Beigelbock. When he saw Beigelbock in the dock, he assaulted him with clenched fists, was restrained by the guards, and then removed from the courtroom and sentenced to ninety days in prison by the judge. According to others (e.g., Kenrick and Puxon, 1972, p. 189), the incident involved two English Gypsies on guard duty at the military tribunal. When one of the SS defendants stood at attention and gave the Nazi salute, one of these Gypsy guards - unable to contain his emotions - bayonetted the Nazi (account based on a private communication to the authors.)

BIBLIOGRAPHY

Arnold, Hermann (1973). Das Zigeunerproblem [The Gypsy problem]. *Deutscher Caritas-Verband* (Caritas) 74(6), pp. 281ff.
A restatement of the old "Gypsy problem" by a controversial post-war "Gypsy expert", a younger contemporary and friend of the old Nazi racial scientists, who entrusted their documents to him after the war. He later donated most of them to the Bundesarchiv.

Arnold, Hermann (1977). Ein Menschenalter Danach: Anmerkungen zur Geschichtsschreibungen der Zigeunerverfolgung [One Generation later: Notes of historical writings on the persecution of the Gypsies]. *Mitteilung zur Zigeunerkunde*, 4.
A skeptical critique of Gypsy survivor testimony published in a journal discontinued soon thereafter.

Arnold, Hermann (1989?) (n.d.). *Die NS-Zigeunerverfolgung: Ihre Ausdeutung und Ausbeutung* [The National Socialist Persecution of the Gypsies: its interpretation and exploitation]. Based on Arnold's inaccessible material in the Bundesarchiv. Available only from Antiquariat Karl-Heinz Gerster, Ligusterweg 5, D 8750, Aschaffenburg.
A privately published counterattack on his critics.

Ayass, Wolfgang et al (1988). *Feinderklärung und Prävention: Kriminalbiologie, Zigeunerforschung und Asocialenpolitik* [Designation of enemies and prevention: Criminal biology, Gypsy research, and "asocial" policy]. Series: N.S. Health & Social Policy 6. Berlin: Rotbuch Verlag. 214 pp.
A leftist critique, by younger scholars, of Gypsy research and government policies in Germany before, during and after the Nazi regime. Includes several articles by one of the principal (ex-)DDR Gypsy researchers, Reimar Gilsenbach, who provides a perspective different from most West German "gypsy experts" of his day.

Bernadac, Christian (1979). *l'Holocauste oublié, le massacre des Tsiganes*. Paris: Ed. France-Empire. 413 pp. (Other edition: 1980: Montreal, Presses Select Ltee.)
One of the few books in any language on the subject, by a prominent French journalist.

Bock, Gisela (1981). Aber ich wollte vorher noch ein Kind [But first I still wanted a child]. *Courage*, 6, 21-24.
Interview with a German Gypsy woman, Theresa Seible, about her sterilization and Mengele's experiments with her twin babies. She became a political activist in the 1970s, began a women's organization. The author (G. Tyrnauer) recorded an interview with her (audiotape) in 1982.

Braun, Hans (1986). *A Sinto Survivor Speaks*. In Grumet, J. (Ed.), *Papers from the Sixth and Seventh Annual Meetings, Gypsy Lore Society, North American Chapter*. New York: Gypsy Lore Society Publications No. 3, pp. 165-71.
Edited transcription of an audiotaped interview. Braun is an Auschwitz survivor.

Buchheim, Hans (1958). Die Zigeunerdeportation vom Mai 1940 [The Gypsy deportation of May 1940]. *Gutachten des Instituts für Zeitgeschichte* (Munich), pp. 51-61. Also: In Frenkel, Marcel (Ed.), *Das Entschädigungsrecht für die Opfer der Nationalsozialistischen Verfolgung*. [The reparations law for victims of National Socialist persecution]. Frankfurt/Main: Abhandlungen Bl., Vol. 1, pp. 136ff.

Documents from the Munich contemporary history archive on the first mass Gypsy deportation .

Calvelli-Adorno (1961). Die rassische Verfolgung der Zigeuner vor dem 1. März 1943 [The racial persecution of Gypsies before March 1, 1943]. *Rechts-sprechung zum Wiedergutmachungsrecht* (Munich), 12, 529-37 (Dec.).
More legal documents on the persecution of Gypsies for possible reparations.

Calvet, Georges (1978). Recit d'un manouche deporté pendant la guerre. *Études Tsiganes* (Paris), 4, 1-7.
A French manouche narrates his story of wartime deportation in the most important journal of Gypsy studies in the French language.

Cargas, Harry J. (1989). The continuum of Gypsy suffering. Chapter in *Reflections of a Post-Auschwitz Christian*. Detroit: Wayne State University Press, pp. 75-90
Cargas is a theologian and one of the founders of the U.S. Holocaust Memorial Council.

Ciechnowski, Konrad (1983). Das Schicksal der Zigeuner und Juden in den Jahren des Zweiten Weltkrieges in Pommerlen [The fate of the Gypsies and Jews in Pomerania during the years of the Second World War]. *The Main Commission for Investigation of Nazi Crimes in Poland*. International Scientific Session on Nazi Genocide in Poland and Europe 1939-1945. Warsaw, April 14-17.
A study comparing the fate of Gypsies and Jews in one locality.

Dambrowski, Amanda (1981). Das Schicksal einer Ostpreussischen Vertriebenen Sinti-Familie im NS-Staat [The fate of an East Prussian persecuted Sinti family in the Nazi state]. *Pogrom*, 80/81, pp. 72ff.
A first-person Sinti narrative.

Dillman, Alfred (1905). *Zigeunerbuch* [Gypsy book]. Munich.
Published for official use by the security office of the Munich police directorate.

Döring, Hans J. (1964). Die Zigeuner im nationalsozialistischen Staat [Gypsies in the NS State]. *Kriminalistik Verlag*, 12. German Criminology Association (Hamburg): Kriminologische Schriftenreihe. 231 pp.
Döring's work deals, in great detail, exclusively with the persecution of the Gypsies in the Third Reich. Utilizing numerous sources difficult to find, the author portrays the development of pertinent NS legislation leading ultimately to the great destruction - above all in KZ Auschwitz. It is the first book to deal with the destruction of the Gypsies, although it began as an academic study of Gypsies as a criminal group.

Erhardt, Sophie (1942). Zigeuner und Zigeunermischlinge in Ostpreussen: Ausder Rassenhygienischen und Kriminalbiologischen Forschungsstelle des Reichsgesundheitsamtes" [Gypsies and Gypsy mixed breeds in East Prussia: From the Racial Hygiene and Population Biological Research Division of the Reich Ministry of Health]. *Volk und Rasse* (Munich), 17(3), 52-57.
The wartime work of a member of the Racial Hygiene Institute's research team. Erhardt became highly controversial in the early 1980s when the politicized Sinti, fearing she would destroy documentary evidence of their genocide in the archive over which she still had control, staged a sit-in at Tübingen University library.

Fein, Helen (1978). Extermination of the Gypsies. In Chertok, R., and Spencer, J., (Eds), *The Holocaust Years: Society on Trial*. New York: Bantam Books, pp. 43-45.
A popular account based almost entirely on Kenrick and Puxon.

Ficowski, Jerzy (1979). Die Vernichtung [The destruction]. In Zülch, T. (Ed.), *In Auschwitz vergast, bis heute verfolgt: Zur Situation der Roma (Zigeuner) in Deutschland und Europa*. Hamburg: Rowohlt Verlag pp. 91-111.
An account of the genocide by the foremost literary scholar of the Gypsies in Poland.

Ficowski, Jerzy (1982). The fate of the Polish Gypsies, In Porter, Jack Nusan (Ed.), *Genocide and Human Rights*. Washington D.C.: University Press of Amerca, pp. 166-177 (original 1950).

Ficowski, Jerzy n.d. (late 1980s?). *The Gypsies in Poland: History and Customs*. Printed in Yugoslavia: Interpress, pp.38-48.
A beautifully illustrated book which has been translated into several languages. Contains a section, "Condemned to Extermination," which includes accounts of Gypsies in Polish forests, ghettoes and concentration camps. Ficowski has translated the poems of Papusza, the best known Gypsy survivor in Poland.

Franz, Philomena (1987). *Zwischen Liebe und Hass: ein Zigeunerleben* [Between Love and Hate: A Gypsy Life] Freiburg, Basel, Wien: Herder (3rd printing).
Autobiography of a Sinti survivor of Auschwitz.

Friedman, Philip (1950) A strange common destiny: The extermination of Gypsies. *Kiyoum*, 8/9, pp. 19661-19667. [In Yiddish]

Friedman, Philip (1980). The extermination of the Gypsies: Nazi genocide of an Aryan people. In Friedman, Ada J. (Ed.), *Roads to Extinction: Essays on the Holocaust*. New York and Philadelphia: Conference on Jewish Social Studies and Jewish Publication Society. pp. 381-386.
Posthumously published collected essays of a distinguished Holocaust scholar includes this piece urging comparative research on Jewish and Gypsy genocides.

Geigges, Anita and Wette, Bernard W. (1979). *Zigeuner heute. Verfolgung und Diskriminierung in der Bundesrepublik* [Gypsies today: Persecution and discrimination in the Federal Republic]. Bornheim-Marten: Lamur Verlag. 475 pp.
An important collection of documents and photos compiled by sympathetic journalists at the dawn of the Sinti political movement.

Gilbert, Martin (1982). *The Macmillan Atlas of the Holocaust*. NY: Macmillan. 256 pp.
Includes a map on the deportation and extermination of Gypsies.

Günther, Hans F. (1926). *Rassenkunde des deutschen Volkes* [Racial science of the German people]. Munich.
The Bible of the racial "scientists."

Hancock, Ian. F. (1980). Gypsies in Germany: The Fate of the Romany. *German Studies*, 2, 247-264.
The author is English born Romani activist in the U.S. and internationally as well as a professor of linguistics at the University of Texas.

Hancock, Ian. F. (1987). Gypsies, Jews, and the Holocaust: Talking through the cracks of history. *Shmate: A Journal of Progressive Jewish Thought*, 17, 6-15.

Hancock, Ian. F. (1987). *The Pariah Syndrome. An Account of Gypsy Slavery and Persecution*. Ann Arbor, MI: Karoma Publishers. 180 pp.
   The first account in English of Gypsy slavery in the Balkans and its relation to other forms of persecution.

Herz, Hugo (1908). *Verbrechen und Verbrechertum in Österreich: Die Kriminalität der Zigeuner und Juden* [Crimes and criminality in Austria: The criminality of Gypsies and Jews]. Tübingen.
   Early 20th century "criminology."

Hohmann, Joachim S. (1980). *Zigeuner und Zigeunerwissenschaft: Ein Beitrag zur Grundlagenforschung und Dokumentation des Völkermord im 'Dritten Reich'* [Gypsies and Gypsy lore: A contribution to the basic research and documentation of genocide in the Third Reich]. Marburg/Lahn: Guttandin und Hoppe. 262 pp.
   An important work documenting the connections between research and genocide in the Third Reich.

Hohmann, Joachim S. (1981). *Geschichte der Zigeunerverfolgung in Deutschland* [The story of Gypsy persecution in Germany]. Frankfurt: Campus. New edition 1988. 248 pp.
   Traces the persecution from the earliest times to present.

Hohmann, Joachim S., and Schopf, Roland (Eds.) (1979). *Zigeunerleben: Beiträge zur Sozialgeschichte einer Verfolgung.* [Gypsy Life: contributions to the social history of a persecution] 2nd ed. Darmstadt: MS edition. 228 pp.
   For a popular audience, profusely illustrated, good material.

Höss, Rudolf (1961). *Commandant of Auschwitz: The Autobiography of Rudolf Hoess.* New York: Popular Library. [First English language edition, 1959]
   Significant passages about the Gypsies in Auschwitz and his attitude towards them.

International Auschwitz Committee (1986). *Nazi Medicine: Doctors, Victims and Medicine in Auschwitz.* New York: Howard Fertig. 700 pp.
   Chapter on Gypsy camp "hospital."

Jelinek, Yeshayahu (1978). The liquidation of Serbs, Jews and Gypsies in the independent Croatian state. *Yalkut Moreshet* (Israel) 26, 61-70. [In Hebrew]
   An Israeli source.

Justin, Eva (1943). Die Rom-Zigeuner [The Rom-Gypsies]. *Neues Volk.* (Berlin) 11(5), 21-24.
   Justin was assistant of Dr. Robert Ritter, director of the racial research division of the Ministry of Health. Written while she was employed there.

Justin, Eva (1979). Zigeuner-Neger-Bastarde [Gypsy-Negro-Bastards]. In Zülch, T. (Ed.), In *Auschwitz Vergast, bis heute verfolgt, op. cit.,* pp. 189-190.
   This piece, reprinted in the earliest book produced by the Sinti political movement, gives the flavor of Justin's approach to her research subjects.

Kanfer, Stefan (1978). *The Eighth Sin.* New York: Random House. 288 pp.
A Gypsy child survivor is transplanted to New York and lives with a Jewish foster family. A fictionalized account interspersed with quotations from Kenrick and Puxon.

Kenrick, Donald, and Puxon, Grattan (1972). *The Destiny of Europe's Gypsies.* New York: Basic Books. (First published in Great Britain, Chatto-Heinemann, Sussex U. Press, 1972). 256 pp.
The most important - and thus far only - work on this subject in English, now out of print. The basis of many other writings. Extensively documented. Translations exist in French, German, Italian, Japanese and Romanes. Essential reading.

Kenrick, Donald; Puxon, Grattan; and Zülch, Tilman (Eds.) (1980). *Die Zigeuner: Verkannt, Verachtet, Verfolgt* [The Gypsies: misunderstood, despised, persecuted]. Hanover: Niedersachsische Landeszentrale für politsche Bildung. 131 pp.
Essays in Gypsy history and persecution by the three authors.

Knobloch, Johann (1974). Zigeuner [Gypsies]. In *Brockhaus Enzyklopaedie*, 20.
The author gathered data for his dissertation research in Lackenbach, a Gypsy transit camp in Austria, *Sonderheft 42*, Innsbruck.

König, Ulrich n.d. *Sinti und Roma unter dem Nationalsozialismus: Verfolgung und Widerstand* [Sinti and Roma under National Socialism: Persecution and resistance]. Studienverlag N. Brockmeyer.
A recent study.

Lakatos, Menyhert (1975). *Füstös Képek* [Smoky pictures]. Budapest (German translation). *Bitterer Rauch* [Bitter Smoke]. East Berlin: Volk and Welt 1978 (2nd edition, 1980).

Martins-Heuss, Kirsten (1989). Reflections on the collective identity of German Roma and Sinta (Gypsies) after National Socialism. *Holocaust and Genocide Studies*, 4(2), 193-211.
A young German scholar who worked in Yad Vashem shortly before her untimely death examines the psychological suffering and coping of surviving Gypsies.

Mazirel, Lau (1973). Die Verfolgung der Zigeuner im Dritten Reich [The persecution of Gypsies in the Third Reich]. In *Essays über Nazi Verbrechen: Simon Wiesenthal Gewidmet* [Essays on Nazi Crimes: Dedicated to Simon Wiesenthal]. Amsterdam.
A Dutch scholar-activist who founded a society for helping nomads, particularly Gypsies. A valuable essay.

Megel, John (1986). The Holocaust and the American Rom. In Grumet, Joanne (Ed.), *Papers from the Sixth and Seventh Annual Meetings, Gypsy Lore Society, North American Chapter*, New York: Gypsy Lore Society, Publications No. 3., pp. 187-90.
An American Rom activist who lobbied the U.S. Holocaust Memorial Council to assure Romani participation.

Milton, Sybil (1990). The context of the Holocaust. *German Studies Review*, 13(2), 269-283.
A very detailed scholarly work on the Gypsies based on archival material now at the U.S. Holocaust Memorial Museum.

Morawek, Karl (1939). Ein Beitrag zur Rassenkunde der Bürgerländischen Zigeuner [A contribution to the racial science of the Gypsies of the Burgenland]. Philosophy dissertation, Vienna.
    The author was a member of the Racial Hygiene and Population Biological Research Center.

Müller-Hill, Benno (1988). *Murderous Science*. Oxford, NY, Tokyo: Oxford University Press. 208 pp.
    The translation of a bold scholarly critique of "racial science" and its contributions to genocide by a leading German geneticist. Includes "conversations" with surving architects of the Nazi genetic theories and their relatives. Originally published as *Todliche Wissenschaft: die Aussonderung von Juden, Zigeunern und Geisteskranken 1933-45*. Hamburg: Rowohlt, 1984.

Musmanno, Michael A. (1961). *The Eichmann Kommandos*. Philadelphia: McCrae Smith.
    Autobiography; about the Einsatzgruppen by one of their judges at Nuremberg; contains some testimony about the killing of Gypsies.

Necas, Ctibor (1981). *The Tragic Fate of the Czech and the Slovak Gypsies between 1939-1945*. Actes de la Faculté Pédagogique, University J.E. Purkyne, Brno.
    The author is the leading Czech scholar on the subject.

Noakes, Jeremy (1985). Life in the Third Reich: Social outcasts in Nazi Germany. *History Today* 35, pp. 15-19.
    A good summary the of Romani predicament in Nazi Germany. Written for lay readers of popular historical magazine.

Nomberg-Prztyk, Sara (1985). *Auschwitz: True Tales from a Grotesque Land*. Chapel Hill: University of North Carolina Press. 185 pp.
    Includes tale of a little Gypsy boy who was Mengele's mascot until his liquidation.

Novitch, Miriam (June 1961). Le second génocide. *Das neue Israel*, 693-694.
    One of the earliest accounts of the Gypsy ordeal by a Jewish (Israeli) survivor of Auschwitz. She founded the first archive of the Gypsy genocide at Kibbutz Lohamei Hagathaot, of which she was a member.

Paulsen, Jens (1936). Biologische Betrachtungen an Zigeunern [Biological reflections about Gypsies]. *Rasse, Monatsschrift der nordischen Bewegung* (Leipzig), pp. 14-17.
    Reflects Nazi thinking on the subject.

Peterson, P., and Liedtke, Ulrich (1971). Zur Entschädigung Zwangssterilisierter Zigeuner: Sozialpsychologische Einflüsse auf psychische Störungen Nationalsozialistisch Verfolgter [Towards the compensation of compulsory sterilized Gypsies: The social psychological influences on the mental disturbances of those persecuted by the Nazis]. *Nervenartzt* (Berlin) 42(4), 197-205. [A monthly journal for neurologists]
    An addition to the growing post-war clinical literature on Holocaust survivors; one of the few related to Gypsies.

Poliakov, Leon (1951). *Bréviaire de la haine*. Paris: Calmann-Lévy. 385 pp. [English translation: *Harvest of Hate* (1954). Syracuse, NY: Syracuse University Press. Later paperback revised edition published by Holocaust Library]
    An early post-war Holocaust classic.

Porter, Jack Nusan (Ed.) (1982). *Genocide and Human Rights*. Lanham, MD: University Press of America. 353 pp.
    Includes four articles on the Gypsy genocide, three of them older reprints, one (Tyrnauer) written for this volume.

Proctor, Robert (1988). *Racial Hygiene: Medicine Under the Nazis*. Cambridge, MA: Harvard University Press. 414 pp.
    An important recent work, carefully documented. Includes some Gypsy material.

Raklemann, Georgia A. (1980) *Zigeuner: Materialen für Unterricht und Bildungsarbeit* [Gypsies: Materials for Teaching and Outreach]. Gesellschaft für entwicklungspolitische Bildung.
    Written by a member of Giessen University's Projekt Tsiganologie.

Regnault, M. (1963). Souvenirs d'une déportée. *Études Tsiganes*, 4, 14-15.
    A French Gypsy recounts his experiences of deportation.

Rinser, Luise (1987). *Wer Wirft den Stein? Zigeuner Sein in Deutschland: Eine Anklage* [Who will throw the Stone? Life of a Gypsy in Germany: An accusation] Berlin: Ullstein.
    By a German writer who had been tried for treason by the Nazis during World War II].

Ritter, Robert (1938a). Mitteleuropaïsche Zigeuner: Ein Volksstamm oder eine Mischlungspopulation [Central European Gypsies: A race or a population mixture]. In *Congrès International de la Population*. Paris: 1937, Part 8, pp. 51-60, Extrait V11.
    Made for international consumption by the director of the Racial Hygiene Research division of the Ministry of Health.

Ritter, Robert (1938b). Zur Frage der Rassenbiologie und Rassenpsychologie der Zigeuner in Deutschland [On the question of racial biology and racial psychology of the Gypsies in Germany]. *Reichsgesundheitsblatt* (Berlin) 13, pp. 425ff.
    Written the same year for internal consumption. Considerably more ideological.

Rose, Romani (1983). "Zigeunerforschung" zur "Tzinganologie" [From "Zigeunerforschung" to "Tziganologie"]. *Wanderbühne, Zeitschrift für Literatur und Politik*, No 6.
    The author is the leader of the Zentralrat der deutschen Sinti und Roma.

Rose, Romani (1985). *Wir wollen Bürgerrechte und keinen Rassismus* [We want civil rights and no racism]. Heidelberg: Zentralrat Deutscher Sinti und Roma. [In 1987 a new expanded edition appeared under the title: Bürgerrechte für Sinti and Roma.]
    Primarily a political document.

Schopf, Roland, and Parusel, Eva Maria (1980). Bericht vom Vernichtungsplatz. In Hohmann, Joachim J., and Schopf, Roland (Eds.), *Zigeunerleben*. Darmstadt: MS edition, pp. 125-141.
    One of the earliest oral histories of a Gypsy survivor, taken by a student of Schopf with an introduction and concluding comment by Schopf, containing a critique of Arnold before he became the center of a political storm.

Schuler, Alfred (1968). Freiheitsentziehung deportierter Zigeuner [Detention of deported

Gypsies]. *Rechtsprechung zum Wiedergutmachungsrecht* (Munich), 19(8), 344-345.
Another Gypsy-related contribution to the formulation of the law regarding reparations.

Scott-Macfie, R.A. (1943). Gypsy persecutions: A survey of a black chapter in European History. *Journal of the Gypsy Lore Society,* 12(3-4), 64-78.
A wartime account by a leading pre-war English scholar on British Gypsies.

Scott-Macfie, R.A. (1956). Gypsies of the Third Reich. *Wiener Library Bulletin.* Nos. 1-2.
A later, fuller document. One of the early post-war accounts.

Seybold, Katrin, Rosenberg, B.; and Spitta, M. (1987). Das falsche Wort [The false word]. Text of video produced by Seybold Film Produktion, Munich.
An extraordinary documentary film about the Nazi extermination of the Gypsies by a German film maker and a Sintezza (Sinti woman) who narrates it.

Steinmetz, Selma (1966). *Österreichs Zigeuner im NS Staat* [Austria's Gypsies in the NS State]. Frankfurt/Zürich/Vienna: Europa-Verlag. 64 pp.
The earliest book on the Nazi destruction of the Austrian Gypsies based on the archives of the Austrian resistance. Contains narratives of survivors.

Steinmetz, Selma (1979). Die Verfolgung der burgenländischen Zigeuner [The persecution of The Gypsies of the Burgenland]. In Zülch, T. (Ed.), *In Aushwitz vergast, bis heute verfolgt. op.cit.,* pp. 112-133.

Stojka, Ceilja (1988). *Wir leben im Verborgenen: Erinnerungen einer Rom-Zigeunerin* [We live in hiding: Memoirs of a Rom Gypsy woman]. Vienna: Picus Verlag.
One of the very few written Gypsy Holocaust memoirs.

Streck, Bernhard (1979). Die Bekämpfung des Zigeunerunwesens: Ein Stück moderner Rechtsgeschichte [The struggle against the Gypsy nuisance: A piece of the modern legal history] In Zülch, T. (Ed.), In *Auschwitz vergast, bis heute verfolgt, op. cit.,* pp. 64-87.
A very well documented account of the legal history of Gypsy persecution in Germany.

Tenenbaum, Joseph (1956). *Race and Reich.* New York: Twayne. 554 pp.
Includes an appendix on the Gypsy genocide.

Thurner, Erika (1980). *Die Zigeuner als Opfer Nationalsozialistischer Verfolgung in Österreich* [The Gypsy as the victim of the NS persecution in Austria]. Dissertation, Salzburg University.
Based on a doctoral dissertation, this is a fine study by an activist modern historian at Linz University. There is new archival material in the form of documents discovered by the author in the remains of the Lackenbach transit camp through which most Austrian Gypsies passed on their way to Auschwitz.

Tyrnauer, Gabrielle (1982). Mastering the past: Germans and Gypsies. In Porter, J.N. (Ed.), *Genocide and Human Rights, op. cit.,* pp. 178-192.
The first publication growing out of work with the Sinti in Germany. Especially written for the Porter book.

Tyrnauer, Gabrielle (1984). Handeln und Ethik in der Angewandten Ethnologie [Action and ethics in applied anthropology]. In Müller, Ernst W. et al, (Eds.), *Ethnologie als Sozialwissenschaft* (Kölner: *Zeitschrift für Soziologie und Sozialpsychologie*) 26, 113-123.
    A study of the Rassenhygienische und Bevölkerungsbiologische Forschungsstelle, its research and its implications for applied anthropology.

Tyrnauer, Gabrielle (1985). *The Fate of the Gypsies during the Holocaust*. Report to the U.S. Holocaust Memorial Council, Washington, D.C. (Unpublished)

Tyrnauer, Gabrielle (1986). Scholars, Gypsies and the Holocaust. In Grumet, J. (Ed.), *Papers from the Sixth and Seventh Annual Meetings, Gypsy Lore Society, North American Chapter*, New York: Gypsy Lore Society Publications, No. 3. pp. 157-164.
    The author organized a panel on Gypsies and the Holocaust, (a first on the subject) critical of traditional Gypsy research (represented by the GLS) which largely ignored the genocide. It included a presentation by American Rom activist, John "Lazo" Megel (see earlier citation).

Tyrnauer, Gabrielle (1991). The forgotten Holocaust of the Gypsies. *Social Education*, 55(2), 111-113.
    Includes a previously unpublished Gypsy survivor oral history.

Tyrnauer, Gabrielle (1993). Holocaust history and the Gypsies. In Eckardt, Alice L. (Ed.) *Burning Memory: Times of Testing and Reckoning*. Oxford and New York: Pergamon Press, pp. 283-295. An earlier version of this piece appeared in *Shofar*, 1978, 7(2), 13-24.
    A critique of some Holocaust scholarship in relation to the Gypsies.

Vossen, Rudiger (1983). *Zigeuner: Roma, Sinti, Gitanos. Gypsies Zwischen Verfolgung und Romantisierung*. [Gypsies: Roma, Sinti, Gitanos. Gypsies between persecution and romanticization]. Ullstein Sachbuch.
    Catalogue for an exhibition at the Hamburg Museum für Völkerkunde. See especially Chap. III, "Die Vernichtung" ("the extermination").

Wiesenthal, Simon (1986). Tragedy of the Gypsies. *Bulletin of Information*, Item 26, p. 6. Dokumentationszentrum des Bundes Jüdischer Vervolgter des Naziregimes.
    Wiesenthal has supported the Gypsies in their struggle for recognition of their "forgotten Holocaust."

Wilczur, Jacek (1983). Zum Matyrium der Zigeuner während Naziokkupation in Polen [On the martyrdom of the Gypsies during the Nazi occupation of Poland]. *The Main Commission for Investigation of Nazi Crimes in Poland*. International Scientific Session on Nazi Genocide in Poland and Europe 1939-1945. Warsaw, April 14-17.

Wippermann, Wolfgang (1986). *Die nationalsozialistische Zigeunerverfolgung: Darstellung Dokumente, didaktische Hinwweise*. Series: das Leben im Frankfurt der NS Zeit [The National Socialist persecution of the Gypsies: Description, documents, teaching guides. Series: life in Frankfurt during the National Socialist period].
    A case study of local history.

Wirbel, Franz (1981). Die Rückkehr von Auschwitz [The return from Auschwitz]. *Pogrom* (Göttingen: Gesellschaft für Bedrohte Völker), 80-81, 142-43.
   Wirbel oral history exists on tape and in transcription.

Würth, A. (1938). Bemerkungen zur Zigeunerfrage und Zigeunerforschung in Deutschland [Observations on the Gypsy question and Gypsy research in Germany]. *Verhandlung des Deutschen Gesellschaft für Rassenforschung*, 9, pp. 95ff.
   A member of the Racial Hygiene research team.

Yates, Dora E. (1949). Hitler and the Gypsies: Fate of Europe's oldest Aryans. In Porter, J.N. (Ed.), *Genocide and Human Rights, op. cit.*, pp. 158-166.
   Yates was long-time president of the British Gypsy Lore Society, founded in 1888.

Yoors, Jan (1971). *Crossings: A Journal of Survival and Resistance in World War II.* New York: Simon & Schuster.
   An account of how the author, who travelled with a Rom tribe in the Balkans during his World War II childhood, now an adult and resistance fighter, was recruited to organize his old Lowara friends to smuggle contraband for the Maquis.

Zülch, Tilman (Ed.) (1979). *In Auschwitz vergast, bis heute verfolgt: Zur Situation der Roma (Zigeuner) in Deutschland und Europa* [Gassed in Auschwitz, persecuted until today: On the situation of Roma (Gypsies) in Germany and Europe]. Hamburg: Rowohlt Verlag.

PART V

The Widening Circle of Destruction and Trauma

8

The Psychiatric Treatment of Holocaust Survivors

Robert Krell

THE ENORMITY OF THE TRAUMA

The psychiatric treatment of survivors has presented mental health professionals of all types a perplexing challenge. No psychiatrist was prepared for persons who had endured the most catastrophic traumas imaginable. The descriptions of unspeakable cruelty by survivor-witnesses fill volumes. And what did they see?

Gisella Perl (1948) describes a 5 year old girl, Julika, "torn from her mother's arms, and thrown into a ditch to be burned alive together with hundreds and hundreds of little boys and girls" (p.50).

Parents witnessed the murders of their children, and children, of their parents. If by chance one survived, survival meant to behold forever the memory of that moment.

Martin Gilbert (1985) has described the sufferings inflicted by the perpetrators, most of which exceed the boundaries of imagination. To this day, an average person might not think it possible that people can inflict such torments as were indeed inflicted.

Ordinary people did extraordinary things. At the time that movie theatres in the U.S. showed Walt Disney's "Snow White" and the technicolor spectacular "Gone With the Wind" was playing to appreciative audiences, *Einsatzgruppen*, S.S. led killing squads, advancing into Eastern Poland and Russia were not only shooting tens of thousands of Jews but set loose anti-

Semitic Poles, Lithuanians and Ukrainians, amongst others, to torture and rape the helpless victims. Synagogues were burned while filled with people. Jewish babies were hurled from rooftops, pregnant women disembowelled, children were torn limb from limb by mobs or used for target practice. It is no wonder that the mind staggers when confronted with such knowledge, and that there was little available to prepare the therapist for the inevitable encounter with the survivor.

EARLY PSYCHOLOGICAL OBSERVATIONS

Curt Bondy, an inmate of Buchenwald *prior* to the war (1938) wrote in 1943, "When the invasion of Europe comes, the allied armies in liberating or conquering the different countries will find millions of people interned in camps." Even more prescient, Bondy states "In writing this paper I felt great uncertainty about the *aftereffects* of internment. As far as I know, not much is known about this subject. We do not know how deeply the stay in a concentration camp or in other camps influences the whole character structure, how long it takes to overcome the difficulties, and what methods of treatment could be used" (p.475).

Bondy's cautious warning stands in sharp contrast to another inmate of pre-war Dachau (1938) and Buchenwald (1939), Bruno Bettelheim (1943) who wrote an authoritative account of the psychologic destruction of pre-war concentration camp inmates. Bettelheim subsequently seldom, if ever, differentiated between survivors of the brutal pre-war period and the far more brutal war-time camps created for the express purpose of torture and murder. Already safely in the United States in the early 40's, Bettelheim's views obscured the more thoughtful comments by Bondy although their articles were published side by side in the same journal. Even the most intelligent and articulate criticism of Bettelheim did not diminish his self-appointed status as *the* expert on understanding survivorhood. His influence severely compromised the evolution of understanding so crucial to treatment of survivors. Attempts to counter Bettelheim's views by the survivor-author, Alexander Donat (1976), and survivor-psychiatrist, Leo Eitinger (1981), failed, the latter noting that while the second world war was in progress, when the killing of millions in the so-called extermination camps reached its greatest momentum, Bettelheim felt "objective enough" - to quote him - to describe his observations from the pre-war camps. He found only regression and "identification with the aggressor" (p.148).

One critic, the writer Terrence des Pres (1976) provides insight into this entire matter in a well-reasoned article, "The Bettelheim Problem." Des Pres argues that Bettelheim's assessment of the survivor experience is accepted by the scholarly community as the "final word on men and women caught in extreme situations" (p.620), when in fact Holocaust survivors of the death camps have qualified or discredited his views as distorted and inaccurate. What strikes Des Pres as most peculiar is how Bettelheim, who was released from Buchenwald in 1939 through wealth and good connections, subsequently became the spokesman for survivors. Des Pres' analysis actually reveals Bettelheim's contradictions, his considerable contempt for victims and survivors, the misapplication of the psychoanalytic approach, and a self-serving and arrogant posture in prescribing what trapped European Jews should have done and how they should have behaved. Bettelheim's pronouncements influenced and misled a generation of writers and mental health professionals who might have done more to assist the survivors with their postwar adjustment, if not for the "Bettelheim Problem."

Des Pres (1976) himself produced a seminal work on life in the concentration camps based on survivor testimony. He attributes a considerable power to the will to survive in order to bear witness. Des Pres also points out the degree to which inmates retained forms of social bonding, organized collective resistance and attempted to keep a degree of dignity. Within this framework, he arrives at very different and more positive interpretations of such concepts as *survivor guilt* than does Robert J. Lifton (1967) or Henry Krystal (1968). Rather than supporting the psychiatric notion that the intense preoccupation of the survivor with the dead is evidence of neurosis, Des Pres suggests that this preoccupation be redefined as a task or responsibility assumed by the survivor. Similarly, he takes issue with the concept that inmates regressed to "childlike" or "infantile" levels of behavior. The appearance of so-called primitive behavior cannot be removed from the context where preoccupation with food derived from starvation, and preoccupation with excreta derived from being forced to live in urine and faeces, one's own and others.

The difficulties in understanding the nature of the trauma are dramatically apparent in interviews conducted by David Boder (1949) in the immediate post-war period. In talking with Abe Mohnblum, an adolescent concentration camp survivor, Boder, a psychologist, attempts to reassure his interviewee of the progress made in the field of psychology and psychological understanding. Mohnblum not only expresses doubts about such claims but also muses, "After all that I have seen, I know that we know nothing yet" (p.126).

The earliest observations of the American psychiatrist, Paul Friedman (1949), and Norwegian psychiatrist, Leo Eitinger (1964), also contain theories not conducive to the understanding and treatment of survivors. Friedman, observing and interviewing survivors on Cyprus, suggested that "in desperate struggle for survival all the forces of the libido are concentrated on the instinct of self-preservation" and follows with an unfortunate lapse into speculation about "the possibility that the continuous death threats re-awakened old castration fears, prohibiting the indulgence in sex, as if the inmates felt that in refraining from sexual activity they would avoid punishment here too, the punishment of the gas chamber and the crematorium" (p.604).

From this extreme and misguided attempt to explain in psychodynamic language diminishing of the libido in a tortured, starving person whose immediate future holds only death, Eitinger in Norway inadvertently erred in the other direction and diminished the psychological sequelae by focusing his studies on the organic consequences of incarceration. In effect, he dilutes the importance of the psychic impact in his study comparing Norwegian non-Jewish resistance fighters who survived concentration camps with a group of Israeli Jewish survivors from concentration camps. Eitinger emphasizes the importance of the "cumulative tainting" of head injuries, encephalitis, or spotted fever, while acknowledging that Jewish inmates would not have survived if incapacitated by any illness. Simply put, the seriously ill inmates are not likely to have remained amongst the survivors available to be examined. In any case, it has become clear that overall, organicity is of relatively little importance in determining the psychological conditions of most Jewish survivors.

While stating that in the subgroup with organic-type illnesses, "the connection between the traumatizing war experiences and the traumatic brain disorder is considered established," Eitinger assumes that war conditions have not played a decisive role in 20 "neurotic" Israeli patients he examined. Their neuroses are viewed to be "independent of their war experiences, inasmuch as it is difficult to prove a direct causal connection" (p.154).

Rappaport (1968) faced squarely Sigmund Freud's doubt "that a terrifying experience can of itself produce neurosis in adult life." Rappaport stated that "he (Freud) could not have foreseen or imagined the terror practices of the S.S. which were designed to exhaust anybody's personality resources regardless of the presence or absence of specific conflicts in the unconscious. An insistence of investigators on finding some latent predisposition for the personality breakdown betrays their unwillingness to imagine the full impact of the terror" (p.720).

The immediate post-war period prepared a climate in which theories were not used in the service of therapy *for* the survivor, but *against* the survivor. German psychiatrists appointed to examine survivors for compensation used either the absence of organicity or the presence of "neurosis" (in the sense of deriving from early infantile 'anlage' or innate predisposition) to deny compensation. If in their opinion, a survivor was predisposed in infancy towards neurosis, then the experience of trauma was incidental.

Eissler (1967) wrote a chilling paper dealing with statements from the opinions of three psychiatrists employed by the German Consulate in New York to determine psychiatric damage in victims of persecution with a view to compensation. Twenty years after liberation, with the gradual acknowledgement and recognition by psychiatrists of the psychologic sequelae of extreme trauma, Eissler documents the existence of psychiatric "opinions" that defy the imagination. Eissler cites statements from the opinions of these psychiatrists.

> Dr. A's opinion concerned "a woman whose parents, brother, three sisters with their children, husband, and an eight year old daughter had been killed during the course of the persecutions; she herself spent years in a ghetto and in several concentration camps and had frequently been beaten to unconsciousness. She complained of depression, anxiety, phobia, feelings of guilt, etc. Dr. A. denied any connection between these symptoms and the experience of persecution. He included in his report the following: ('Despite such grave experiences, of which no one is spared, most people continue their lives and have no chronic depressions') (p.1353).
>
> Dr. B. examined "a 57 year-old man, whose mother, sister, wife and four children had been killed in a concentration camp and who complained about cardiac symptoms, pins-and-needles sensations in the hands and feet, dyspnea at night, daily headaches, dizziness, hoarseness, weariness, and inability to work. At the age of 39 he had been forced to live in a ghetto. Subsequently he went through three concentration camps. He claimed that once he was thrown from a truck, which necessitated eye surgery; since then his vision had been impaired. The ophthalmologist of the Consulate diagnosed high-grade myopic changes as the result of dilation in the retina and choroid of both eyes. All signs of eye surgery were denied, however, and no connection with persecution was found with regard to the eye symptoms, which were said to be of constitutional origin" (p.1354).
>
> And Dr. C. offered an expert opinion on "a 40 year-old married woman who had an uneventful history up to the age of 15, when her home country was occupied by the Germans. The principal pathogenic events among the many traumata she suffered were the following: She witnessed a six-day old infant, the child of a neighbour, being killed by being thrown against a truck. When the windows of the house in which she lived were searched at night with searchlights in order to discover any Jews who might be hiding there, and she had to conceal herself with her sister behind a curtain, this was followed by a bout of diarrhea. This same symptom recurred in connection with the loss of her father, when he did not return from services at the synagogue.
>
> "The family had to go into hiding, and the claimant spent 15 months in complete isolation in a hayloft, separated from her family, her only contact being the person who brought her some food once a day. Personal hygiene was impossible: her infrequent menstrual periods were experienced by her as catastrophes and at times she suffered from diarrhea and vomiting. She was exposed to periods of terror, since the Germans frequently passed by and she was not at all certain of her host's reliability. After liberation she suffered from phobias, among which were inability to stay in her apartment unless all the doors were open, diarrhea, severe bouts of headache, dysmenorrhea, frigidity and disgust with intercourse, insomnia, and neurodermatitis. All this Dr. C. diagnosed as a case of anxiety neurosis, 'caused by constitutional factors' (anlagebedingt), in an emotionally labile personality with low stimulus threshold" (p.1356).

Eissler concluded that his examination of the rejection of claims in the United States reflected the examining psychiatrists' contempt for the victims.

This attitude in milder forms and even in well-meaning psychiatrists, can be detected in subsequent years as well. After all, the burden of proof of victimization remained with the victims, even though the conditions in which they survived were common knowledge.

In view of the "negative attitudes on the part of so-called experts (who, it must be added are not always German physicians)" (p.236), Niederland (1961) urged familiarization with the more common psychiatric disorders to be found in surviving victims. Niederland deliberately omitted mental symptoms due to organic brain damage or cerebral concussions caused by beatings. He focused on the responses of the psychic apparatus, the symptom-free interval, and pointed out the overwhelming impact on personality of terror. He notes the difficulties of describing prolonged terror, and likens it to a "protracted life-in-death existence" (p.239).

Niederland described the "survivor syndrome," the probable descriptive precursor of the contemporary diagnostic term, PTSD, or Post-Traumatic Stress Disorder, although Hermann and Thygesen (1954), in a series of Danish studies had already named the "concentration camp syndrome" on the basis of evaluations of 120 concentration camp prisoners.

The problems of treatment are evident in the inherent contradictions of investigators of the time, as well as the overall response of the psychiatric profession.

Basically, psychiatrists and psychologists responded to the challenge posed by survivors with unflattering (to put it mildly) comments about survivor psychopathology, and about untreatability in response to the survivors' use of denial and an apparent unwillingness to relate the experience. The therapist's personal silence in response to the needs of the survivor was not addressed at all.

It is the silence on the part of therapists which is most dramatic given the virtual absence of any discussion about the treatment of survivors in any major psychiatry textbook written in the sixties, seventies and eighties save one, Arieti's *American Handbook of Psychiatry* which contained an article by Paul Chodoff (1966). It was Chodoff who suggested in an earlier article (1963) that "possibly, psychodynamic psychiatry has gone too far in its at least implied insistence that every state of emotional illness must result from the impact of a trauma on a personality somehow predisposed to react adversely to the trauma; cases of the kind described here must be taken into account before such explanations can be regarded as universal" (p.327).

In effect, the original descriptions of the concept of PTSD elaborated on the basis of post-war studies of various kinds of survivors in the fifties disappeared until 1980 when they re-emerged in connection with the descriptions of the traumas experienced by the Vietnam veterans, and were subsequently, finally, enshrined as a diagnostic category in the DSM III.

Klaus Hoppe's (1966) description of survivors with "hate addiction" and

Henry Krystal's (1968) findings of survival guilt in 92% of survivors laid a burden on the already burdened survivors. How could a survivor present to a therapist when already labeled as obsessed with hatred, consumed with guilt, and perhaps most insulting of all, viewed as the personification of a Nazi persecutor through "identification with the aggressor"?

Gradual recognition and study of the problems in survivors who succumbed to symptoms led to more rational treatment approaches such as those pioneered in Holland by Jan Bastiaans (1957, 1976), in Israel by Hillel Klein (1963, 1972) and Shamai Davidson (1967, 1992), and in the United States by Paul Chodoff (1966) and Judith Kestenberg (1980). In Canada, attention was being drawn to the treatment of the children of survivors by Vivian Rakoff (1966), John Sigal (1966) and Nathan Epstein (1966) at the Jewish General Hospital in Montreal in the early 1960's.

Bastiaans (1979) established a center for the treatment of victims of war and employed a wide variety of carthartic techniques for the emotionally incapacitated survivors. Klein (1972) expanded the treatment possibilities with the judicious application of psychodynamic principles combined with great personal insight from his own concentration camp experience. Davidson (1980) expanded the care of the survivor to include family as did Axel Russell (1974) and Robert Krell (1982) in the early seventies in Canada.

LATER OBSERVATIONS AND CONTEMPORARY KNOWLEDGE

The understanding of the survivor's predicament and treatment has regained impetus from contemporary insights offered by leading psychiatrists who themselves were victims during World War II including Haim Dasberg (1987), Dori Laub (1985) and Anna Ornstein (1985).

Dasberg (1987) points out that throughout the western world there is increased interest in the plight of victims, whether of political regimes and torture, or of rape victims and battered wives. This heightened sensitivity has contributed to a renewed interest in Holocaust victims.

Dasberg redefines the target groups which may require psychosocial support as those survivors aged 65 and over (the elderly), survivors aged 45-55 (the child survivors) and the second and third-generation offspring. The latter may challenge, through curiosity and activities, the "carefully guarded armistices and conspiracies of silence between their parents (second generation) and grandparents (first generation)" (p.247).

Dori Laub and Nanette Auerhahn (1985) have opened an area of inquiry which goes to the heart of the therapeutic issues. There is a chasm between what the survivor knows and what he can actually tell others. Much of knowing is dependent on language. These therapists suggest that, "Because of the radical break between the Holocaust and what culture is, the survivor often cannot find categories of thought or words for his experience" (p.3).

It follows that a therapist's task is, at least in part the joining with the survivor-patient in a search for words that convey meaning, that place in context even the fragments of memory.

Ornstein (1985) carefully dissects a problem central to therapeutic approaches to the survivor. She protests the Krystal and Niederland view of dismissing individual differences in face of the massiveness of the trauma, thereby creating the impression in the minds of mental health professionals that survivors are, psychologically speaking, the products of the Holocaust. In Krystal and Niederland's views, if massive psychic trauma was capable of overwhelming any and all of an adult's defenses, then pre-Holocaust personality organization had no particular relevance for post-Holocaust adjustment. Theoretically, the victims suffered a massive blocking of all affect and suffered a psychologic death. Ornstein does not agree nor does Davidson (1992) whose life work collated by Israel Charny reflects a more balanced view of the survivor's affective life.

The failure of language between therapist and patient has led to there being a better description of Holocaust survivors in the literature of our time than in mental health writing. Lawrence Langer's writings, particularly his "Versions of Survival" (1982), Elie Wiesel's "Night" (1960) and "The Forgotten" (1992), and Primo Levi's (1989) "The Drowned and the Saved" are necessary prerequisite reading to understanding the survivor experience.

The failure of language to convey the experience of the survivor appears to be a major problem in treatment. No satisfactory language has developed which encompasses the survivor's reality and allows for therapeutic communication towards a meaningful healing encounter.

Krell (1984) has addressed some of the problems related to psychiatric terminology which could become an obstacle to empathic understanding. He cautions against the cavalier manner with which otherwise meaningful concepts are carelessly applied in the survivor literature. If there is a general understanding that the massiveness of the assault on human life and dignity in Nazi persecutions is so extreme as to render therapeutic responses problematic, then it behooves professionals to examine whether pre-war concepts still apply in the diagnostic observations of survivors of the worst imaginable.

Anna Freud (1936) had explained the concept of "identification with the aggressor" as the child's means of dealing with anger and hurt over aggressive acts towards the child as, for example, in a child's visit to the dentist. Upon returning home, that child might diminish his personal pain and fear by performing "dentistry" on a doll, thereby identifying with the dentist. This useful prewar psychoanalytic construct was used too extremely and inappropriately postwar to explain the behavior of Jewish Kapos in the

Camps. The brutal behaviors of non-Jewish Kapos who were selected from the ranks of criminals and/or anti-Semites were not examined psychologically. The destructive behaviors of the Jewish Kapos were examined not in the light of cowardice, coercion or fear but as examples of Nazi-like behavior explained by the dynamic "identification with the aggressor." Interestingly, no effort has been made to see if the non-Jewish Kapos fit this psychodynamic interpretation of their brutal behavior.

Not only do such analyses confuse unconscious identification with conscious imitation to curry favor with the masters, but the concept is used to explain subsequent survivor behavior in the area of aggression and rage as if it were similar to that of the perpetrators! Through a simplistic perversion of terminology, the survivor of Nazism is then described as acting Nazi-like when pent-up anger is released.

Danieli (1982) likewise cautions against any stereotypical approach to survivor families and her categorization helps to understand the profound individual differences in a group which is so often discussed as if homogeneous. She attempted to clarify types of survivorhood and to delineate experiences which may have different personality outcomes. Danieli chose family as the unit of data analysis for a variety of reasons including the "centrality of the family unit in the lives of Holocaust survivors and their offspring" (p.405) and "interest in the psychological sequelae of the Holocaust on children of survivors." She identified two major categories of survivors, "the fragile, helpless, martyred victims, present more often in homes of former concentration camp survivors" (p.408), and the "superhumanly strong, capable, heroic fighters, generally found in homes of former partisan and resistance fighters" (p.408).

Children of the first category were 'allowed' physical but not psychological problems; they were trained to mistrust others and to survive future Holocausts. Their parents demanded devotion, discouraged autonomy, and equated happiness with security thereby emphasizing achievement and diminishing personal joy or self-fulfillment. Invariably, the child delayed leaving home, behaved protectively towards the parents, and saw his or her mission as repairing the parental wounds.

The second category of survivors were preoccupied with an intense desire to achieve, combined with compulsive activity. Their children were encouraged to stand up for themselves; manipulate, not avoid the outside world; and were expected to be in charge, leading them to find challenges in order to live up to the fantasized image of what is heroic.

It is evident that the problem of extreme psychologic trauma defies the language of the ordinary and continues to hamper even sophisticated observers like Krystal (1990) in his book summating a lifetime of work.

Leo Eitinger (1981) who had been preoccupied with organic consequences in his earlier studies, turned his attention in later years to the psychological and examined in some detail the defense mechanism of denial *in the* concentration camps. He distinguishes between the rigid denial exercised upon learning of the reality of a death camp (life-saving at first) and a differentiated degree of denial with awareness of the threat to life but accompanied by a more rational assessment. It is in differentiation that an inmate might change from thoughts of suicide to thoughts of trying to stay alive to be a witness and tell the story. Eitinger cites as one example of denial the fact that inmates who were doctors offered medical help, such as it was, to sustain life even though the patient was returned to the sufferings in the camp and probable death. Eitinger points out that denial is considered a primitive defense and that in normal life, problems cannot be solved without awareness, but in these extreme situations, with no realistic possibility of solving the problem, denial in some cases was of immediate life-saving value (p.151).

In light of the camps, the relatively traditional definitions of denial, guilt, identification with the aggressor, isolation of affect and other concepts require re-examination and redefinition if they are to be relevant and useful to professionals working with the survivors of atrocity. The areas of psychological explorations of coping and vulnerability, stress and resilience, memory and aging all have added a dimension to the understanding of the potential vulnerability of the Holocaust survivor. In turn, the survivor literature has provided perspectives on each of these topics which has aided the exploration by those who are concerned with the effects of trauma and its treatment.

PROSPECTS FOR ADVANCES

In some small measure, the medical and psychiatric literature on Holocaust survivors compiled by Eitinger and Krell (1985) provided impetus towards the understanding of the long-term consequences of mass trauma. The plight of the Vietnam veteran and the introduction of the diagnosis of PTSD revived interest in various dimensions of the psychological and psychophysiological consequences of chronic trauma. While van der Kolk (1989) has re-examined the concepts of stress as conceptualized first by Pierre Janet, and Lenore Terr (1991) has described the consequences of extreme childhood trauma, others returned to an examination of Holocaust survivors with respect to contemporary adaptation (Nadler and Ben-Shushan, 1989), coping (Moskovitz and Krell, 1990), and physiologic concomitants like sleep disturbance (Rosen et al, 1991). Lawrence Kolb (1987) has applied neuropsychological research to extend thinking about the findings related to the emotional consequences of PTSD.

With the rapidly evolving interest in a wide variety of traumas, all of which come under the rubric of PTSD, Holocaust survivors may be submerged as simply one category of victims. This would be to the detriment of research, since it was the uniqueness of the trauma which focused the interest of various investigators. From the examination of the impact of this tragedy, it has been possible to examine victimization in its broader aspects. Few advances are likely if the unique context in which Holocaust survivors experienced their personal tragedy is lost in the spectrum of traumas under investigation.

As survivors age, with the attendant problems of retirement, physical infirmities, and the ever present impact of re-triggered memory, therapists must remain sensitive to their particular plight. The issues of the aging survivor (Danieli, 1981) have been addressed to a point, but interestingly, do not involve the younger survivors who are also aging and vulnerable.

It is the child survivors of the Holocaust who form the group of trauma victims which is presently struggling with emotional difficulties, some requiring treatment. The child survivor presents with psychologic themes related to persecution which require resolution but on the basis of an understanding different than that commonly associated with existing survivor literature (Krell, 1985)

It has become evident that the postwar experiences of survivors who were over 16 in 1945 were vastly different from those under 16. The older survivor (youth or young adult) was more likely to marry, to stay close to other survivors in the community where they settled, and to enter the work force. The younger survivor was often placed with foster families, returned to school and completed some kind of education. The latter group also had less recall for family, Jewish traditions and Jewish learning, which may have set them apart. In fact, many of the children owed their survival to adopting Christianity and living in hiding.

In therapy, the child's survival experience demands that issues such as hiding, enforced silence, change from the religion which caused their persecution, be addressed. Moreover, in addition to the loss of family and home, hidden children frequently endured physical and sexual abuse.

A variety of strategies with respect to treatment are presented in a recent book edited by Paul Marcus and Alan Rosenberg (1989) titled *Healing Their Wounds: Psychotherapy with Holocaust Survivors and Their Families*. This remarkable work collates contemporary thinking on the treatment of survivors and respects the diversity of approaches necessary to explore the wellbeing of survivors. In contrast to the earlier pessimism which pervaded the field when psychopathologic constructs and individual psychodynamic theory prevailed, the writers of these chapters demonstrate a variety of successes in individual, group and family therapy. Of course, the objectives for wellness have changed dramatically. For example, for most therapists, the process of working through inconsolable losses and chronic mourning has been replaced with encouragement to properly commemorate those who were lost. There is a new-found modesty amongst therapists who tend to have become more respectful listeners and who are less reluctant to involve family where appropriate.

There is also a gradual acknowledgement that survivors as individuals rather than "the survivor" collectively require the same courtesy as any other patient, namely the opportunity to be viewed within the framework of each person's particular and unique life. The editors have therefore included not only different therapies but also different survivors - among them child survivors, adult survivors who are now elderly, religious survivors and survivor - families.

SURVIVOR GUILT AND RAGE

With all the theories that have evolved around the concepts of guilt, aggression and denial, the driving force which is often alluded to but seldom elaborated, is rage. Krystal and Niederland (1968) observed several decades ago that 92% of survivors admitted to survival guilt and this observation fostered the notion of guilt as the substrate for subsequent psychopathology and/or an explanation of survivor behavior.

The failure to define guilt in its existential dimension (*'Why did I live when so many others, better than myself, perished?'*), from the guilt of choices (*'How could I have abandoned my mother to her fate?'*), to the guilt of definite acts (*'I stole bread from my father as he lay dying'*) creates problems in understanding the survivor's postwar psychologic dynamics. Even more complex, the various choices which survivors made were largely enforced within an environment where free choice was impossible, this so aptly described by Langer (1982) as the "choiceless choice."

In order to feel guilt in the definitive sense, the survivor would have had to do something deserving of guilt. The vast majority ascribe their survival to luck, fate, and the help of God (not necessarily personal actions at the expense of others (Leon, 1981). Rappaport (1971) states simply, "Survival guilt is a term with the unequivocal implication that freedom from guilt could have been obtained by non- survival " (p.46).

Danieli (1984) in discussing this issue states succinctly, "Guilt presupposes the presence of choice, and the power, the ability, and the possibility to exercise it" (p.38). She postulated that "one of the most powerful functions of survivor guilt is to serve against existential helplessness" (p.38).

I would speculate that the preoccupation with the concept of guilt, a rather familiar concept and used all too readily to explain much of survivor behavior, protects the therapist from dealing with survivor rage. To witness atrocity, to endure barbarity and to be helpless in face of it, engenders rage.

The suppression and containment of rage may well be the single most common feature in survivors. Neither adults in concentration camps, nor children in hiding, nor even partisan or resistance fighters could vent rage freely for fear of discovery and death.

It is easier to deal with presumed guilt than unbridled rage, so we have not asked about it. Perhaps it was missed. While American and Russian soldiers sought revenge in the closing days of war, very few survivors did. Those who were offered revenge upon their captors, generally did not accept. Why? What is it about the survivor's rage that made vengeance impossible? Were the victims simply too malnourished to exact retribution? Were the crimes committed too great for response?

I believe we face here a rage so great it numbs the mind. Kosinski (1965) lapsed into several years of silence. I know a dozen more who described an inability or unwillingness to speak for months or years following liberation. Rage is cloaked in silence. Krell (1984) noted elsewhere that, "It is as if the concepts of identification with the aggressor and survivor guilt serve to distance the therapist from the emotion neither the survivor nor the therapist can handle - a rage which if it could be heard... Faced with this potential rage, the therapist confronts the survivor with all his skills in order to contain it. If it were unleashed, it would mean for the therapist a confrontation with his mortality, a trip with the survivor to `that place'" (p.525). It served both therapist and patient to accept survivor guilt as an explanation of feelings in turmoil, a turmoil so great that means of expression could not be found.

It is no surprise that psychiatrists and psychologists who are themselves survivors also avoided the arena of rage. While on one hand armed with a greater understanding of the Nazi universe, on the other they too struggled for control, alongside their patients, of indescribable feelings of rage. Rage is the common denominator of the abused. Victims of many types of chronic abuse understand this. Their likely response: silence. *Future therapies of survivors of extreme trauma, including those of torture and rape, must deal with the victim's rage, expressed or not.* The therapist need not necessarily uncover this rage, for some traumatic memories should indeed stay defended. What is required is the therapist's understanding of the fundamental injustice, the scale of the human affront, the subsequent aloneness of the victim. It is the therapist's *attempt* to understand which diminishes the anquish of the lonely victim. When Holocaust survivors tell the therapist how alone they are, they are no longer alone.

Elie Wiesel's suggestion in an address to physicians at Cedars-Sinai Hospital in 1982 remains relevant in this context. When asked how to treat the Holocaust patient, he offered the following, "Listen to them. Listen to them carefully. They have more to teach you, than you them."

REFERENCES

Bastiaans, Jan (1979). De behandeling van oorlogsslachtoffers. (The treatment of war victims. *Tijdschrift Voor Geneesmiddelen Onderzoek (Journal of Drug Research)*, 1, 352-358.

Boder, David P. (1949). *I Did Not Interview the Dead*. Urbana: University of Illinois Press.

Chodoff, Paul (1963). Late effects of the concentration camp syndrome. *Archives of General Psychiatry*, 8, 323-333.

Danieli, Yael (1984). Psychotherapists' participation in the conspiracy of silence about the Holocaust. *Psychoanalytic Psychology*, 1(1), 23-43.

Davidson, Shamai (1967). A clinical classification of psychiatric disturbances of Holocaust survivors and their treatment. *Israel Annals of Psychiatry*, 5, 96-98.

Dasberg, Haim (1987). Psychologic distress of Holocaust survivors and offspring in Israel - forty years later. *Israel Journal of Psychiatry*, 24, 243-256.

Des Pres, Terrence (1976). *The Survivor. An Anatomy of Life in the Death Camps*. New York: Oxford University Press.

Donat, Alexander (1976). Jewish resistance. In Friedlander, Albert H. (Ed.), *Out of the Whirlwind: A Reader of Holocaust Literature*. New York: Schocken Books, pp. 50-67.

Eitinger, Leo (1981). Denial in concentration camps. *Nord. Psykiatr. Tidssk.*, 5, 148-156.

Freud, A. (1946). *The Ego and the Mechanisms of Defence*. New York: International Universities Press. First published in 1936.

Gilbert, Martin (1985). *The Holocaust: A History of the Jews of Europe During the Second World War*. New York: Henry Holt and Company.

Klein, Hillel; Zellermayer, Julius; and Shanan, Joel (1963). Former concentration camp inmates on a psychiatric ward. *Archives of General Psychiatry*, 8, 334-342.

Kosinski, Jerzy (1965). *The Painted Bird*. New York: Bantam Books.

Langer, Lawrence L. (1982) *Versions of Survival: The Holocaust and the Human Spirit*. Albany: SUNY Press.

Leon, Gloria R; Butcher, James N; Kleinman, Max; Goldberg, Alan; and Almagor, Moshe (1981). Survivors of the Holocaust and their children: Current status and adjustment. *Journal of Personality and Social Psychology*, 41(3), 503-516.

Levi, Primo (1989). *The Drowned and the Saved*. New York: Vintage International Books.

Lifton, Robert J. (1967). *Death in Life: Survivors of Hiroshima*. New York: Random

House.

Perl, Gisella (1984). *I Was a Doctor in Auschwitz*. Salem, New Hampshire: Ayer Publishers. First Published by International Universities Press, New York, 1948.

Rakoff, Vivian; Sigal, John; and Epstein, Nathan (1966). Children and families of concentration camp survivors. *Canada's Mental Health*, 14, 24-26.

Rappaport, Ernest (1971). Survivor guilt. *Midstream*. August-September, 41-47.

Wiesel, Elie (1960). *Night*. New York: Bantam (originally published in French in 1958).

Wiesel, Elie (1992). *The Forgotten*. New York: Summit Books.

Wiesel, Elie (1982). The Holocaust Patient. Lecture at Cedars-Sinai Hospital, Los Angeles. Audio-Visual Library.

BIBLIOGRAPHY

Bastiaans, Jan (1957). *Psychosomatische Gevolgen Van Onderdrukking en Verzet (Psychosomatic Sequelae of Persecution and Resistance)*. Amsterdam: Noord-Hollandsche Uitgevers Maatschappij.
    A pioneer in the treatment of victims of war, Bastiaans studied primarily ex-members of the Dutch resistance, many of whom spent time in various concentration camps. In the English summary of the book (pp.467-472), Bastiaans states that "in previously well balanced and healthy people neuropsychiatric and psychosomatic syndromes only manifest themselves after more severe stress than in less stabilized and adapted people. When it can be shown that certain sequelae of war stress are genetically related to disturbances of childhood one must still attach *great value* to the *stresses of the war period...*" (p.470) (my italics).
    Bastiaans very early attributed to massive trauma the power to cause illness in otherwise well people. In fact, in his introduction (which may not have been generally available since it was published in Dutch), Bastiaans finds it understandable that those who were spared the atrocities (including doctors) would prefer to avoid the reality presented by these particular patients. Bastiaans also intimates that the extraordinary stress experienced by concentration camp inmates will not be found in the medical-psychiatric literature to that time, yet cites the works of doctor-inmates, E.A. Cohen (1952) and E. de Wind (1946).
    This book contains a discussion of the classic work of Thygesen and Hermann (1951-52) who examined Danish resistance fighters and who found that 63% were symptomatic with a constellation of symptoms labelled the KZ syndrome - the definitive forerunner of PTSD. Although the Danes emphasized the effects of famine, it was the combination of famine and severe emotional stress that caused the syndrome. It should also be noted that these survivors of camps were not primarily in the most severe camps nor specifically targeted for death.

Bettelheim, Bruno (1943). Individual and mass behavior in extreme situations. *American Journal Abnormal and Social Psychology*, 38, 417-452.
    The relevance of this article is that it was considered authoritative when in fact, in light of post-war literature by and about survivors, it should have been dismissed. Bettelheim's theses expressed in 1943 and not revised in his lifetime was that camp

inmates regressed to "infantile behavior," that their obsession with food related to "food as the most available and basic symbol of security," and that prisoners who survived, survived because they had adjusted to the camp situation accepting "various values of the SS as his own." Bettelheim's emphasis on negative coping as prevalent is countered by most later observers who emphasize that the few who were able to survive, did so through a tendency to organize and support one another.

"Infantile regression" on the part of all prisoners as Bettelheim claims, could hardly explain the underground organizations and active revolts in Sobibor, Treblinka and Birkenau.

Bondy, Curt (1943). Problems of internment camps. *American Journal Abnormal and Social Psychology,* 38, 453-475.

This important article opens with the following sentence "When the invasion of Europe comes, the Allied armies in liberating or conquering the different countries will find *millions* of people interned in camps." Bondy describes his personal experiences of Buchenwald in 1938 and states even then "About the concentration camps no exaggeration is necessary; the most gruesome fantasies are reality."

Bondy describes not only group differences in those interned in different camps, but examines the destructive effects of all such camps, indicating that sooner or later, no-one escapes undergoing radical changes. He suggests that means of dealing with the camps and camp inmates be made even before the invasion of Europe including preparation for those who are ill, maimed, or insane. Next to food and drink, he prescribes love and friendliness.

Chodoff, Paul (1966). Effects of extreme coercive and oppressive forces: brainwashing and concentration camps. In Arieti, Sylvano (Ed.), *American Handbook of Psychiatry.* New York: Basic Books, pp. 384-405.

Chodoff distinguishes carefully between his two topics and one wonders why they did not deserve separate chapters.

Chodoff's review is thoughtful and constructive. He correctly emphasizes that survival depended far more on fate and chance than on coping behaviour, not minimizing the importance of the latter in matters of survival.

He discusses that regression may have had an adaptive function as did varieties of emotional detachment. Chodoff points to post-war studies which indicate that the vast majority of survivors were indeed symptomatic, many with features of the "concentration camp syndrome."

Chodoff's discussion of the nature of the syndrome leans toward the conclusion that the traumatic events themselves caused the symptoms rather than any personality predisposition.

Chodoff's perspective of survivor guilt as perhaps related to an unwillingness to forget and give up memories which include memories of family, is closer to the truth than actual guilt over survival.

Danieli, Yael (1981). The aging survivor of the Holocaust. Discussion: On the achievement of integration in aging survivors of the Nazi Holocaust. *Journal Geriatric Psychiatry,* 14, 191-210.

Danieli reacts to a paper by Krystal with praise and without criticism. Her critique offers a meaningful and therapeutically helpful approach to the aging survivor. She de-emphasizes the capacity for the aging survivor to heal through personal reintegration in the absence of the broader context - namely their relationship to their own children.

Krystal emphasizes the natural tasks of the elderly, the need to recall, review and evaluate and examines the obstacles to these tasks derived from the Holocaust experience.

Danieli correctly points out that this particular experience cannot be integrated nor can its devastation be faced alone. She suggests a wide variety of individual, family and group therapies might provide the mutual caring required for both the aging survivors and their children.

She also points out the potential healing value of reconnections with religion (not only for religion but for familiar melodies and languages), the establishment of centres of education, of memorials to serve as gravesites and documentation of personal memoirs.

Danieli, Yael (1982). Families of survivors of the Nazi Holocaust: Some short and long term effects. In Spielberger, Charles, and Sarason, Irwin (Eds.); and Milgram, Norman (Guest Ed.), *Stress and Anxiety*. Volume 8. Washington, Hemisphere Publishing Corp., pp. 405-421.

This remarkable paper describes not only the various effects of the Holocaust experience on its survivors, but distinguishes the consequences according to whether the primary family identification centered on the survivor(s) as victim or fighter.

Danieli's contribution marked a turning point in the approach to survivor-families because the particularities of each allows the therapist to understand the differences in consequences for the children of these respective "types" of families.

This paper provides the reader with a quick and intelligent overview of the unique features complicating the lives of Holocaust survivors. As Danieli writes, "The individual survivor's war as history is crucial to the understanding of survivor's offspring."

Davidson, Shamai (1980). Transgenerational transmission in the families of Holocaust survivors. *International Journal Family Psychiatry*, 1, 95-112.

Davidson's pioneering work in Israel with survivor families, provides a perceptive examination of the "psychosocial interior of the survivor family." His clinical work led him from observations of the second generation to an emphasis on the individual survivor, then logically to the family. In addition, the psychopathologic constructs of a "survivor syndrome" could not account for his encountering "the considerable adaptive capacity shown by survivors in their reintegration into society, despite the massive trauma they suffered..."

Davidson points out that children were "intensely involved by the parents in their parents' early attempts at recovery" and therefore it was inevitable that there were transgenerational consequences.

He demonstrated with case vignettes, that with treatment of some second generation adult children, their recovery was not possible without simultaneous therapy of the parent.

Davidson, Shamai (1992). *Holding on to Humanity - The Message of Holocaust Survivors*. The Shamai Davidson Papers. Edited by Israel W. Charny. New York: University Press.

Charny's introduction to this seminal work is itself a most enlightening and insightful commentary on survivors. In recounting Davidson's struggle with the general notion that the vast majority of survivors were indeed damaged while ensuring that this neither necessarily implied psychopathology nor diminished in any way the individual survivor's creative accomplishments, Charny provides invaluable insights into the nature of massive trauma.

These insights should be required reading for mental health professionals. With such an auspicious beginning, this book then reveals the treasure of Shamai Davidson's lifetime of observations. Davidson states that survivors who insisted on telling of their trauma had their experiences converted into psychiatric symptoms to be dealt with by the "expert." Since the experts themselves exercised denial in facing the Holocaust experience, they avoided the topic even in long-term psychotherapy and psychoanalysis.

Davidson's depth of understanding is evident in his analysis of feelings held towards the survivor in Israeli society. In the process of his discussion, Davidson points the way to dealing with victims of massive trauma. For example, he set up counseling services for non-clinical survivors. Free from stigmatization, Holocaust survivors began to offer their unexpressed feelings in order to heal. Trauma survivors should not have to experience breakdowns in order to receive assistance.

Throughout his writings, Davidson provides thoughtful and relevant contributions to the treatment of victims generally, and to Holocaust survivors, specifically.

Des Pres, Terrence (1979). The Bettelheim problem. *Social Research,* 46, 619-647.
The author examines how Bettelheim came to be seen as an authority on the concentration camp experience when in fact he was already in America by 1939. Bettelheim emerged as the authoritative voice on survivorhood to the literary and scholarly community while in fact discredited by survivors who endured the post-1939 camps of Auschwitz, Treblinka, and Bergen-Belsen.

Bettelheim was responsible for descriptions which "characterized" camp behaviour using terminology generally reserved for psychopathology. He ignored instances of resistance in Sobibor and Treblinka, equated walking into the gas chamber with suicide by "submitting to death without resistance" while in fact advocating that nothing short of liberation by the Allies could save the inmates. This article must be read before the reader tackles any of Bettelheim's "survival" work.

Eissler, Kurt R. (1967). Perverted psychiatry. *American Journal Psychiatry,* 123(11), 1352-1358.
Eissler's remarkable article deserves the widest circulation and the most intensive study. For here can be detected the seeds of the perversion of medicine and psychiatry. That which took place within German medicine in the 30's and contributed to the progress of victimization, continues unabated in the postwar 50's and 60's, directed against the few surviving victims.

Eissler's discussion is required reading because it tackles the issue of experts who hold theories. He questions the morality of theory when it is less likely to favour the victim. To avoid injustice being done, Eissler prefers to err on the side of connecting the postwar suffering with the persecution. Those biased toward a "constitutional etiology" (without scientific proof as yet) he considers guilty of a moral offence.

Eissler continues to explore the ethics and morality concluding that "the feeling of contempt for suffering is something of a universal reaction still very much alive in almost all of us." His words appear prophetic in uncovering a malady so common in the practitioners of mental health care who almost invariably must deal with victims - their secret contempt for victims.

Eitinger, Leo (1972). *Concentration Camp Survivors in Norway and Israel.* The Hague: Martinus Nijhoff. (First published in 1964).
Eitinger's book is a landmark work but seriously flawed. He investigated the concentration camp syndrome (C.C.S.) in 2 groups of former camp inmates. His stated purpose was to examine whether the severe psychic and physical stress situations to which human beings were exposed in the concentration camps have had lasting

psychological results. Dr. Eitinger's descriptions of patients and their ordeals are straightforward and relevant, not so his conclusions.

Amongst Israeli survivors who are "schizophrenic" he carefully avoids blaming the illness on captivity. This leaves the reader wondering how a schizophrenic person could have survived a concentration camp.

He fails to connect the "neuroses" of 20 patients from the "Israeli Neurotic Group" to their war experiences. Yet he describes one patient who lost both parents and five siblings by age 19, another who lost his wife and two sons, and a third who lost her husband but whose two children were saved in hiding.

Eitinger is on firmer ground when relating organic cerebral changes to psychiatric illness in the Norwegian group.

While swinging back and forth inconclusively, Eitinger continues to make valuable observations. Of one survivor he notes (page 160) "it is obvious that experiences of the traumatic magnitude we are dealing with here, must act almost independently of the premorbid personality." After discussing possible connections with organicity he adds once again "it would be within the bounds of reason to assume that psychic trauma of a serious and chronic nature could also be responsible for changes which resemble the concentration camp syndrome."

Eitinger denoted certain factors as 'cumulative tainting' including head injuries, encephalitis and spotted fever and concluded that "a sum of injurious somatic factors may be regarded as the reason for the changes which have taken place." He nevertheless points out that Jews with such injuries/illnesses had no chance to survive.

Eitinger, Leo, and Krell, Robert (1985). *The Psychological and Medical Effects of Concentration Camps and Related Persecutions on Survivors of the Holocaust: A Research Bibliography*. Vancouver: University of British Columbia Press.

This is probably the most comprehensive listing of references pertaining to survivor literature to 1984. This volume comprises a collection of 1100 references from all language sources plus related books and theses.

Friedman, Paul (1949). Some aspects of concentration camp psychology. *American Journal Psychiatry*, 105, 601-605.

This is one of the earliest descriptions of psychologic consequences and is based on the psychiatric examination of 172 persons detained in Cyprus including 84 children up to the age of 18, and 88 adults. Paul Friedman provides important descriptions of the children's extreme fatigue and sleepiness, the shallowness of emotions and sexual disinterest (in adolescents). The speculative psychodynamic explanations for most conditions mentioned are weak or inaccurate; for example: "The abstention from sex, which was one of the most striking effects in life in the concentration camps, is characteristic of the primitive and narcissistic stage to which the inmates had regressed."

Hermann, K., and Thygesen, P. (1954). Le syndrome des camps de concentration 8 ans apres la liberation. (The concentration camp syndrome 8 years after the liberation). In Thygesen, P. *La Deportation dans les Camps de Concentration Allemands et ses Sequelles*, pp. 56-72. Paris: F.I.R.

Danish medical doctors who had themselves been in German concentration camps, began their examinations of former prisoners in 1947. In 1954, Hermann and Thygesen reported on 120 concentration camp survivors with "concentration camp syndrome" characterized by uniform asthenic and vegetative symptoms associated with emotional disturbances as well as signs of intellectual deterioration. The visible physical decline in many cases, showed evidence of an accelerated aging process. This article is the first to describe a syndrome secondary to this particular massive psychic trauma.

Hoppe, Klaus D. (1966). *The Psychodynamics of Concentration Camp Victims. Psychoanalytic Forum*, 1, 76-80. Discussions by: Niederland, William 80-81; Chodoff, Paul 81-83; Friedman, Paul 83-84; Jacobson, Edith 84.

The problem with Hoppe's exploration of the dynamics is evident in the discussion of "chronic reactive depression" as connected in some way to "narcissistic regression." This thesis bolstered by theories of regression and fixation - all derived from studies in the non-concentration camp world.

He accurately identifies in his patients their hatred of the persecutors where it remains fixed. Why this fixation on appropriate hatred is interpreted as the pathology of "hate-addiction" is hard to understand.

Hoppe then explores guideposts for psychotherapy in assisting the victims as patients, and the role of the therapist. The underlying premise for conducting relatively traditional psychotherapy is weak. Hoppe does emphasize the need for the therapist to work through his own guilt feelings in order to be helpful.

Chodoff points out in his comments that regression may have served an adaptive function in the camps and that it was not the basis for later psychopathologic conditions. Nor do predisposing personality factors determine the later picture so much as the intensity of trauma which produces similar effects by sheer force of the psychologic and physical assault.

Hoppe, Klaus D. (1972). Chronic reactive aggression in survivors of severe persecution. *Comprehensive Psychiatry*, 12, 230-237.

This paper is a peculiar mix of relevant insights and unrelated observations. Of 190 survivors examined by the author, he diagnosed 5% to have "chronic reactive aggression." The anger, hate and rage he describes is an important feature in survivors of atrocities and both more common and less pathologic than the author infers. For some unknown reason, there is an inappropriate discussion of the fate of survivors of the Nazi persecution with the plight of the black minority in the United States.

Hoppe does sensitively identify the survivors' re-experience of pesecution within the framework of restitution examinations and how such examinations can elicit renewed anger and rage.

Kestenberg, Judith (1980). Psychoanalysis of children of survivors from the Holocaust: case presentations and assessment. *Journal American Psychoanalytic Association*, 28, 775-803.

This article represents both the best and worst of analytic thinking about this complex topic and mirrored the difficulties inherent in treatment.

While commenting astutely on the various reasons accounting for the intense relationship between survivor-parents and their children, the recycled classic theories dilute the points made. Kestenberg attempts to explain survivor-parenting on the basis of a shift in identification with parents (their own lost family) to an identification with the persecutor. With this notion in mind, adolescents were seen in therapy without the professional meeting the (persecuting) parents.

The analyst was dependent entirely on the adolescent's knowledge of the Holocaust past and that knowledge was usually limited.

Nevertheless, Kestenberg points to important themes to consider in treatment, particularly the childrens' roles in reincarnating the losses and providing redemption for the deprived parents. She also noted the replay by survivor parents of starvation and the absence of toilet facilities, with constant reminders related to both.

An important contribution is the notion that a measure of pathology and unusual ego strength can both originate from the stress associated with living "under the shadow of the Holocaust." Moreover, Kestenberg suggests that children of survivors can resolve "problems creatively by reliving the Holocaust and undoing its effect in works of art, in political action, education, as well as in one's own parenthood"...

Klein, Hillel (1972). Holocaust survivors in Kibbutzim: readaptation and reintegration. *Israel Annals Psychiatry & Related Disciplines*, 10, 78-91.

Klein's study of 25 "survivor couples" demonstrates how some survivors overcame the trauma through continuity of earlier Zionist ideas. The fulfillment of the dreams of murdered family members mitigated the personal suffering and provided meaning to life (and survival).

The traumatic past is acknowledged but the focus is on present-day successes and achievements. Klein noted differences between those who had been in concentration camps and partisans or members of the ghetto resistance. The latter retained their identity as leaders.

Kolb, Lawrence C. (1987). A neuropsychological hypothesis explaining posttraumatic stress disorders. *American Journal Psychiatry*, 144, 989-995.

Kolb's clinical experiences in diagnosis and treatment of hospitalized men in Wold War II combat led to further observations of posttraumatic stress disorders in over 300 Vietnam veterans.

Fourteen of 18 patients who provided only sketchy accounts of their combat experience, without associated affect, required only a 30 second combat sound stimulus to re-enact a Vietnam combat experience under neurosynthesis.

The intense emotional abreaction was not elicited by musical stimuli or silence.

With colleagues, he then examined the autonomic arousal patterns and psychophysiological concomitants. Kolb suggests that there are some combat veterans "with chronic, delayed, or remitted forms of posttraumatic stress disorder who have a persisting conditioned emotional response to stimuli reminiscent of battle."

He postulates a neuropsychological construct of stimulus overload where excessive emotional stimulation overwhelms "the cortical defensive structural processes concerned with perceptual discrimination and effective adaptive responses for survival."

Such stimulation may effect neuronal synaptic changes and account for the subsequent behavioural manifestations of PTSD.

Krell, Robert (1982). Family therapy with children of concentration camp survivors. *American Journal Psychotherapy*, 4, 513-522.

For children of Holocaust survivors who experience emotional problems, the parental background may complicate their symptomatology and therapy. The psychiatric literature is replete with failures of therapy with survivors' children, sometimes remarkably with the therapist altogether unaware of the Holocaust background!

The inclusion of family for information-gathering in assessment and in resolution of complex and mysterious contemporary interrelationships based on the past, is paramount.

This paper describes two patients where involvement of family clarified otherwise incomprehensible behaviours.

With the therapist's resolve it is usually possible to involve and engage the family in the treatment process, if not family therapy per se.

Krell, Robert (1984). Holocaust survivors and their children: comments on psychiatric consequences and psychiatric terminology. *Comprehensive Psychiatry,* 25, 521-528.

Progress in the description and therapy of Holocaust survivors and their children has been hampered by unsatisfactory terminology, denial on the part of the therapist, and occasionally hostility to the survivor. The author suggests that the therapist's inability to comprehend the extent of Nazi sadism has unwittingly led clinical researchers to attempt to understand the perpetrators by investigating survivors. To survivors are attributed "Nazi-like" behaviours through such mechanisms as identification with the aggressor. These behaviours are then scrutinized as if they belonged to the victim, rather than the persons who committed the original aggression. Aggression has been misunderstood in the context of Holocaust survivors, as has the concept of survivor guilt, which is less commonly present than has been assumed. The failure to refine survivor terminology has at times misdirected treatment and obscured the remarkable adaptations and coping styles of the majority of the survivor generation and its offspring.

Krell, Robert (1985). Child survivors of the Holocaust: 40 years later. *Journal American Academy Child Psychiatry,* 24(4), 378-380.

Child survivors of the Holocaust have only recently been identified as a group of individuals deserving attention separate from survivors in general. The psychiatric literature pertaining to the Holocaust differentiates between Holocaust survivors and their children (the second generation) but does not generally distinguish between those survivors who were children or adults at the time of liberation. This special section points out some differences between the "child" and "adult" survivors in respect to the role of memories, methods of coping, and long-term adaptation.

Krell, Robert (1985). Therapeutic value of documenting child survivors. *Journal American Academy Child Psychiatry,* 24, 397-400.

For many survivors who offer their accounts for historical or educational purposes, it is the first time they have attempted to provide a chronological account of life experiences. Intensive and repetitive fragments of emotion-laden memory may find a niche in such an account which explains to the teller where it fits.

The author suggests that integrating seemingly disparate fragments into a coherent sequence, is healing.

Krell, Robert (1989). Alternative therapeutic approaches to Holocaust survivors. In Marcus, Paul, and Rosenberg, Alan (Eds.), *Healing Their Wounds: Psychotherapy with Holocaust Survivors and Their Families.* New York: Praeger, pp. 215-226.

The actual condition of "survivorhood" is beyond therapy, for survivors readily acknowledge the existence of irreparable damage. Therapy is directed toward the survivor living satisfactorily despite the damage. In order to be therapeutically effective, the therapist must put aside commonly held notions about denial, guilt and aggression. Their original prewar meanings, are confusing and often irrelevant to the postwar survivor experience.

Survivor rage is so great that therapists avoid tapping into it, thereby assuring the failure of therapy. However, rage can be re-worked in the service of remembrance and therefore it may help for the survivor to relate or record his/her entire experience, particularly for high school students.

Psychiatric conditions such as depression and psychotic episodes must be treated not only with contemporary methods but be examined as well in light of the Holocaust experience. Examples are offered, one where the receipt of minimal compensation provided relief because of the implied acknowledgement by the perpetrators, of a great injustice.

The therapist may assist therapeutically by helping relate the account, in the quest for compensation, and through acquiring an understanding of the survivor's struggle against chronic despair.

Krystal, Henry (Ed.) (1968). *Massive Psychic Trauma*. New York: International Universities Press.

The contents of this book came from the Wayne State University Workshops on The Late Sequelae of Massive Psychic Trauma.

Because of its nature, it is an uneven work with many valuable insights and considerable chaff. It did serve to galvanize further work. With respect to Krystal's contribution, a problem arose with their (Krystal and Niederland) hypothesis "that the major pathogenic force is survivor guilt." They closely related features of depression to survivor guilt and then noted that "92 percent (of 151 patients) expressed self-reproach for failing to save their relatives."

There is much of value in the discussion where the authors sometimes demonstrate a great depth of understanding as in their observations that survivors of persecution are suspected of unfair play or collaboration and that therefore "we tend to blame the survivor for the guilt of the perpetrator."

This understanding becomes somehow suspended in the discussion of the "two pathogenic forces in survivors of Nazi persecution," namely survivor guilt and problems of aggression. The theoretic connection of these "pathogenic forces" to the experienced reality of the survivor fails to connect. For example, the authors offer that "survivor guilt is a form of pathological mourning in which the survivor is stuck in a magnification of the guilt which is present in every bereaved person."

What is pathologic mourning? How does the loss of an 87 year old mother of illness (normal mourning of up to one year) compare with the murder of parents, wife and children, brothers and sisters at one time, some of the murders witnessed by the survivor? It cannot be a magnification of guilt experienced by a *normal* bereaved person because it would be a magnification of *normal* bereavement. There is *nothing* normal to be found and comparisons of language, particularly the theoretic, fail. The authors redeem themselves partially when acknowledging that the dreams in survivors' nightmares, cannot be completely explained theoretically.

Krystal, Henry (1990). *Integration and Self-Healing: Affect, Trauma, Alexithymia*. Ann Arbor, Michigan: The Analytic Press.

This erudite book, written many years after Krystal's initial contributions to "Massive Psychic Trauma," ultimately disappoints where survivors are concerned. The chapter on Trauma and Affect provides a valuable discourse on the nature of trauma and its understanding. While explaining the psychologic phenomenon of helplessness in face of overwhelming and inevitable danger, Krystal falls into the trap of describing this as the reason why European Jews "obeyed orders in an automaton like fashion, took off their clothes, and together with their children descended into a pit..." The reason for obeying orders in the face of machineguns lay in the fact that there was no escape, and resistance resulted in the murder of children in front of parents, the rape of daughters in front of fathers, the mutilation and torture of grandparents before one's eyes.

To cooperate with one's inevitable murder is not tantamount to suicide as Krystal intimates. Here he follows Bettelheim into an arena of thought which defies both reality and the imagination.

Where Krystal shines as a psychoanalyst and one who is himself, a survivor, is in the posing of incisive questions, e.g., "What happens to people who surrender to what they experience as overwhelming danger, but do not die?" And in examining childhood trauma "How can we imagine the child's *timeless* horror?" His discussion of early trauma is masterful, particularly the notion that "among the *direct* effects of severe childhood trauma in adults is lifelong *dread* of the traumatic state and the *expectation* of it."

Laub, Dori, and Auerhahn, Nanette (Eds.) (1985). Knowing and not knowing the Holocaust. *Psychoanalytic Inquiry, 5*(1).
This special edition devoted to the Holocaust contains several seminal contributions to contemporary knowledge. This collection reflects the editors' wide range of experience in treatment approaches with survivors as well as the work done in obtaining audiovisual testimony from hundreds of eyewitnesses to the Holocaust.
Authors include Bergmann, Jucovy, Prince, Marcus, Ornstein and Krystal.

Marcus, Paul, and Rosenberg, Alan (1989). *Healing Their Wounds: Psychotherapy With Holocaust Survivors and Their Families.* New York: Praeger.
This finely edited book reflects the best of contemporary thinking with respect to Holocaust survivors. Much can be learned from it for the treatment of victims generally.
For example, Janet Hadda's chapter, "Mourning the Yiddish Language and Some Implications for Treatment," should alert mental health professionals to the disruption of self-identity caused by the loss of a meaningful language and its unique usage.
Rabbi Martin Cohen's, "The Rabbi and the Holocaust Survivor," proposes the healing encounter of survivor and Rabbi studying together in an attempt to unravel the mysteries of how we can accept the concept of a loving God in light of the Holocaust experience. Here too are therapeutic implications for traumatized victims from other cultures and religions. The reimmersion in once meaningful traditions may assist in one's confrontation with despair.
The editors included a sufficient number of viewpoints to provide a satisfying perspective on the complex clinical challenge posed by Holocaust survivors.

Moskovitz, Sarah, and Krell, Robert (1990). Child survivors of the Holocaust: Psychological adaptations to survival. *Israel Journal Psychiatry Related Sciences, 27*(2), 81-91.
This paper addresses the means by which children who survived the Holocaust made sense of their survival in later years. Inevitably, these children, now adults, have lived their lives with a series of perplexing questions and fragmented memories. The normal developmental tasks of growing up were mutilated beyond recognition by the trauma of loss and grief, danger and fear, hatred and chaos. The awesome tasks faced by child survivors included the reconstruction of a terrible past into a sensible present. In order to imbue life with meaning, a sense of continuous self had to be derived from the most fragile and discontinuous beginnings. The authors suggest that over a lifetime the child victim has to struggle with three fundamental questions: 1) Why me? 2) Since it happened to me, how shall I live my life? 3) In living life, what must I do with my grief and my memories? These three inextricable questions are discussed.

Nadler, Arie, and Ben-Shushan, Dan (1989). Forty years later: Long term consequences of massive traumatization as manifested by Holocaust survivors from the city and the kibbutz. *Journal Consulting and Clinical Psychology, 57*, 287-293.
These authors explored the long-term consequence of massive trauma on city-dwellers as compared with survivors living in Kibbutzim. The survivors and controls were

drawn from non-clinical populations.

The psychological effects were measured with a variety of instruments and found to be still evident 40 years later. The "survivors rated themselves as less emotionally stable, with lower feelings of self-discipline and self-control, lower feelings of dominance and assertiveness, and lower levels of energy."

This rather sound methodological study was followed with personal interviews to which 30 of 34 survivors agreed. The survivors suffered significantly more than controls from psychosomatic symptoms, insomnia, anxieties and fears, nightmares and depression.

Finally, a comparison of the two groups of survivors reveal "that city survivors were worse off psychologically than Kibbutz survivors."

The kibbutz provided a stronger ideological environment with stronger institutional and psychological support than city dwellers forced to rely more on family alone.

Men were found to be more emotionally closed than women and suffering more as a result.

Niederland, William G. (1961). The problem of the survivor: Some remarks on the psychiatric evaluation of emotional disorders in survivors of Nazi persecution. *Journal Hillside Hospital,* 10, 233-247.

This paper firmly establishes a causal connection between the experience of extreme persecution and subsequent emotional problems. Niederland emphasizes his points with case histories in which survivors deserving of compensation were denied because of psychiatrists who preferred to believe the pre-existence of "innate defects which no one has yet demonstrated to exist" rather than acknowledge the facts of terror and trauma experienced by the victims as formative in psychologic illness.

The reason for the rejection of the various claims reveals another dark chapter in psychiatry.

Niederland attempts a dynamic explanation of the symptom-free interval, connecting it to repression of guilt feelings rather than the more likely delay due to preoccupations with finding work, housing and a measure of security.

In another case he somehow connects a former concentration camp inmate's "demand to be killed herself and bitten to death" as perhaps connected to cannibalism. Since his paper advocates fact, a more reasonable association could be made to the deaths witnessed by many - German guard dogs unleashed on prisoners.

Ornstein, Anna (1985). Survival and recovery. *Psychoanalytic Inquiry,* 5(1), 99-130.

Ornstein's article reviews the "survivor syndrome" as one borne of necessity to describe a previously unknown condition for restitution purposes. She cautions against its general use for the non-clinical population of survivors and its usage to explain symptoms of children of survivors who present to psychotherapists. In a footnote to discuss "transmission" of effects, she questions the relevance of information solicited from a patient in analysis which is not offered spontaneously.

On this point she is wrong. It has been shown that therapists have repeatedly colluded in avoiding the possible impact of the Holocaust on their patients and *should* inquire about it.

Ornstein provides a masterful discussion of adaptation to extreme conditions and of the process of mourning and recovery. While recognizing the obvious impact of this catastrophic event, she emphasizes the need of the survivor to reconstruct the "totality of their life history." Therapists need to recognize the capacity of survivors to resume life meaningfully in the total context of their cumulative experiences. This paper has many insights essential to the successful therapy of Holocaust survivors. She successfully demolishes a variety of assumptions expressed by early investigators which simply do not hold up under scrutiny, e.g., Krystal's view of the Holocaust having had "the same impact on the adult psyche as did severe infantile traumatization."

Ornstein's discussions of the survivor's anger as it relates to healing, her differentiation between therapists reacting to the Holocaust itself rather than to the patient's transference, and her perceptive review of the "Pawnbroker" provide essential insights into the nature of massive trauma and treatment of traumatized individuals.

Rappaport, Ernest (1968). Beyond traumatic neurosis - a psychoanalytic study of late reactions to the concentration camp trauma. *International Journal Psychoanalysis*, 49, 719-731.

This paper, first presented in 1964, is extremely valuable. Rappaport points out how this particular trauma exceeds what was known and for which there are no words. He describes the existence of guilt of those who were spared the trauma, rather than guilt in the victims, thereby pointing to the failure of the listener/therapist. As a pre-war inmate of Buchenwald, Rappaport in Block 13, challenges Bettelheim's (Block 12) observations.

He cites case histories of victims to illustrate the irrefutable connection between late psychic reactions and the concentration camp experience. Rappaport's patients did not show the usual features of traumatic neurosis, neither predisposition or infantile conflict. He adds "they cannot be approached therapeutically in the usual manner." Rappaport reveals his own late reactions to traumas sustained in a camp which he felt does not even compare to the camps yet to follow.

Rosen, Jules; Reynolds, Charles; Yeager, Amy; Houck, Patricia; and Hurwitz, Linda (1991). Sleep disturbances in survivors of the Nazi Holocaust. *American Journal Psychiatry*, 148, 64-66.

The authors examine sleep disturbances and note these as particularly significant symptoms in that disturbed sleep and frequent nightmares may persist 45 years after the stresses occurred, while other symptoms abate.

Forty-two survivors were compared with 37 depressed patients and 54 healthy comparison subjects.

Of 166 survivors, 25.3% responded to questionnaires. Sleep disturbances were significant in two-thirds of this sample and were distinct in severity and profile compared to the elderly depressed and healthy companion subjects.

Interestingly, the survivors "reported significantly more disturbed sleep due to bad dreams but less loss of enthusiasm during the day than did the depressed group."

There was a positive correlation between the frequency of nightmares and the number of years spent in a concentration camp.

Russell, Axel (1974). Late psychosocial consequences in concentration camp survivor families. *American Journal Orthopsychiatry*, 44, 611-619.

This study of 34 concentration camp survivor families treated in family therapy for a six month period, provided suggestions for therapeutic interventions. All families were referred with a child as the identified patient, frequently an only child. Russell describes a pessimistic picture of these children whom he saw in the 60's and tried to assist with individuation issues against overwhelming odds. He noted improvement in only 40% of his patients.

However, in light of the even greater failure to engage in individual therapy, these children may have been better served. Russell suggests that therapy should be much longer than six months.

Terr, Lenore C. (1991). Childhood traumas: an outline and overview. *American Journal Psychiatry*, 148, 10-20.

This important theoretical paper on trauma in childhood assists in re-conceptualizing etiology. Terr divides trauma-stress conditions with Type I - "the results of one sudden blow," and Type II - "the results of long-standing or repeated ordeals."

It is type II that is particularly relevant to understanding child survivors of the Holocaust and their subsequent preoccupations.

Terr notes and discusses each of four characteristics important in traumatized children: 1) strongly visualized or otherwise repeatedly perceived memories, 2) repetitive behaviours, 3) trauma-specific fears and 4) changed attitudes about people, aspects of life, and the future.

A subsequent discussion of denial and psychic numbing, self-hypnosis and dissociation, and rage, are particularly relevant to survivors of chronic trauma. Her comments on rage and its negative extreme, passivity, provide some understanding of the dynamics in victims of persistent abuse.

Van der Kolk, Bessel, A; and Van der Hart, Onno (1989). Pierre Janet and the breakdown of adaptation in psychological trauma. *American Journal Psychiatry*, 146(12), 1530-1540.

Janet was amongst the first psychiatrists to explore how trauma causes psychopathology. His clinical observations led to the theory that trauma or frightening experiences produced a narrowing of consciousness through a dissociation of feelings or memories related to that experience.

His work on trauma was re-discovered in light of renewed interest over the past two decades, in victims of a variety of abuses.

The authors' review of his work demonstrate the contemporary relevance of Janet's contributions on a wide variety of topics related to traumatic sequelae. Particularly he showed that overwhelming trauma results in dissociative reactions which become fixed and remain outside of conscious awareness. Yet these fixations continue to exert influence over affect, perceptions and behaviour.

Memories are stored on a variety of levels - "as narratives as well as sensory perceptions, visual images (nightmares and hallucinations), and "visceral" sensations (anxiety reactions and psychosomatic symptoms)."

9

The Massive Mortality of Children

George Kent

MASSIVE NUMBERS

The number of children dying each year has been declining, but the numbers are still enormous. Recent estimates of the number of under-five deaths in the developing world for selected years are as follows (Grant, 1993):

1960	18,900,000
1970	17,400,000
1980	14,700,000
1990	12,700,000

With an estimated 12.7 million children in the developing world dying before their fifth birthdays in 1990, we have about 35,000 dying each day, more than a million each month.

Even with the best of care, the children's mortality rate can never be reduced to zero. In 1991, the lowest rate in the world was in Sweden where there were only 5 deaths of children under 5 years of age for every 1000 children born. If the world's resources were fully devoted to minimizing children's mortality, presumably the children's mortality rate could be reduced to about 5 everywhere. But that is a very demanding standard. It is quite reasonable, however, to suggest that if our worldwide priorities called for it, the worldwide average children's mortality rate could be reduced to, say, 10 per 1000 live births. In 1991, twenty one countries had children's mortality rates of 10 or less.

If the children's mortality rate had been 10 for all countries in 1991, children's deaths would have numbered 1,410,000. We can take that as a conservative estimate of the "minimum possible" number of children's deaths. The actual estimated number of children's deaths for 1991 was 12,821,000 (Grant, 1993, pp. 68-69). The difference, 11,411,000, can be taken as a reasonable estimate of the number of "unnecessary" or excessive children's deaths. Thus about 89 percent of the total number of deaths of children under five were "unnecessary" or excessive.

Children's deaths account for about one-third of all deaths worldwide. In northern Europe or the United States, children account for only 2 to 3 percent of all deaths. In many less developed countries, more than half the deaths are deaths of children, which means there are more deaths of young people than of old people. The median age at death in 1990 was 5 or lower in Angola, Burkina Faso, Ethiopia, Guinea, Malawi, Mali, Mozambique, Niger, Rwanda, Sierra Leone, Somalia, Tanzania, and Uganda. This means that in these 13 countries at least half the deaths were of children under 5. In the United States the median age at death in 1990 was 76, and in the best cases, Japan, Norway, Sweden, and Switzerland, it was 78 (World Bank, 1993, 200-201).

In the United States, in 1910 the infant mortality rate - the number of children dying before their first birthdays for every thousand born alive - was 124. The rate dropped steadily from 47 in 1940 to 10.9 in 1983, but then the speed of decline diminished rapidly. The infant mortality rate has been going down in the United States, but not as fast as in many other nations, with the result that the United States' standing in the rankings has deteriorated. In 1983 the United States ranked only seventeenth among the nations of the world (Sivard, 1986, p. 37). In 1991 data, the United States' infant mortality rate was 11, and 21 other countries had even lower rates. According to a report of the United States Congress, "in contrast to the dramatic decline in the rate of infant mortality between 1950 and 1980, progress on reducing infant deaths has slowed to almost a halt in recent years" (United States House of Representatives, 1989, p. 170).

The number of children who die each year can be made more meaningful by comparing it with other mortality figures.

There have been an estimated 101,550,000 fatalities in wars between the years 1700 and 1987 (Sivard, 1988, p. 28). That yields an average of 353,833 fatalities per year. William Eckhardt (1992) estimated that the total number of civilian and military deaths due to warfare in 1991 was 443,500, and that the yearly average between 1986 and 1991 was 427,800. These figures can be compared to the more than 12 million children's deaths in each of these years.

The most lethal war in all of human history was World War II. There were about 15 million battle deaths (Small and Singer, 1982, p. 91) over a period of almost six years, for a rate of about 2.5 million deaths a year. If we add in civilian deaths, including genocide and other forms of mass murder, the deaths in and around World War II totaled around 51,358,000 (Wright, 1965, p. 1542). Annualized for the six year period, the rate comes up to about 8.6 million deaths a year - when children's deaths were running at well over 25 million per year. This most intense war in history resulted in a lower death rate, over a very limited period, than results from children's mortality year in and year out.

Counting late additions, at the end of 1987 there were 58,156 names on the Vietnam War Memorial in Washington, D.C. That is less than the number of children under five who die every two days throughout the world. A memorial for those children who die worldwide would be more than 250 times as long as the Vietnam memorial, and a new one would be needed every year.

Historically, governments have killed many of their own citizens outside of warfare. According to R. J. Rummel (1990), in the twentieth century "independent of war and other kinds of conflict - governments probably have murdered 119,400,000 people... By comparison, the battle-killed in all foreign and domestic wars in this century total 35,700,000 (p. xi)." His more recent estimates bring the total number of people killed by governments outside of war to about 170 million in this century. While this figure is far higher than the numbers killed in warfare, it is far lower than the number of children's death over the twentieth century. Early in the century the world's population was smaller but the children's mortality rate was higher. If we estimate an average of, say, 20 million children's deaths per year, we arrive at a figure of over 1.8 billion for the number of children's deaths in this century, more than ten times the number of people killed by governments.

Children die for many different reasons. Historically the practice of infanticide has been widespread (deMause, 1974; Piers, 1978; Rose, 1986). Even if children were not directly murdered, they were often abandoned or "exposed" in ways that, but for the "kindness of strangers" who might rescue them, could lead to their deaths (Boswell, 1988). In some cases children have been killed as a matter of government policy. King Herod, angered at the flight of Jesus, Mary and Joseph to Egypt, ordered the killing of all the male infants of Bethlehem.

Child abuse and neglect is still widespread in modern times, in both rich and poor countries, and many children die as a result. Millions of children live and die on the streets. In some countries street children are systematically killed. Children are being counted among the casualties of warfare at a steadily increasing rate over the past century. Often children are pressed to participate in armed combat as soldiers (Boothby, 1986; Ressler, Boothby, and Steinbock, 1987; Leveille, 1988; Kent, 1990; Kent, 1991). Children are sometimes deliberately targeted, even outside of warfare.

State-sponsored torture of children has taken place in Argentina, El Salvador, Iraq, and South Africa.

Many children have been killed in genocide events. It is generally agreed that about one million of the six million victims of the Holocaust were children. However, the number of children who die in genocides (as that term is usually understood), is only a small proportion of all the deaths of children.

The immediate cause of death for most children is not murder or incurable diseases such as AIDS, but a combination of malnutrition and quite ordinary diseases (Grant, annual; Kent, 1991). Table 1 shows the distribution of causes for 1986. Given adequate resources, diseases such as diarrhea, malaria, and measles are readily managed problems.

Table 1. Estimated Annual Deaths of Children Under 5 by Cause, 1986

CAUSE	NUMBER (millions)	PROPORTION (percentage)
Diarrhea	5.0	35.4
Malaria	3.0	21.3
Measles	2.1	14.9
Neonatal Tetanus	0.8	5.7
Pertussis (Whooping Cough)	0.6	4.3
Other Acute Respiratory Infections	1.3	9.2
Other	1.3	9.2
ESTIMATED TOTAL	14.1	100.0

Source: James P. Grant, *The State of the World's Children 1987* (New York: Oxford University Press, 1987), p. 111.

We know the immediate causes of the massive deaths of children in clinical terms, but we also need an understanding in social terms. Why are the world's children devastated by so much malnutrition and disease? Describing the conditions of children around the world is not nearly as difficult as deciding how we should understand it or deciding what should be done about it.

SOCIAL PRIORITIES, NOT POVERTY

If we consider not only the clinical factors but also the social context we would see that almost all deaths of small children are due to some form of abuse or neglect, whether by the immediate family or by the society at large. Even congenital birth defects are largely preventable with improved prenatal care; even accidents are to a large degree preventable (Stanton, 1990).

If enough resources and attention are given to small children, most would thrive. Many do not do well because their families are desperately poor. But focusing on the children and their families alone blinds us to the ways in which their conditions reflect the policies and actions of their societies. What is the role of government policy?

Many countries spend very little on children. Poverty is their explanation. But contrary to common assumptions, poor countries, like poor people, do have money. Poor countries are not uniformly poor; most have a middle class and a wealthy elite. They all manage to muster sufficient food and medical services for the wealthy. Soldiers don't go hungry. Even poor countries find money for monuments and armaments. Poor countries are constrained in what they can do, but viewed globally, surely the limited allocation of resources to serving the interests of poor children is due more to the ways in which available funds are used than to the absolute shortage of funds (Sivard, 1991; United Nations Development Programme, 1991).

Working through UNICEF and other agencies, the international community has some programs designed to promote child survival, but these are meager in comparison with the effects of international economic forces on children. The most glaring example in recent history is the combined effects of excessive export promotion, debt bondage, and then structural adjustment policies imposed by the developed world on Africa.

Specific deaths may be beyond the control of the immediate family or community, but *patterns* of mortality can be influenced by public policy. The failure to introduce effective policies and programs for reducing children's mortality (immunization, for example) should sensibly lead to charges of abuse or neglect by government.

The failures of governments in relation to children are partly due to bad policies and programs, but more often to absent and inadequate programs resulting from the treatment of children's programs as low-priority items in national budgets. Children could be fed adequately in almost every country in the world, even the poorest among them, *if* that were regarded as high priority in government circles. Massive children's mortality is not necessary and inevitable.

That the problem is national priorities rather than national poverty is nowhere more clear than in the richest country in the world. The infant mortality rate in the United States is now about 10 per 1000, which is quite good. But how do we come to terms with the fact that about twenty other developed countries have even lower rates, rates that are declining even faster than in the United States? Twenty percent of the children in the United States are under the official poverty line. That is not because the United States is a poor country (Children's Defense Fund, 1984, 1987, 1992).

Government officials say that of course they don't want children to go hungry or die - and they don't. The problem is that they place so many other concerns at a higher priority. Where there are serious problems of hunger or homelessness or children's mortality, decision-makers claim that they *cannot* deal with the problem because they don't have the resources. Often the truth is that they *will not* respond to the problem. Children's welfare could be sharply improved if that objective was of high priority to governments. *Cannot* is an attempt to evade responsibility. The *cannot* defense should not be accepted as an excuse where low priority - *will not* - is the truthful explanation.

Children, especially poor children, are not attended to because they do not have the power to demand attention from public and private agencies. For some children the situation is worse than being ignored. The powerful often find ways to use children to serve their own interests, whether those interests are economic or sexual or military. Whether it is a matter of neglect or direct abuse, it is the interests of others that are served; the interests of children are ignored.

Small children cannot make their own claims for recognition of their rights; they require surrogates to speak on their behalf. A number of organizations, private and public, national and international, have emerged to take up the advocacy of children, e.g., United Nations Children's Fund, Defense for Children International, and Save the Children. But much remains to be done. Millions upon millions of children still die unnecessarily each year.

INTENTIONALITY

In some killings, witnesses observe the accused caught with a "smoking gun," and the accused is known to have motives for taking the life of the victim. In other cases, the accused may acknowledge having caused the death but argue that the gun went off accidentally, or say that he was temporarily insane and thus not responsible for his action. In criminal trials, distinction are made according to the nature of the intentions:

> Homicide is divided into four different types: *Criminally negligent homicide* (sometimes called vehicular homicide) is an unintentional killing resulting from indifference or reckless disregard for human life, such as speeding through a school zone. *Manslaughter* is killing someone intentionally in the heat of passion; unintentionally while committing a violation or a misdemeanor; or unintentionally while performing a lawful act in a negligent manner, such as while cleaning a loaded gun. *Second-degree murder* involves malice, which means that the killer must have intended to cause death or to inflict severe bodily harm. *First-degree murder*, the most serious form of homicide, involves both malice and a premeditated decision to kill someone. (Yates, 1988, p. 601)

We can make similar distinctions in connection with other sorts of death scenarios. Are the widespread deaths of children worldwide intentional in some sense? There is also the question of where the locus of these intentions might be. Who exactly is the responsible agent?

Most children's deaths cannot be described as murders, but that does not mean that they are accidental or natural or inevitable. Many can be described as resulting from a form of negligent homicide. Negligent homicide is still homicide in that the deaths are avoidable and unnecessary.

Governments do commit negligent homicide. It should be possible to charge governments with crimes of omission or neglect. Consider the case of Joshua DeShaney vs. Winnebago County Department of Social Services, brought before the United States Supreme Court. The child, Joshua, had been beaten by his father, causing him to be retarded and permanently institutionalized. A county social worker who knew of the abuse took no action. A majority of the court ruled that the state had not inflicted the violence, and thus was blameless. In his dissent Justice William J. Brennan argued, "Inaction can be every bit as abusive of power as action... I cannot agree that our Constitution is indifferent to such indifference (DeShaney, 1988, p. 212)."

Most criminal law deals with those who take actions that should not have been taken; it does not deal so effectively with failures to take action that should have been taken. This is true whether the failure to act is attributed to individuals or to governments.

This skew means that child abuse gets much more attention than child neglect, despite the fact that far more children's deaths can be associated with neglect. Neglect may be difficult to observe in individual households, but at the societal level the systematic neglect of children shows up in high morbidity and mortality rates.

We tend to draw too sharp a line between *deliberate* and *neglectful*. *Deliberate neglect* describes the pattern of many governments' responses to the needs of children. The term is not an oxymoron; it is not self-contradictory. If the failure to attend to children's needs persists over time, even in the face of repeated complaints and appeals, that neglect can be described as intentional or deliberate. Neglect can be understood as the failure to do something that should be done - and that failure may or may not be intentional. If it persists and it is obvious, it must be regarded as intentional.

Piers (1978) speaks of "infanticide by deliberate neglect." She illustrates the concept by reference to a South American barrio in which "the seventh or eighth child in a poor family was the one doomed to die. The means of killing were starvation and neglect (pp. 15-19)." The famous *Black's Law Dictionary* (Black, 1968) describes a disputed concept in law of "willful negligence," defined as "willful determination not to perform a known duty, or a reckless disregard of the safety or the rights of others, as manifested by the conscious and intentional omission of the care proper under the circumstances (p. 1186)."

There is a difference between not knowing what your actions will lead to and what is described in law as "reckless disregard" for the predictable consequences of one's action. Manufacturers of cars and pharmaceuticals are expected to pull their products off the market if they learn they have serious harmful effects. When infant formula was first promoted in the third world, it may not have been anticipated that it would kill babies. But when international governmental and nongovernmental organizations documented and warned and campaigned about the problem, and the World Health Assembly passed guidelines to control the behavior of sellers of infant formula, and still the sellers persist in selling the product in a way that is known to kill babies, that is unforgivable (Ritchie, 1991). It is a form of killing.

Usually killings are concentrated in a particular time and space. The deaths of children, however, are dispersed all over the globe, and they are sustained over time. There certainly is no central command structure causing these deaths to happen. There is nothing like the Wannsee Conference of January 1942 at which the Nazis systematically elaborated their plans for the extermination of the Jews of Europe. There is that difference. The widespread deliberate and sustained neglect of children is not the calculated program of a few madmen assembled at a particular moment in history. Yet, the massive mortality of children is also deeply frightening precisely because it occurs worldwide with no central coordination mechanism. The culpability is not individual but systemic.

HATRED?

The plight of children can be explained by the indifference of policymakers to the welfare of children. Children are ignored or they are used to serve other people's interests, and apparently the interests of the children themselves simply do not matter very much.

Is it just a matter of indifference, or do some societies harbor a desire to harm children? Marian Wright Edelman, president of the Children's Defense Fund in Washington, D.C., is one of the most articulate advocates for change in United States policy toward children. Reporting on her views, on May 19, 1991, the *San Jose Mercury News* headlined "There's a War on: Our Children Are the Target." In May/June 1991, *Mother Jones* magazine, also reporting Edelman's views, offered a cover highlighting "America's Dirty Little Secret: We Hate Kids." Could they really mean *hate*? Do we really *target* children, or is that just hyperbole designed to attract attention? Do our societies go beyond simply ignoring children and actually want to harm them?

In *History of Childhood* (1974), Lloyd deMause has argued that it is not simply a matter of neglect. There are darker forces at work, a real deep-rooted malice, an urge to sacrifice children. More recently deMause (1990) has suggested that "Direct budget cuts in child aid and recessions that mainly affect children are modern equivalents of ancient child sacrifice - only our sacrificial priests are now presidents, budget committees and Federal Reserve chairmen (p. 139)."

On the whole, is public policy merely indifferent to the welfare of children, or does it show signs of actual hatefulness? Is there an active desire to hurt children?

In my view there is no widespread societal motivation to harm children for its own sake, out of intrinsic hatefulness. But there is a well-established pattern of accepting the sustained and undeniable harm that befalls children as societies pursue other interests. While there may be no widespread intention to harm children directly, there is widespread acceptance of their being harmed indirectly, as a kind of "collateral damage" from other activities regarded as more important. In that sense there is instrumental hatefulness. The idea is frightening, but given the history of human capacity to do - or tolerate - violence to other human beings, it cannot be dismissed.

There are many programs to serve children, in the United States, in other countries, and in the world as a whole. But the persistent inadequacy of these programs, especially for poor children, does result in persistent harm, and often death.

The point is ultimately inescapable: *Deliberate* neglect of children, sustained over an extended period, leads to definite harm. Thus, morally it *is* hateful behavior. It should not be forgiven before the law in the way that momentary inattention might be forgivable. The conventional distinction between negligent homicide (manslaughter) and deliberate homicide (murder) is meaningful only as it refers to a singular, fleeting event. You may get away with the story that your gun went off accidentally the first time, but if the same thing happened repeatedly the story would not be accepted. No court would view repeated, sustained killings, with full knowledge, as accidental.

In sum, the widespread deliberate neglect of children by governments must be understood as being, in its way, intentional. At the same time, it is also important to distinguish deaths by neglect from deliberately targeted deaths motivated by hateful desire to destroy, as in the Holocaust, or the Armenian genocide, or King Herod's systematic killing of the children of Bethlehem.

INTERNATIONAL OBLIGATIONS

So far I have discussed the obligations of national governments to care for their own citizens. However, obligations should not end at national borders. Poor children in poor countries should be viewed as the responsibility not only of their national governments, but of the entire international community. In a world as wealthy as ours, children should not have to die of starvation anywhere.

As pointed out earlier, structural adjustment policies imposed by the international lending agencies may be harmful to children. Surely there is a minimum requirement that international policy, whether of individual countries or international agencies, should not do anything to increase child mortality rates anywhere. There is also a positive obligation to work to reduce those mortality rates. Rich countries have some responsibility because they have the opportunity and the resources to do something substantial about the problem. They should devote more to the problem than the few hundreds of millions of dollars they now spend on international child survival programs.

International responsibility for massive children's mortality can also take other forms. With the increasing vulnerability of children in warfare, warring parties need to give more attention to the welfare of children in armed conflict situations. Some children are killed directly in combat, and many more die as a result of the disruption of food, health, sanitation, and other systems.

The idea of inviolable national sovereignty has served the international system well since the Treaty of Westphalia of 1648, but times have changed. There have been massive violations of human rights by national governments, especially in this century. Also in this century, there is new international law with regard to human rights, and there are new international mechanisms for implementing and monitoring that law, especially in the United Nations system. There is increasing acknowledgment that the doctrine of non-interference in the internal affairs of nations should be revised. The practice of nations has already moved ahead of international law in this area, as illustrated by the delivery of international humanitarian assistance without the consent of the national governments in the case of U.S. protection of Kurds following the Persian Gulf War, and also in Somalia and also in Bosnia in 1992-93.

The historical shift from a doctrine of inviolable sovereignty to acceptance of humanitarian intervention under special circumstances has its parallel in the historical evolution of the family. Until late in the nineteenth century, parents in New York City could abuse and torture their children, but police would not intervene in "family matters." Parents in effect had sovereign control over their families. Now, however, it is widely accepted that when there are gross violations of a child's rights, outside agencies should intervene to protect that child. The rights of supervising adults are not absolute, but must be balanced by consideration of the best interests of the child; under some special circumstances it may be necessary to intervene on behalf of the child. That same principle should now be acknowledged at the societal level.

DOES CHILDREN'S MORTALITY CONSTITUTE GENOCIDE?

Would it be reasonable to suggest that the treatment of children worldwide, allowing the deaths of over 12 million children under five each year, amounts to a form of genocide?

The *Convention on the Prevention and Punishment of the Crime of Genocide* was adopted by the United Nations General Assembly on December 9, 1948 and entered into force on January 12, 1951. According to article II:

> In the present Convention, genocide means any of the following acts committed with intent to destroy, in whole or in part, a national, ethnical, racial or religious group as such:
>
> (a) Killing members of the group;
> (b) Causing serious bodily or mental harm to members of the group;
> (c) Deliberately inflicting on the group conditions of life calculated to bring about its physical destruction in whole or in part;
> (d) Imposing measures intended to prevent births within the group;
> (e) Forcibly transferring children of the group to another group.

Paradoxically, although children do constitute a group, they are not a national, ethnic, racial, or religious group, the only victims recognized in the Genocide Convention. It could also be argued that the massive mortality of children is not the deliberate action of readily identified actors in the pattern characteristic of other commonly recognized genocides.

Some argue that genocide should be defined narrowly to prevent the debasement and trivialization of the concept. The difficulty is that a narrow definition may suggest that other kinds of large-scale mortality that are permitted to take place are less important. The sensible alternative is to systematically acknowledge that there are different kinds of genocide associated with different categories of victims and different forms of intentionality. This is the approach advocated by Charny (1993, in press) in his taxonomic scheme. He defines genocide in the generic sense as the willful destruction of a large number of human beings, except as that might be necessary in self defense.

Charny argues that, along with distinguishing different categories of genocide, including a category of intentional genocide, the degree of willfulness or intentionality should be assessed, in all other categories of genocide as well, leading to rating of different degrees of the crime of genocide. Perhaps the definitions used in assessing homicides could be adapted. Just as there can be first, second, or third degree murder, so too there might be first, second, or third degree genocide. Further distinctions must be made, however, to take account of sustained deliberate neglect.

The deaths of children throughout the world differ in many ways from the Holocaust and other atrocities we commonly describe as genocides. The differences, however, are not sufficient to dismiss the issue. The conclusion is virtually inescapable: *children's mortality is so massive, so persistent, and so unnecessary it should be recognized as a kind of genocide.*

Anne Frank, the girl who wrote the famous diary while hiding from the Nazis in Amsterdam, died in the Bergen-Belsen concentration camp in Germany in March 1945. She was not shot or gassed, but died of typhus. Is her death any less of an atrocity because the immediate cause of death was a disease and not gas or a bullet? Does it matter that the Nazis did not specifically plan the typhus?

Why is it that we are deeply concerned with the abuse and neglect of children by their families but give so little attention to the abuse and neglect of children by their societies and their governments? No matter what the intentions of political leaders and no matter what name we give it, there are massive horrors that befall children around the world. We are asked to remember the Holocaust, but sometimes we forget why we are to remember.

REMEDIES: RECOGNIZING CHILDREN'S RIGHTS

We have focused here on the dark side of the massive mortality of children, but of course there are many individuals and organizations, governmental and nongovernmental, that do wonderful things for children. Thousands of organizations provide services and work as advocates for children in many different ways.

However, the remarkable thing is that, with few exceptions, this work is all so persistently inadequate. This is not because the children's service and advocacy organizations are incompetent but because societies invest so little of their resources into serving the needs of children - especially poor children. Certainly health and education budgets are high in some countries - the United States, Japan, the Nordic countries - but if we look at the pattern worldwide we see that on the whole children are beggars despite the world's bounty. The budget for day care for children in the city of Stockholm has been higher than the entire global budget for UNICEF. Within the borders of the United States alone, we see enormously high expenditures for health and education, but too little of it serves the interests of poor children. Programs designed especially for the poor such as the Special Supplemental Food Program for Women, Infants and Children (WIC) program or Aid to Families with Dependent Children (AFDC) are persistently underfunded.

Advocates for children usually press for improved government funding for children's programs, but that leaves children vulnerable to the see-saw of the budgeting process. Funding may be increased for a time, but with the next war or drought or recession the budget-makers say there is not enough money, and funding for the programs is ratcheted down again. The demand should be not merely for increased funding, but for recognition that children have clear *rights* to certain levels of health, nutrition, education, and other services. If powerlessness is the source of much of children's woes, then pressing for the recognition of children's rights is one way of empowering them.

After ten years of negotiation by a working group of the Commission on Human Rights, on November 20, 1989 a new *Convention on the Rights of the Child* was approved by the United Nations General Assembly. Weaving together the scattered threads of earlier international statements of the rights of children, the convention's articles cover civil, political, economic, social and cultural rights. It includes not only basic survival requirements such as food, clean water, and health care, but also rights of protection against abuse, neglect, and exploitation, and the right to education and to participation in social, religious, political, and economic activities. Most of the world's nations have agreed to the convention, and many are now reviewing and strengthening their national laws relating to the rights of children.

Where children's mortality rates are much higher than they need to be, the government's policies may amount to a form of genocide. When children as a class are not adequately nourished and cared for, that constitutes an ongoing crime by society. As a crime, there should be mechanisms in law for correcting that manifest injustice, including means for calling not only parents and local communities but also governments to account. The foundation of that mechanism would be the clear recognition in law and practice of children's rights.

REFERENCES

Black, Henry Campbell (1968). *Black's Law Dictionary: Definition of the Terms and Phrases of American and English Jurisprudence, Ancient and Modern*. Fourth Edition. St. Paul, Minnesota: West Publishing Co. 1882 pp.

Boothby, Neil (1986). Children and war. *Cultural Survival Quarterly*, 10(4), 28-30.

Children's Defense Fund (1984). *American Children in Poverty*. Washington, D.C.: CDF. 88 pp.

Children's Defense Fund (1987). *A Children's Defense Budget, FY 1988: An Analysis of Our Nation's Investment in Children*. Washington, D.C.: CDF. 305 pp.

deMause, Lloyd (1990). It's time to sacrifice... our children. *Journal Psychohistory*, 18(2), 135-144.

DeShaney v. Winnebago County Department of Social Services. *United States Reports*, 489 (Cases Adjudged in the Supreme Court at October Term, 1988), 189-213.

Eckhardt, William (1992). Wars and Peaces of 1991. *COPRED Peace Chronicle*, 17(1), 8.

Kent, George (1990). *War and Children's Survival*. Honolulu: Spark Matsunaga Institute for Peace. 33 pp.

Leveille, Dominique (1988). Children used by the guerrilla in Mozambique: younger than the war itself. *International Children's Rights Monitor*, 5(1), 24.

Piers, Maria W. (1978). *Infanticide*. New York: W. W. Norton. 139 pp.

Ressler, Everett M.; Boothby, Neil; and Steinbock, Daniel J. (1987). *Unaccompanied Children: Care and Protection in Wars, Natural Disasters and Refugee Movements*. New York: Oxford University Press. 421 pp.

Ritchie, Mark (1991). Challenging global monopolies: Citizen movements take on infant formula giants. *Why Magazine* 7, 18-20.

Rose, Lionel (1986). *The Massacre of the Innocents: Infanticide in Britain 1800-1939*. London: Routledge & Kegan Paul. 215 pp.

Sivard, Ruth Leger (annual). *World Military and Social Expenditures*. Washington, D.C.: World Priorities.

Small, Melvin J. and Singer, J. David (1982). *Resort to Arms: International and Civil War, 1816-1980*. Beverly Hills, California: Sage. 373 pp.

Stanton, Marietta (1990). *Our Children Are Dying*. Buffalo, New York: Prometheus Books. 217 pp.

United States House of Representatives, Select Committee on Children, Youth, and Families (1989). *U.S. Children and their Families: Current Conditions and Recent Trends*, 1989. Washington, D.C.: U.S. Government Printing Office. 297 pp.

Watts, Michael (1991). African development in an age of market idolatry. *Transitions*, 51, 124-41.

World Bank (1993). *World Development Report 1993: Investing in Health*. Washington, D.C.: World Bank.

Wright, Quincy (1965). *A Study of War*. Second edition. Chicago: University of Chicago Press. 1637 pp.

Yates, Sharon Fass, ed. (1988). *The Reader's Digest Legal Question & Answer Book*. Pleasantville, New York: Reader's Digest Association. 704 pp.

BIBLIOGRAPHY

Note

While there is a great deal of literature on children, few studies examine their conditions in a political framework. Fewer still examine children's mortality from this perspective. The brevity of this bibliography should convey a sense of how few are the voices that speak for children, and how much important work remains to be done.

Aries, Philippe (1962). *Centuries of Childhood: A Social History of Family Life*. New York: Alfred A. Knopf. 447 pp.
   A major history, arguing that there was no distinct concept of childhood in premodern Europe. For a review of critical responses see Boswell, 1988, pp. 36-38.

Black, Maggie (1986). *The Children and the Nations: The Story of UNICEF*. New York: UNICEF. 502 pp.
   Recounts the history of the United Nations Children's Fund from its beginnings in the aftermath of World War I to its current work in countries throughout the world. Despite its limited budget, UNICEF has worked effectively with national governments to curtail children's misery and promote their development.

Boswell, John (1988). *The Kindness of Strangers: The Abandonment of Children in Western Europe from Late Antiquity to the Renaissance*. New York: Pantheon Books. 488 pp.

A thorough scholarly analysis of the history of abandonment or "exposure" of small children. Boswell shows that although abandonment or "exposure" was widespread in premodern times, it did not lead to death so often as many assume. "The overwhelming belief in the ancient world was that abandoned children were picked up and reared by someone else" (p. 131). Also shows that, paradoxically, the creation of foundling homes resulted in increased infant mortality.

Charny, Israel W. (1993, in press). Towards a generic definition of genocide. In Andreopoulos, George (Ed.), *The Conceptual and Historical Dimensions of Genocide.* Philadelphia: University of Pennsylvania Press.
    In this paper, which was presented on the occasion of the Yale University Law School Raphael Lemkin Symposium on Genocide in February, 1991, the author proposes a far-reaching classification of different types of genocide but where all are subsumed under a generic definition of all cases of mass murder as genocide. Thus, it would not be, as others have claimed, that only if the mass murders were intentional are they to be called genocide in the first place: but intentional genocide is a category, and an important concept, in the classification system. Charny also proposes assigning first, second and third degree classifications to genocide as in homicide law.

Children's Defense Fund (1992). *The State of America's Children 1992.* Washington, D.C.: Children's Defense Fund. 132 pp.
    One of a broad variety of publications by the Children's Defense Fund, one of the leading children's advocacy organization in the United States. Provides a thorough analysis of the conditions of children in the United States, nationally and in the separate states, with regard to health, child care, income, housing, education, etc. Shows that infant mortality rate for both blacks and whites has been decreasing steadily since 1940, but the rate for whites has been going down more rapidly than for whites. Includes numerical data, political analysis, and concrete recommendations for action.

Cornia, Giovanni Andrea, and Sipos, Sándor, (Eds.) (1991). *Children and the Transition to the Market Economy: Safety Nets and Social Policies in Central and Eastern Europe.* Aldershot, England: Avebury. 251 pp.
    The socialist countries have had extensive safety nets, but some of the social services are being dismantled as they make the transition to market economies. In some cases children, the poor, and the elderly are being disadvantaged. This major study from UNICEF's International Child Development Centre in Florence, Italy analyzes the problems and offers a number of concrete recommendations.

deMause, Lloyd (Ed.) (1974). *The History of Childhood: The Untold History of Child Abuse.* New York: Psychohistory Press. Republished in 1988 by Peter Bedrick Books. 450 pp.
    Ten experts review the treatment of children through history and argue that child abuse has been dominant. However, they acknowledge that there has been a steady improvement in the treatment of children over time.

Freeman, Michael, and Veerman, Philip (Eds.) (1992). *The Ideologies of Children's Rights.* Dordrecht: Martinus Nijhoff/Kluwer. 369 pp.
    With the United Nations *Convention on the Rights of the Child* coming into force in 1990, it has become important to understand not only the content but also the philosophies and ideologies underlying those rights. The 25 articles in this volume

describe those foundations and also their application in specific issue areas such as children right to health, child abuse, children in armed conflicts, and juvenile justice.

Grant, James P. (annual). *The State of the World's Children*. New York: Oxford University Press/UNICEF.
UNICEF's annual report on the conditions of the world's children and the organization's activities to improve those conditions. Detailed data are provided on children's mortality. In the 1993 edition, corrections were made adjusting global mortality figures that had been reported earlier to slightly lower levels.

Kent, George (1991). *The Politics of Children's Survival*. New York: Praeger. 224 pp.
Study of the societal factors underlying massive children's mortality throughout the world, including food systems, poverty, war, repression, and population growth. Argues that remedies should center on strategies of empowerment, including full use of national and international law to assure recognition of children's rights.

Kent, George (forthcoming, 1994). *Children in the International Political Economy*. London: Macmillan.
Children around the world are victims of massive mortality, poverty, and abusive working conditions, and they are often forced to serve as soldiers and prostitutes. This study shows that current methods of operating the international political economy work against the interests of the weak, especially children. When all others have failed them, children look to the international community as their last resort. There is no escaping the conclusion that responsibility for children should be recognized not only at local and national levels but also at the international level.

Kohler, Lennart, and Jakobsson, Gunborg (1987). *Children's Health and Well-Being in the Nordic Countries*. London: Mac Keith Press. 140 pp.
Powerful demonstration of how public policy can improve children's well-being if that is a high priority concern. The Nordic countries are world leaders in assuring their children's well-being.

Myers, Robert (1992). *The Twelve who Survive: Strengthening Programmes of Early Childhood Development in the Third World*. London: Routledge/UNESCO. 468 pp.
Myers points out that 12 of every 13 children born live to see their first birthdays (thus the title), so it is important to pay attention not only to children's survival but also to their development. Provides an excellent overview of methods and programs for child care and development and makes many useful recommendations. Shows that child care services can be effective in improving the quality of life of children, but does not give enough attention to the need to motivate governments to support such services. Effectiveness is not enough.

Ressler, Everett M.; Tortorici, Joanne Marie; and Marcelino, Alex (1993). *Children in War: A Guide to the Provision of Services*. New York: UNICEF. 288 pp.
Study commissioned by United Nations Children's Fund to guide the provision of services for children caught in armed conflict. Reviews methods for dealing with injury, illness, malnutrition, disability, torture, abuse, imprisonment, recruitment, psychosocial distress, etc. Follows Ressler's 1988 study, *Unaccompanied Children: Care and Protection in Wars, Natural Disasters, and Refugee Movements*, published by Oxford University Press. Establishes that even in the worst of conditions there is much that can be done for children.

Rummel, R. J. (1990). *Lethal Politics: Soviet Genocide and Mass Murder Since 1917.* New Brunswick, New Jersey: Transaction Books. 268 pp.

The first of a series of books by Rummel providing detailed accounts of mass killing of civilians by governments outside of warfare, a phenomenon he describes as democide. Through his systematic examination of all such events in the twentieth century, he now estimates there have been about 170 million victims of democide in this century.

Tesón, Fernando R. (1988). *Humanitarian Intervention: An Inquiry into Law and Morality.* Dobbs Ferry, New York: Transnational Publishers. 272 pp.

A philosophical, moral, and legal argument for the necessity of overriding national sovereignty when nations commit gross violations of human rights. Tesón acknowledges the parent-child analogy in justifying humanitarian intervention in cases of gross human rights violations, but does not apply it to the international protection of children (pp. 83-85).

United Nations (1992). *Child Mortality Since the 1960s: A Database for Developing Countries.* New York: United Nations. 400 pp.

Review of currently available data and methodologies for estimating children's mortality for 82 countries. The volume was assembled by the Population Division in the Department of Economic and Social Development of the United Nations. Unfortunately, it does not provide comparable data for developed countries, and it does not provide global totals.

United Nations Development Programme (1991). *Annual Human Development Report.* Cary, North Carolina: Oxford University Press.

Compilation by the United Nations Development Programme on several different dimensions of the quality of life. Shows that in many developing countries less than one-tenth of public spending is on human priority goals. Only about one-twelfth of foreign aid spending is earmarked for human priority goals. Provides data and analyses that help to demonstrate and explain the disadvantaged position of children, especially poor children, throughout the world.

10

Horizontal Nuclear Proliferation and Its Genocidal Implications

Samuel Totten[1]

Horizontal nuclear proliferation (the acquisition of nuclear weapons by an increasing number of countries across the globe) has profound ramifications vis-a-vis the issues of genocide and omnicide. With the exception of a miniscule number of scholars, policymakers, and activists, most individuals have ignored the problems posed by the horizontal spread of nuclear weapons across the globe. In doing so, humanity has basically resigned itself to the fact that nuclear weapons are part and parcel of the technological advances of the mid-to-late twentieth century, and something to be "lived with." In fact, it seems that unless they are directly threatened by a nation that possesses or is suspected of possessing nuclear weapons, most people would rather ignore the dangers posed by the destructive power of such weapons and/or the ramifications of the spread of such weapons across the globe. That said, this author agrees with psychologist Robert Jay Lifton's (1982) trenchant observation that "it is a fact of the greatest absurdity that we human beings threaten to exterminate ourselves with our own genocidal technology" (p. 15).

As the historical events surrounding the dawn of the nuclear age recede into the haze of the past so does remembrance of the horrific destruction wrought by the two relatively small atomic bombs that were dropped on Hiroshima and Nagasaki by the United States. That does not bode well for the future. And as more and more nations acquire nuclear weapons and then mechanistically and mindlessly go about stockpiling and developing increasingly sophisticated weapons of their own, it certainly seems likely that there is an ever greater possibility that at some point in time, somewhere in the world, nuclear weapons may be used once again.

Many have argued that nuclear deterrence has staved off a third world war and that possession of nuclear weapons by a nation can serve to both deter nuclear and conventional attack. In other words, the possession of nuclear weapons is a "necessary evil." In contradistinction to this point of view, there are those who would agree with Santoni when he says "...because nuclear policies (of deterrence, for example), express the willingness, under certain circumstances, to incapacitate the adversary nation, they are genocidal in intention and imply "multiple genocide" (quoted in Gay and Santoni and, 1988, p. 174). Santoni's point represents the spirit of this essay.

As nuclear weapons have become both more powerful and greater in number, some scholars have discussed the possibility of "nuclear omnicide" or "the irreversible extinction of all sentient life" (Gay and Santoni, 1988, p. 174). In *The Fate of the Earth*, Schell (1982) also discusses the possibility of the extinction of all life if a nuclear war were fought. Finally, numerous scientists have discussed the devastating effects of what they have referred to as "nuclear winter" and "nuclear fall" (Ackerman, et al., 1985; Turco, et al., 1983).

HISTORY OF HORIZONTAL NUCLEAR PROLIFERATION

The first nuclear weapons were developed by the United States during the early to mid-1940s while it was engaged in World War II. The United States was also the first, and thus far only, nation to use nuclear weapons in an act of war. On August 6, 1945, the United States dropped an atomic bomb on the Japanese city of Hiroshima, and three days later, on August 9, it dropped another atomic bomb on the city of Nagasaki. While the use of such weapons brought a swift end to the war, there has been lengthy and heated debate over the need for as well as the legitimacy of the use of such destructive weapons in that situation (Alperovitz, 1965; Amrine, 1959; Bernstein, 1974; Herken, 1982; Sherwin, 1977).

In 1949, the Soviet Union developed its first nuclear bomb. The distrust and enmity of the United States and the Soviet Union, which resulted in the so-called Cold War, set off a nuclear arms race that resulted in the ever-increasing buildup of evermore powerful and sophisticated weapons by each side. One of the results of this putative race was the development of the hydrogen bomb by the U.S. in 1953 and the U.S.S.R. in 1954.

Over the next twenty years, three more nations developed, tested, and began stockpiling their own atomic bombs: Great Britain (1958), France (1961), and China (1964). They, too, eventually developed their own hydrogen bombs: Great Britain in 1958, China in 1967, and France in 1968. In the parlance of the nuclear weapons field, all of the aforementioned nations are commonly referred to as "the nuclear club members."

In 1974, India developed its first atom bomb and conducted what it called its "peaceful nuclear explosion." In doing so, Indian government officials disingenuously claimed that its bomb was for civilian and not military purposes. Furthermore, as Scherr and Stoel (1979) note:

> The Government of India immediately claimed that the plutonium device it had exploded was all-Indian: "Not a single thing used in it was foreign." The statement sought to mask twenty years of U.S. and Canadian assistance to Indian development of nuclear power.
> ...The Indian nuclear explosion...came as a shock to the American public. The official U.S. response was muted. The CIRUS reactor provided by the Canadians had been identified as the source of the plutonium used in the explosive. It was argued that the incident was a matter between India and Canada...The fact that U.S. heavy water had been provided for the CIRUS reactor was not mentioned... (pp.19-20, 21)

Since the early 1980s, various nuclear experts across the globe have suggested that South Africa may have developed and built its own nuclear weapons. While South Africa officials asserted that South Africa was "capable of building weapons[,...] they had remained deliberately vague about whether it had built any" (Albright, 1993b, p. 3). But on March 24, 1993, South African President F. W. de Klerk cleared away the ambiguity when he "admitted to a joint session of parliament that South Africa had once had a supply of nuclear weapons; six of seven planned devices had been completed" (Albright, 1993b, p. 3). He went on to say that "the weapons were dismantled and their weapon-grade uranium-metal cores melted down and re-cast before South Africa signed the Nuclear Non-Proliferation Treaty (NPT) on July 10, 1991" (Albright, 1993b, p. 3). In addition to dismantling the weapons, de Klerk reported that all nuclear weapon components and design information were also destroyed.

Two other nations (three counting India) have acquired *the ability* to develop nuclear weapons. These nations, often referred to as "defacto nuclear club members," are Israel (the late 1960s), India (the early 1970s), and Pakistan (the mid -1980s). Israel refuses to say whether it possesses nuclear weapons, consistently repeating the deliberately ambiguous statement, "Israel will not be the first nation to introduce nuclear weapons into the Middle East."

Over the past twenty years or so, at least eight other nations have, at one time or another, appeared to be working toward the development of nuclear weapons programs. The eight nations most frequently mentioned are: Argentina, Brazil, Iran, Iraq, Libya, North Korea, South Korea, and Taiwan. As political, security, and/or economic circumstances have changed over the past twenty years in various regions, so has the drive by the aforementioned nations to develop or not develop such weapons.

As disturbing as these trends are, Dennis (1984) notes that

...the proliferation of nuclear powers has not been as great as had been thought likely. During the sixties and seventies many countries had the technological capacity and the industrial and material resources to build nuclear weapons but did not do so: Australia, Canada, West Germany, Japan, Italy, Sweden. In fact, most of these countries have publicly stated their intention not to acquire nuclear weapons...

There are many good reasons. The responsibilities and pitfalls are great. A nuclear explosive is of little value without a practical delivery system against a foreseeable adversary. A country may believe it can rely for protection on its alliances with other powers. Countries realize that as they equip themselves with nuclear arms, the potential enemy may well respond in kind. Possessing nuclear weapons may very well lessen a nation's security instead of improving it. (p. 362)

Be that as it may, in December of 1991, humanity faced a new and startling development vis-a-vis horizontal nuclear proliferation, and that had to do with the final breakup and demise of the Soviet Union into a number of independent republics. Immediately, eleven of the twelve former Soviet republics (Russia, Byelorussia - now called Belarus, Ukraine, Armenia, Azerbaijan, Kazakhstan, Kirgizia, Moldavia, Tadzhikistan, Turkmenistan, and Uzbekistan) proclaimed independence and formed a new commonwealth. According to one Soviet expert, the late Marshal Sergei Akhromeyev, "tactical nuclear weapons are deployed in practically all Union republics" (Norris and Arkin, 1991, p. 48). More specifically, Norris and Arkin (1991) report that "Of the 27,000 nuclear weapons currently estimated to be in the Soviet arsenal, 95 percent are in four republics. Seventy percent are in Russia, 15 percent in the Ukraine, 7 percent in Kazakhstan, and 5 percent in Belorussia. The Caucasus republics have 3 percent, and the central Asian republics - Turkmenia, Uzbekistan, Tajikistan, Kirgizia - have less than 2 percent" (pp. 48-49). In March 1993, Sergei Kiselyov reported that "Experts from the London Institute of Strategic Research believe that 20 percent of the former Soviet Union's nuclear arsenal was located outside Russia. Within the last two years, 7,000 weapons, supposedly on Russian territory, were in fact evacuated from the Baltic states, the republics of the Caucasus, and the Central European states. It is impossible to say where, in the countries of the former Soviet Union, at least 2,000 weapons still reside" (p. 33). That said, he does note that Russia, Ukraine, Belarus, and Kazakhstan have all retained portions of the Soviet arsenal (Kiselyov, 1993, p. 31). "According to the governments of these four republics, all tactical (i.e., battlefield and short-range) nuclear weapons were returned to Russia as one of June 1992. Each of these four republics still retain some strategic (large-yield, long range) nuclear weapons."[2]

What all of this means in regard to the ultimate stability of the Commonwealth and its control over both conventional and nuclear weapons remains to be seen. At this writing, it is too early to predict anything with certainty. What is known, though, is that the situation in the former Soviet Union is far from stable. Almost every day, it seems, at least one of the commonwealth nations seems to experience yet another painful tremor as it goes through the throes of birth. As for the nuclear situation in the Commonwealth nations, Joseph Nye, director of Harvard University's Center for International Affairs, has perspicaciously noted that: "The command-and-control system for nuclear weapons is no stronger than the social system supporting it" (Budiansky, and Auster, 1992, p. 38).

Some of the most crucial problems that remain unresolved in regard to the control of nuclear weapons and nuclear technology spread out amongst the new commonwealth states are: Whose responsibility is it for dismantling the strategic nuclear weapons, and who will pay for it? What is to be done with "those factories that provide nuclear weapons grade fuel?" (Post, et al., 1992, p. 26). How will former Soviet nuclear experts make a living now that their services are no longer needed?

There has been speculation about the possibility that the thousands of out-of-work or poorly paid nuclear scientists of the former Soviet Union may offer their services to the highest bidder. This is particularly disturbing when one realizes that U.S. officials estimate that up to "2000 [former Soviets] have the technical know-how to design atomic bombs" and that an "additional 3,000 to 5,000 people have experience in enriching uranium or manufacturing plutonium" (Post, et al., 1992, p. 29). A key worry is that these people may assist current non-nuclear weapons states in developing nuclear weapons. There also is concern that such individuals might be tempted to sell nuclear fuel or other materials to the highest bidders. Concomitantly, there has also been speculation that military personnel in charge of the former Soviet Union's nuclear arsenals may be tempted to sell a weapon(s) to outside parties (including sale to non-weapons states or terrorists).

On a positive note, in late January 1992, Russian President Boris Yeltsin announced that he was making deep cuts in Russia's nuclear arsenals. He asserted that approximately 600 strategic nuclear missiles had been taken off alert, that production of long-range nuclear bombers was being cutback, and that battlefield nuclear weapons in both Russia and the former Soviet republics were being dismantled. At the same time, then U. S. President George Bush also announced that he had ordered a halt to the development of new nuclear weapons as well as cutbacks in the current U.S. nuclear arsenals (e.g., an elimination of 1,500 of 2,000 nuclear warheads on U.S. land-based missiles, reduction by one-third the number of nuclear warheads on sea-based missiles, and the conversion of some nuclear bombers to non-nuclear roles). In February 1992, Bush proposed that the U.S. and the commonwealth nations each cut their arsenals by more than half (e.g., to about 4, 700 strategic nuclear warheads and bombs for the U.S. and to about 4,400 for the commonwealth). Yeltsin immediately countered by proposing that each side cut its nuclear weapons to about 2,500 nuclear warheads. Finally, in January 1993, Bush and Yeltsin signed the START II treaty, which "[i]f fully implemented by the year 2003..., the United States will have reduced its strategic nuclear forces to 3,500, and Russia will have cut its warhead to 3,000. These numbers would compare to 1990 strategic totals of 12,000 for the United States and 11,000 for the Soviet Union. Never before in history have two countries agreed to destroy more than two-thirds of their most dangerous weapons" (Isaacs, 1993, p. 10). The successful execution of such cuts are contingent on a host of concerns, not the least of which is the stability of the new Commonwealth. These hopeful events were, of course, triggered by both the end of the Cold War as well as the demise of the Soviet Union.[3]

Nonetheless, as hopeful as the latter events are, it is still a fact that there exists enough nuclear weapons across the globe to cause devastating and unprecedented destruction. That is a concern that demands to be addressed by people across the globe.

THE DRIVE TO OBTAIN NUCLEAR WEAPONS

Most experts agree that there are three key reasons as to why a nation might wish to develop its own nuclear arsenal: security, prestige, and influence. In regard to the issue of security, certain nations have made the decision to "go nuclear" due to one or more of the following reasons: (1) They either felt threatened and/or had been overtly threatened by another nation's nuclear arsenal (or suspected nuclear arsenal); (2) they felt threatened by a neighbor's superior conventional weapons arsenal; and/or, (3) they were concerned that a neighboring country might be working on the development of a nuclear arsenal.

In regard to the issue of prestige, numerous analysts suggest that certain nations may desire a nuclear arsenal in order to gain prestige (in its own region and/or internationally) that it cannot muster in more conventional ways (e.g., through being an economic powerhouse, having an exceptionally strong conventional military force, being strategically significant, or being a regional or international leader). Finally, some have suggested that a nation may wish to obtain nuclear weapons in order to wield more influence in regional or international affairs. In this way such nations could "use nuclear weapons as a bargaining tool or to threaten and thereby obtain its wishes in international affairs" (Dennis, 1984, p. 349).

MEANS OF OBTAINING NUCLEAR CAPABILITY

Up to this point in time, those nations known to definitely possess nuclear arsenals have either developed and built the weapons themselves or have done so with the technical assistance of another nation (as opposed to purchasing or stealing the weapons).

While there has been much discussion about the possibility that terrorist groups could steal or purchase a nuclear weapon, there is no hint or hard evidence that that has happened yet. Concomitantly, while there has been considerable discussion in the last months of 1991 and throughout 1992 and 1993 that out-of-work and disenfranchised Soviet nuclear experts/scientists might be willing to sell their knowledge and skills to parties that desire nuclear weapons, and/or that disenfranchised Soviet military personnel might be willing to actually steal and sell nuclear weapons to the highest bidders, that too is speculation at this time. However, as the horizontal proliferation of nuclear weapons continues, the possibility of the theft or the sale of nuclear weapons increases.

In regard to the knowledge that it would take to design a nuclear weapon, Jack Dennis (1984), a professor of computer science and engineering at M. I. T., has noted the following: "The designer of a nuclear weapon must have knowledge of the physical process and the properties of nuclear materials on which weapon designs are based. None of the fundamental knowledge is secret, and much of it is just as essential to competent work in nuclear energy as it is to weapons development. Through the worldwide exploitation of nuclear energy..., this fundamental knowledge is accessible to any country having a technically educated group and access to published scientific literature" (p. 347). And as Tsipis (1984) has noted, "...the physical processes involved [in developing nuclear weapons] ...are treated in textbooks on nuclear physics" and can even be found in certain encyclopedia articles (e.g., a case in point is Edward Teller's article on the hydrogen bomb in the 1981 volume of *Encyclopedia Americana*) (p. 204).

The nuclear power/nuclear weapons connections

Only those who are disingenuous or outright duplicitous will not readily admit the inextricable link between nuclear power and nuclear weapons. Stated another way, there is only one type of atom, not two (the "peaceful atom" and "the military atom") as some in the past have asserted. As Lovins and Lovins (1980) have cogently stated, "All concentrated fissionable materials are potentially explosive. All nuclear fission technologies both use and produce fissionable materials that are or can be concentrated.

Unavoidably latent in those technologies, there is a potential for nuclear violence..." (p. 9).

In a discussion regarding the amount of fissionable material needed to design a nuclear weapon, Lovins and Lovins (1980) note that

> Little strategic material is needed to make a weapon of mass destruction. A Nagasaki-yield bomb can be made from a few kilograms of plutonium, a piece the size of a tennis ball...Yet these amounts are a minute fraction of plutonium flows in normal fuel cycles. A large power reactor annually produces, and an experimental "critical assembly" may contain, hundreds of kilograms of plutonium; a large fast breeder reactor would contain thousands of kilograms; a large reprocessing plant may separate tens of thousands of kilograms per year, or more than one bomb's worth per hour.
>
> Nor is it only fissionable materials that lead to bombs...[I]t is at least equally important that most of the knowledge, much of the equipment, and the general nature of the organizations relevant to making bombs are inherent in civilian nuclear activities, and are "in much of their course interchangeable and interdependent" for peaceful or violent uses. (pp. 9-10)

It is because of this "inextricable link" between civilian and military uses of the atom that some critics have been so vehement in their criticism of President Eisenhower's (1953) "Atoms for Peace" program, which vigorously promoted the peaceful uses of atomic energy both domestically and internationally.

It should be clearly noted that, "Nuclear power plants by themselves do not present a proliferation risk. It is the 'sensitive' nuclear facilities - enrichment plants and reprocessing plants - that provide the essential link between nuclear power and nuclear weapons. Although the United States has barred commercial reprocessing and use of plutonium at home, several other nations in the industrialized and developing world have refused to follow the U.S. example" (Leventhal, 1990, p. 147).

It is because of the aforementioned link that nonproliferation experts have called for the implementation of measures by both individual states and the international nonproliferation regime as a means to attempt to staunch the spread of nuclear materials and technology across the globe. Among these measures are the following: halting commercial production and use of nuclear-explosive materials, tightening export controls of nuclear materials and technology, reducing reliance on and/or totally phasing out nuclear power, promoting and implementing non-nuclear energy alternatives, and strengthening the international non-proliferation regime - particularly the practices of the International Atomic Energy Agency (IAEA) in such areas as developing tighter safeguards and conducting more rigorous inspection policies, and addressing the current weaknesses and loopholes in the Treaty on the Non-Proliferation of Nuclear Weapons (NPT).

DANGERS INHERENT IN THE
SPREAD OF NUCLEAR WEAPONS

There are numerous dangers inherent in the spread of nuclear weapons, including but not limited to the following: the possibility that a nation threatened by destruction in a conventional war may resort to the use of its nuclear weapons; the miscalculation of a threat of an attack and the subsequent use of nuclear weapons in order to stave off the suspected attack; a nuclear weapons accident due to carelessness or flawed technology (e.g., the accidental launching of a nuclear weapon); the use of such weapons by an unstable leader; the use of such weapons by renegade military personnel during a period of instability (personal, national or international); and, the theft (and/or development) and use of such weapons by terrorists. While it is unlikely (though not impossible) that terrorists would be able to design their own weapons, it is possible that they could do so with the assistance of a renegade government.

As recent events in both Eastern Europe and in the former Soviet Union have vividly illustrated, geopolitical situations can (and do) change radically and quickly. The same is true in those regions where coup d'etats are a regular feature of the political landscape (in South America, for example). The point is, there is absolutely no guarantee that a country with nuclear weapons today will not erupt in civil war, fracture into new entities with entirely different political agendas, and/or create new and radically different allies which could possibly result in the further spread of nuclear materials. Thus, in one sense there is *no absolute control over nuclear weapons*.

Not to be overlooked is the destructive nature of nuclear weapons. As Spector (1990) notes, compared to the worst chemical weapons: "...even nuclear weapons that are considered small by today's standards, like those used against Hiroshima and Nagasaki, can cause death and destruction on a scale immeasurably more severe. Indeed, it has been estimated that if a dozen nuclear weapons were used by India against Pakistan or vice versa, they could cause over a million casualties, even if the weapons were aimed at military installations, rather than deliberately targeted against cities" (p. 143).

And while the end of the Cold War certainly seems to bode well for the future, it is still a fact that even after the United States and Russia (as well as the other Commonwealth nations) follow through and drastically cut back the number of weapons in their nuclear arsenals, there still will be thousands of nuclear weapons spread across various parts of the globe. And as long as they remain in place, they constitute a great and immediate danger to the citizens and ecology of the earth.

MANAGING VERSUS HALTING
HORIZONTAL NUCLEAR PROLIFERATION

A major issue that has plagued humanity since the outset of the nuclear age is the problem of how the spread of nuclear proliferations can be controlled and/or slowed, if not prevented. It has been an extremely divisive issue, and certainly one reason is the fact that there is no clear cut agreement as to what constitutes the most efficacious means for solving the problem.

Since the 1950s there have been numerous efforts to stem the horizontal spread of nuclear weapons. The major thrust of this international effort is commonly referred to as the "nuclear nonproliferation regime." The nonproliferation regime is a collection of treaties, bilateral arrangements, supplier-country efforts, ad hoc diplomacy, and international institutions that collectively attempt to prevent the spread of nuclear weapons. In addition to the NPT, other treaties in effect whose purpose is to prevent the spread of nuclear weapons to various geographical areas are the Outer Space Treaty, which prohibits nuclear weapons in space, the Treaty for the Prohibition of Nuclear Weapons in Latin America (which is also known as the Treaty of Tlatelolco), and the Treaty of Rarotonga which established a regional nuclear free zone in the South Pacific.

Heading up the nonproliferation effort is the International Atomic Energy Agency (IAEA), which is an affiliate of the United Nations and based in Vienna, Austria. Founded in 1957, it currently has over 100 member countries. The IAEA's "key function is to conduct on-site inspections of nuclear installations around the globe to verify that nuclear materials are being used exclusively for peaceful energy and research and not for nuclear arms. Today the agency inspects more than 95 percent of all nuclear facilities outside of the five declared nuclear weapons states, auditing operating records and performing physical inventories of nuclear materials to make certain that none have been diverted for military purposes" (Spector, 1990, p. 144).

The IAEA has key strengths as well as alarming weaknesses. As for its major strength, Donnelly (1990) argues that the "IAEA's well established safeguards mark an unprecedented yielding of national sovereignty to an international organization and are seen as able to detect systematic diversions of enough nuclear materials to make an arsenal" (p. 157). In fact, it is generally argued that if the IAEA did not exist, there would be a greater push across the globe by nations to develop their own nuclear arsenals and that there would be a wide-open and totally uncontrollable market for nuclear weapons technology and materials.

Critics argue that the IAEA's standards are not stringent enough, that its inspections are not rigorous enough, and that it is not tough enough in meting out penalties. A recent case that illustrates many of the weaknesses of the IAEA's efforts vis-a-vis preventing the horizontal proliferation of nuclear weapons is the surprise discovery in 1991 of Iraq's nuclear weapons program.

It is also true that under the current mandate of the IAEA there can be no absolute guarantee that proliferation will be prevented. As Michael J. Wilmshurst (1990), Director of External Relations at the IAEA, has written: "IAEA safeguards are not now and will not be in the 1990s adequate for that purpose. For such time as there are states - whether nuclear-weapon states or non-nuclear-weapons states - which have not placed all of their nuclear activities under safeguards, it would be impossible for the Agency to confirm that there has been *no* proliferation" (p. 14).

The centerpiece of the nonproliferation regime's efforts is the Treaty on the Non-Proliferation of Nuclear Weapons (NPT), which went into force in 1970. Prior to the dismemberment of the Soviet Union, Spector (1990) noted the following about the NPT:

> More than 135 nonnuclear-weapon countries are now parties to the pact. Under the treaty, these parties pledge not to manufacture or acquire nuclear weapons and have agreed to place *all* of their nuclear plants under IAEA inspection, effectively ruling out the use of any part of the nuclear program for nuclear arms. In return for this, the nuclear weapons states that sponsored the accord - the United States, the Soviet Union, and Great Britain - are required to negotiate in good faith to end the nuclear arms race and (along with other advanced countries) to assist other parties in peaceful nuclear projects. To ensure that nuclear sales do not contribute to weapons programs, all parties are also required to make sure that the recipient of any export places it under IAEA safeguards.
>
> Unfortunately, Israel, India, South Africa [South Africa eventually signed the NPT on July 10,1991], and Pakistan - the four countries with undeclared nuclear weapons capabilities - have not signed the treaty, nor have Argentina or Brazil. All six of these countries [South Africa no longer does] have some nuclear installations (usually imported ones) that are under IAEA oversight. They also have other facilities, including enrichment plants or reactors and plutonium extraction plants, that are not under these safeguards and are therefore legally free to be used for the manufacture of nuclear arms. Iran, Iraq and Libya have ratified the Non-Proliferation Treaty, but many observers fear they are not committed to it. (p. 144)

The NPT has its proponents and its detractors. Its key supporters generally assert that while the NPT is certainly not perfect, it has been relatively effective and the world is a safer place for it. They argue that those who have predicted a world bristling with nuclear weapons in regions across the globe over-estimated, to a large degree, the projected spread of nuclear weapons. They further argue that the both the existence and impact of the NPT and other components of the international nonproliferation regime are key reasons why the current number of nuclear and near-nuclear states is so low.

Others are less sanguine and argue that many of the NPT's components need to be revised, some radically. It should be noted that not all critics of the NPT are critical of the same components. For example, some critics have argued that "in its goal of stemming the proliferation of nuclear weapons the treaty's two key weaknesses are: there are many nations not party to the treaty, and the provision in Article X allows any party to withdraw if 'extraordinary events, related to the subject matter of the Treaty, have jeopardized the supreme interests of its country'" (Dennis, 1984, p. 360). Others argue that for years the superpowers only gave lip service to Article VI (which calls on each of the Parties to the Treaty to undertake "to pursue negotiations in good faith on effective measures relating to cessation of the nuclear arms race at an early date and to nuclear disarmament, and on a treaty on general and complete disarmament under strict and effective international control") and that this has weakened the treaty. Still others argue that Article IV ("All the Parties to the Treaty undertake to facilitate, and have the right to participate in, the fullest possible exchange of equipment, materials and scientific and technological information for the peaceful uses of nuclear energy") of the Treaty is a major stumbling block to effectively controlling or managing horizontal nuclear proliferation. Critics of this article assert that such an exchange provides any nation that is willing to sign the NPT with the building blocks of nuclear weapons. Still others argue that a major weakness of the NPT is that it is "pushing nuclear energy and technology" when it would be wiser to encourage nations to use alternative sources of energy which do not lend themselves to the development of nuclear weapons.

As previously mentioned, Iraq serves as a case in point that illustrates many of the weaknesses of the current international nonproliferation regime. Among the key weaknesses the Iraqi case highlights are: (1) the lack of real control that the IAEA has over the sale and purchase of key nuclear materials/technologies that can be used in the manufacture of nuclear weapons, (2) the relative ease with which nations can divert nuclear materials from so-called "peaceful nuclear programs" to military programs, and (3) the lack of honesty by some signatories in regard to living up to the agreements set out in the NPT.

Furthermore, as Weiss (1991) notes in "Tighten Up On Nuclear Cheaters": "Iraq could have put into place every element of a nuclear weapons program, including production facilities, without violating a single provision of the NPT or of its safeguards arrangements with IAEA. When Saddam Hussein was ready to produce the weapons, he could have invoked the NPT clause that allows a signatory to withdraw from the treaty after giving 90 days notice by declaring that 'extraordinary events, related to the subject matter of this Treaty, have jeopardized' its 'supreme interests'" (p. 11).

What is most disturbing is that Iraq had ample assistance in developing its surreptitious nuclear weapons program, and that that assistance came from companies based in nations that are signatories of the Treaty on the Non-Proliferation of Nuclear Weapons (e.g., France, Germany, and the U.S.).

THE CRITICAL CHALLENGES AND ISSUES WHICH FACE THE FIELD TODAY

The *most* critical challenge facing humanity vis-a-vis the issue of nuclear weapons proliferation is the development and sustainment of a political will, by both individual nations as well as the international community of nations, to halt the vertical and horizontal proliferation of nuclear weapons. Without political will, all efforts will be undermined. At this time, it is a simple but disturbing fact that such *a political will to prevent the horizontal proliferation of nuclear weapons does not exist.* Clear evidence of the lack of political will is the ambiguity-riddled focus of the NPT and IAEA. Simply stated, at the same time that the NPT and IAEA call for the prevention of horizontal nuclear proliferation, they both promise and make provisions for providing nuclear materials and technology (the very building blocks of nuclear weapons) to nations across the globe. In order to make any sense of such a policy one has to conduct a series of tortuous rationalizations.

Two of the most basic premises of the NPT underlie the problem. First, there is an assumption that there is an overwhelming need by nations across the globe for nuclear power materials and technology in order to meet their energy needs. That is simply not so. Second, there is an assumption that as long as countries agree to abide by a set of agreements (which include safeguards against using so-called civilian nuclear technology for military purposes), the best way to prevent the horizontal proliferation of nuclear weapons is by providing countries with nuclear materials and technology. In light of the on-going fiasco in Iraq, the sagacity of such a stance should be seriously reconsidered.

The notion of "sharing the wealth" of nuclear technology and materials in order to prevent horizontal proliferation of nuclear weapons is set out in both the Treaty's Preamble as well as in Article IV of the Treaty. In regard to the inconsistency of this position, Lovins and Lovins (1980) have argued as follows:

> The International Atomic Energy Agency was established in 1957 to promote the spread of nuclear energy for peaceful purposes, especially in developing countries, and to see that this was 'not used in such a way as to further any military purposes.' The IAEA's promotional zeal, however, conflicts with the practical difficulty of finding any exclusively peaceful nuclear technologies. This tension is mirrored in the Non-Proliferation Treaty, whose primary obligation is the promise of weapons states in Article I (reciprocated by non-weapons states in Article II) not to transfer bombs or 'in any way to assist

[or] encourage' others' acquisition of bombs. Yet in Article IV, all parties undertake 'to facilitate,' and have a right 'to participate in, the fullest possible exchange of equipment, materials and scientific and technological information for the peaceful uses of nuclear energy," and have an 'inalienable right' to peaceful uses 'without discrimination' - subject to Articles I and II. This ambiguous compromise does not resolve but embodies the underlying dilemmas of classical nonproliferation policy: reconciling national sovereignty with world order and the promotion of reactors with the prohibition of bombs. (p. 126)

Nowhere in the treaty, it should be noted, is there a single hint that there are alternative (cleaner and safer) sources of energy that could be used in place of nuclear energy which in turn would alleviate the "need" for spreading nuclear materials and technology across the globe. (For a detailed and cogent argument along this line, see Lovins and Lovins' (1980), *Energy/War: Breaking the Nuclear Link - A Prescription for Non-Proliferation*, and O'Heffernan, Lovins, and Lovins' (1983), *The First Nuclear World War: A Strategy for Preventing Nuclear War and the Spread of Nuclear Weapons.)*

If the international community hopes to make real progress on halting the horizontal proliferation of nuclear weapons, then the current nuclear weapons states also need to quit giving lip service to the notion of arms control and nuclear disarmament, and make real and *lasting* cuts in their arsenals to the point where they do away with their nuclear weapons. Many, of course, argue that the latter will never happen and that one is naive to even suggest such a notion. They assume that, at best, major cuts are all that can be expected.

That said, it seems as if the United States and Russia are finally going to act in accordance with the spirit of the treaty. Up until very recently, most nations talked about nuclear arms control (rarely, if ever, was the issue total nuclear disarmament), and when they did agree to cut weapons from their arsenals they generally replaced them with even more powerful and more sophisticated weapons. The result, of course, was that many non-nuclear weapons states looked askance at such actions and raised the question: "If other states can have nuclear weapons, why can't we?" As long as states continue to maintain a nuclear arsenal, the aforementioned question will not only continue to be legitimate but it will be one that will not go away. It, in fact, will not even begin to fade until the nuclear states act in *full* accordance with Article VI of the Treaty: "Each of the Parties to the Treaty undertakes to pursue negotiations in good faith on effective measures relating to cessation of the nuclear arms race at an early date and to nuclear disarmament, and on a treaty on general and complete disarmament under strict and effective international control."

Some assert that since the "nuclear genie," i.e., knowledge about how to build nuclear weapons, is out of the bottle, it is naive to think that we can go back to a non-nuclear age. But that is not what is being argued here.

What is being argued is that it makes absolutely no sense at all to attempt to prevent horizontal nuclear proliferation while (1) allowing (or promoting) the spread of the very materials that are needed to build the weapons, or (2) to continue to listen to nuclear club members call for a nuclear-weapons free world while they continue to build their own arsenals.

On the other hand, if the international community solely wishes to "manage" or attempt to control the horizontal nuclear proliferation of nuclear weapons (and at this point in time that seems to be its aim) there are still certain issues it needs to address. Two of the foremost among these are: (1) the need to overhaul the functions and activities of the IAEA, and (2) the need to revise (in some instances, radically) several of the stipulations and articles in the NPT in order to strengthen them so that they are more effective and, ultimately, leak-proof.

The IAEA needs to develop more stringent safeguard standards, develop more rigorous methods for ascertaining whether a nation is abiding by IAEA agreements (including, of course, those set by the NPT), conduct more thorough inspections of nuclear facilities, and establish stronger penalties for those who abrogate the treaty and find the means for putting those penalties into effect.

Over and above the previously mentioned weaknesses of the NPT, it is also true that (1) many nations are not party to the treaty, and (2) "...the provision in Article X allow[s] any party to withdraw if 'extraordinary events, related to the subject matter of the Treaty, have jeopardized the supreme interests of its country'" (Dennis, 1984, p. 360).

There are numerous other challenges that face humanity vis-a-vis the issue of horizontal nuclear proliferation. More specifically, there is a need to: prevent illicit nuclear trade and/or assistance; halt the export and spread of sensitive nuclear technologies; support the "'once-through uranium fuel track,' which ends with disposal of spent fuel deep in the earth without separating the plutonium (this prevents the introduction of bomb material at any stage of the nuclear power program)" (Nuclear Control Institute, 1990, p. 1); halt the use of the "plutonium fuel cycle," which leads to the accumulation of "enormous stockpiles of separated plutonium that represent a 'latent' proliferation risk - that is, once produced, they remain available to future governments for weapons use" (Leventhal, 1990, p. 148); "defer or eliminate programs for introducing separated plutonium and highly enriched uranium into domestic and world commerce," both of which can be used for the development of nuclear explosive materials (Leventhal, 1990, p. 150); "offer positive incentives to nations across the globe to forego production and use of nuclear-explosive materials" (The Working Group on Nuclear Explosives Control Policy, 1984, p. vi); prod the international community to place a higher priority on encouraging non-NPT nations to ratify the Treaty; encourage nations to reduce reliance on nuclear power, and encourage and support their use of alternative energy sources; develop and implement the means to protect against the theft and use of nuclear weapons and weapons-usable nuclear materials by terrorists and any other parties (Leventhal and Alexander, 1987); and, halt nuclear weapons testing by all nuclear states.

THE REAL PROBABILITIES OF PROGRESS IN THE FIELD

The probabilities of progress in regard to controlling or managing horizontal proliferation, let alone halting it, are mixed. In some areas, the chances for progress are good, in others the chances seem dim.

As for the issue of political will, if the record of the recent past is any indication, the prospects over the long-haul for halting horizontal nuclear proliferation are not all that good. Massive amounts of the technology and materials are located across the globe and the knowledge needed for developing such weapons is fairly well known. As the geopolitical landscape continues to change and/or heat up, different nations under different leadership will undoubtedly be tempted to develop their own nuclear arsenals. At the same time, if the political will were harnessed, there are workable plans that could be put into effect today that could eventually result in denuclearization.

The discovery of the Iraqi nuclear program has ostensibly made the international community more aware of the dangers of horizontal nuclear proliferation. Hopefully, that will result in more stringent regulations and safeguards on both the international level (e.g., the efforts of the IAEA and the focus of the NPT) as well as on the state and regional (e.g., bilateral agreements, etc.) levels. Then again, while the surreptitious development of a nuclear weapon by India shocked the world back in 1974, it did not take long for complacency to set back in once again. The point is, nation states, like people, often have short memories and/or do not learn from past mistakes or problems.

On a more positive note, at the end of 1991 Chinese legislators voted to sign the NPT. This has been hailed in the West as a major move toward meeting Western demands that China join the international community in its nonproliferation efforts. At the conclusion of 1991, South Korea and North Korea signed a pact that was to denuclearize the Korean peninsula. It was signed as part of a larger peace pact, but also in order to remove the danger of a nuclear war. The agreement allows both nations to use nuclear energy "for peaceful purposes" but bans them from manufacturing, possessing or deploying any type of nuclear weapons. But then "[o]n March 12, 1993, North Korea announced that it was withdrawing from the Nuclear Non-Proliferation Treaty (NPT)" (Albright, 1993a, p. 9). North Korea has since, however, "indefinitely suspended" its withdrawal. No matter what, the agreement with South Korea has been left hanging.

With the end of the Cold War, the break-up of the Soviet Union, and the current efforts by the U.S. and the former USSR to (1) dismantle parts of its nuclear arsenals, (2) call down certain systems, and (3) possibly hold off on the development of new weapons systems, there may be a golden opportunity for the first time in the nuclear age for the nuclear weapons states to "take substantial steps towards nuclear arms control and disarmament and downgrade the role of nuclear weapons in international relations and their own dependence on them" (Fischer and Szasz, 1985, p. 163). It seems imperative that the United States should not only support and assist the former republics of the Soviet Union to dispose of their weapons but also continue the process of curtailing the production of its own new nuclear weapons as well as disarming those in its current arsenal. The other nuclear states should, of course, follow suit. It would be naive, however, to believe that any of the nuclear state nations will totally disarm (at least in the near future) its nuclear arsenals, but any serious step in that direction could prove fruitful. Such a move could be the first significant step towards truly stemming the drive by other states to obtain their own nuclear arsenals.

Some nuclear experts argue that the current nuclear weapons states could provide a sign of good faith that they are serious about arms control and disarmament issues by agreeing to a Comprehensive Nuclear Weapons Test Ban (CTB). Proponents of a CTB argue that "...meaningful disarmament cannot occur until all nuclear testing is stopped, which will both slow the superpowers' weapons development and close off entry into the nuclear club" (Wurst, 1990/91, p. 45). While some weapons labs in the U.S. and elsewhere still claim that tests are needed to assess the reliability of weapons, it has been proved that "the testing and replacement of non-nuclear parts would be sufficient to maintain the reliability of already well-tested designs. Nuclear tests [are] simply not necessary" (Von Hippel and Zamora-Collina, 1993, p. 31). Recently, "the [U.S.] weapons labs and weapons experts sold Congress on the idea that warhead safety was the primary reason for permitting a limited schedule of tests [; h]owever, the air force, the navy and, the Defense and Energy Departments have all concluded that the safety modifications proposed by labs are not worth the cost" (Von Hippel and Zamora-Collina, 1993, p. 31). When all is said and done, the time is ripe for a solid commitment to the CTB by the nuclear powers.

As for the probability of overhauling the function and activities of the IAEA and radically revising the articles/stipulations in the NPT in order to strengthen them, the hope for progress is also mixed. In light of the Iraq debacle, it seems as if the international community should be open to the possibility of addressing some of the most sorely needed changes in the IAEA and the NPT. An NPT Conference will be held in 1995 at which time it will be decided whether the Treaty shall continue in force indefinitely or shall be extended only "for an additional fixed period or periods." However, once again, it would be naive to think that any radical changes are likely to be made in either the focus or running of the IAEA or in the make-up of the NPT. That seems to be true because most nations, along with the IAEA, have had a tendency to take a short-term and narrow approach to the issue of horizontal nuclear proliferation.

Finally, the probability that the international community or a large number of individual nations will, in the near future, pursue a "non-nuclear future" (in which they replace nuclear energy with renewable energy sources such as passive and solar technologies, industrial co-generation, biogas, small-scale hydroelectricity, windpower, etc.) in conjunction with energy conservation (e.g., "weatherstripping, insulation, heat exchangers, greenhouses, window overhangs and coatings") is rather dubious.

Speaking to the significance of such a move, Lovins and Lovins (1980) have argued that

> ...the search for practical ways to stop and even to reverse proliferation - the transcendent threat of our age - leads by inexorable logic to the necessity of phasing out nuclear power, as part of a coherent package of policies addressing both the vertical and the horizontal spread of bombs...eliminating nuclear power is a *necessary* condition for nonproliferation. But how far is it a *sufficient* condition? Suppose that nuclear power no longer existed...[W]ith trivial exceptions, there would no longer be any innocent justification for uranium mining, nor for possession of ancillary equipment such as research reactors and critical assemblies, nor for commerce in nuclear-grade graphite and beryllium and zirconium, tritium, lithium-6, more than gram quantities of deuterium, most nuclear instrumentation - in short, the whole panoply of goods and services that provides such diverse technological routes to bombs. If these exotic items were no longer commercially available, then - they would be much harder to obtain; efforts to obtain them would be far more conspicuous; and such efforts, if detected, would carry a high political cost for both supplier and recipient because for the first time they would be unambiguously military in intent. (p. 36)

CONCLUSION

While the global community has much to rejoice over today as the U.S. and the Commonwealth nations set about making drastic cuts in their nuclear arsenals, one should be circumspect in one's rejoicing. As previously mentioned, the nuclear firepower that remains in the world is still awesome. As long as current nuclear club members states continue to maintain their nuclear arsenals and as long as other nations pursue their own development of nuclear weapons, the world is not safe. The survivors of Hiroshima and Nagasaki know that. They remember only too well what it was like to suffer the results from a "small nuclear weapon":

The next day I woke up very early, and saw the city was completely flat! I found lots of sick and burned persons; they were alive and dead, their skin peeling off like old clothes. Some were crying "kill me, kill me," because of the pain. Half of the people in the city were dead, but the dead just lay there because no one could do anything...The survivors saw the end of the world in 1945 - the end of all human life. But I don't think people have learned that lesson from us yet. (Kanji Kuramoto quoted in Totten and Totten, 1984, p. 77, 79)

There is a desperate need to awaken the world once and for all to the perils of nuclear proliferation, and to prod the international community to address the problem *before* nuclear weapons are used against a people once again.

NOTES

1. The author wishes to sincerely thank Mr. Steven Dolley, Research Director at the Nuclear Control Institute, Dr. Art Hobson, Professor of Physics at the University of Arkansas at Fayetteville, and Dr. David Kreiger, President of the Nuclear Age Peace Foundation, for their critiques of this chapter as well as their valuable suggestions.

2. Correspondence with Steven Dolley, Research Director of the Nuclear Control Institute in Washington, D.C., July 6, 1993.

3. The author believes that the dangers posed by horizontal nuclear proliferation hold true despite the deep and welcome cutbacks in nuclear weapons currently being made by the U.S. and the new Commonwealth nations formed out the former USSR. First, it needs to be recognized that some experts have asserted that such cutbacks may take up to ten years to implement. Second, assuming that the agreement will be fulfilled (in light of the constant tremors and radical changes taking place in the former Soviet Union, this certainly is not a given), the "nuclear situation" still is not something that one can be sanguine about. This is true because even after the cutbacks have been made, both the United States and Russia will still have enough firepower to wipe humanity off the face of the globe several times over. It is also worth noting the caveat that Boris Yeltsin mentioned in a speech at the United Nations on January 31, 1992: if the new Commonwealth nations should fail, there is a better than even chance that the world could find itself facing a renewal of the Cold War and the nuclear saber-rattling of the "superpowers" once again. Third, the dangers posed by the nuclear arsenals of the other nuclear club members - China, France, and Great Britain - as well as those by undeclared nuclear states such as Israel [and formerly, South Africa] will remain.

REFERENCES

Ackerman, et al. (1985). *The Environmental Consequences of Nuclear War*. New York: John Wiley & Sons.

Albright, David (May 1993a). North Korea drops out. *Bulletin of the Atomic Scientists*, 49(4), 9-11.

Albright, David (May 1993b). South Africa comes clean. *Bulletin of the Atomic Scientists*, 49(4), 3-5.

Alperovitz, Gar (1965). *Atomic Diplomacy: Hiroshima and Potsdam*. New York: Simon and Schuster.

Amrine, Michael (1959). *The Great Decision: The Secret History of the Atomic Bomb*. New York: G. P. Putnam's.

Bernstein, Barton, J. (Ed.) (1974). *The Atomic Bomb: The Critical Issues*. Boston: Little, Brown.

Budiansky, Stephen, and Auster, Bruce B. (January 20, 1992). Tackling the new nuclear arithmetic. *U.S. News & World Report*, 112(2), 38.

Clines, Francis X. (December 2, 1991). 11 Soviet states form Commonwealth without clearly defining its powers," *New York Times*, pp. 1, 8.

Dennis, Jack (1984). Nuclear weapons proliferation. In Dennis, Jack (Ed.) *The Nuclear Almanac: Confronting the Atom in War and Peace*. Reading, MA: Addison-Wesley Publishing Co, pp. 345-365.

Donnelly, Warren H. (1990). Managing proliferation in the 1990s, "Something borrowed, something new..." *Social Education, 4*(3), 156-158.

Gay, William C., and Santoni, Ronald E. (1988). Philosophy and the contemporary faces of genocide: Multiple genocide and nuclear destruction. In Charny, Israel W. (Ed.), *Genocide: A Critical Bibliographic Review*. New York: Facts on File, pp. 172-190.

Herken, Greg (1982). *The Winning Weapon: The Atomic Bomb in the Cold War 1945-1950*. New York: Vintage.

Isaacs, John (1993). A bouquet for Bush. *Bulletin of the Atomic Scientists, 49*(2), 10, 46-47.

Kiselyov, Sergei (1993). Ukraine: Stuck with the goods. *Bulletin of the Atomic Scientists*, 49(2), 30-33.

Leventhal, Paul (1990). The nuclear power and nuclear weapons connection. *Social Education*, 54(3), 146-150.

Leventhal, Paul, and Alexander, Yonah (Eds.) (1987). *Preventing Nuclear Terrorism: The Report and Papers of the International Task Force on Prevention of Nuclear Terrorism*. Lexington, MA: Lexington Books.

Lifton, Robert Jay (Fall 1982). Beyond nuclear numbing. *Teachers College Record, 84*(1), 15-29.

Post, Tom, et al. (January 13, 1992). Selling nuclear missiles -- and minds. *Newsweek*, p. 29.

Schell, Jonathan (1984). *The Fate of the Earth*. New York: Alfred A. Knopf.

Sherwin, Martin J. (1977). *A World Destroyed: The Atomic Bomb and the Grand Alliance*. New York: Vintage.

Spector, Leonard S. (1990). The new nuclear nations. *Social Education, 54*(3), 143-145, 150.

Teller, Edward (1981). Hydrogen bomb. *Encyclopedia Americana, 14*:654-656. Danbury, CT: Grolier, Inc.

Totten, Sam, and Totten, Martha Wescoat (1984). *Facing the Danger: Interviews With 20 Anti-Nuclear Activists*. Trumansburg, NY: The Crossing Press.

Tsipis, Kosta (1984). The physics of nuclear weapons, pp. 195-204. In Dennis, Jack (Ed.), *The Nuclear Almanac: Confronting the Atom in War and Peace*. Reading, MA: Addison-Wesley Publishing Company.

Turco, R. P.; Toon, O. B.; Ackerman, T. P.; Pollack, J. B.; and Sagan, C. (1983). Nuclear winter: Global consequences of multiple explosions. *Science , 222*, 1283-1300.

Von Hippel, Frank, and Zamora-Collina, Tom (July/August 1993). Nuclear junkies: Testing, testing, 1, 2, 3, - Forever. *Bulletin of the Atomic Scientists, 49*(6), 28-32.

Wilmshurst, Michael J. (1990). The adequacy of IAEA safeguards for the 1990s. In Fry, M.P.; Keatinge, N.P.; and Rotblat, J. (Eds.), *Nuclear Non-Proliferation and the Non-Proliferation Treaty*. New York: Springer-Verlag, pp. 13-18.

The Working Group on Nuclear Explosives Control Policy (1984). *Stopping the Spread of Nuclear Weapons: Assessment of Current Policy - An Agenda for Action*. Washington, D.C.: Nuclear Control Institute.

Wurst, Jim (Winter 1990/91). The neglected link: Test ban & proliferation. *Nuclear Times, 8*(4), 44-45.

BIBLIOGRAPHY

Microfiche

U.S. Nuclear Non-Proliferation Policy, 1945-1991 (Available from Chadwyck-Healey Inc. 1101 King St., Alexandria, VA 22314).
  "Spanning the bombings of Hiroshima and Nagasaki through the recent IAEA inspections of Iraq's nuclear program, this collection offers researchers the most complete available set of primary source materials related to U.S. non-proliferation policy. Included are secret cables and memoranda, briefing papers, confidential letters, and more."

Journals

Bulletin of the Atomic Scientists, c/o Educational Foundation for Nuclear Science, 6042 S. Kimbark Ave., Chicago, IL. 60637.
     The journal is published monthly except February and August. It frequently contains articles, essays, and editorials on the issue of horizontal nuclear proliferation.

Articles, Essays, Monographs, Booklets, and Books

Albright, David, and Hibbs, Mark (January/February 1992). Iraq's bomb: Blueprints and artifacts. *The Bulletin of the Atomic Scientists, 48*(1), 30-40.
     Reports on the findings of the U.N. and International Atomic Energy Agency's inspectors concerning Iraq's nuclear weapons program.

Aspen Strategy Group (1990). *New Threats: Responding to the Proliferation of Nuclear, Chemical, and Delivery Capabilities in the Third World.* Lanham, MD: University Press of America. 286pp.
     The authors examine the dimensions and dangers inherent in the proliferation of nuclear, chemical and missile technology in the Third World, the strengths and weaknesses of the global regimes that have been developed and those that are currently being negotiated to control nuclear proliferation, and the need for specific regional and country policies to support the efforts of nonproliferation at the international level.

Barnaby, Frank (1989). *The Invisible Bomb: The Nuclear Arms Race in the Middle East.* London: I. B. Tauris & Co. 223 pp.
     This book is comprised of three parts and nine chapters: Part I. Israel (Israel's Nuclear Requirements, Israel's Nuclear Capability, and What Are Israel's Nuclear Weapons For?); Part II. The Position in the Region and the Islamic World (The Arab States, An Islamic Bomb, and Could the PLO Go Nuclear?), and Part III. The Issue of International Control (The International Non-Proliferation Regime, and Reducing the Importance of Nuclear Weapons in the Middle East). The information on Iraq is, of course, dated in light of the revelations in 1991 and 1992 concerning the extensiveness of Iraq's nuclear weapons program.

Beckman, Robert L. (1985). *Nuclear Non-Proliferation: Congress and the Control of Peaceful Nuclear Activities.* Boulder, CO and London: Westview Press. 446pp.
     This work examines the Nuclear Non-Proliferation Act of 1978 and other non-proliferation laws that sought to tighten U.S. nuclear export criteria and strengthen "the international non-proliferation regime." Beckman juxtaposes the efforts of nuclear managers with those of "nuclear reformers" who favor strong safeguards.

Beres, Louis Rene (Ed.) (1986). *Security or Armageddon: Israel's Nuclear Strategy.* Lexington, MA: Lexington Books. 242pp.
     The contributors to this volume explore Israel's nuclear capability as it relates to security issues. Among the twelve chapters are: "Going Public With the Bomb: The Israeli Calculus," "Deliberate Ambiguity: Evolution and Evaluation," "A Regional Non-Proliferation Treaty for the Middle East," "The Armageddon Factor: Terrorism and Israel's Nuclear Option," "Israel's Choice: Nuclear Weapons or International Law."

Beres, Louis Rene (1979). *Terrorism and Global Security: The Nuclear Threat.* Boulder, CO: Westview Press. 161pp.
An early and important book on the issue of nuclear terrorism. In Part 2, "Preventing Nuclear Terrorism," Beres discusses the issue of nonproliferation.

Boardman, Robert, and Keeley, James F. (Eds.) (1983). *Nuclear Exports & World Politics: Policy and Regime.* New York: St. Martin's Press. 256pp.
The authors in this collection of essays examine the trends that were evident in the early 1980s vis-a-vis the nuclear supply policies of six western nations: Australia, Canada, France, the United Kingdom, the United States, and West Germany.

Bolt, Richard (December 1988). Plutonium for all: Leaks in global safeguards. *Bulletin of the Atomic Scientists,* 44(10), 14-19.
A very disturbing article about the weaknesses and holes in the safeguards that are currently in place to prevent the diversion of plutonium. Bolt notes that "according to a confidential report of the International Atomic Energy Agency, the theft of a bomb's worth of material would have a one-in-twenty chance of going unnoticed - even if the Agency met its own inspection goals."

Boutwell, Jeffrey (1990). *The German Nuclear Dilemma.* Ithaca, NY: Cornell University Press. 247pp.
Boutwell examines West German's nuclear politics as developed and implemented under both Helmut Kohl and Helmut Schmidt, and speculates about the possible nuclear options a unified Germany might pursue.

Britto de Castro, Antonio Rubens; Majlis, Norberto; Rosa, Luiz Pinguelli; and de Souza Barros, Fernando (May 1989). Brazil's nuclear shakeup: Military still in control. *Bulletin of the Atomic Scientists,* 45(4), 22-25.
Discusses the Brazilian military's intent to develop a nuclear arsenal.

Bulletin of the Atomic Scientists (1990). *Special Issue: Haves vs. Have-Nots - Nonproliferation Treaty on the Line. 46*(5).
Includes such essays as: "Non-Proliferation Treaty: A Broken Record?"; "Nonproliferation's Divided Agenda"; "France and the Nuclear Free-for-All"; "It Ain't Broke -- Don't Fix It"; "Dump the Treaty"; "Eastern Europe After Pax Sovietica"; "Western Europe Needs Treaty"; "Disappointment in the Third World"; "The Nuclear Testing Threat"; and, "Nonproliferation Agenda: Beyond 1990."

Bulletin of the Atomic Scientists (1993). Special Issue: Nuclear Temptations. 49(5).
Includes a sample of the papers that were delivered at a symposium on the proliferation of nuclear weapons that was sponsored by the American Academy of Arts and Sciences. Includes such essays as: "A Proliferation Primer," "Europe's Leaky Borders," "Asian Ambitions, Rising Tensions," "An Equal-Opportunity NPT," and "Myth-making: The 'Islamic' Bomb."

Charles, Dan (April 1989). Exporting trouble - West Germany's freewheeling nuclear business. *The Bulletin of the Atomic Scientists,* 45(3), 21-27.
Examines how Germany's nuclear export policy virtually disregards the inextricable connections between nuclear power and nuclear weapons.

Dewitt, David B. (Ed.) (1987). *Nuclear Non-Proliferation and Global Security*. New York: St. Martin's Press. 283pp.

All but one of the original drafts of the sixteen papers herein were presented at the Conference on Global Security and the Future of the Non-Proliferation Treaty: A Time for Reassessment. The volume is divided into three parts: I. Global Security and the Treaty on the Non-Proliferation of Nuclear Weapons: The Agenda; II. Nuclear Non-Proliferation Policies and Perspectives; and, III. The Treaty on the Non-Proliferation of Nuclear Weapons in Review.

Doble, John (1986). *The Spread of Nuclear Weapons: The Public's View*. Washington, D.C.: Roosevelt Center for American Policy Studies. 24pp.

A sample assessment ("derived from six focus group discussions") of U. S. citizens' views vis-a-vis the horizontal proliferation of nuclear weapons.

Ehteshami, Anoushiravan (1989). *Nuclearisation of the Middle East*. London: Brassey's. 201 pp.

The author presents a scenario of a future Middle East which is based on the assumption of the development of nuclear weapons by various states in that region. In developing it, he explores the various factors (ethnic, national, religious, changing alliances) that could contribute to such a scenario.

Eisenhower, Dwight D. (1953). *Atomic Power for Peace*. Washington, D. C. : U.S. Government Printing Office. 14pp.

This is the address (which has become known as the "Atoms for Peace Speech") President Eisenhower gave before the General Assembly of the United Nations on December 8, 1953. It is herein that Eisenhower proposed the need for nuclear nations to share "peaceful power from atomic energy" with other nations.

Feiveson, Harold A.; von Hippel, Frank; and Albright, David (March 1986). Breaking the fuel/weapons connection. *Bulletin of the Atomic Scientists, 42*(3), 26-31.

The authors argue that by halting both the military and civilian production of weapons-usable material, the result could be the halt of the spread of nuclear weapons.

Feldman, Shai (1982). *Israeli Nuclear Deterrence: A Strategy for the 1980s*. New York: Columbia University Press. 310pp.

In this volume, Feldman "examines the risks and benefits that may be involved in a possible shift of emphasis in Israel's political-military strategy: from one dominated by principles of conventional defense-offense to one of overt nuclear deterrence."

Fieldhouse, Richard (May 1991). China's mixed signals on nuclear weapons. *Bulletin of the Atomic Scientists, 47*(4), 37-42.

A discussion of the make-up of China's nuclear arsenal as well as its policy and actions vis-a-vis horizontal nuclear proliferation.

Findlay, Trevor (1990). *Nuclear Dynamite: The Peaceful Nuclear Explosions Fiasco*. Sydney, Australia: Brassey's Australia. 339pp.

Findlay examines the issue of "peaceful nuclear explosions," and the use of such explosions by various countries (the U.S., Russia, Argentina, Australia, Brazil, and India). The primary purpose of the work is to show the deceit and folly behind the notion of peaceful nuclear explosions, and the need for a comprehensive test ban.

Fischer, David A.V. (1987). *The International Non-Proliferation Regime*. New York: United Nations. 81pp.
Provides a succinct but fairly detailed overview of the efforts to prevent the horizontal proliferation of nuclear weapons.

Fischer, David, and Szasz, Paul (1985). *Safeguarding the Atom: A Critical Appraisal*. London and Philadelphia: Taylor and Francis. 243pp.
A detailed examination of the types of international safeguards in place to prevent the diversion of nuclear material from so-called peaceful activities to the development of nuclear weapons. The authors conclude that "Technical improvement of safeguards is feasible, but their main limitations and weaknesses are political not technical."

Florini, Ann (1983). *Nuclear Proliferation: A Citizen's Guide to Policy Choices*. New York: United Nations Association of the United States of America. 48pp.
The primary purpose of the booklet was to assist local chapters of UNA and other community members to examine the issue of horizontal proliferation.

Fry, M. P.; Keatinge, N. P.; and Rotblat, J. (Eds.) (1990). *Nuclear Non-Proliferation and the Non-Proliferation Treaty*. New York: Springer-Verlag. 198pp.
This volume is comprised of four main parts and twenty essays. The four parts are: Part I. Nuclear Proliferation: Technical and Economic Aspects; Part II. Nuclear Proliferation: Political Priorities; Part III. Nuclear Proliferation and Soviet-American Relations; and Part IV. Priorities for Pursuing the Objectives of Article VI of the NPT. While Part III is dated, the other pieces in the volume address a host of key issues vis-a-vis the problem of nonproliferation in the 1990s.

Goldblat, Jozef (1985). *Nuclear Non-Proliferation: A Guide to the Debate*. London: Taylor & Francis. 95pp.
This book summarizes the findings of a study on the non-proliferation policies of fifteen countries (Argentina, Brazil, Canada, Egypt, France, India, Israel, Pakistan, South Africa, South Korea, Spain, Sweden, Switzerland, and Taiwan) that were originally presented in *Non-Proliferation: The Why and Wherefore* edited by Goldblat.

Goldblat, Jozef (Ed.) (1985). *Non-Proliferation: The Why and the Wherefore*. London and Philadelphia: Taylor & Francis. 343pp.
The authors "examine the reasons why the ruling elites" in various countries (e.g., China, France, Argentina, Brazil, India, Israel, Pakistan, South Africa) "have been in favor of acquiring nuclear weapons or at least of keeping open the option to do so."

Goldman, Joe (July/August 1990). U.S. endorses Menem's nuclear plans. *Bulletin of the Atomic Scientists, 46*(6), 9-10.
Discusses how the United States Ambassador at Large, Richard Kennedy, endorsed Argentina's so-called "nuclear nonproliferation credentials" despite the fact that Argentina still has not ratified the Non-Proliferation Treaty or the Treaty of Tlatelolco.

Graham, Thomas W., and Evers, Ridgely, C. (Eds.) (1978). *Bibliography: Nuclear Proliferation*. Washington, D.C.: U.S. Government Printing Office. 159pp.
Includes annotations of books, articles in periodicals, U.S. government documents, and other materials.

Greenwood, Ted; Feiveson, Harold A.; and Taylor, Theodore B. (1977). *Nuclear Proliferation: Motivations, Capabilities, and Strategies for Control.* New York: McGraw-Hill Book Co. 210pp.
An early and important work, this volume is comprised of two major parts: "Discouraging Proliferation in the Next Decade" by Greenwood, and "Alternative Strategies for International Control of Nuclear Power" by Feiveson and Taylor.

Hersh, Seymour M. (1991). *The Samson Option: Israel's Nuclear Arsenal and American Foreign Policy.* New York: Random House. 354pp.
A controversial volume in which Hersh, an investigative reporter, discusses both Israel's nuclear weapons program as well as its nuclear strategic plans.

Hewlett, Richard, and Holl, Jack M. (1989). *Atoms for Peace and War, 1953-1961: Eisenhower and the Atomic Energy Commission.* Los Angeles and Berkeley: University of California Press. 696pp.
An indepth examination of the nuclear policies of the Eisenhower Administration, particularly its "atoms for peace" program.

Hoenig, Milton M. (1991). Eliminating Bomb-Grade Uranium from Research Reactors. Washington, D. C. : Nuclear Control Institute. 8pp.
In this paper, which was published as an individual paper in a series, Hoenig argues that certain nuclear weapons materials - highly-enriched uranium and plutonium - should be banned universally.

Holdren, John P. (1983). Nuclear power and nuclear weapons: The connection is dangerous. *Bulletin of the Atomic Scientists, 39*(1), 40-45.
A measured discussion that examines such issues as the motivations and barriers to acquiring nuclear weapons, technological and political issues, a short history of nuclear power-related proliferation, and prospects for further proliferation.

Jain, J.P. (1974). *Nuclear India.* New Delhi: Radiant Publishers. 2 volumes. Volume 1 - 200pp; Volume 2 - 440pp.
Volume one examines India's role in the International Atomic Energy Agency (IAEA) as well as its attitudes towards the IAEA. Concomitantly, it discusses the significance and ramifications of India's so-called "peaceful nuclear explosion." Volume 2 consists of 187 documents germane to the issues discussed in Volume 1.

Joeck, Neil (1986). *Strategic Consequences of Nuclear Proliferation in South Asia.* London: Frank Cass. 109pp.
The key focus of this volume is on "the consequences for particular states should Indian and Pakistan decide to deploy nuclear weapons."

Jones, Rodney W. (Ed.) (1984). *Small Nuclear Forces and U. S. Security Policy: Threats and Potential Conflicts in the Middle East and South Asia.* Lexington, MA: D. C. Heath and Co. 289pp.
The contributors examine the "potential impact of small nuclear forces in the Middle East and South Asia on U.S. security policy, and address "... the potential dangers of not arresting the development of small nuclear force capabilities."

Kapur, Ashok (1987). *Pakistan's Nuclear Development.* New York: Croom Helm. 258pp.
The author provides a historical overview of Pakistan's "nuclear history."

Karp, Regina Cowen (1991). *Security Without Nuclear Weapons? Different Perspectives on National Security*. New York: Oxford University Press. 412pp.
    Karp traces the development of security in the nuclear age through case studies of countries that have nuclear weapons as well as those that do not.

Kessler, Richard (May 1989). Peronists seek "nuclear greatness." *Bulletin of the Atomic Scientists*, 45(4), 13-15.
    Discusses Argentina's ultra nationalists' headlong effort to establish a nuclear fuel cycle that is totally independent of outside suppliers or control.

Leventhal, Paul (1991). *Latent and Blatant Proliferation: Does the NPT Work Against Either?* Washington, D. C.: Nuclear Control Institute. 8pp.
    In this paper, which was published as an individual paper in a series, Leventhal outlines the current weaknesses of the Non-Proliferation Treaty, and suggests ways it can immediately be strengthened.

Leventhal, Paul, and Alexander, Yonah (Eds.) (1987). *Preventing Nuclear Terrorism: The Report and Papers of the International Task Force on Prevention and Nuclear Terrorism*. Lexington, MA: Lexington Books. 472pp.
    A major work on the issue of nuclear terrorism, this volume includes numerous chapters that address various issues vis-a-vis horizontal nuclear proliferation (e.g., "Clandestine Nuclear Trade and the Threat of Nuclear Terrorism," "International Safeguards and Nuclear Terrorism," "Civilian Inventories of Plutonium and Highly Enriched Uranium," and "The Front End of the Nuclear Fuel Cycle: Options to Reduce the Risks of Terrorism and Proliferation").

Lewis, John Wilson, and Litai, Xue (1988). *China Builds the Bomb*. Stanford, CA: Stanford University Press. 329pp.
    A detailed and well researched examination of why (including China's sense of a nuclear threat from the United States and the deterioration of its relationship with the Soviet Union) and how China built its first atomic bomb and subsequent nuclear arsenal (including thermonuclear weapons).

Library of Congress, Arms Control and Disarmament Bibliography Section (Ed.) (Winter 1964-Spring 1973). *Arms Control & Disarmament: A Quarterly Bibliography with Abstracts and Annotations*. Volumes 1-9. Washington, D.C.: U. S. Government Printing Office.
    Each of these quarterly issues contains abstracts and annotations of literature in the area of arms control (including the issue of horizontal nuclear proliferation) in English, French, and German. Sources surveyed include trade books, monographs, selected government publications, publications of national and international organizations and societies, and approximately 1,200 periodicals.

Lovins, Amory B. (1977). *Soft Energy Paths: Toward A Durable Peace*. San Francisco: Friends of the Earth. 231pp.
    An important and early work by Lovins wherein he delineates both the need for and the methods on how to move from hard energy paths (coal, oil, gas, and nuclear fission) to soft energy paths (renewables such as solar, wind, and biomass conversion) in order to provide a safe and constant supply of energy for everyone across the globe. Such a policy would avoid contributing to the spread of nuclear technology which can lead to the development of nuclear weapons by non-nuclear states.

Lovins, Amory B., and Lovins, L. Hunter (1980). *Energy/War: Breaking the Nuclear Link*. San Francisco: Friends of the Earth. 161pp.

An outstanding book that at the outset discusses the disingenuous notion that there are two atoms - the peaceful atom and the military atom. The authors also discuss the irrelevance of nuclear power, the fatuity of U.S. nuclear policies (tellingly, the argument is still as relevant today as it was in 1980 when this volume was published), methods for implementing non-nuclear futures, the problem with the spread of nuclear technology, and a call for "rethinking the NPT Article IV obligation" (e.g., "the transfer of civilian nuclear technology by advanced countries to less advanced countries").

Lovins, Amory B.; Lovins, L. Hunter; and Ross, Leonard (Summer 1980). Nuclear power and nuclear bombs. *Foreign Affairs, 58*(5), 1137-1177.

An essay whose premise is that "the nuclear proliferation problem, as posed by "nuclear experts and policymakers, is insoluble." The authors argue that nuclear power is "the main driving force behind proliferation"; and that as long as it is provided to countries that desire it, the problem of horizontal proliferation will not only remain but increase in intensity. They go on to argue that nuclear power could be phased out and replaced with cleaner, safer energy sources which do not lend themselves to the proliferation of nuclear weapons.

Meyers, Stephen M. (1984). *The Dynamics of Nuclear Proliferation*. Chicago: The University of Chicago Press. 229pp.

Meyers examines the various capabilities and incentives that motivate nations to make the decision to develop nuclear arsenals, including the "technological" and "motivational" bases of the nuclear proliferation process.

Molander, Roger, and Nichols, Robbie (1985). *Who Will Stop the Bomb?: A Primer on Nuclear Proliferation*. New York: Facts on File. 150pp.]

A primer on nuclear proliferation for the "average" citizen.

Moore, J.D.L. (1987). *South Africa and Nuclear Proliferation*. New York: St. Martin's Press. 260pp.

Moore examines the nuclear capabilities and intentions of South Africa vis-a-vis the context of international proliferation policies. In doing so, he argues that South Africa is definitely capable of producing nuclear weapons and speculates on the numbers it could produce.

Muller, Harald (Ed.) (1987). *A European Non-Proliferation Policy: Prospects and Problems*. Oxford, England: Clarendon Press. 416 pp.

Examines the non-proliferation policies of various countries in Europe, the opportunities and limits of European cooperation in the area of non-proliferation, and the scope of influence that western European countries could possibly have on nuclear threshold countries (e.g., India, Pakistan, Iran, Libya, Brazil, Argentina, etc.).

Norris, Robert S., and Arkin, William M. (November 1991). Where the weapons are. *Bulletin of the Atomic Scientists, 47*(9), 48-49.

Addresses the location and number of nuclear weapons throughout the various republics of the Soviet Union.

O'Heffernan, Patrick; Lovins, Amory B.; and Lovins, L. Hunter (1983). *The First Nuclear World War: A Strategy for Preventing Nuclear Wars and the Spread of Nuclear Weapons*. New York: William Morrow and Co. 444pp.
   In this fascinating volume, the authors explore the likelihood of Third World countries "going nuclear" (e.g., obtaining nuclear weapons) and the ramifications if they succeed in doing so (e.g., the possibility of terrorists using nuclear weapons; a regional nuclear war in the Middle East, South Africa, or Latin America; etc.). Its last section, "The Soft Path to Peace," provides valuable insights vis-a-vis solving the aforementioned problems -- primary among the solutions is the development of "soft energy strategies."

Patterson, Walter C. (1984). *The Plutonium Business and the Spread of the Bomb*. San Francisco: Sierra Club Books. 272pp.
   Patterson provides a historical overview of the development and uses of plutonium from 1940 through the mid-1980s. He discusses the dangers inherent in the global spread of plutonium (which can be separated from spent fuel in civil nuclear power plants and used in nuclear weapons development) and a plutonium economy (the primary one being its accessibility for the development of nuclear weapons by anyone who has the commitment, desire, know-how, or technology).

Perlmutter, Amos; Handel, Michael; and Bar-Joseph, Uri (1982). *Two Minutes Over Baghdad*. London: Vallentine, Mitchell, & Co. 191pp.
   An account of the events leading up to and resulting in the Israeli bombing of the Osriak Iraqi nuclear reactor on June 7, 1981.

Pilat, Joseph F., and Pendley, Robert E. (Eds.) (1990). *Beyond 1995: The Future of the NPT Regime*. New York: Plenum Publishing. 276pp.
   The collective chapters in this work basically constitute a panegyric regarding the value of the Treaty on the Nonproliferation of Nuclear Weapons and argue in favor of its continuance when it comes up for reconsideration in 1995.

Potter, William C. (Ed.) (1990). *International Nuclear Trade and Nonproliferation: The Challenge of the Energy Suppliers*. Lexington, MA: Lexington Books. 426pp.
   Numerous experts examine key issues vis-a-vis horizontal nuclear proliferation: the ever-increasing capacity of states to obtain nuclear materials through trade, which they can ultimately use to develop nuclear weapons; the inadequacy of international agreements to control the exports of nuclear materials; and, a review of policy suggestions.

Ramberg, Bennet (1986). *Global Nuclear Energy Risks: The Search for Preventive Medicine*. Boulder, CO and London: Westview Press. 128pp.
   A critique of policies in place to prevent horizontal nuclear proliferation, and suggestions on how to strengthen such efforts.

Robles, Alfonso Garcia (1979). *The Latin American Nuclear-Weapon-Free-Zone*. Muscatine, IA: The Stanley Foundation. 31pp.
   A discussion of the process that led to the Tlatelolco Treaty, also known as the Treaty for the Prohibition of Nuclear Weapons in Latin America.

Scheinman, Lawrence (1987). *The International Atomic Energy Agency and World Nuclear Order*. Washington, D.C.: Resources for the Future. 336pp.

Provides a detailed historical overview of nuclear non-proliferation issues and the role of the IAEA, whose job it is to insure compliance with the nonproliferation treaty. Scheinman is very critical of what he calls the "implicit" politicization of the IAEA, especially in its attempt to find a balance between implementing safeguards and providing technical assistance to developing nations.

Scherr, Jacob, and Stoel, Thomas (Summer 1979). Atoms for peace? Controlling the spread of nuclear weapons. *Amicus, 1*(1), 18-64.
Delineates how the U.S.'s "Atoms for Peace" program failed in its intention to maintain worldwide control over peaceful uses of nuclear energy by sharing it.

Schiff, Benjamin N. (1983). *International Nuclear Technology Transfer: Dilemmas of Dissemination and Control.* Totowa, NJ: Rowman & Allanheld, Publishers. 226pp.
A detailed examination of the issue of nuclear technology transfer.

Simpson, John (Ed.) (1987). *Nuclear Non-Proliferation: An Agenda for the 1990s.* Cambridge, MA: Cambridge University Press. 237pp.
This collection of essays examine a whole host of non-proliferation issues as they relate to the 1990s: nuclear trade relations, new technologies and the nuclear non-proliferation regime, options for strengthening the non-proliferation regime in the 1990s, amending the Nuclear Non-Proliferation Treaty and methods for enhancing the Regime, and the pros and cons of extending the Nuclear Non-Proliferation Regime beyond 1995.

Spector, Leonard (1987). *Going Nuclear.* Cambridge, MA: Ballinger. 379pp.
The third in a series on the status of horizontal nuclear proliferation across the globe, this volume examines so-called "nuclear threshold states" (Israel, India, South Africa, and Pakistan), and the state of affairs vis-a-vis horizontal nuclear proliferation in other parts of the world (e.g., Libya, Iraq, Iran, Argentina, and Brazil). Spector cogently delineates how legally acquired nuclear technology (including nuclear power plants) are the key to the development of nuclear weapons programs.

Spector, Leonard S. (1985). *The New Nuclear Nations.* New York: Random House. 367pp.
This volume is the second annual report on horizontal nuclear proliferation by Spector. It not only provides detailed updated information on the status of emerging nuclear states originally highlighted in volume one (*Nuclear Proliferation Today*) but adds a chapter on South Africa and a chapter on the facets of clandestine nuclear trade.

Spector, Leonard S. (1984). *Nuclear Proliferation Today.* Cambridge, MA: Ballinger Publishing Co. 478 pp.
The first in a series of annual reports on nuclear proliferation issued by the Carnegie Endowment for International Peace, this volume provides a detailed and comprehensive country-by-country examination of nations that were then (in the early 1980s) considered to be on the nuclear threshold.

Spector, Leonard S. (1988). *The Undeclared Bomb: The Spread of Nuclear Weapons 1987-1988.* Cambridge, MA: Ballinger Publishing Co. 320pp.
The fourth volume in Spector's annual series on the status of horizontal proliferation of nuclear weapons across the globe, it highlights key developments in states with

emerging nuclear capabilities. In doing so, he discusses the use of freely offered - or smuggled - Western and Soviet rocket technology to assist other nations in establishing nuclear forces, the growing technological breakthroughs (particularly in the area of nuclear delivery systems), violations of non-proliferation promises, and the problem of new nuclear suppliers in the international marketplace.

Spector, Leonard S., with Smith, Jacqueline R. (1990). *Nuclear Ambitions: The Spread of Nuclear Weapons 1989-1990.* Boulder, CO: Westview Press. 450pp.
Nuclear Ambitions is the fifth of five volumes in a series on the spread of nuclear weapons. Like the other volumes, this one "surveys the status of nuclear developments in each of the emerging nuclear states in a country-by-country format." In doing so, it assesses the increasing threat of nuclear conflict in the Third World and analyses key long-term trends.

Stockholm International Peace Research Institute (1980). *The NPT: The Main Political Barrier to Nuclear Weapons Proliferation.* London: Taylor and Francis. 66pp.
An examination of the major problems connected with the Non-Proliferation Treaty (NPT), and suggestions on how to strengthen the NPT. Still relevant today.

Sweet, William (1988). *The Nuclear Age: Atomic Energy, Proliferation and the Arms Race.* Washington, D.C.: Congressional Quarterly, Inc. 340pp.
At the outset Sweet examines the connection between nuclear power and nuclear weapons. He then argues that the rate of acquisition of nuclear technologies like fuel reprocessing by non-nuclear nations will have "an important bearing on whether the spread of atomic weapons can be stopped and even reversed or only slowed."

Synder, Jed C., and Wells, Samuel F. (Eds.) (1985). *Limiting Nuclear Proliferation.* Cambridge, MA: Ballinger Publishing Co. 363 pp.
The essays in this volume focus on the so-called "threshold states" (or those countries on the verge of developing nuclear weapons) and on possible constraints that could be used to dissuade them from going "nuclear."

Takagi, Junzaburo, and Nishio, Baku (October 1990). Japan's fake plutonium storage. *Bulletin of the Atomic Scientists, 46*(8), 34-38.
Discusses and criticizes Japan's decision to ship reprocessed plutonium from France and Britain to Japan. The authors also discuss the dangers inherent in Japan's "buying" into a "plutonium economy."

Toscano, Louis (1990). *Triple Cross: Israel, the Atomic Bomb and the Man Who Spilled the Secret.* New York: A Birch Lane Press Book. 321pp.
A "journalistic" account of the so-called Mordechai Vanunu affair. Vanunu, an Israeli who worked as a control room technician at the Dimona nuclear research center, disclosed information to the world press which indicated that the Israelis have a nuclear arsenal of over 200 nuclear weapons.

Totten, Samuel, and Kleg, Milton (Eds.) (1990). *Special Issue: Nuclear Proliferation: Political Issues. Social Education, 54*(3).
This special issue of *Social Education* includes pieces on teaching about horizontal nuclear proliferation, the defacto and emerging nuclear nations, the nuclear power/nuclear weapons connection, environmental hazards of nuclear arms proliferation, and managing/preventing proliferation.

United Nations (1981). *South Africa's Plan and Capability in the Nuclear Field*. New York: United Nations Publications. 40pp.
A speculative report by the United Nations on South Africa's possible nuclear program. The report was initiated due to reports that South Africa was constructing a possible nuclear test site in the Kalahari Desert in 1977 and the suspicion that South Africa may have conducted a nuclear bomb test in the Indian Ocean in 1979.

United Nations (1982). *Study on Israeli Nuclear Armament*. New York: United Nations Publications. 22pp.
Concerned about the possibility of the development of a nuclear arsenal by the Israelis, the General Assembly of the United Nations commissioned this study. The report examines Israel's nuclear development, Israel's nuclear weapons potential, factors affecting Israel's nuclear policy, and international reports concerning Israeli nuclear armament.

United Nations (1991). *Towards a Nuclear-Weapons-Free Zone in the Middle East*. New York: United Nations Publications. 88pp.
Discusses verifiable measures that could possibly facilitate the establishment of a nuclear-weapons-free zone in the Middle East.

U.S. Congress, Office of Technology Assessment (1977). *Nuclear Proliferation and Safeguards*. Washington, D.C.: U.S. Government Printing Office. 270 pp.
Provides a survey of key technical issues. Includes valuable tables and charts.

U.S. Congress. Senate. Committee on Foreign Relations (1955). *Atoms for Peace Manual: A Compilation of Official Materials on International Cooperation for Peaceful Uses of Atomic Energy - December 1953-July 1955*. Washington, D.C.: U.S. Government Printing Office. 615pp.
Provides valuable insights into the focus of the United States so-called "atoms for peace" program whose primary goal was to "sell" the public on the usefulness of the atom and to spread the wealth of the "peaceful" atom to other nations.

United States Congressional Research Service (1980). *Reader on Nuclear Proliferation*. Washington, D.C.: U.S. Government Printing Office. 344pp.
Prepared for use by the U.S. Senate's Subcommittee on Energy and Nuclear Proliferation, this reader is comprised of 25 articles that express a wide-range of views on an eclectic array of issues regarding nuclear proliferation.

United States Senate, Committee on Foreign Affairs (1988). *Nuclear Proliferation in South Asia: Containing the Threat*. Washington, D.C.: U.S. Government Printing Office. 42pp.
This report "evaluates the dynamics of the South Asia nuclear programs [in India and Pakistan], the impact of U.S. nonproliferation policies, and regional perspectives on nuclear weapons issues."

United States Senate, Committee on Government Operations (1975). *Peaceful Nuclear Exports and Weapons Proliferation*. Washington, D.C.: U.S. Government Printing Office. 1335pp.
Includes "a selected but comprehensive review of the legal, technical and policy aspects of the close relationship [that] exists between the export of peaceful nuclear technology and the proliferation of nuclear weapons." It is comprised of 112 essays,

articles, and speeches on such issues as nuclear terrorism, nuclear theft, the non-proliferation treaty of nuclear weapons, the spread of nuclear materials, and nuclear safeguards.

United States Senate, Committee on Governmental Affairs (1978). *Reader on Nuclear Nonproliferation*. Washington, D.C.: U.S. Government Printing Office. 504pp.
This volume is comprised of 43 selected readings on the issue of horizontal nuclear proliferation. All but two of them were written and published in the years 1976-1977.

Weiss, Leonard (1991). Tighten up on nuclear cheaters. *Bulletin of the Atomic Scientists, 47*(4), 11-12.
Argues that Iraq pursued the development of nuclear weapons for years without ever violating the Non-Proliferation Treaty (NPT) or the IAEA's safeguards agreements. Weiss issues a call for strengthening both the NPT and the policies of the IAEA.

Weissman, Steve, and Krosney, Herbert (1981). *The Islamic Bomb: The Nuclear Threat to Israel and the Middle East*. New York: Times Books. 339pp.
In this journalistic account, the authors delineate why and how various Middle Eastern and South Asian countries (Iraq, Israel, Libya, Pakistan, and India) have aggressively sought nuclear technology, materials, and know-how in order to develop their own nuclear arsenals. In doing so, the authors clearly detail the weaknesses inherent in the Non-Proliferation Treaty and other so-called safeguards.

Williams, Robert C., and Cantelon, Philip L. (Eds.) (1984). *The American Atom: A Documentary History of Nuclear Policies from the Discovery of Fission to the Present 1939-1984*. Philadelphia, PA: University of Pennsylvania Press. 333pp.
This volume includes copies of numerous key reports, addresses, and treaties that are germane to the issue of horizontal nuclear proliferation. Among these are: The MacMahon Bill (Atomic Energy Act of 1946); The Baruch Plan (a plan put forth by the U.S. concerning the control of nuclear materials); President Eisenhower's "Atoms for Peace" address; and the "Treaty on the Nonproliferation of Nuclear Weapons."

Williams, Robert H., and Feiveson, Harold A. (July/August 1990). Diversion-resistance criteria for future nuclear power. *Energy Policy, 18*(6), 543-549.
The authors argue that "in order for nuclear power to make a major contribution to global energy, it would have to be made not only safe and cost effective but also highly diversion-resistant" so that the technology and nuclear materials could not be used for nuclear weapons development.

Wohlstetter, Albert (1977). *Swords from Ploughshares: The Military Potential of Civilian Nuclear Energy*. Chicago: University of Chicago Press. 229pp.
Considered a landmark study, this is a detailed analysis of the connections between civil nuclear technology and the proliferation of nuclear weapons as well as the forces that drive proliferation. It examines both the historical and political dimensions of proliferation as they relate to the economic and military picture.

PART VI
Professional Study of
Genocide and Its Prevention

11

Non-Governmental Organizations Working on the Issue of Genocide

Samuel Totten

Humanity's record in preventing genocide has been nothing short of abysmal. Ample evidence of that is the fact that in the twentieth century alone, it is estimated that over 50 million people have perished in genocidal acts, and that number is probably low. In fact, Rummel (1990) estimates that since 1900 governments are responsible for the genocide and mass murder - "independent of war and other kinds of conflict" - of 119,400,00 people (p. xi). In a recent study of genocide and politicide (killing members of political groups), Harff and Gurr (1988) assert that since 1945 "between seven and sixteen million people" perished (p. 359).

One would have thought that following the horror of the Holocaust, the international community would not only have made a concerted effort to develop efficacious means and methods to detect ominous signs of potential genocidal occurrences, but also mustered the will and means to intervene and/or prevent genocide from taking place.

That hope obviously has not come to fruition, but it is noteworthy that over the past decade a good number of individuals and organizations outside of government have committed their time and energy to working on these and related issues. More specifically, they have been engaged in work on one or more of the following fronts: the study of the preconditions and patterns of genocide, conflict resolution in nations and regions where various preconditions have occurred, the development of models and components for a genocide early warning system, and educational efforts. This essay and the subsequent bibliography will highlight some of the key organizations working in these areas.

THE STATE OF AFFAIRS TODAY

Human Rights Organizations

Prior to 1945, there was a limited number of organizations working for the protection of international human rights, e.g.: the Anti-Slavery Society (London); the International Committee of the Red Cross (Geneva); the Ligue francaise pour la defense des droits de l'homme et du citoyen (Paris); and the International League for Human Rights (New York) (Wiseberg and Scoble, 1981, p. 229); and, with few exceptions during the Holocaust years, there were virtually no organizations that exclusively focused on the issue of genocide. Since the founding of the United Nations and the ratification of the U.N. Universal Declaration of Human Rights, the world has seen a burgeoning of non-governmental human rights organizations. In the early 1980s, *Human Rights Internet* identified close to 2,000 nongovernmental organizations working on various issues vis-a-vis the protection of international human rights (Wiseberg and Scoble, 1982).

As Kuper (1985) has noted:

> The proliferation of organizations has been associated with considerable diversification. Some organizations, such as the scientific and professional ones, are highly specialized in terms of their objectives or of their constituencies. Others have broad objectives and a grass-roots constituency. Many are transnational, maintaining contact with other bodies in the local areas of their branches, as well as internationally. And recently we have seen the establishment of national networks of associations. These provide a structural base for coordinated national campaigns and for effective liaison with organizations and networks in other countries. There are all the indications of the growth of a vigorous international human rights association parallel to that of the United Nations (pp. 217-218).

The work of such human rights organizations is, indeed, eclectic. Depending on the focus of the organization, work may include: research; archival development and collection; publishing reports, essays, journals, books; organizing conferences; serving as observers at trials of political prisoners and others; serving as advisors to governments and non-governmental organizations; organizing letter writing campaigns on behalf of those being deprived of their rights; conducting urgent action campaigns, e.g., an organization detects a situation or conflict that either has resulted in or is on the verge of becoming violent and contacts its members to immediately send letters to state and international officials and bodies in habitually deprive their citizens of their human rights by pushing for withdrawal of economic, military and/or diplomatic support they receive; conducting field missions in order to collect data on human rights abuses; serving as liaisons for groups that are endangered and/or lacking their own powerbase; working to strengthen conventions and laws for the protection of human rights; working to develop more effective means in regard to intervention and prevention measures vis-a-vis human rights infractions; attempting to strengthen current and/or develop new legal machinery for bringing perpetrators of human rights infractions to trial; and, working to actually bring perpetrators to trial.

The vast majority of these human rights organizations have *not* specifically worked on the issue of genocide, but they often key in on various human rights wrongs including but not limited to denial of civil rights, arrest without trial, torture, extrajudicial killings, and "disappearances" that can, under certain circumstances, constitute preconditions to a genocidal occurrence. Such work is not only crucial in protecting people's rights, but also in bringing the issue of human rights to the attention of the global community.

Organizations Concerned with Indigenous Peoples

Throughout this period there are a number of organizations whose primary concern has been the plight of indigenous peoples across the globe and these *have* focused on the issues of ethnocide and genocide. Among the major organizations working on this front are: Cultural Survival (Cambridge, MA); Gesellschaft für Bedrohte Volker (Goettingen, Germany); the International Work Group for Indigenous Affairs (Denmark); and, Survival International (London and Washington, D.C.). A major function of many of these groups is that they specifically serve as advocates for people who find themselves voiceless and/or powerless against governments or business interests that encroach upon their land, threaten their way of life, and/or endanger their lives. These organizations also assist indigenous groups that are already active on their own behalf. In doing so, they conduct research into the problems faced by indigenous peoples, serve as advocates for the groups in international and national meetings and governmental and nongovernmental forums, and educate the general public about the fate of indigenous peoples. In light of the fact that the United Nations Genocide Convention is so weak and that to date the United Nations and member states have chosen *not* to strengthen the Convention and/or act upon its mandate to prosecute genociders, the work of such organizations is crucial to the welfare of many indigenous peoples across the globe (Kuper, 1985; Whitaker, 1985). The efforts of both groups of non-governmental organizations (those whose focus is international human rights and those whose focus is the plight of indigenous peoples) have been impressive. Kuper (1985) has commented:

> Given the poor record of intergovernmental organizations and of states in the punishment of genocide and mass murder and the paucity of formal interstate complaints, the major initiative rests with individuals and nongovernmental organizations. And they have been taking this initiative with increasing impact on international public opinion and on intergovernmental organizations, as notably in the campaigns against disappearances and torture. They act in both the international and domestic spheres. In the international organizations they are the main source of charges of gross violations of human rights. Nongovernmental organizations, in particular, carry out the important task of investigating and publishing the facts, and the reports of such bodies as Amnesty International have high credibility in international circles. Domestically, these organizations, and individuals, may be able to exert pressure on their own governments to take some action against offending states by diplomacy and by the more positive restraints of trade sanctions and the denial of aid. They themselves may organize boycotts and protests (p. 188).

Organizations Devoted to the Holocaust and/or Genocide

Since the end of World War II, and particularly since the early 1970s, there also has been a proliferation of organizations whose primary focus is the Holocaust. These organizations have been founded by both religious as well as secular groups. The primary focus of most of them has been remembrance and education. A smaller number focus on research. There are literally hundreds of such organizations located across the globe.

It has only been fairly recently that various organizations across the globe have begun to focus their attention on the specific issue of genocide. In one regard, this is not surprising; it is, in matter of fact, a statement that *the field of genocide studies is essentially relatively new*. Among the most active organizations working in this field today are the following: Gesellschaft Für Bedrohte Voelker (Society for Threatened Peoples) (Goettingen, Germany); the Institute on the Holocaust and Genocide (Jerusalem); the Institute for the Study of Genocide (New York City); International Alert (London); the Montreal Institute for Genocide Studies (Montreal); and the Cambodia Documentation Commission (New York City).

GESELLSCHAFT FÜR BEDROHTE VOELKER (SOCIETY FOR THREATENED PEOPLES), GERMANY

Gesellschaft für Bedrohte Voelker (Society for Threatened Peoples) was established in 1970. It is a membership organization with about 5000 members. Its main mandate is "at the least, to provide information about genocide; and possibly, help to avoid it." It conducts research into the suppression of minority groups' rights and cases of genocide, and disseminates its findings through its journal *Pogrom* and other publications.

INSTITUTE ON THE HOLOCAUST AND GENOCIDE, JERUSALEM

The Institute on the Holocaust and Genocide in Jerusalem (which was originally called the Institute of the International Conference on the Holocaust and Genocide, but was later changed in order to streamline its name) was established following the International Conference on the Holocaust and Genocide that was held in Tel Aviv in 1982. (For a discussion about the controversy that arose around the Conference, see Charny, 1988, p. 8.) As Charny (1988) has noted, the Conference "represented a pioneering effort to bring together many different peoples, such as Jews and Armenians, who normally are involved in the memorial of their own history of genocide, and to bring together many different professions in the interdisciplinary study of genocide as a process" (p. 8).

Under the leadership of Israel Charny, the Institute is devoted to the study of the genocides of all peoples; and in doing so, it hopes to gain an understanding of the generic genocidal process. It also has the further explicit goal of developing new concepts for intervention and prevention of genocide in order to protect all peoples in the future. In carrying out its mandate, the Institute sponsors and conducts studies on various aspects of genocide, publishes standard reference works, and serves as an international center of information for the field. In 1988, the Institute inaugurated its bibliographical review series on genocide (*Genocide: A Critical Bibliographic Review*). Thus far, three volumes in the series (including this one) have been published and several more are currently under way. The Institute also publishes the *Internet on the Holocaust and Genocide*, a newsletter that includes updates on the plight of peoples around the world vis-a-vis genocidal actions, scholarly findings on various aspects of genocide, information on projects that address the issue of genocide, book reviews, etc.

The Institute is now in the process of completing the first *Holocaust and Genocide Computerized Bibliographic Database* for the period 1980-1990, and has plans to expand it in the future. It is also currently developing the first thesaurus on genocide, *The Thesaurus of Holocaust and Genocide Terms*.

Most significantly, the Institute is working on the development of a genocide early warning system (which it currently identifies as a proposed World Genocide Early Warning System). At this point in time, work on the system is at an incipient stage, but each project of the Institute is specifically aimed at contributing to its development. (For a more detailed discussion of this genocide early warning system, see Charny,1988, pp. 24-26).

INSTITUTE FOR THE STUDY OF GENOCIDE, NEW YORK

The Institute for the Study of Genocide (ISG) in New York City was founded in 1982 "to promote and disseminate scholarship on the causes, consequences and prevention of genocide." In order to advance its goals, the ISG engages in research, education and communication. Among the many projects that ISG has engaged in and/or sponsored since its inception are the following: historical and contemporary research on the causes of genocide, genocidal massacres and mass political killings as well as methods for predicting them; research which monitors signs of gross violations of human rights which may lead to genocide; and, conferences and meetings "to advance research on genocide, to study patterns of recognition and denial, to assess the effects of genocide, and to consider how to detect and stop genocide." It also "maintains liaison with human rights organizations, research institutes and legislators to obtain and to publicize information."

The ISG is "exploring the possibilities of and resources needed for a data-bank and computer-network which would enable both the ISG and nongovernmental human rights organizations to monitor, evaluate, and respond to several related phenomena: life-integrity, signs of group persecution, and ideologies justifying expelling or eliminating particular groups" (correspondence with Helen Fein, February 17, 1992).

Among the conferences ISG has sponsored or co-sponsored are: "How to Detect and Deter Genocide (which brought together activists and members of the academic community working on various human rights issues to consider problems and strategies), and the "Conference on Teaching About the Holocaust."

ISG publishes *The ISG Newsletter*, which addresses the aforementioned issues and highlights reports, new books, conferences, and other scholarly activities that address the issue of genocide. ISG also publishes occasional papers on various aspects of genocide, and is currently in the process of compiling teaching guides and syllabi on genocide. Two of its most noted works are: *Lives at Risk: A Study of Violations of Life-Integrity in 50 States Based on the Amnesty International 1988 Report* by Helen Fein, and *Genocide Watch* (which is comprised of essays presented at ISG's conference entitled "Detect and Deter Genocide").

INTERNATIONAL ALERT, LONDON

In 1985, International Alert - Standing International Forum on Ethnic Conflict, Genocide, and Human Rights (IA) (which is commonly known as

International Alert) was established by a group of experts concerned with anticipating, predicting and preventing genocide and other mass killings. IA basically has two main aims: First, the organization is concerned with conflict resolution and conflict avoidance (conflicts of interest between ethnic or other groups within a recognized state that have already resulted in violence or are likely to do so unless solutions or accommodations are found) in accordance with international standards. In that regard IA aims at promoting internal peace and conciliation through dialogue. Second, as its name implies, it works to "alert" international opinion to situations of ethnic violence which are assuming genocidal proportions.

The establishment of International Alert was intended as an experiment in international relations in defining a role for an international NGO in the field. The first Secretary-General of IA was the late Martin Ennals who had successfully led Amnesty International through its formative growth period, and had become convinced that more needed to be done about collective mass persecution. In regard to its efforts thus far, IA officials state that "IA can more easily point to successful 'interventions' than 'prevention.' An example of this is our role in promoting the right of the indigenous peoples of the Northern Philippines to declare their villages to be 'Peace Zones.' Equally important has been our continued work in Sri Lanka, and to a somewhat lesser extent in Tibet, in contributing to the 'international pressure' to see a peaceful resolution to those disputes which recognizes the rights and aspirations of all peoples in those areas."

IA reports that "it aims to keep in close cooperative contact with both the international community of academics (peace and conflict researchers as well as those working on ethnic conflicts and genocide) and we work closely with local and international peace and human rights activists." IA also asserts that "What sets IA apart [from most other organizations in the field] is that it is an activist-oriented NGO. That is, it gets involved actively, in association or collaboration with a local organization or a coalition of local organizations and individuals, in constructive initiatives which promote both careful analysis of the root causes *and* the promotion of dialogue between the parties." IA has published a series of papers and reports on its efforts in the areas of the development of an early warning system as well as on its work in various parts of the world (e.g., southern Africa, Uganda, Suriname, the Philippines, Sri Lanka, and Tibet) to resolve conflict before it erupts into violence.

Finally, IA (along with the Peace Research Institute of Oslo - PRIO) has been hosting a number of roundtable discussions on the development of an early warning (conflict forecasting) system as well as on the role that NGOs can play in its development.

THE MONTREAL INSTITUTE FOR GENOCIDE STUDIES

The Montreal Institute for Genocide Studies (MIGS) was established in 1986 by Frank Chalk and Kurt Jonassohn and is based at Concordia University in Montreal. "Its approach is comparative and historical, involving scholars in Canada, the United States, Great Britain, and France. It collects and disseminates knowledge about the historical origins of...mass killings...The Institute accomplishes its objectives through research, teaching, and publication."

The Institute has published a series of "Occasional Papers" on various topics relating to genocide. Among those are Chalk and Jonassohn's "The History of Genocide - A Selective Bibliography"; Gregory H. Stanton's "Blue Scarves and Yellow Stars: Classification and Symbolization in the Cambodian Genocide"; Jonassohn's "Prevention Without Prediction"; Gabrielle Tyrnauer's "Gypsies and the Holocaust: A Bibliography and Introductory Essay"; and Jack Nusan Porter's "Sexual Politics in the Third Reich: The Persecution of the Homosexuals During the Holocaust: A Bibliography and Introductory Essay."

CAMBODIAN DOCUMENTATION COMMISSION, NEW YORK

Of especial note is the focus and efforts of the Cambodian Documentation Commission (CDC) which was established in 1982 and is based in New York City. It was founded by David Hawk, Dith Pran, Haing Ngor, Kassie Neou, Yang Sam, and Arn Chorn. Pran, Ngor, Neou, and Sam are all survivors of the Cambodian genocide. Hawk, a U.S. citizen, is a tireless researcher into the Khmer Rouge-perpetrated genocide and an individual who has dedicated many years in an attempt to bring the perpetrators of that genocide to trial. CDC's focus is four-fold: to document the genocide in Cambodia, seek accountability (either through an international or domestic tribunal) for those responsible for planning and carrying out the genocide, prevent the Khmer Rouge from returning to power, and to promote human rights in Cambodia. In an effort to carry out its mandate, CDC has arduously worked along the following lines: presented petitions and appeals to states that are parties to the U.N. Convention on Genocide, member states of the United Nations, and Cambodian political leaders; given testimony to the U.N. Commission on Human Rights as well as United States Congressional hearings; and, produced translations of archives that document repression of the Cambodian people under the Khmer Rogue. The latter were translated from Khmer to English. CDC also has translated international human rights declarations and conventions from English to Khmer for the purpose of disseminating them to key parties in Cambodia. It also has worked for and supported the strongest anti-genocide and pro-human rights provisions in United Nation's resolutions on the Cambodian conflict and the Cambodia Peace Treaty. Furthermore, Hawk and Hurst Hannum have written "The Case Against Democratic Kampuchea," a model legal brief for an Article IX complaint, and issued it to the International Court of Justice. While CDC was successful in getting several states that are party to the U.N. Convention on Genocide to consider lodging complaints to the International Court under Article 9 of the Genocide Convention against the Khmer Rouge, not a single state chose to issue the complaint.

WHAT ARE THE CRITICAL CHALLENGES AND ISSUES WHICH FACE THIS FIELD TODAY?

While certain organizations working on the issue of genocide have already made significant contributions to humanity's understanding of various aspects of genocide through their theoretical and research efforts and are making headway in regard to both promoting the notion that genocide is a scourge of humanity and that it needs to be the concern of all humanity, their efforts to develop effective means for intervening and/or preventing genocide are at an incipient stage. Kuper (1992) has noted, while ["t]here is no dearth of related interests [among the various organizations,] the problem is that of their coordination for effective campaigning" against genocide (p. 148). That is not to say that the efforts currently underway to address the chasm between the recognition of the problem and the reality of amelioration are insignificant. In fact, they are vitally significant. As delineated above, among such efforts are the development of typologies, the implementation of "international alert" programs, and the development of various plans for the development of a genocide early warning system. However, at best, only the initial groundwork is being done to date. This section of the essay shall delineate some of the critical challenges facing the field today.

A good deal of the information presented here is based on an open-ended questionnaire that the author sent to over 70 organizations that are working on the issues of human rights, refugee problems, the plight of indigenous peoples, ethnocide, and/or genocide. The first part of this section shall highlight the answers that were provided in regard to the following question: "What do you perceive as being the greatest impediment(s) to progress in your area of concern, and why?" along with the author's own insights. Interestingly, over ninety percent of the respondents did not address the "why" aspect of the aforementioned question. The second half of this section provides numerous suggestions as to how organizations could possibly strengthen their efforts in regard to the issues of intervention and prevention of genocide.

Impediments to Progress

The impediments to progress will simply be listed here, and then discussed in some detail under the section, "What Are the Real Probabilities of Progress in this Field?" The two impediments most frequently mentioned by the respondents were cynical geopolitics (or realpolitik) and the lack of adequate funding. Other areas that were mentioned by various organizations are as follows: the United Nations, e.g., its lack of political will to be an effective force; the lack of ready access to both print and electronic media; the lack of widespread concern by the masses about the issue of genocide, deprivation of human rights, and the plight of peoples far removed from them; the difficulty in dealing with the bureaucracy of governments and other organizations; and the difficulties of implementation of solutions which are obvious and necessary to save lives.

Suggestions for Strengthening Efforts

In the questionnaire, not a single organization mentioned being a part of a systematic or formal network comprised of various organizations (and as far as the author can ascertain, no formal network currently exists); rather, they inferred that: they were part of an informal network whose members meet at various international meetings, they read and/or contribute to one another's newsletters, and occasionally they may work in conjunction with another organization on research and/or writing projects. It seems as if some sort of formal network is definitely needed in order to facilitate and strengthen the efforts already under way to prevent future genocides from taking place. (For a discussion regarding the need for such a network, see Kuper, 1982; Kuper, 1984, pp. 301-305, Kuper, 1992.)

At the very least, it seems that it would be valuable for the various organizations to form an international computer network so that they could share ideas and information, and generally keep one another apprised of the type of work in which they are engaged. This could be set up in a number of ways, depending on how structured the organizations desired the network to be. At its loosest, it simply could be comprised of a computer bulletin board service in which items of interest were posted for members of the network to read. If more structure is desired, an archival or library service could be arranged where items are posted and stored for future use. If a more interactive structure were desired, a "discussion" group could be set up whereby members of the various organizations could regularly discuss, via the computer network, items of interest. Such technology is already available, and assuming that most of the researchers have computers, it would not take much effort or money to put any one of these systems into effect.

Eventually, it would be ideal for the individual organizations to form a more structured and formal network - something along the lines of a coalition. It seems as if such a coalition would greatly strengthen the overall efforts of individual organizations in their efforts to, ultimately, prevent genocide. While individual organizations could still pursue their particular goals and fill their unique mandates, a coalition could provide them with the means to bring together scholars, activists, and others in order to: combine their knowledge-bases in various areas and to strengthen their efforts; co-conduct and widely disseminate research (possibly via "yearbooks" which provide a country-by-country or region-by-region update concerning genocidal situations); collaborate on the collection, documentation, and examination of key archives; exchange ideas more easily; develop increasingly sophisticated and comprehensive databases on various issues vis-a-vis genocide; develop more efficacious methods and means for disseminating information of all types on the issue of genocide; carry out the dissemination of all types of information on the issue of genocide; work collectively (and in conjunction with educators at all levels) to educate the general public and students of all ages (elementary school through graduate school) about the issue of genocide and/or the plight of threatened peoples; develop more effective means for gaining access to the media; develop effective means for keeping a genocidal situation in the news as opposed to the current situation where genocide is often reported in a perfunctory manner and then ignored even as the genocide continues to take place; work in concert to alert (via the print and electronic media, computer networks, and other means) the international community whenever a genocidal situation rears its head; develop and implement methods for conducting urgent action campaigns which would not only alert the world and policymakers about genocidal situations but bring together a critical mass to voice its concern and to put pressure on the perpetrators as well as other bodies and governments to halt the genocide; co-sponsor field missions (e.g., observation teams and researchers) that have the ability to immediately descend on a location where genocide is either likely to take place and/or is taking place in order to gather key and accurate data in order to alert the rest of the world to the problem (The author readily acknowledges that in certain situations this might be an impossibility. In that case, field missions could be sent to areas where those who are in danger (refugees) are fleeing, and then they could conduct interviews and gather as much data as possible and relay it to a central data collection area); lobby for the strengthening of current conventions/laws and assist in the development of new legal machinery for the intervention and prevention of genocide (for a cogent discussion of the weaknesses of the U.N. Convention on Genocide, see Kuper, 1985; for a discussion regarding the need for the development of new legal machinery, see Charny, 1988, and Whitaker, 1985); argue and lobby for the establishment of "universal jurisdiction" vis-a-vis the crime of genocide (Whitaker 1985); lobby for and assist in the development and the implementation of an effective means (possibly an international body) to arrest and prosecute the perpetrators of genocide (e.g., something along the lines of an International Penal Tribunal, see Kutner and Katin, 1984; Whitaker, 1985, p. 40); apply pressure on the United Nations to strengthen its efforts (which are extremely weak and do not constitute much more than lip service) to work toward the intervention and prevention of genocide; lobby for and help to establish an "impartial international body to deal with genocide - one that would concern itself primarily with questions of fact rather than with questions of law" (Whitaker, 1985, pp. 43-44); raise funds for special projects such as a genocide early warning system; and work together to develop and implement an effective genocide early warning system that could be put into effect as soon as possible. Again, ideally such a collective effort would contribute to a situation in which the work of the various organizations is more efficacious; that is, it would assist groups to work on projects that complement and integrate the efforts of one another, cut down on redundant efforts, and address gaps that are currently being overlooked.

Ideally, at least once a year, such a coalition could sponsor a conference. During such a conference, the following could take place: representatives of the executive boards of each individual group could report on its group's efforts and projects; and the coalition's members could assess the collaborative projects the various organizations are engaged in, and develop new projects on which they could collaborate. They could also discuss and develop methods for encouraging and influencing international bodies and governments to take a more active role in the intervention and prevention of genocide.

As research on genocide continues to expand, it seems as if the establishment of an international research center by the aforementioned coalition would be valuable. The center could: serve as the lead agency in raising funds for research and development projects; support research projects (including interdisciplinary research into the causes, patterns, and ramifications of genocide); house a major archive, library and database on genocide; be a place where scholars could co-conduct research, plan major projects, and hold conferences; and be the site of an international genocide early warning system.

A research center along this line also could be the home-base for a computer network which each of the coalition's members would have access to (as would other human rights organizations and interested scholars, activists, journalists, public policy makers, etc.). A computer network such as this would obviously facilitate and expedite the sharing of information on research, new and ongoing projects, the most current situation across the globe vis-a-vis genocide, et al.

On another note, it would be extremely useful to scholars and activists to have a journal that *specifically focused on the issues of intervention and prevention of genocide*. Such a journal could not only encourage and support research into such issues, but also keep readers (researchers, activists, and others) abreast of the latest genocidal situations (either situations that constituted possible precursors to genocide or actual genocidal situations) as well as efforts that were either under way or needed to be initiated in order to intervene and prevent genocide from taking place.

Over the past decade or so, numerous scholars and/or organizations have either called for and/or begun working on what is commonly become referred to as a genocide early warning system (Charny, 1982; Charny 1988, pp. 20-38; Coliver, 1990; Knight, 1982; Kuper, 1981; Kuper, 1982; Kuper, 1984; Kuper, 1985, pp. 218-228; Howard and Howard, 1984, pp. 324-329; Rupesinghe and Kuroda, 1992; Stavenhagen, 1990; Whitaker, 1985, pp. 41-45). These are systems that identify criteria for detecting conditions which increase the possibility of genocide occurring, and then bring the situation to the world's attention in order to urge intervention and prevention. As Whitaker (1985) has noted: "Punishment after the event does not meet the priority problem of preventing great loss of life. Those personalities who are psychologically prepared to commit genocide are not always likely to be deterred by retribution... Intelligent anticipation of potential cases could be based on a data bank of continuously updated information, which might enable remedial, deterrent or averting measures to be planned ahead" (p. 41).

While a complete operational system has yet to be developed, various components of such a system have been designed and are being implemented. For example, there are the previously mentioned efforts of International Alert to "to promote awareness by sounding international alerts on threatening crises in intergroup relations" (personal correspondence from Leo Kuper, August 10, 1990). And as previously mentioned, International Alert, in conjunction with the Peace Research Institute of Oslo (PRIO), has been discussing the development of an Early Warning (conflict forecasting) system as well as the way in which NGOs could play a part in the development of such a system. There is also the effort of Israel W. Charny, who is heading up the development of a major data base on information relating to all aspects (including preconditions) of genocide.

Other scholars have written about what forms and methods such an early warning system might take. For example, Kuper (1985) has noted that a starting point for collecting key information about possible genocidal actions would be organizations such as Amnesty International and the investigative reports completed by the International Commission of Jurists (p. 220). Whitaker (1985) has suggested that a satellite could possibly assist in the collection of the data needed for the implementation of such a system. Totten (1991) has stated that a key component of any early warning system should be the collection and analysis of eyewitness accounts of events that might be leading up to a genocide and/or of particular genocidal acts themselves. "Time and again throughout this [the twentieth] century, some of the first warnings that a genocidal act was taking place were the appearance of first-person accounts by members of the victim group who either managed to escape or smuggle out reports, and/or accounts by others witnesses (e.g., journalists, consular officials, relief workers)" (Totten, 1991, p. lvii).

The point is that while there are numerous ideas for an early warning system, there has been no central effort to bring the ideas together, evaluate them, and then fashion them into a single system. The genuine interest on the part of so many different researchers in such a system simply undergirds the great need for both individuals and organizations to come together to share ideas and resources. Again, a coalition of groups under the auspices of a central research center could facilitate the developmental work needed to design such a direly needed system.

It would also behoove those working on the issue of the prevention of genocide to follow the lead of human rights activists, and encourage members of the legal profession across the globe to become more involved with the issue. Their talents and skills could prove extremely valuable in a wide array of areas: documenting situations that seem to be slouching towards genocide and/or actual genocidal situations; "evaluating the potential effects of economic sanctions and other viable methods of enforcement" (Wiseberg and Scoble, 1981, p. 244); educating members of the law and judiciary professions about their duties and obligations with regard to upholding the law as it relates to the intervention and prevention of genocide; providing assistance in strengthening the legal machinery concerning the intervention and prevention of genocide; and, bringing to trial and prosecuting perpetrators of genocide.

The significance of education was mentioned at the outset of this section, but it is so vitally important that additional attention will be given to it. Whitaker (1985) and others have suggested that what is needed is a worldwide effort "starting at an early age" to educate "against such aberrations" as genocide (p. 42). Whitaker (1985) has also noted: "Without a strong basis of international public support, even the most perfectly redrafted Convention will be of little value. Conventions and good governments can give a lead, but the mobilization of public awareness and vigilance is essential to guard against any recurrence of genocide and other crimes against humanity and human rights... As a further safeguard, public awareness should be developed internationally to reinforce the individual's responsibility, based on the knowledge that it is illegal to obey a superior order or law that violates human rights" (p. 42).

Current efforts to educate about genocide are neither as widespread nor as strong as they could or should be. They are also extremely fragmented. Research needs to be done in regard to the most effective ways for teaching about genocide and in regard to the impact such educative activities on have on the individual concerning his/her moral actions (See Darsa, 1991; Totten, 1991). Again, a coalition of researchers and activists could facilitate such an effort.

While more and more scholars in various disciplines at the college and university levels are beginning to focus on the issue of genocide, there is still a lot that needs to be done in order to both facilitate such study and to expand interest in the field. First, individual organizations and/or a coalition could fund scholarships and fellowships in order to encourage graduate students to pursue studies which prepare them to make contributions to the field of genocide studies. Second, in a similar but different vein, at some point in time it would be valuable for individual organizations and/or a coalition to take the lead in establishing and/or encouraging the establishment of endowed research chairs in the field of genocide studies at various colleges and universities across the globe. Such chairs already exist in the field of Holocaust studies and human rights, and there is no reason why something similar could not be done in the field of genocide studies. Third, individual organizations and/or a coalition need to encourage college- and university-based scholars already active in the field to encourage their professional organizations to establish special interest groups on genocide. When all is said and done, though, those individuals and organizations working on these issues need to constantly assess the efficacy of their efforts and approaches.

As Kuper (1992) perspicaciously notes,

> In the first place, we must guard against the illusion that moral considerations will prevail in the circles of power, without, however, totally excluding the possibility that in certain circumstances they might contribute a supportive argument. Then, too, we must guard against the resort to meaningless surrogates for action or placebos. An approach is made to a member of parliament, who expresses sympathetic understanding through an aide and will see what can be done. Or a nongovernmental organization presents a submission to the U. N. Commission of Human Rights and leaves with a sense of accomplishment - or more realistically with the hope that perhaps something may come of it. But the probability is that these representations will have little or no effect unless they are part of an informed campaign of systematic actions. (p. 139)

WHAT ARE THE REAL
PROBABILITIES OF PROGRESS IN THIS FIELD

The probabilities of progress in the previously mentioned areas are mixed. It is fairly certain that current organizations working on genocide (especially those that are small, primarily focused on research and not supported by the dues of members) will continue to be plagued with financial hardship. This is a serious problem for a number of reasons. In order to maintain a functioning organization, many organizations are plagued by the necessity to spend an inordinate amount of their time each and every year seeking grants and other funding sources. This, of course, cuts into the precious time that they could otherwise dedicate to substantive issues. In some cases, it has slowed down the progress on a number of important projects. Due to a lack of adequate funding, some organizations have either had to temporarily halt important projects midway to completion or altogether abandon them. The lack of adequate funding drastically limits the number of projects that an organization can take on, limits the breadth and depth of certain projects, and precludes hiring the number of researchers, activists, computer experts, and secretarial help that is crucial to running an effective organization. If for no other reason than to address the issue of inadequate funding, it would behoove the various organizations to meet once a year in order to put their collective "minds" together in an attempt to solve this dire problem.

What is needed to assist these organizations are major funding sources that would provide long-term assistance to those organizations and/or a coalition that are engaged in cutting-edge work vis-a-vis the issues of genocide. On another note, as more and more nations continue to work together to solve problems that plague the earth (e.g., the depletion of the ozone layer), it might be worth looking into a situation where either the United Nations or even individual nations agree to "tithe" a certain amount of funding every year to those organizations that are working to prevent future genocides. There is also the possibility, of course, that if the various organizations did form some sort of formal network or coalition, the efforts to raise badly needed monies might be facilitated through a collective effort. There is also the possibility that as the issue of genocide gains more attention, just as the issue of human rights did in the 1970s and 1980s, membership in various organizations will increase and with it the revenue brought in by membership fees. Directly tied to the latter point is the need for organizations to "expand constituency support, whether they are directed toward the national or the international arenas" (Wiseberg and Scoble, 1981, p. 255). This will not only bring in additional monies; but more significantly, it will help to raise the consciousness of the global community about the issue of genocide and possibly bring about a critical mass of support of the efforts at intervention and prevention of genocide.

It also seems to be a foregone conclusion that the centrality of realpolitik (see Beres, 1984) and the ostensible primacy of the issue of "internal affairs" in our world will militate at least for now and well into the future against the development of the political and moral will that is needed in order to once and for all put into place the most effective machinery to prevent future cases of genocide. Such moral and political will is sorely needed on the international scene if humanity hopes to effectively combat the scourge of genocide.

As for the role of the United Nations in fighting genocide, it too has become entangled in the noose of realpolitik. As previously mentioned, many respondents to the aforementioned questionnaire complained that rather than being part of the solution in the fight against genocide, the U.N. has been part of the problem. Such sentiments corroborate what Kuper (1984) noted close to a decade ago: "Given the unwieldly bureaucratic procedures of the U.N., its deep cleavages, and protective stance toward offending governments, there is a need for some supranational institution to transcend the present limitations" (p. 302). Until such a supranational organization is established, the world is going to have to depend on non-governmental organizations both to lead the battle and to set a sterling example (for the U.N. and individual governments) in regard to what can be done when the moral and political will are harnessed and brought to bear upon a situation. Certainly one way in which non-governmental organizations are having and will continue to have a direct influence on the U.N. is through their consultative status with such bodies as the U.N.'s Economic and Social Council.

There is no reason why an international network could not be established in the near future. As previously mentioned, on the simplest level the development of a computer bulletin board could be established at this very time. It simply would require establishing a central location for the messages to be routed, along with an individual or group of individuals to head up the effort. It is also likely that an international network such as HURIDOCS (a global network of over a hundred non-governmental human rights organizations) could be established that focuses on the issue of genocide. The aim of such a project could, like HURIDOCS, be to "improve access to and dissemination of public information on [genocide] through more effective, appropriate and compatible methods and techniques of information handling. [While] HURIDOCS itself does not collect documents,...it services the organizations participating in the network by providing basic tools for information handling and documentation control, development of new standards, teaching and training in techniques, advice on software and hardware and coordination among the different documentation centres." There seems to be a good possibility that a coalition of groups could come together. Many of the directors and board members of the various organizations are already in contact, sharing ideas, and working together on various projects. As research on genocide continues to proliferate and as the drive by various organizations to move from research to action becomes more intense, it is likely that the organizations will eventually decide to form a coalition.

At the same time, many of the problems raised by Wiseberg and Scoble (1981) regarding the "probable limits of effective cooperation" by various human rights groups across the globe could also plague the collective efforts of organizations addressing the issue of genocide. Among such problems are: "...the diverse interests, ideologies, and strategies that different sections of the human rights community bring to bear on the human rights issue" (p. 251). Wiseberg and Scoble (1981) go on to note that "Generally, calls for cooperation are interpreted as a request that they [individual organizations] diminish the significance of precisely those issues they have made uniquely their own" [and,] "there are bound to be disagreements over strategy and tactics, even where they can agree on the salience of an issue" (p. 252). It is also a fact that many human rights organizations have, in fact, risen above such concerns and are acting collectively on a number of fronts, and organizations addressing the intervention and prevention of genocide can do the same. It is primarily a matter of moral and political will, and this author believes that those can be mustered - one way or another - for the benefit of the greater good.

CONCLUSION

As mentioned at the outset of this essay, organizational work vis-a-vis the issue of genocide is still in its most incipient state. That is not surprising in light of the fact that it has only been over the course of the last several decades or so that the issue of genocide has become a major focus of scholarly study and a central issue of certain activists. That being the case, there is a good deal to be hopeful about. A new field of genocide studies is emerging, and out of these efforts scholars and others are increasingly focusing on developing the methods and means for efficaciously intervening and preventing genocides from taking place. Thus, while there is a long, long way to go until effective machinery will be put into place vis-a-vis intervention and prevention, the process has begun and that, in and of itself, is both a quantum leap and a vitally significant step in the right direction.

REFERENCES

Beres, Louis Rene (1984). Reason and realpolitik: International law and the prevention of genocide. In Charny, Israel W. (Ed.), *Toward the Understanding an Prevention of Genocide: Proceedings of the International Conference on the Holocaust and Genocide.* Boulder, CO: Westview Press, pp. 306-323.

Chalk, Frank, and Jonassohn, Kurt (1988). The history and sociology of genocide - A selective bibliography. (A paper in the Institute's "Occasional Paper" series.) Montreal: Montreal Institute of Genocide Studies.

Charny, Israel W. [in collaboration with Chanan Rapaport] (1982). *How Can We Commit the Unthinkable?: Genocide, The Human Cancer.* Boulder, CO: Westview Press. [Republished in paperback by Hearst Books (William Morrow) in 1983 under the title *Genocide, The Human Cancer.*]

Charny, Israel W. (1988). Intervention and prevention of genocide. In Charny, Israel W. (Ed.), *Genocide: A Critical Bibliographic Review.* New York: Facts on File, pp. 20-38.

Coliver, Sandy (1990). *Early Warning and Conflict Resolution.* London: International Alert.

Darsa, Jan (1991). Educating about the Holocaust: A case study in the teaching of genocide. In Charny, Israel (Ed.), *Genocide: A Critical Bibliographic Review, Volume 2.* London and New York: Mansell Publishing and Facts on File, respectively, pp. 175-193.

Fein, Helen (Spring, 1990). *Genocide: A Sociological Perspective.* In *Current Sociology*, 38(1), whole issue, 126 pp.

Fein, Helen (Ed.) (1992). *Genocide Watch.* New Haven, CT: Yale University Press.

Fein, Helen (1990). *Lives at Risk: A Study of Violations of Life-Integrity in 50 States in 1987 based on the Amnesty International Report.* New York: Institute for the Study of Genocide.

Harff, Barbara, and Gurr, Ted Robert (1988). Toward empirical theory of genocides and politicides: Identification and measurement of cases since 1945. *International Studies Quarterly, 32*(3), 359-371. See also *Internet on the Holocaust and Genocide*, Special Issue 13, December, 1987.

Howard, Ephraim M., and Howard, Yocheved (1984). From theory to application: Proposal for an applied science approach to a genocide early warning system. In Charny, Israel W. (Ed.), *Toward the Understanding and Prevention of Genocide: Proceedings of the International Conference on the Holocaust and Genocide.* Boulder, CO: Westview Press, pp. 324-329

Jonassohn, Kurt (July 1990). Prevention without prediction. (A paper in the Institute's "Occasional Paper" series). Montreal: Montreal Institute for Genocide Studies.

Knight, Gerald (1982). A Genocide Bureau (Editor's title]. Text of talk delivered at the Symposium on Genocide, London, 20 March (sponsored by a group that later created the organization International Alert). Mimeographed, 14 pp. Available from the Baha'i International Community, 866 United Nations Plaza, New York, NY 10017.

Kuper, Leo (1981). *Genocide: Its Political Use in the Twentieth Century*. New Haven, CT: Yale University Press.

Kuper, Leo (1984). The United Nations and genocide: A program of action. In Charny, Israel W. (Ed.), *Toward the Understanding and Prevention of Genocide: Proceedings of the International Conference on the Holocaust and Genocide*. Boulder, CO: Westview Press, pp. 296-305.

Kutner, Luis, and Katin, Ernest (1984). World Genocide Tribunal: A proposal for planetary preventive measures supplementing a genocide early warning system. In Charny, Israel W. (Ed.), *Toward the Understanding and Prevention of Genocide: Proceedings of the International Conference on the Holocaust and Genocide*. Boulder, CO: Westview Press, pp. 330-346.

Porter, Jack Nusan (June 1991). Sexual politics in the Third Reich: The persecution of the homosexuals during the Holocaust: A bibliography and introductory essay. (A paper in the Institute's "Occasional Paper" series). Montreal: Montreal Institute for Genocide Studies.

Rummel, R. J. (1990). *Lethal Politics: Soviet Genocide and Mass Murder Since 1917*. New Brunswick, NJ: Transaction Publishers.

Rupesinghe, Kumar, and Kuroda, Michiko (Eds.) (1992). *Early Warning and Conflict Resolution*. London: Macmillan; and New York: St. Martin's. 238 pp.

Stanton, Gregory H. (April 1989). Blue scarves and yellow stars: Classification and symbolization in the Cambodian genocide. (A paper in the Institute's "Occasional Paper" series.) Montreal: Montreal Institute for Genocide Studies.

Stavenhagen, Rodolfo (1990). *Early Warning and Conflict Resolution*. London: International Alert.

Totten, Samuel (1991). Educating about genocide: Curricula and inservice Training. In Charny, Israel W. (Ed.), *Genocide: A Critical Bibliographic Review, Volume 2*. London and New York: Mansell Publishing and Facts on File, respectively, pp. 194-225.

Totten, Samuel (1991). *First-Person Accounts of Genocidal Acts Committed in the Twentieth Century: An Annotated Bibliography*. Westport, CT: Greenwood Press.

Tyrnauer, Gabrielle (May 1991). *Gypsies and the Holocaust: A bibliography and introductory essay*. (A paper in the Institute's "Occasional Paper" series.) Montreal: Montreal Institute for Genocide Studies.

Whitaker, B. (1985). *Revised and Updated Report on the Question of the Prevention and Punishment of the Crime of Genocide*. New York: United Nations Economic and Social Council. E/CN.4/Sub.2/1985/6. 2 July 1985.

BIBLIOGRAPHY

Note: It is impossible for this annotated bibliography to be all-inconclusive. There are several thousand non-governmental human rights organizations worldwide as well as hundreds of organizations whose focus is on the Holocaust. In light of that, numerous directories and bibliographies that list upwards of a score or more of institutions/ institutes/organizations have been included in this bibliography. It is inevitable that by the time this volume reaches the reader additional organizations will have been established, others may be defunct, and still others may have changed locations.

A great many of the annotations will be found to be direct quotes. They were either obtained from the survey that was sent out by the author to over 70 institutions and organizations and/or from the brochures and materials produced by such institutions and organizations.

In light of the fact that many institutions/institutes/organizations address various concerns (some, for example, solely address the Holocaust, while others may address both the Holocaust as well as other genocides), it would be awkward and misleading to place the organizations under separate headings (e.g., Holocaust, genocide, refugees, international human rights, et al.). Thus all of the institutions, institutes, and organizations are listed in alphabetical order.

The words "Membership organization" placed in brackets at the end of the address of an institution, institute or organization signifies that individuals may join its membership.

ESSAYS/PAPERS/REPORTS

Blaser, Art (1981). Assessing human rights: The NGO contribution. In Nanda, Ved P.; Scarritt, James R.; and Shepherd, Jr., George W., (Eds.), *Global Human Rights: Public Policies, Comparative Measures, and NGO Strategies*. Boulder, CO: Westview Press, pp. 261-287.
An informative discussion of NGO contributions.

Kuper, Leo (1981). *International Action Against Genocide*. London: Minority Rights Group. 19 pp.
Examines a wide-range of strategies for "activating an international alert against impending genocides," and the role that organizations could play.

Kuper, Leo (1985). *The Prevention of Genocide*. New Haven, CT: Yale University Press. 286 pp.
Throughout this sterling volume, Kuper offers perspicacious insights into the value of non-governmental organizations and speaks to the need for a strong international non-governmental organizational structure to combat genocide.

Kuper, Leo (1992). Reflections on the prevention of genocide. In Fein, Helen (Ed.), *Genocide Watch*. New Haven, CT: Yale University Press, pp. 135-161.
A thought-provoking essay that addresses, in part, both the strengths and weaknesses of current efforts by scholars, activists and organizations to prevent genocide.

Kuper, Leo (1984). The United Nations and genocide: A program of action. In Charny, Israel W. (Ed.), *Toward the Understanding and Prevention of Genocide: Proceedings of the International Conference on the Holocaust and Genocide*. Boulder, CO: Westview Press, pp. 296-305.
Brief comments on the need to develop an organizational base of nongovernmental organizations to work on the intervention and prevention of genocide.

Luling, Virginia (forthcoming). Campaigning for indigenous peoples: The work of Survival International. In Morris, C. Patrick, and Hitchcock, Robert K. (Eds.), *International Human Rights and Indigenous Peoples*. [Publishing arrangements are still to be finalized.]
> An overview of the work of Survival International. (For a succinct statement about Survival International's focus and efforts, see the annotation about the organization in this bibliography.]

Wiseberg, Laurie, and Scoble, Harry (1982). *An international strategy for NGOs pertaining to extra-legal executions*. Paper presented at Amnesty International Conference on Extra-Legal Executions, Amsterdam.
> "In an excellent discussion of an international strategy for NGOs, [they] analyze the human rights function of these NGOs as they relate to fact-finding, dissemination of information, techniques of mass action and humanitarian relief. They conclude with an emphasis on the need for a coordination of effort in campaigning against extra-legal executions" (Kuper, 1984, p. 303).

Wiseberg, Laurie, and Scoble, Harry (1981). Recent trends in the expanding universe of NGOs dedicated to the protection of human rights. In Nanda, Ved P.; Scarritt, James R.; and Shepherd, George W. (Eds.), *Global Human Rights*, Boulder, CO: Westview Press, pp. 229-260.
> Discusses the proliferation and focus of NGOs working on the issue of the promotion and protection of international human rights.

DIRECTORIES/BIBLIOGRAPHIES

Cultural Survival (Ed.) (1985). "Identity and Education." *Cultural Survival Quarterly*, 9(2): B-1 to B-7 (an insert).
> Includes a directory of 140 indigenous/indigenist organizations located across the globe, and a listing of over 170 "organizations, which share common concerns with indigenous peoples."

Burek, Deborah (Ed.) (1992). *Encyclopedia of Associations' National Organizations of the U.S.* Detroit, MI: Gale Research Inc., 3 volumes, 395 pp.
> This three-set volume provides information on "over 22,000 nonprofit American membership organizations of national scope." It lists one key genocide organization located in the U.S. as well as several hundred organizations working on humans rights and related issues.

Holocaust Educational Trust (Ed.) (1988). *Directory of Holocaust-Related Activity in Britain*. London: Author. 15 pp. (To obtain a copy, write to: The Holocaust Educational Trust, BCM Box 7892, London WCIN 3XX, England).
> This booklet contains the description and addresses of various Holocaust organizations based in Britain. The organizations are listed under the following headings: survivors and refugees, education, libraries and research, and universities.

Irvin, Linda (Ed.) (1992). *Encyclopedia of Associations' International Organizations*. Detroit, MI: Gale Research Inc. 2 parts, 2344 pp.
> This two-set volume provides information on over 11,000 international nonprofit membership organizations located outside of the United States. It lists a number of

the key organizations working on the issues of genocide and ethnocide as well as several hundred organizations working on human rights and related issues.

Lawson, Edward J. (Ed.) (1991). *Encyclopedia of Human Rights*. Bristol, PA: Taylor & Francis. 2,080 pp.
Includes a section that provides information on intergovernmental and nongovernmental organizations that work on various human rights issues.

Schirmer, Jennifer; Renteln, Alison Dundes; and Wiseberg, Laurie (1988). Anthropology and human rights: A selected bibliography. In Downing, Theodore E., and Kushner, Gilbert (Eds.), *Human Rights and Anthropology*. Cambridge, MA: Cultural Survival, Inc, pp. 121-196.
A short section (pp. 193-196) included within the larger bibliography is entitled "NGO Resources." It lists sixteen organizations working on the behalf of indigenous groups' human rights.

Shulman, William L. (1990). *Directory - Association of Holocaust Organizations*. Bayside, NY: Holocaust Resource Center and Archives, Queensborough Community College. 72 pp.
This directory lists 58 institutions and organizations in the United States and two in Canada that provide services related to the Holocaust.

Szonyi, David M. (1985). *The Holocaust: An Annotated Bibliography and Resource Guide*. New York: KTAV Publishing House. 396 pp.
Chapter V is entitled "Holocaust Education and Commemoration Centers and Research Institutes and Archives" (pp. 259-275). It contains the listings of 40 institutions and organizations.

Totten, Samuel (1991). *First-Person Accounts of Genocidal Acts Committed in the Twentieth Century: An Annotated Bibliography*. Westport, CT: Greenwood Press. 351 pp.
Includes annotations of those organizations across the globe that hold first-person accounts of various genocidal acts committed in the twentieth century.

UNESCO (Ed.) (1988). *World Directory of Human Rights Teaching and Research Institutions*. Oxford, England: Berg Publishers Limited. 216 pp.
While few of the 331 organizations listed here specifically cite genocide and/or ethnocide as a focus of concern, many do deal with concerns that are germane in one way or another to such issues, e.g., determination of indigenous populations and their right to cultural identity, interethnic relations and/or conflict, international law, enforcement of human rights.

U.S. Holocaust Memorial Council (Ed.) (1988). *Directory of Holocaust Institutions*. Washington, D.C.: Author. 56 pp.
This directory includes listings of 98 Holocaust institutions in the United States and Canada (19 Holocaust museums, 48 Holocaust resource centers, 34 Holocaust archival facilities, 12 Holocaust memorials, 26 Holocaust research institutes, and 5 Holocaust libraries).

Whalen, Lucille (1989). *Human Rights: A Reference Book*. Santa Barbara, CA: ABC-CLIO. 218 pp.
A useful volume whose contents include, in part, a directory of organizations, and a

listing of computer networks and databases.

Wiseberg, Laurie S. (Ed.) (1987). *Human Rights Internet Directory: Eastern Europe & the USSR.* Cambridge, MA: Human Rights Internet. 304 pp.
 Provides information on over 225 human rights organizations which exist or have existed in Eastern Europe and the Soviet Union since the mid-1970s, official human rights bodies in that region, and organizations elsewhere in the world concerned with human rights in the region. In light of the drastic changes that have occurred in these regions over the past several years, much of the information needs updating.

Wiseberg, Laurie S. (Ed.) (1987). *Human Rights Directory: Latin America.* Cambridge, MA: Human Rights Internet. 244 pp.
 Provides information on human rights organizations based in Latin America and those based elsewhere whose focus is on human rights in that region.

Wiseberg, Laurie S. (Ed.) (1984). *North American Human Rights Directory.* Cambridge, MA: Human Rights Internet. 264 pp.
 Provides information on over 500 organizations in the United States and Canada engaged in human rights work.

INSTITUTIONS/INSTITUTES/ORGANIZATIONS

Altruistic Personality and Prosocial Behavior Institute, Department of Sociology, Humboldt State University, Arcata, CA 95521. [Membership organization.]
 Founded in 1982 as the Altruistic Personality Project by Samuel and Pearl Oliner, the institute serves the dual purpose of studying specific examples of heroic and conventional altruism and to seek out ways to enhance altruism and prosocial behavior in society. Its researchers are interested in the consequences of bystanders, bigotry, heroism, and applying the institute's resources and research findings in helping people know better how to recognize and act in a prosocial manner. It focuses on both research and education.

Amnesty International, International Secretariat, 1 Easton St., London, WC1X 8DJ, United Kingdom. FAX: 44-71-956-1157. [National Offices are located in many countries throughout the world. Membership organization.]
 Amnesty International (AI) is a worldwide voluntary movement that works to prevent some of the grave violations by governments of people's fundamental human rights. The main focus of its campaigning is to: free all prisoners of conscience; ensure fair and prompt trials for political prisoners; abolish the death penalty, torture, and other cruel treatment of prisoners; and end extrajudicial executions and "disappearances." AI is impartial, and is independent of any government, political persuasion or religious creed.
 While Amnesty International does not itself seek to determine whether or not a particular set of human rights violations constitutes the crime of genocide, Amnesty International works against the fundamental violations of human rights which occur in the context of genocide, including extrajudicial executions and torture.
 Amnesty International advocates ratification by all states of international conventions on human rights and humanitarian law, including the Convention on the Prevention and Punishment of the Crime of Genocide. AI considers that ratification of, or accession to, the Genocide Convention, demonstrates a state's commitment to

an international legal system which would restrain large-scale executions by governments. AI's sections have worked alongside other organizations to encourage their governments to ratify the Genocide Convention.

Centro de Formacion y de Investigacion Sobre las Culturas Indias - Chitakolla (Center for Promotion of, and Research on, Indian Culture - Chitakolla). Calle Ingavi No. 1047, 2do. Patio, Altos, La Paz, Bolivia.
This organization works for the preservation of indigeous cultures and attempts to systematically keep abreast of human rights violations of indigenous peoples throughout Latin America. It publishes a bulletin entitled *Boletin Chitakolla*.

Comité de Defense des Droits de L'Home Au Burundi, BP 1716, Bruxelles I, Belgique.
Established in 1986, the committee's main focus is the defense of human rights in Burundi. Its staff has published several essays/works on the issue of genocide in Burundi - (e.g., "Burundi, La Spirale D'un Genocide," Les "Petits" et Les "Grands," and Deux Mille Collines Pour).

Cambodia Documentation Commission, 251 W. 87th St., Apartment 74, New York, NY 10024.
Established in 1982 under the leadership of David Hawk, the Commission has four key purposes: to document the genocide in Cambodia, seek accountability through either an international or domestic tribunal for those responsible for the genocide perpetrated between 1975-1979, prevent the Khmer Rouge from returning to power, and promoting human rights in Cambodia. In addition to conducting research and educating about these issues, the Commission carries out its mandate by petitioning and issuing appeals to state parties to the Genocide Convention, member states of the U.N., and Cambodian political leaders. It also presents testimony to the U.N. Commission on Human Rights, various U.S. Congressional hearings, and other bodies. A large part of its efforts revolve around translating Khmer Rouge archives that document the atrocities from Khmer to English, and international human rights documents and conventions from English to Khmer.

Consejo Indio de Sudamerica (CISA), Apartado Postal 2054, Lima 700, Peru.
CISA's (Indian Council of South America) main goal is the defense of indigenous peoples' rights across South America. Its publication, *Pueblo Indio*, highlights humans rights issues vis-a-vis indigenous peoples in South America.

Consejo Regional Indigena del Cauca (CRIC), Calle 20 N., No. 13-53, Barrio Cadillal, Popayan, Cauca, Colombia.
Founded in 1971, CRIC (Indigenous Regional Council of Cauca) works to preserve the indigenous way of life in Colombia including fighting against human rights violations. It publishes a monthly report entitled *Unidad Indigena: Unidad Tierra y Cultural (Indigenous Unity: Unity of Land and Culture)*, which also highlights human rights violations against indigenous peoples in Colombia.

Cultural Survival, 53A Church St., Cambridge, MA 02138. FAX: 1-617-495-1396. [Membership organization.]
Cultural Survival (CS), a non-profit foundation, advocates the rights of indigenous peoples and ethnic minorities worldwide. It was founded in 1972 by a group of Harvard-based social scientists who were distraught by the human rights abuses being suffered by indigenous peoples and ethnic minorities across the globe. It achieves its goal of supporting indigenous human rights through an integrated program of

research, publication, education, public policy, and field projects. CS supports projects on five continents, serving to guarantee the land and resource rights of tribal peoples, strengthen their organizations, and support sustainable economic projects. Its research papers are published with the aim to guide governments, international aid organizations and other institutions in their relations with minorities and smaller societies.

Gesellschaft für Bedrohte Volker (in English - Society for Threatened Peoples), Duestere Strasse 20A, P.O. Box 2024, D-3400 Goettingen, Germany. FAX: 49-551-58028 [Membership organization.]
Established in 1970, its primary focus is conducting research, documenting and disseminating information about genocide with an eye towards preventing its occurrence. Two specific concerns are the plight of indigenous peoples and the protection of the rights of minorities. It publishes a journal entitled *Pogrom*. The Society has also produced a series of monographs and reports on the issues of discrimination of minorities and indigenous peoples, and the threat of genocide and ethnocide.

Facing History and Ourselves National Foundation, 25 Kennard Rd., Brookline, MA 02146. FAX: 1-617-232-0281. [Membership organization.]
Established in 1976 by William S. Parsons and Margot Stern Strom, Facing History and Ourselves is a non-profit organization providing educators with services and resources for examining the history of the Holocaust, genocide, racism, anti-semitism, and issues related to adolescent and adult development. It publishes a quarterly newsletter entitled, *Facing History and Ourselves News*. It has also published several books, including *Facing History and Ourselves: The Holocaust and Human Behavior* by Margot Stern Strom and William S. Parsons (Watertown, MA: Intentional Education, 1982), and *Facing History and Ourselves: Elements of Time - Holocaust Testimonies* by Facing History and Ourselves (Brookline, MA: Facing History and Ourselves Foundation, 1989).

Human Rights Internet (also known as Internet: International Human Rights Documentation Network), c/o Human Rights Centre, University of Ottawa, 57 Louis Pasteur, Ottawa, Ontario K1N 6NF Canada. FAX: (613) 564-4054. [Membership organization.]
Human Rights Internet (HRI) was established in 1976 on the premise that accurate and timely information is a precondition to effective action for the defense of human rights. It seeks to encourage dialogue and communication between three constituencies: human rights scholars from all disciplines, human rights advocates/activists, and policymakers with responsibilities in the area of human rights at both the governmental and intergovernmental levels. Its aim is to build a worldwide network especially with frontline human rights nongovernmental organizations (NGOs) in countries suffering widespread repression. HRI publishes the *Human Rights Reporter* (quarterly), human rights directories (which describe the work of human rights organizations on all continents), resources for teaching and research, and special reports. It also edits a special microfiche collection on human rights NGO documents, and has a database on international human rights.

Human Rights Watch, 485 Fifth Ave., New York, NY 10017-6104. FAX: 1-212-371-0124. [Membership organization.]
Human Rights Watch (HRW) is comprised of five regional divisions - Africa Watch, Americas Watch, Asia Watch, Helsinki Watch, and Middle East Watch. Most of

HRW's work is done in the name of one of its divisions. On matters of general human rights policy that cut across divisional lines, HRW speaks in its own voice. HRW monitors the human rights practices of governments: murder, disappearances, kidnapping, torture, discrimination of racial, gender, ethnic or religious grounds, etc. It publicizes violations of human rights and launches international protests against governments that commit abuses. It also generates pressure on the U.S. and other governments, as well as on international bodies to respond to abuses. It sends fact-finding missions to countries where abuses take place, attends court proceedings, and examines court records. It applies pressure on a country abusing rights by pushing for enforcement of U.S. law requiring withdrawal of U.S. economic, military and diplomatic support from governments that regularly abuse the rights of its citizens. The various divisions of HRW collect information on human rights abuses in countries in their areas of specializations and publishes it in document reports and briefer topical bulletins. Some of its many publications include: *The Search for Brazil's Disappeared, Guatemala: Getting Away With Murder, Destroying Ethnic Identity: Gypsies of Bulgaria,* and *The Miskitos in Nicaragua, 1981-1984.*

Indian Law Resource Center, 601 E. St, S.E., Washington, D.C. 20003.
Founded in 1978, the Indian Law Resource Center is a non-profit law office and advocacy organization established and directed by Indians. It provides legal help in the U.S. and Central and South America without charge to Indian nations and tribes in major cases of important Indian rights abuses, e.g., where Indian people are being killed, imprisoned, and driven from their lands in great numbers. It also carries out research and educational work for the development of Indian rights at both the national and international levels.

Institute for the Study of Genocide, John Jay College of Criminal Justice (City University of New York), 899 10th Ave., Room 623, New York, NY 10019). [Membership organization.]
The Institute for the Study of Genocide (ISG) was founded in 1982 to promote and disseminate scholarship on the causes, consequences and prevention of genocide. It focuses "on the relation between genocide in the making and contemporary violations of life integrity (or gross violations of human rights) in the modern world systematically, regardless of perpetrators or victims." In doing so, it conducts research which monitors signs of gross violations of human rights and genocide; sponsors conferences and meetings to advance research on genocide, study patterns of recognition and denial, assess the effects of genocide, and consider how to detect and stop genocide; publishes a newsletter with analysis of current situations; publishes occasional papers clarifying issues about genocide; and maintains liaison with human rights organizations, research institutions and legislators to obtain and to publicize information. "The ISG is exploring the possibilities of and resources needed for a data-bank and computer network which would enable both the ISG and nongovernmental human rightrs organizations to monitor, evaluate, and respond to several related phenomena: states (and non-state actors) committing gross violations of life-integrity, signs of group persecution, and ideologies justifying expelling or eliminating particular groups" (correpondence with Helen Fein, February 17, 1992). Among its publications are *Genocide Watch* edited by Helen Fein (New Haven, CT: Yale University Press, 1992), which is comprised of essays presented at the Institute's 1989 conference ("How to Detect and Deter Genocide") and *Lives at Risk: A Study of Violations of Life-Integrity in 50 States Based on the Amnesty International 1988 Report* by Helen Fein (New York: Institute for the Study of Genocide, 1990).

Institute on the Holocaust and Genocide, P.O. Box 10311, 91102 Jerusalem, Israel. FAX: 972-2-720424

Established in 1979, the Institute on the Holocaust and Genocide is devoted to the study of the genocides of all people. It aims to understand the generic genocidal process and aims at the further explicit goal of developing new concepts for intervention and prevention of genocide to all peoples in the future. In carrying out its mandate, the Institute sponsors and conducts studies on the Holocaust and genocide, holds conferences, and publishes a newsletter (*Internet on the Holocaust and Genocide*). It has (in 1988 and 1991) and continues to sponsor and publish a series of bibliographies entitled *Genocide: A Critical Bibliographic Review* in which professionals from well over a dozen different disciplines have participated. It has also developed the first *Holocaust and Genocide Computerized Bibliographic Database* and is now in the process of developing the first *Thesaurus on Holocaust and Genocide Terms*. Its major unfulfilled project is a World Genocide Early Warning Center, for which it has completed and published noteworthy theoretical work but has never succeeded in devleoping the financial means required to launch the actual Center.

International Alert - Standing International Forum on Ethnic Conflict, Genocide, and Human Rights (IA). 379-381 Brixton Rd., London SWD 7DE, United Kingdom. FAX: 44-71-738-6265

From the outset International Alert (IA) was envisaged as an experiment in international relations, an attempt to define a role for nongovernmental organizations vis-a-vis intra-state conflict resolution and conflict avoidance in areas where the conflicts had already resulted in violence or were likely to do so unless solutions or accommodations were found. IA is concerned with anticipating, predicting, and preventing genocide and other mass killings. As its name implies, it also works to help "alert" international opinion to situations of ethnic violence which are assuming genocidal proportion.

In carrying out its mandate, IA conducts research on countries identified as politically volatile areas; organizes seminars, and issues comparative reports. It publishes texts based on its "conflict transformation" initiatives, and it is currently in the process of developing a newsletter. Among its numerous publications are: *Early Warning and Conflict Resolution*, a report by Rodolfo Stavenhagen, Rapporteur of the Consultation on Early Warnings; *Early Warning and Conflict Resolution*, a report by Sandy Coliver, Rapporteur of the Second Annual Consultation on Early Warnings; *Tibet in China: An International Alert Report*; and, *Tibet - An International Consultation*.

In collaboration with the Peace Research Institute of Oslo (PRIO), IA has been hosting a number of roundtable discussions on the issue of developing an early warning (conflict forecasting) system, and the role that NGO's could play in its development. It is also closely following the developments of the U.N.'s working group on a similar system.

The International Commission of Jurists (ICJ), P.O. Box 120, 1224 Chene-Bougeries, Geneva, Switzerland. FAX: 41-22-493145.

Founded in 1952, the ICJ is a nongovernmental organization devoted to promoting throughout the world the understanding and observance of the Rule of Law and the legal protection of human rights. Among its many activities are: sponsoring proposals within the United Nations and other international organizations for improved procedures and conventions for the protection of human rights; conducting studies or inquiries into particular situations or subjects concerning the Rule of Law and publishing reports upon them; sending international observers to trials of major significance; and intervening with governments concerning violations of the Rule of Law. While membership of the Commission is limited to 45 eminent jurists, others in sympathy with the goals of the ICJ are welcome to become Associates.

International Federation of Human Rights (F.I.D.H.), 27 rue Jean Dolent, 75014, Paris, France. FAX: 33-1-43363543.
The International Federation of Human Rights was founded in 1922 in order to work for the promotion of the ideal of human rights and to fight against violations of human rights. Since its founding it has worked for the establishment of an International Criminal Court and beginning in 1927 it began promoting a "World -Wide Declaration of Human Rights." During the period of the Holocaust, the FIDH fought against and became a target of nazism. Since December 10, 1948, it has had as its primary goal the concrete implementation of the Universal Declaration of Human Rights through international procedures and control. All FIDH affiliates recognize the principles found in the Universal Declaration on Human Rights and strive for their actual and effective enforcement in their own country. Each FIDH affiliate fulfils a three-fold action: defense of individuals and groups when subjected to the abuse of power; public action to mobilize opinion and sensitize governments; and policy proposals on human rights and their implementation. The Executive Board conducts investigations of human rights violations and fact-finding missions. The FIDH publishes a weekly newsletter and the reports of its mission.

International Helsinki Federation for Human Rights, Rummelhardtgasse 2/18, A-1090 Vienna, Austria. FAX: 43-1-408744
The International Helsinki Federation for Human Rights (IHF), which was founded in 1982, is a nongovernmental, non-profit organization which monitors compliance with the human rights provisions of the Helsinki Final Act and its accompanying documents. It coordinates the work of national Helsinki committees in 20 countries and has direct links with human rights activists in countries where no Helsinki Committees exist. It criticizes human rights abuses regardless of the political system of the state where these abuses occur. It publishes *The Helsinki Monitor*, a quarterly that focuses on the human rights issues addressed by the IHF.

International Human Rights Law Group, 1601 Connecticut Ave., NW., Suite 700, Washington 20009. FAX: 1-202-232-6731. [Membership organization.]
The International Human Rights Law Group, which was founded in 1978, is a nongovernmental, public interest law center which mobilizes the special skills of the legal community to promote and protect human rights. One of its many functions involves sending fact-finding missions to investigate human rights abuses in countries across the globe. Much of the Law Group's work is carried out by a large cadre of attorneys who contribute their time and expertise to pro bono projects and cases.

International Peace Research Institute, Oslo (PRIO), Fuglehauggt. 11, N-0260, Oslo 2, Norway.
PRIO was founded in 1959, originally as a department of the Institute for Social Research in Oslo. In 1966, it became an independent, international institute. Since 1987, research has focused on three main programs: security and disarmament studies, studies in environmental security, and conflict theory and the study of ethnic conflicts. The program on Conflict Theory and Ethnic Conflict deals with the theoretical basis for conflict management and resolution. In progress are studies of

techniques for early warning conflicts whose purpose would be to identify indicators of potential conflict and methods for exercising conflict resolution at an early stage; different constitutional systems in multi-ethnic societies; and, processes for peaceful redistribution of power to protect ethnic identity through varying degrees of political autonomy, democratization and demilitarization. In 1990 a new study group devoted to internal conflicts and their resolution, International Conflict and Resolution - ICON, was established. It is concerned, in particular, with conflicts that involve violence. The Institute publishes the *Journal of Peace Research*, the *Bulletin of Peace Proposals*, *PRIO Reports*, and the PRIO Book Series.

The International Romani Union, Manchaca, Texas 78652. [Membership organization.] Established in 1979, a key focus of IRU's work is to combat anti-Gypsy racism in all its forms, to monitor media misrepresentation, and to work for the improvement of health and civil and social rights of Roma everywhere. It has published numerous works on the genocide of the Roma.

International Work Group for Indigenous Affairs (IWGIA), 10 Fiolstraede, DK-1171 Copenhagen K, Denmark. FAX: 45-33-147749
IWGIA is an independent, international organization, which supports indigenous peoples in their struggle for self-determination and against oppression. It is oriented towards the goal of supporting indigenous peoples themselves so they can present their cases before the international community. IWGIA organizes campaigns to put pressure on governments and international organizations, and mobilizes public opinion to protest against suppression and violation of indigenous peoples' human rights. These efforts are often coordinated with human rights organizations in other countries. In order to document and investigate specific cases, IWGIA initiates and supports research projects. IWGIA publishes the following publications: *Newsletters*, which are published 3-4 times a year and documents the most recent situations facing indigenous peoples; *Documents*, which are indepth analyses of the situation of a specific people or deals with a selected theme; and the *Yearbook*, which presents an overview of the year's main events relating to indigenous peoples across the globe. While IWGIA has no regular membership, individuals can join national groups and subscribe to its publications, give donations, and forward material concerning indigenous peoples. Among its many publications on genocide and ethnocide are as follows: *The Ache Indians: Genocide in Paraguay* by Mark Munzell (Copenhagen: IWGIA, 1973); *The Yanomami in the Face of Ethnocide* by Jacques Lizot (Copenhagen: IWGIA, 1976); *Genocide in the Chittagong Hill Tracts, Bangladesh* by Wolfgang Mey (Copenhagen: IWGIA, 1984); and *The Indigenous Voice: Vision and Realities* (Volume 1 focuses on present-day struggles against genocide and land grabbing).

Leo Baeck Institute, 129 East 73rd St., New York, NY 10021. FAX 1-212-988-1305.
The Leo Baeck Institute promotes and facilitates the study of the life and history of German Jewry from its inception to its demise in the Third Reich. It has published well over 100 books in English, German, and Hebrew.

Minority Rights Group, 379 Brixton Rd., London SW9 7DE, England. FAX: 44-71-738-6265.
The Minority Rights Group (MRG), an international human rights group, investigates the plight of minority and majority groups suffering discrimination and prejudice, and works to educate and alert public opinion. It also works to prevent problems from

developing into dangerous and destructive conflicts and to foster international understanding of the factors which create prejudiced treatment and group tensions. It has published numerous reports on the issues of ethnocide and genocide, including the following: *What Future for the Armerindian of South America?; Selective Genocide in Burundi; The Armenians; The Tibetans: Two Perspectives on Tibetan-Chinese Relations; ROMA: Europe's Gypsies; The Kurds; International Action Against Genocide*; and *The Miskito Indians of Nicaragua.*

Montreal Institute for Genocide Studies, Concordia University, 1455 De Maisonneuve Blvd., West Montreal, Quebec, Canada H36 IM8. FAX: 1-514-848-3494.
Established in 1986, the Institute collects and disseminates knowledge about the historical origins of mass killings. It accomplishes its objectives through research, teaching, and publication. It seeks to acquire and improve access to scholarly resources on genocide. The Institute sponsors and publishes an "Occasional Papers Series" and has jointly published, with Yale University Press, a text entitled *The History and Sociology of Genocide: Analyses and and Studies* by Frank Chalk and Kurt Jonassohn (New Haven, CT: Yale University Press, 1990).

Refugees International, 220 I St., N.E., Suite 2240, Washington, D.C. 20002. FAX: 1-202- 547-3796. [Membership organization.]
Through a wide network of international contacts, R.I. monitors and analyzes refugee crises in order to develop and promote strategies and solutions that address specific refugee needs. Using both quiet diplomacy and the power of public opinion, RI presses governments and international organizations to improve protection for refugees. In doing so, it works to help "people out of potentially genocidal situations by giving them hope and shelter outside of their home countries if they are in danger of and/or fear persecution, political upheaval or other intense suffering." It also "attempts to anticipate life-threatening situations, assess and recommend key protection and care remedies, and influence the relevant governments and international organizations to adopt these solutions."

Simon Wiesenthal Center, 9760 West Pico Blvd., Los Angeles, CA 90035-4792. FAX: 1-310-277-5558. [Membership organization.]
Established in 1977, the Center is dedicated to the study of the Holocaust, its contemporary implications and related human rights issues. The Center (whose membership is comprised of over 385,000 families) is headquartered in Los Angeles but it also maintains offices in New York City, Chicago, Toronto, Miami, Jerusalem, and Paris. The Center is dedicated to the preservation of the memory of the Holocaust through education and awareness. To accomplish its goals it has developed programs in the areas of Holocaust studies and research, educational outreach, and international social action. The Center "closely interacts with a variety of public and private agencies, meeting with elected officials, U.S. and foreign governments, diplomats and heads of state." Among the issues that have been the focus of discussion have been the "prosecution of Nazi war criminals, antisemitism, contemporary attitudes of intolerance and bigotry, terrorism, and genocide. The Center also tracks, investigates and counters antisemitc manifestations worldwide." It recently opened its musuem on the Holocaust, "The Musuem of Tolerance."

Survival International, 310 Edgware Rd., London W2 IDY, England. FAX: 44-71-7234059. [Membership organization.]
Established in 1969, Survival International (S.I.) is a worldwide movement to support tribal peoples. It stands for their right to decide their own future and helps them to

protect their lands, environment and way of life. Through research, field missions, authoritative publications, media outreach and a grassroots membership, S.I. works around the world to support tribal peoples as they exercise their right to self-determination. It specifically campaigns for "justice and an end to genocide." In order to organize and target action, it has established an Urgent Action Bulletin Letter Writing Network. *Urgent Action Bulletins*, which are sent to all members, report on recent and serious abuses of tribal peoples' rights. They invite the recipient to take action by writing to those in power. It also publishes a newsletter entitled *Survival International*. Among its many publications that focus on the issue of genocide and/or ethnocide are: *Threatened Cultures; Natives of Sarawak: Survival in Borneo's Vanishing Forests;* and, *Witness to Genocide: The Present Situation of Indians in Guatemala.*

TAPOL, Indonesia Human Rights Campaign, 111 Northwood Rd., Thornton Heath, Surrey CR4 8HW, England. FAX: 44-81-6550322.
    Organized in 1973, TAPOL's main focus is to develop awareness in the general public and governmental agencies concerning human rights violations committed by the Indonesian military regime in Indonesia, East Timor, and West Papua. In addition to publishing the *TAPOL Bulletin*, it has also published such reports as *An Act of Genocide, Indonesia's Invasion of East Timor*, and *West Papua: The Obliteration of a People.*

Ukrainian Canadian Research and Documentation Centre (UCRDC), 620 Spadina Ave., Toronto, Canada M5S 244.
    The UCRDC conducts research and educational programs into the Soviet manmade famine in Ukraine. Its main focus is the acquisition of archival materials relating to the 1932-1933 famine in Ukraine and the fate of the Ukraine during World War II. It collects official state documents, photographs, film footage, newspapers, letters, and conducts oral histories (audio and video tapes) with eyewitnesses of the famine. It has contributed to a number of works on the Ukraine famine, including but not limited to the following: *The Foreign Office and the Famine: British Documents on Ukraine and the Great Famine of 1932-1933* edited by Marco Carynnyk, Lubomyr Y. Luciuk, and Bohdan S. Kordan (Vestal, NY: The Limestone Press, 1988), and *Investigation of the Ukrainian Famine, 1932-1933: Report to [the U.S.] Congress* edited by the U.S. Commission on the Ukraine Famine, 2 volumes (Washington, D. C.: U. S. Government Printing Office, 1987 and 1988). It has also produced a documentary on the famine, "Harvest of Despair" (55 min, color, VHS or BETA formats. Available in English and French formats. Available from UCRDC).

U.S. Committee for Refugees, 1025 Vermont Ave., NW, Suite 920, Washington, D.C. 20005. FAX: 1-202-347-3418.
    The U.S. Committee for Refugees is dedicated to ensuring the protection of more than fifteen million refugees in asylum countries around the world, and of countless numbers of displaced people trapped within their countries. USCR's mandate is: to defend the basic human rights of refugees, most fundamentally, the principle of nonrefoulement (no forced return of a person with a well-founded fear of persecution to his or her homeland) to defend the rights of asylum seekers to a fair and impartial determination of their status; and to defend the right to decent and humane treatment for all internally displaced persons. USCR pursues its mandate through a process of documentation and objective reporting on the conditions of refugees, asylum seekers, and internally displaced persons worldwide, regardless of ideology, nationality, race,

religion, or social group. In pursuit of its goals, it lobbies government and nongovernmental organizations and frequently testifies before Congress on refugee issues. It publishes the *World Refugees Survey*, an annual report with comprehensive articles and detailed statistics on the world's refugees and internally displaced persons; *Refugee Reports*, a monthly news service focusing on domestic refugee issues; and, *Issue Papers and Issue Briefs*, which report on critical refugee issues and policy matters.

United States Holocaust Memorial Museum (100 Raoul Wallenberg Place, SW, Washington, D.C. 20024). FAX: 1-202-488-2690. [Membership organization.]
"The primary mission of the U.S. Holocaust Museum is to promote education about the history of the Holocaust and its implications for those living today. Opened in April 1993, the Museum's permanent exhibition encompasses 36,000 square feet...The exhibition presents a comprehensive history of the Holocaust through artifacts, photographs, films, and eyewitness testimonies." Housed within the musuem is the United States Holocaust Research Institute which includes: the Holocaust Library, the Holocaust Archive, the Photo Archive, the Film and Video Archive, and the Benjamin and Vladka Meed National Registry.

YIVO Institute for Jewish Research, 1048 Fifth Ave., New York, NY 10028. FAX: 1-212- 734-1062 and 1-212-879-9763.
YIVO is dedicated to examining and preserving the rich Yiddish cultural heritage of East European Jews and their American descendants. "Its library has over 300,000 volumes and contains the worlds' largest collection of Yiddish books and Judaica items." It houses an extensive archive including key materials on the Holocaust and has a Center for Advanced Jewish Studies.

Zentralrat Deutscher Sinti Und Roma (Documentation and Cultural Center of German Sinti and Roma), Bluntschlistr. 4, 6900 Heidelberg, Germany. FAX: 49-6221-981190.
Its primary work involves historical documentation and research vis-a-vis the plight of the Sinti and Roma (Gypsies) during the Holocaust. It holds a central archive and has published a bibliography and numerous reports.

Index

Bold-face page numbers following an author's name refer to an annotated bibliographic entry for that author. (In the case of a chapter from a larger work, only the annotated entry relating to that chapter is distinguished by the use of bold face, not the entry for the larger work itself.) The occurrence of more than one annotated bibliographic entry for a particular author on the same page is indicated by a numeral in parentheses following the page number. Note that on pages where an author appears in an annotated bibliographic entry, there may also be other references to that author in other entries in that page, but the page number is not listed a second time.

In Vahakn Dadrian's chapter, boldface entries direct the reader to the sections where the listed person is discussed and/or publications are given. Additional points to be noted are the following: 1. Ottoman officials were often known and addressed either by their first or last name only; some entries, therefore, reflect this condition. 2. The insertion of a third name in parentheses in some entries indicates a reference to a surname adopted in the 1930s by the subjects in accommodation of the strong urging of Mustafa Kemal Atatürk. 3. Occasional inconsistencies in the spelling of some Turkish names such as Ahmed or Ahmet, Hamid or Hamit are due to the lack of uniformity prevalent in the existing literature. 4. Brief descriptions are attached to certain names in order to avoid confusion about their identity and the posts they occupied.